ULSTER 1912-22
Change, controversy and conflict

Top: Captain John Redmond, chaplain and later vicar of Ballymacarrett, Belgium, 1917.
Bottom: Willie Redmond MP for east Clare in Volunteers uniform, Maryborough, c. 1915

See chapter 7, pp 134–5 for how these two men met at Messines in 1917

ULSTER 1912–22
Change, controversy and conflict

EDITED BY
ALAN F. PARKINSON AND BRIAN M. WALKER

ULSTER HISTORICAL FOUNDATION

COVER DESIGN
Front cover: Detail from the 'The Kidnappers' by Hy Mayer (New York 1914),
(Library of Congress control no. 2011649829).
Courtesy of the Library of Congress
Rear: Soldiers of the Royal Irish Rifles in Chichester Street, Belfast, 8 May 1915.
Courtesy of the Royal Ulster Rifles Museum

FRONTISPIECE IMAGES
Willie Redmond in Volunteers uniform, holding flag
with other Volunteers parading with rifles. Maryborough, *c.* 1915.
Courtesy of the National Library of Ireland (NLI, NPA RED 3)

Rev. John Redmond at Dranouter, West Flanders,
Belgium, 12 June 1917.
Courtesy of the Imperial War Museum (IWM)

Ulster Historical Foundation is pleased to acknowledge support for this publication provided by the Esme Mitchell Trust and the patrons, donors and subscribers listed on page ix. All contributions are gratefully acknowledged.

Published in 2024
by Ulster Historical Foundation
www.ulsterhistoricalfoundation.com

Except as otherwise permitted under the Copyright, Designs and Patents Act 1988, this publication may only be reproduced, stored or transmitted in any form or by any means with the prior permission in writing of the publisher or, in the case of reprographic reproduction, in accordance with the terms of a licence issued by The Copyright Licensing Agency. Enquiries concerning reproduction outside those terms should be sent to the publisher.

© Ulster Historical Foundation and the individual contributors
ISBN: 978-1-913993-61-0

DESIGN AND FORMATTING
FPM Publishing

COVER DESIGN
J.P. Morrison

PRINTED BY
GPS Colour Graphics Ltd, Belfast

Contents

ACKNOWLEDGEMENTS	vii
LIST OF PATRONS, DONORS AND SUBSCRIBERS	ix
FOREWORD	xi
AUTHORS' BIOGRAPHIES	xiv
INTRODUCTION	xvii
ABBREVIATIONS	xxii

1 James Brown Armour: 1
   Irish Presbyterian minister and Home Ruler revisited
   – the case for a re-examination of Armour and his role
   RICHARD McMINN

2 Friends in Fleet Street: 22
   British press support for Ulster's anti-Home Rule
   campaign, 1912–14
   ALAN F. PARKINSON

3 Beyond the Somme: 42
   Northern Ireland's Great War ex-servicemen
   RICHARD S. GRAYSON

4 The Easter Rising and Belfast republicanism   60
   JAMES McDERMOTT

5 Ulster unionism and the Irish Convention, 1917–18   81
   NEIL C. FLEMING

6	Combating the 'flu': Regional responses to the 1918–19 influenza pandemic in Ulster PATRICIA MARSH	113
7	Rev. John Redmond, vicar of Ballymacarrett: Army chaplain, peace maker and temperance advocate BRIAN M. WALKER	132
8	The USC and the formation of the Northern Ireland state, 1920–22 BRIAN BARTON	149
9	The life and career of Denis Henry (1864–1925): An Irish political misfit: Catholic unionist politician and first Lord Chief Justice of Northern Ireland ÉAMON PHOENIX	172
10	The Swanzy riots: Lisburn, 1920 CHRISTOPHER MAGILL	187
11	Perceptions of the king's visit to Belfast, 22 June 1921 HEATHER JONES	204
12	Lady Cecil Craigavon and the reclamation of history DIANE URQUHART	220
13	The Boundary Commission and border minorities CORMAC MOORE	238
	INDEX	256

Acknowledgements

The editors would like to thank the following people and groups for their kind assistance in the making of this book: the contributors of the essays for all their efforts and patience during the book's 'gestation' period (as is normal in such a collection, the views and interpretations expressed in the essays are solely those of their authors); Professor Lord Paul Bew for kindly writing the Foreword; Fintan Mullan of the Ulster Historical Foundation for commissioning and supporting this project; his colleague Dr William Roulston for his vital contribution as copy-editor; and Jill Morrison for producing the jacket design. We are also grateful to the Esme Mitchell Trust and to the individuals who generously subscribed to the publication of this volume. Finally, it is with sadness that we note the loss of another of our contributors to this book during its publication phase. Dr Richard McMinn was a prominent Northern Ireland educationalist, serving as Principal of Stranmillis University College in Belfast for many years. He was also a fine historian whose wide areas of interest included Protestant Home Rulers and the history of the Irish circus.

ALAN F. PARKINSON
BRIAN M. WALKER

'An American funeral in Belfast', 11 Oct. 1918 for 12 American soldiers, victims of the Otranto disaster, and men who died from pneumonia after being landed in Ireland from a troopship (LOC control no. 2017675939)
Courtesy the Library of Congress

List of Patrons, Donors and Subscribers

The publication of this work was made possible by the generosity of the individuals and organisations listed below. Ulster Historical Foundation would like to thank all patrons, donors and subscribers for their support.

The Esme Mitchell Trust

PATRONS

Terry Eakin

Johnny Andrews Doreen McBride
Gerrard Burnett Francis McGrath
Alan Esdale I.M.O. Mary Schranz
John Gordon Rosana Trainor

DONORS

James Cannon Yvonne Cowieson Dr George McBride
Niall McSperrin Colin Walker

SUBSCRIBERS

Kathleen Oliver Blanchard
Rodney Brown
David Byers
Aaron Callan
Dr G. Johnston Calvert
Sheriff Vincent J. Canavan
I.M.O. Mary Jane Carroll
Ross R. Cooper
Mark Dingwall
James Elliott
Kieran Fagan

Dr Ronan Fawsitt
Dr Jennifer FitzGerald
Ioan Fleming
David Gibson
Fred W. Gibson
Cecily Kelleher
Robert Kilpatrick
Thomas Colvill
Holmes Lyons
Derek McAuley
Dr I.W. McCay
Goffinet McLaren
Ian Montgomery
David Moore

Gareth Neighbour
John M. Noble
Ron Pagan
Tom Parkinson
Dr R. Rees
Mark John Richardson
Antony Sellers
John Sharpe
Kelly Stadelbauer, Canada
Jim Thomson
Sharol Ward
Gerard Woods
Terry Wright

JONATHAN BARDON (1941–2020)

GEORGE BOYCE (1942–2020)

ÉAMON PHOENIX (1953–2022)

Foreword

It is a pleasure and an honour to provide a foreword to this book. The volume is full of fine essays dedicated to the memory of three great scholars of Northern Ireland. As long as people care about this place, they will care about the work of Jonathan Bardon, George Boyce, and Éamon Phoenix.

Jonathan Bardon was a Dublin-born scholar who became absorbed by Northern Ireland. His most important book, *A History of Ulster* (Belfast, 1993), was formally presented to Bill Clinton when the US president visited Belfast. There could have been no better guide for a politician anxious to learn about the region's peculiar and particular history. Bardon's work represents a kind of old school historiographic liberalism of the best sort – going back to Professor J. C. Beckett. His style, always calm and measured, gives a particular force to those moments when strong judgements are registered. His work was always buttressed by the most impeccable scholarship. Alas, Jonathan Bardon's pre-existing serious chest condition made him particularly vulnerable when Covid hit. He is a great loss to the community of Northern Irish historical scholars. But I should add that he, like George Boyce and Éamon Phoenix, was an excellent and renowned teacher, and he, like them, will always be a presence in the mind of his students.

George Boyce (1942–2020) enjoyed a lengthy academic career in Wales. He was Lecturer, then, after 1989, Professor, in the Department of Politics and International History. Yet he was always intimately engaged with Northern Ireland. Whilst he loved Wales, there were always certain things he missed from home. I recall when he was an external examiner in the Queen's Politics Department, having to stop on the road back to the airport to allow him to buy wheaten bread at an Ulster bakery. His first book, based on the empirical research of his PhD, *Englishmen and Irish Troubles: British Public Opinion and the Making of Irish Political Policy 1918–1922*, was characterised by a scrupulous determination to get the facts straight. This was inevitable: a young scholar must provide proof of his professionalism. But in later years Professor Boyce was more than willing to face up to the big intellectual questions – most notably the democratic basis of Irish nationalism and indeed Irish unionism. He was not afraid of the big theoretical questions, as his entry on 'Parnell and Bagehot', Chapter 5 in *Parnell in Perspective* (London, 1991), the volume he co-edited, as so many with Alan O'Day, shows clearly.

I recall with pleasure one night in our house, my wife, Dr Greta Jones, who had been proud to contribute an essay to one of George's volumes, challenged him on one of the key 'what might have been' questions in Irish history: What would have happened if Napoleon had defeated the British and successfully conquered Ireland? Napoleon later concedes, after all, that his failure to prioritise Ireland may have been his greatest mistake. Many Irish nationalists – going back to Watty Cox – have seen this as Ireland's great missed opportunity, leading to the demise of a progressive, relatively democratic development. George Boyce was, however, a sceptic on this score – basing himself not primarily on a view of Ireland's potential, or otherwise, for such a development but on the selfish strategic and economic behaviour of all Napoleon's satellite regimes. George's mode of argument was typical of the man – never bombastic, quiet, assured and calm, but always lucid. It was a pleasure, we both felt, to know him. But he would not, I know, regard this tribute as complete without reference to his co-operation on many edited volumes with his dear friend Alan O'Day. Between them they performed an enormously progressive role in keeping Irish historical debate alive.

Éamon Phoenix was the *doyen* of northern nationalist historiography. Nobody could match him in his level of research. I can myself personally acknowledge too that he was enormously generous with his knowledge. I recall that during the centenary celebrations for Northern Ireland, as chair of the historical advisory committee, I was keen that Dr Phoenix was invited to meet Prince Charles in the City Hall. A generous and understanding seminar followed, enlivened as always by Éamon's exceptional grasp of detail and understanding for the oddities of Belfast life – the friendship between Joe Devlin, the West Belfast MP, and Hugh Pollock, the most cerebral of the interwar unionist cabinet ministers. Éamon was a great son of Belfast and without him a good part of the city's history would have been lost. Indeed, all three scholars did much to preserve the truth about the place.

The essays in this fine volume have a focus on the 1912–22 period. All aspects from radical republicanism to mainstream unionism are carefully surveyed in new and fresh perspectives. It is a particular pleasure to see Lady Craig at last receive the attention she has long deserved. Éamon Phoenix brought Joe Devlin and Cahir Healy to life; it is good to see Diane Urquhart do the same for Lady Craig. Despite the current, largely polemical public debate about the alleged subjugation or 'suspension' of the Act of Union of 1800, the key constitutional infrastructure of partition – two parliaments on the island of Ireland – is established with the

Government of Ireland Act of 1920 in this period. It is modernised by the Good Friday Agreement but its underlying principles remain in place. Hence, the editors are to be commended for the selection of topics and the centrality of the main theme. The essays are not only a worthy tribute to three fine scholars but a reminder to the public of the things that really matter.

Jonathan, George and Éamon were, in the best sense of the word, public historians. Éamon, in particular, made a large-scale contribution to the *Irish News*, but the work of George and Jonathan attracted widespread attention. But it is worth adding that the essays in the book are in the best tradition of public history. They engage with the important matters in a decisive way. The editors and authors are to be congratulated. When the three scholars who are honoured in this book were starting out their professional careers, much that passed for public history in this country was politicised myth-making. The great exception to this general rule was the professionalism of the Irish Historical Society, founded by Professors Moody and Edwards in 1938. It provided a helpful context for serious young scholars. Now, happily, things have changed for the better. It is not just a matter of increased professionalism.

The Good Friday Agreement insisted that Irish unity would require the consent of a majority of the people in Northern Ireland. The dropping of the Irish territorial claim to Northern Ireland embodied in Articles 2 and 3 of the 1937 Constitution allows the Good Friday Agreement to sit alongside the victory of Sinn Féin in the 1918 election which signalled the decisive end of classic Irish unionism.[1] These essays reflect a new self-confidence and vigour in the matter of Irish history writing as scholars, with an impressive lack of inhibition, face up to some of the most difficult and interesting questions of our past, a past which, of course, includes Protestant nationalists like J.B. Armour as well as Catholic unionists like Denis Henry.

PAUL BEW

Note

[1] See Paul Bew, *Ancestral Voices in Irish Politics: Judging Dillon and Parnell* (Oxford, 2023), pp xi–xii.

Authors' biographies

DR BRIAN BARTON taught at the College of Business Studies, Belfast, and the Open University. He is author of *The Belfast Blitz: The City in the War Years* (2015) and *The Secret Court Martials: Records of the Easter Rising* (2010).

LORD PAUL BEW is Professor Emeritus of Irish Politics at Queen's University Belfast, and an independent cross-bench peer in the House of Lords. His publications include *Ireland: The Politics of Enmity, 1789–2006* (2010) and *Ancestral Voices in Irish Politics: Judging Dillon and Parnell* (2023).

NEIL FLEMING is Professor of Modern History, University of Worcester. He is editor of *Aristocracy, Democracy and Dictatorship: The Political Papers of the Seventh Marquess of Londonderry* (2022) and author (with J.H. Murphy) of *Ireland and Partition: Contexts and Consequences* (2021).

PROFESSOR RICHARD S. GRAYSON is Head of the School of Education, Humanities and Languages at Oxford Brookes University. His previous publications include *Belfast Boys: How Unionists and Nationalists Died Together in the First World War* (2009) and *Dublin's Great Wars: The First World War, the Easter Rising and the Irish Revolution* (2018).

HEATHER JONES is Professor of Modern and Contemporary History at University College London. She is author of *For King and Country: The British Monarchy and the First World War* (2021) and *Violence Against Prisoners of War: Britain, France and Germany, 1914–1920* (2011).

DR CHRISTOPHER MAGILL was awarded a PhD by Queen's University Belfast in 2014. He is author of *Political Conflict in East Ulster, 1920–22: Revolution & Reprisal* (2020). His research interests include loyalist violence during the Irish revolution and the formative years of the Ulster Special Constabulary.

AUTHORS' BIOGRAPHIES

DR PATRICIA MARSH is currently working as an archivist in the Public Record Office of Northern Ireland. She is author of *The Spanish Flu in Ireland: A Socio-Economic Shock to Ireland, 1918–1919* (2021).

JIM McDERMOTT is a former school history teacher and has also taught history at Stranmillis University College, Belfast. He is the author of *Northern Divisions: The Old IRA & the Belfast Pogroms 1920–22* (2001).

DR RICHARD McMINN was Principal of Stranmillis University College, Belfast, where he also taught history. His publications include *Against the Tide: J.B. Armour, Irish Presbyterian Minister and Home Ruler* (1985). Richard passed away in November 2023.

DR CORMAC MOORE is an historian-in-residence with Dublin City Council. He is author of *Birth of the Border: The Impact of Partition in Ireland* (2019) and *Laois: The Irish Revolution, 1912–23* (2023).

DR ALAN F. PARKINSON is a former Senior Lecturer in History and Education at London South Bank University. He is author of *A Difficult Birth: The Early Years of Northern Ireland, 1920–5* (2020) and *Friends in High Places: Ulster's Resistance to Irish Home-Rule, 1912–14* (2012).

DR ÉAMON PHOENIX was Principal Lecturer in History at Stranmillis University College, Belfast. His publications include *Northern Nationalism: Nationalist Politics, Partition and the Catholic Minority in Northern Ireland 1890–1940* (1994). He died in November 2022.

DIANE URQUHART is Professor of Gender History at Queen's University Belfast. She is author of *Irish Divorce: A History* (2020) and *The Ladies of Londonderry: Women and Political Patronage, 1800–1959* (2007).

BRIAN M. WALKER is Professor Emeritus of Irish Studies at Queen's University Belfast. He is author of *Irish History Matters: Politics, Identities and Commemoration* (2019) and *A Political History of the Two Irelands: From Partition to Peace* (2012).

Royal procession in front of St George's Church, Belfast, 1921
Alex. Hogg (Private collection)

Introduction

ALAN F. PARKINSON AND BRIAN M. WALKER

'Anniversaries are the curse of Ireland' Sir Kenneth Bloomfield wrote about the 1960s: 'Like saints' days, the dates of historically resonant events punctuate the Northern Ireland calendar, calling for an orgy of reminiscence, celebration and demonstration from some section or other of the population.' He continued: 'It does not seem to matter that some of these demonstrations annoy or infuriate other people: that is, indeed, for some of the participants, a principal attraction'.[1] It has been argued that the passion and confrontation aroused by the large number of commemorations in the 1960s, especially in 1966, was one of the factors that helped to destabilise political society and led to the outbreak of the 'Troubles'. Since then, however, new ways of viewing and celebrating these commemorations have emerged. This was notable in the 1990s when the tercentenary of the Battle of the Boyne and the bicentenary of the 1798 rebellion were marked with strong efforts to see these crucial events in their historical context and to avoid confrontational and simplistic approaches to the past.

This new approach has been very much in evidence in how the recent 'decade of centenaries', has covered events during the key formative years 1912–22. There have been significant exhibitions, lectures and commemorative occasions, which have enjoyed wide public support and involvement. Important also has been new historical writing which has cast critical light on these years. This collection of essays adds to such work. It has a special emphasis on northern events, from the signing of the Ulster Covenant in 1912 to partition and the formation of Northern Ireland. The volume also pays tribute to three recently deceased, and greatly respected, historians who contributed enormously to our better understanding of this period in modern Irish history.

The contributors to this volume bring with them a range of research expertise, but all have written about their chosen subject and most have participated in media discussion during this decade-long period of commemorating anniversaries. The major events of the period all feature heavily in this collection. They include unionist resistance to Irish Home Rule; the impact upon communal relationships across Ulster of the seismic events during 1916 in Dublin and on the Western Front; the severe sectarian violence in the Greater Belfast area during the early 1920s; and the crucial diplomatic and political interventions aimed at solving the North's political difficulties. However, a number of essays explore other significant events and influences during this period, including Patricia Marsh's piece on the 'Spanish flu' pandemic in Ulster in 1918/19 and Diane Urquhart's exploration of the understated political influence of Lady Craig and other leading female unionists.

While some essays are set within the context of these seminal events, the specific subject for examination is sometimes less well-known and 'different' in its choice. The lives of a number of fascinating people are outlined in detail in this collection. They include Richard McMinn's revisionist analysis of the career of pro-Home Rule Presbyterian minister J.B. Armour; Éamon Phoenix's essay on the unique political and legal career of Catholic unionist Denis Stanislaus Henry; and Brian Walker's contribution on the extraordinary and varied life of Rev. John Redmond.

Other essays investigate the significance of British newspapers' sympathetic coverage of Edward Carson's unionist movement's opposition to Home Rule between 1912 and 1914 (Alan F. Parkinson); the shared experiences of Somme soldiers both during and after the great battle (Richard S. Grayson); and Jim McDermott's investigation into the often neglected area of Northern republican engagement in the 1916 Rising. The early 1920s conflict is explored in a number of contributions, ranging from Heather Jones's analysis of the importance of King George V's visit to Belfast to formally open N. Ireland's first Parliament in June 1921; Brian Barton's examination of the role played by the Ulster Special Constabulary during these disturbances; and Chris Magill's case study observing the sectarian violence which occurred outside Belfast (chiefly in Lisburn). Finally, political and diplomatic developments are traced in Neil Fleming's account of the Irish Convention (1917–18); and Cormac Moore's account of the key developments which led to the report of the Boundary Commission in 1925.

This collection is a festschrift, or tribute volume, to the memory of three outstanding northern historians, Jonathan Bardon, D. George Boyce, who both passed away in 2020, and Éamon Phoenix, who died in November 2022. All three men left a deep mark on Irish historiography, and have also influenced the subsequent work of many other historians, including – as noted below several contributors to this volume. Even academics who did not know these men acknowledge their impact on the field of modern Irish history. Professor Richard S. Grayson writes that George and Jonathan were 'both giants of the field and their books were some of the first I encountered when I started doing my own research in Irish history'. Richard admits that he and many other scholars 'owe them a tremendous debt for their publications.'

JONATHAN BARDON (1941–2020) was a Dubliner who moved north in 1963 after graduating from Trinity College. He would remain living in Belfast for close to 60 years. Jonathan also gained a teaching diploma at Queen's University before moving into teaching. Most of his career was spent at Belfast College of Business Studies, though he also taught at the School of History at Queen's University. Jonathan was involved in numerous publications relating to Irish history, particularly those pertaining to the North. His books included *Belfast: An Illustrated History*, *The Plantation of Ulster* and *Beyond the Studio: A History of BBC Northern Ireland*. He was also a prolific writer for radio and television, and his best-known work in this area was the BBC Radio series *A Short History of Ireland*, which ran to over 240 episodes. However, Jonathan Bardon is best remembered for his magisterial, but also highly readable, account of the history of his adopted North, from prehistoric times right up to the early 1990s. *A History of Ulster* (1993) is a monumental, epic work which is usually a first base for historians researching the region's history, and it won warm praise from a host of readers, including former American President Bill Clinton, who avidly devoured its contents during the long-running Irish peace process.

Shortly after Jonathan's death in April 2020, Éamon Phoenix described Jonathan as 'a lovely man and great scholar who carried his learning lightly'. Jonathan was 'a great story-teller who wrote with passion about his adopted city of Belfast'. Éamon had first met Jonathan when they were researching the recent releases of state papers, and it was during one of these meetings that Jonathan disclosed his highly unorthodox approach to writing up his lengthy tome (some 800 pages), *A History of Ulster*. Apparently, he wrote up sections of this classic text 'in snatches during the last years of the Troubles when he was waiting in his car to collect his (then) teenage daughter from her friends' houses!' Richard McMinn worked with Jonathan in preparing a new history course for schools in Northern Ireland, which had the aim of promoting improved community understanding and respect, as well as endeavouring to foster peace and reconciliation. Richard knew Jonathan for many years, and recalled that his books and lectures were 'always stimulating and easy to follow, and like all of his work, certainly made a difference to the understanding of the subject across the whole of the Northern Ireland history curriculum.'

D. GEORGE BOYCE (1942–2020) was born in County Armagh and educated at Lurgan College and Queen's University Belfast, where he also completed a PhD in history. After a short spell working in the Department of Manuscripts at Oxford University's Bodleian Library, George moved into academia in 1971. He spent the rest of his career – from 1971 until 2004 – working in the Department of Politics and International History at Swansea University, first as a lecturer and, from 1989, as Professor. A Fellow of the Royal Historical Society, George served as an external examiner at several Irish universities. He was involved in about 20 publications, including *Englishmen and Irish Troubles: British Public Opinion and the Making of Irish Political Policy, 1918–22*; *Nationalism in Ireland*; *Nineteenth Century Ireland: The Search for Stability*; and *The Irish Question and British Politics, 1868–1996*. Later in his career, George turned his attention to editing books containing the work of many scholars in the field of Irish history (his chief collaborator was the late Professor Alan O'Day).

Several contributors to this volume knew George well. Richard McMinn knew George from his spell as a doctoral student at Queen's, when he was himself on the undergraduate history course with Kathleen, George's future wife. Richard described George Boyce as 'a true son of Lurgan and County Armagh, who never lost his love for the land of his birth'. Alan Parkinson was a doctoral student of George's at Swansea during the first half of the 1990s. Like George, he was fascinated by how the media and public opinion in Great Britain impacted upon Irish political developments, and he regularly visited George in south Wales for close to six years. He recalls that George, although 'a modest man, had an enormous amount of knowledge of Irish history in particular', but also points out that he was 'an ideal tutor, with realistic expectations and plans for a hard-pressed, part-time student like myself.' Alan used to enjoy his termly visits to Wales and frequent correspondence with George, when 'we shared our concerns about the political and security situation in the North, as well as talking about imminent holidays 'back home', where George enjoyed sailing around the Ards peninsula'.

ÉAMON PHOENIX (1953–2022) was a former pupil of St Mary's Christian Brothers' Grammar School and a graduate of Queen's University Belfast, where he also gained a PhD on the history of northern nationalism. After a period teaching history at St Malachy's College and working as a Fellow at Queen's University's Institute of Irish Studies, Éamon spent most of his career as a history lecturer at Stranmillis University College, Belfast. He eventually became responsible for Stranmillis's Lifelong Learning Programme and spoke regularly at conferences, while also leading historical walking tours across the North and much wider afield. He was also prominent in the local media and took a leading role in the commemorations marking the Decade of Anniversaries programmes organised by local authorities and other groups. One of his numerous pieces of work for the media included a prominent role as historical adviser on the well-known 'Year 21' podcast, commemorating the centenary of Northern Ireland. Éamon's work in this area was recognised by a Community Relations Council award in 2022 for his service to the community and work in the field of reconciliation.

Dr Phoenix's publications included works on the Friar's Bush graveyard in south Belfast; a centenary edition of the history of the *Irish News*; the history of Stranmillis College; and a co-edited collection of essays, *Conflicts in the North of Ireland, 1900–2000*. However, his most celebrated work was *Northern Nationalism* (1994), which remains the standard text for this subject. Alan Parkinson worked with Éamon on the 2010 essay collection and also collaborated with him in giving lectures and talks on a variety of subjects in the Greater Belfast area. Alan recalls that Éamon had an encyclopaedic understanding of modern Irish history, as well as being 'a master of the historical anecdote'. He was also 'incredibly energetic and his schedule, even in retirement, would have worn out people half his age.' Éamon was 'passionate about the history of the North and loved taking it to audiences across the region – he really was "The People's Historian".' Jim McDermott also worked alongside Éamon and often assisted him in teaching history classes at Stranmillis College. On the eve of his funeral, Jim wrote about Éamon:

> He was an outstanding historian, a gifted writer and charismatic public speaker, as well as being one of the nicest people you could ever wish to meet. His wide range of friendships embraced viewpoints across the religious and political spectrums, and his audiences were completely engaged by his grasp of detail, his obvious appreciation of other points of view, and the lightness which he brought to the most complex of political and historical issues.

Éamon's essay in this volume was commissioned before his death.

Note

[1] Ken Bloomfield, *Stormont in Crisis: A Memoir* (Belfast, 1994), p. 92.

Abbreviations

AOH	Ancient Order of Hibernians
BMH WS	Bureau of Military History Witness Statement
COFMLA	Cardinal Tomás Ó Fiaich Memorial Library and Archive
HC	House of Commons
IPP	Irish Parliamentary Party
IRA	Irish Republican Army
IRB	Irish Republican Brotherhood
LGBI	Local Government Board for Ireland
MOH	Medical Officer of Health
MSOH	Medical Superintendent Officer of Health
NAI	National Archives of Ireland
NLI	National Library of Ireland
PRONI	Public Record Office of Northern Ireland
RAMC	Royal Army Medical Corps
RIC	Royal Irish Constabulary
TNA	The National Archives (London)
USC	Ulster Special Constabulary
UUC	Ulster Unionist Council
UVF	Ulster Volunteer Force
UWUC	Ulster Women's Unionist Council

1

James Brown Armour

Irish Presbyterian minister and Home Ruler revisited – the case for a re-examination of Armour and his role[1]

RICHARD McMINN

During the recent so-called 'decade of centenaries' the relatively well-known Presbyterian clerical advocate of Home Rule, Rev. James Brown (J.B.) Armour (1841–1928), minister of Trinity Presbyterian Church, Ballymoney, County Antrim, did receive a mention in some of the attempts to reconstruct the events of the crisis which was created by the introduction of the third Home Rule Bill by Herbert Asquith's Liberal government, supported by John Redmond's Irish National Party. However, the references to Armour's views and precise role were invariably brief. There was also very little mention of the famous Ballymoney Protestant protest meeting against 'Carsonism', held in Ballymoney Town Hall and often seen as being associated with Armour, the exact centenary of which fell on 24 October 2013. By contrast, the Ballymoney Museum, located in the now-refurbished building which was the original venue for that meeting, has understandably given rather more treatment, in one of its exhibition galleries, to the Armour phenomenon and specifically to the famous meeting which was once upon a time held on its premises.

The Ullans Speakers Association, itself based in Ballymoney and supported by the Ulster-Scots Agency, published an anonymously authored pamphlet entitled, *A Ripple in the Pond: The Home Rule Revolt in North Antrim* (2012).[2] This sought to explore the Home Rule crisis in the context of the 'radical Route', to provide brief biographical portraits of the principal actors, both local and national, in the Home Rule drama and concluded with an account of the actual Ballymoney meeting of 24 October 1913 and its immediate aftermath. Given the absence of endnotes etc, the publication was clearly aimed at a general rather than an academic audience. The

Ballymoney meeting has also featured to a greater or especially a lesser extent in recent accounts of the life and political career of Sir Roger Casement, and in Conor Morrissey's work on Protestant nationalism in this period, Leo Keohane's recent biography of Captain Jack White and Brian Feeney's analysis of the 'Irish Revolution' in County Antrim between 1912 and 1923.

Taking into account that this author's 1985 Public Record Office of Northern Ireland publication, *Against the Tide: A Calendar of the Papers of Rev. J.B. Armour, Irish Presbyterian Minister and Home Ruler 1869–1914*,[3] is no longer in print and given that his more recent biographical profile of Armour in the *Oxford Dictionary of National Biography* (2004),[4] because of word length restrictions, makes no specific mention of the 1913 Ballymoney meeting, it is perhaps appropriate and timely to revisit both Armour and his precise role in the events of the autumn of 1913. The recent acquisition by the Public Record Office of Northern Ireland of a further, relatively small *cache* of Armour papers, photographs and family history material[5] could be cited as a further justification for a 'cold case' review. Unfortunately, the new set of papers contains little political material, apart from some additional letters written by Armour to his beloved son, Rev. Max Armour, which date from the period 1914–16 and some notes by Max Armour on his father's life.

The former contain further examples of Armour's support for Asquith's Liberal government during the Curragh Mutiny crisis, his admiration for Asquith as a leader and tactician ('a real master'[6]), his view in 1914 that any partition of Ireland as a compromise solution would be economically disastrous for Ulster ('it spells ruin commercially'[7]), his somewhat naïve belief that Lloyd George could engineer 'a settlement' between the Carsonites and the Redmondites,[8] his foreboding at the formation of a Coalition government in May 1915 ('a leap in the dark'[9]) his somewhat optimistic conviction in November 1915 that Edward Carson was 'a punctured bladder'[10] and, in the context of reports of a Zeppelin raid on the Scottish port of Leith in April 1916, a condemnation of the Germans as a 'Satanic crew'. 'The Huns have their friends in every town. One can only hope that some of the ruffians will be caught and hung up to decorate the lamp posts'.[11] However, none of these comments do anything other than reinforce the picture of Armour's personality and views revealed by the main body of Armour material contained in the original archive and described in detail in *Against the Tide* in 1985.[12]

But the new *cache* of material does contain a fascinating, but easily overlooked, item which raises some fundamental historiographical and research issues that are particularly relevant to the intriguing intersection between family history and political history and to the practitioners of both. The donor of the new material, J.B. Armour's Canadian, clerical grandson, Rev. J.S.S. Armour, has included with the deposit a family history volume. 'It All Began with a Silver Spoon: a Family History Volume of the Armours, Stavelys and Annesleys' (2011) is an unpublished, but very professionally produced, printed book with copious photographs.[13] It is clear that J.S.S. Armour has devoted his retirement to the writing of a most comprehensive account, for the benefit 'of his grandchildren', of the history of both the maternal and paternal lines of his family, based around various artefacts and heirlooms still very much in use in his home.

As an example of its kind, one can only express admiration for both the research effort involved and for the skill with which the writer has presented the results, often with healthy flashes of scepticism and humour. However, chapter seven, which is entitled 'My Grandfather's Clock – the Story of the Armour Family', highlights the interesting and perhaps inevitable culture clash which occurs if a celebration of family history comes up against the work of political historians, who may, or may not, share the sympathetic, uncritical interpretations of the writers of the history of a particular family especially when dealing with their own ancestors who were significant political figures. For both kinds of writer some challenging dilemmas arise and the J.B. Armour case provides a good example of them. To put it succinctly, J.S.S. Armour feels that recent publications by historians such as Gordon Lucy and indeed this author have been insufficiently generous in their treatment of his grandfather's personality and character and also of his inclusive vision for the political future of Ulster.[14]

Gordon Lucy sees Armour as a 'thrawn Ulster Scot', but presents a largely factual short account of his career, which in the main endorses the conclusions in McMinn's earlier volume. Lucy's conclusion that 'the mainspring of Armour's politics was his hostility to Toryism, landlordism and the Church of Ireland' is certainly borne out by the contents of the Armour archive in PRONI. Lucy's final sentence that: 'What was unusual about Armour was the tenacity with which he clung to his world view long after both disestablishment of the Church of Ireland … and land purchase schemes in the late 19th and early 20th century, might have appeared to render his politics largely anachronistic' is perhaps somewhat open to question, given the emergence of organisations, such as the Presbyterian Unionist Voters Association in 1898, the Russellite land purchase movement after 1900, and even as late as the 1920s, the Unbought Tenants Association, a thorn in the flesh of the Craigavon unionist government. Certainly, J.S.S. Armour is unhappy with Lucy's argument that J.B. Armour's politics were 'largely anachronistic' and regrets that Lucy makes no mention of J.B. Armour's generous views on higher education provision for Roman Catholics at Maynooth, at University College Dublin and at Queen's University Belfast.

As for McMinn, J.S.S. Armour feels strongly that he 'is not entirely objective nor indeed overly sympathetic to the North Antrim point of view' ('It All Began with a Silver Spoon', p. 147) and that while J.B. Armour may have been blunt and did not 'suffer fools gladly', he was never 'bitter'. This is presumably a reference to the final sentence of the introduction to *Against the Tide* about J.B. Armour: 'But generally he was at his bitter and brilliant best in opposition – to landlordism, to Anglicanism, to Home Rule, to Unionism and to the General Assembly, often against the tide' (p. lx). For his grandson J.S.S. Armour, as for his sons William, Max and Kenneth, J.B. Armour was 'a prophet whose vision for Ireland was that of a united dominion in which Protestants would play a moderating and significant role' ('It All Began with a Silver Spoon', p. 146). For perfectly understandable reasons, J.S.S. Armour prefers the highly sympathetic analysis of J.B. Armour's journalist son, William, in his 1934 biography, along with that of William's brother, Max, contained in the unpublished, typescript notes which, as mentioned above, have now been placed in PRONI.[15]

Thus, the underlying potential tension that often exists between a certain kind of family history and political history is brought into sharp relief by this fascinating case study. However, in evaluating such conflicting arguments it is perhaps important to remind ourselves of the late E.H. Carr's famous dictum that history is a dialogue between the present and the past.[16] As Professor Arthur Marwick put it in his classic 1970 volume, *The Nature of History*, 'each age writes its own history, for each age will make a different evaluation of what is "significant" in its own past, will tend to see the past in the light of its own preoccupations and prejudices.'[17] This led Marwick to the sobering and salutary conclusion that 'the definitive historical work on any topic has not been written and never will be.'[18]

Who was James Brown Armour?[19]

The highly sympathetic 1934 biography of the controversial cleric written by his journalist son, William (W.S.) can fortunately be supplemented by, and tested against, the very substantial Armour archive, deposited in PRONI by family members. This collection of papers and correspondence provided the basis for my own somewhat revisionist biographical essays of 1985 and 2004.

J.B. Armour was born on 20 January 1841 in the townland of Lisboy, in the parish of Kilraghts (usually spelled 'Kilraughts'), near the town of Ballymoney, County Antrim, the youngest of six children of William Armour (*c*. 1795–1864), a farmer, and his wife, Jane Brown, daughter of William Brown of Ballynaloob, in the parish of Killagan near Ballymoney.

Lisboy was, and still is, a strongly Presbyterian farming community, so the youthful Armour attended Kilraughts Presbyterian Church, and received his early education at the nearby Ganaby National School. The Kilraughts area in the nineteenth century was a centre of tenant-right agitation and Armour quickly came to share such radical sentiments.

After some initial hesitation when he was drawn to the possibility of a legal career, Armour decided to become a Presbyterian minister and was ordained on 19 July 1869 by the Route Presbytery, as assistant and successor to Rev. J.L. Rentoul of Second or Trinity Presbyterian Church, Ballymoney. Known as 'the black wolf', the young Armour had black hair and sharp features, wore spectacles, and invariably sported a beard. A later portrait by the well-known Ulster artist William Conor shows him to have become white-haired, with the gold-rimmed spectacles and beard still in evidence. Armour was in many respects a man of generous and liberal instincts but he also had a considerable temper and frequently used quite violent language to denounce political opponents. While he was an advocate of generous treatment of Irish Roman Catholic demands for denominational educational provision, for example at university level, he was extremely hostile towards the Anglican church in Ireland, with regard not only to its doctrines and its clergy, but above all, as he believed, because of its role as part of the Conservative landlord ascendancy. In particular, he constantly stressed the sufferings of Presbyterians at the hands of the Church of Ireland. Although theologically orthodox, he could best be described as something of a natural non-conformist in other matters.

Armour did not marry until he reached the age of 42. His bride, whom he married on 19 March 1883, was a widow, Jennie Adams Hamilton (née Stavely). She already had two sons by a previous marriage to her deceased cousin, A.M.S. Hamilton, and was to have three sons with Armour – Max, William and Kenneth. The Armour family lived in the manse adjoining the church. The Stavely family, as members of the Reformed Presbyterian Church, had something of a radical political history, stretching back to the 1790s and the United Irishmen. Armour was to remain in Ballymoney for the rest of his life, retiring as a minister of the Trinity congregation on 2 September 1925. He was actively involved in the fields of temperance and education, acting as the first principal of Ballymoney Intermediate School in 1878 (later to become Dalriada School); teaching classics on a part-time basis at Magee College, Londonderry, until 1908 and serving on the first senate of the newly-established Queen's University of Belfast (1910–14). He enjoyed a brief period of official favour after 1906, when he was appointed as one of the personal chaplains to the new Liberal viceroy, Lord Aberdeen, a Scottish Presbyterian.

Armour's political activities

However, it was Armour's political activities which made him a well-known figure in the north of Ireland and beyond. His views were expressed at the local level in north Antrim through his involvement in election campaigns and also on the wider stage of the annual general assemblies of the Presbyterian Church in Ireland, for example in 1893 and, after a considerable lull, again in 1913, following an initial intervention, through various newspapers, in the debate over the third attempt at a Home Rule Bill in early 1911. These views were given considerable press coverage and he contributed a chapter entitled 'A Presbyterian View' to J.H. Morgan (ed.), *The New Irish Constitution* (1912). Prior to the introduction at Westminster of Gladstone's first Home Rule Bill in 1886, Armour was an enthusiastic supporter of the Gladstonian Liberal cause, as were considerable numbers of Ulster Presbyterians. His support for land reform and the aggressive character of his Presbyterianism were important factors influencing Armour's political outlook. For him, Conservatism was closely linked to the Anglican church and the landlord class.

Following the split in the Liberal Party over Home Rule in 1886, Armour at first favoured the Liberal Unionist position. However, he became increasingly unhappy, principally because of the allegedly unfair treatment of Liberal Unionists by their Conservative Unionist allies, especially with regard to the selection of parliamentary candidates. Indeed, he continued to complain of discrimination against Presbyterians in the whole area of public appointments. From the 1892 election campaign onwards he was to be publicly identified as a supporter of Home Rule, perhaps more for negative than positive reasons. Inevitably, this commitment exposed him to considerable public and private criticism and even threats over the years.

Armour's political views

Armour was not a nationalist in the Irish-Ireland sense, hence his hostility to cultural nationalism, the Sinn Féin movement, and subsequently to the Easter Rising of 1916. Like John Redmond, he conceived of Home Rule as a means of strengthening rather than weakening the bonds between Ireland and Britain. Thus, Armour gave his patriotic support to Ireland's participation in the First World War. He saw Home Rule as a force for reconciliation, undoing 'the evils of the paper union of 1800'. He believed it would stimulate Ireland's commerce and trade, but he also justified it on the grounds that it was the principle of Presbyterian church government applied to secular affairs. Home Rule would benefit Protestantism generally by ending the political monopoly of Anglicanism. As far as Presbyterians were concerned, the vital consideration was that they 'cannot possibly under Home Rule have a lesser share in the offices of emolument and dignity than they had all down the years from 1800 to 1912' (Armour, 'A Presbyterian View'). When partition became a reality in 1920, Armour condemned it in principle but also because he saw the new government of Northern Ireland as anti-Presbyterian.

The following report in the *Irish News* demonstrates that even as late as June 1921, the clerical veteran was still prepared to defy his age and go into battle at the General Assembly of his church yet again to condemn the partition of Ireland, now a *fait accompli*.

CLERGYMAN ON FOLLY OF PARTITION

At the Presbyterian General Assembly yesterday, the veteran County Antrim clergyman, Rev. J.B. Armour said that for twenty-nine years he had taken a prominent part in the discussion of [the Irish Question] and he had stood very much alone. 'You have had your elections and there was a great deal of applause over the results. But there was a certain amount of personation and intimidation. (Cries of No and Shame). Is it a shame that this Partition is to take place? I agree. You have practically handed over your destinies to … the Landlord Party of the Church of Ireland.

'I hope this Parliament will turn out alright, but I am afraid that what Grattan said about the [Old] Irish Parliament will probably be true of this assembly. He said – "I have witnessed its cradle; I have followed its hearse". Sir James Craig deserves better than to be a kind of wet-nurse to a kind of bastard parliament. In my opinion the time will come when he will rejoice that the hearse has arrived (Laughter).'

The Moderator expressed the hope that the Rev. Armour will be spared to see the Ulster Parliament an undeniable success.[20]

Ironically, Armour caught a chill at a local luncheon in Ballymoney given in honour of the unionist Prime Minster Sir James Craig in 1928. This subsequently developed into pneumonia and his death followed at the Trinity manse, Ballymoney, on 25 January 1928. He was buried three days later in Ballymoney cemetery. His widow survived him until 1931.

In evaluating J.B. Armour's political views, it is instructive and illuminating to compare his career with that of fellow Ulster Presbyterian cleric, Rev. James Alexander H. Irwin, the republican-sympathising Presbyterian minister from Killead, Co. Antrim, who accompanied Éamon de Valera on a leg of the latter's marathon political lobbying and fund-raising tour of the United States in 1919–20. The Sinn Féin President (sometimes described as the 'President of the Irish Republic') was keen to demonstrate Protestant enthusiasm for Irish independence. Irwin provided both visual and oratorical support on a series of platforms for this objective and for de Valera's argument that the conversion of Ulster Protestants was imminent.

Inevitably, the spirit of 1782 and 1798 was frequently referred to, with de Valera at a rally held in April 1920 in Carnegie Hall, New York, highlighting, as Conor Morrissey has pointed out, the significance of Irwin's appearance as proving the success of Sinn Féin's ideas in penetrating Ulster. On Irwin's return to Ulster and Killead he was the victim of a campaign of harassment by church members, seeking his removal. After a brief period in prison, following the discovery of a revolver, ammunition and an Irish Volunteer badge in his house, Irwin was eventually forced to seek refuge after 1926 in Edinburgh and then as a minister in Lucan, Co. Dublin, from 1935. He died in his manse there in 1954. J.B. Armour was certainly no J.A.H. Irwin!

The 'Radical Route' 1869–1914?[21]

It is important to place any discussion of the events of the autumn of 1913 in the Ballymoney area into the wider context of the political history of north Antrim in the immediately preceding years. Such an analysis would certainly have enhanced the somewhat limited recent description of the background to the Protestant Home Rule meeting of 24 October 1913 contained in *A Ripple in the Pond*. The same could also be argued in the case of Brian Feeney's recent account of developments and events in County Antrim during the 'Irish revolution' from 1912–23.[22] The question of just how 'radical' the Route really was is investigated in some detail in two journal articles which this author published back in 1982.

The first of these, in the journal *Éire-Ireland*, pointed out that, leaving aside the vexed question of defining the term and indeed the geographical area precisely, the Route between 1869 and 1900 did produce a number of prominent individuals who became active in non-unionist politics such as Rev. J.B. Armour, John Pinkerton (nationalist MP for Galway City, 1886–1900) and Samuel Craig McElroy (auctioneer, tenant-right campaigner and editor of the *Ballymoney Free Press*). The article acknowledged that the area was the heartland of the Ulster tenant-right movement in the last three decades of the nineteenth century and the scene of considerable activity by the Liberal Party both before and after the split on the issue of Home Rule in 1886.

All of this does, at first sight, seem to add up to a convincing historical case in favour of the folk tradition of a pocket of sturdy political independence, with the town of Ballymoney at its centre. However, a careful scrutiny of both the nature of the somewhat narrowly focused and self-regarding tenant-right movement in the area, led by S.C. McElroy and of the limited electoral success enjoyed by the Liberal Party in the County Antrim constituency (1869–85) and in the new post-1885 North Antrim seat (following the enfranchisement of the agricultural labourers and the split over Home Rule) led me to a rather negative conclusion about the radical legend. 'Sometimes historical or archaeological investigation can confirm legend, sometimes the opposite. Ballymoney, it would appear, is not the Troy of the North.'

There was however a Liberal revival in the North Antrim constituency after 1900, which was examined in the second article, published in the journal *Irish Historical Studies*. The campaign for compulsory sale to secure owner occupancy for tenant farmers orchestrated by T.W. Russell (Liberal Unionist MP for South Tyrone from 1886), combined with the rise of the Independent Orange Order (led in North Antrim by its Grand Chaplain, Rev. D.D. Boyle of Ballymoney), which appealed to agricultural labourers as well as Protestant urban artisans, helps to explain something of a Liberal breakthrough in the 1906 general election. A strong unionist candidate, William Moore QC, had been returned unopposed for North Antrim in 1900 but was narrowly defeated in 1906 by the Russellite R.G. Glendinning, a Belfast Baptist and linen manufacturer. Glendinning enjoyed the support of Russell's Ulster Farmers and Labourers Union and its local manifestation, the North Antrim Land Purchase Association (NALPA), along with the Independent Orange Order and, in the absence of a nationalist candidate, of some of the approximately 2,000 nationalist voters in the constituency. Glendinning subsequently joined the newly-created Ulster Liberal Association and sat on the Liberal benches in the House of Commons.

Asquith now led a Liberal government after his landslide victory nationally and, as noted above, there was a Scottish Presbyterian Liberal peer, Lord Aberdeen, installed as viceroy in Dublin. Liberal patronage, in part the result of lobbying by J.B. Armour, was dispensed to a number of mainly Presbyterian middle class supporters of Glendinning in the shape of appointments as justices of the peace. The Liberal Chief Secretary for Ireland, Augustine Birrell, proudly announced in Ballymoney Town Hall on 25 November 1907 that he was speaking 'in the very nest of Irish radicalism'.

However, R.G. Glendinning was no radical or enthusiastic nationalist. In reality he was a self-confessed and unrepentant Liberal Unionist and his new constituency organisation, the North Antrim Reform Association, was largely Presbyterian in its make-up and very much identified with the land purchase issue. Glendinning had a poor attendance record at Westminster, was an uninspiring orator and by December 1909 was ready to retreat from politics to the more familiar world of his linen business. The Independent Orange Order, which played such a key role in electing him, was now in decline, following a schism over Home Rule and the expulsion of its crypto-nationalist leader, Lindsay Crawford.

Glendinning's replacements, Sir William Baxter, a Coleraine councillor and shop owner and then William Macafee, a young lawyer, were unsuccessful in the general elections of January and December 1910, in the face of the increasing tension over Home Rule, the failure of the Asquith government to enact compulsory sale or rebuild the harbours at Ballycastle and Rathlin Island, and the selection by the unionists of a more popular Presbyterian standard bearer, Peter Kerr-Smiley. However, the margins of victory by the unionist candidate in the general elections of January and December 1910 were relatively small (384 and 584 votes respectively). Allowing for nationalist votes for the Liberal candidates, it is clear that some 1,000–1,500 Protestant Liberal voters had remained loyal. Nonetheless, I was left in 1982 with the conclusion that: 'The "radicalism" of the Route was honeycombed with limitations and qualifications. It was a structure built upon the sand of political illusion, rather than on the rock of political reality.'

Brian Feeney has asserted that 'the Presbyterian minister, Revd. John [sic] B. Armour ... was prominent in the Ulster Liberal Association, which was resurrected in 1906 before the general election of that year.'[23] In fact, Armour had played little part in the local electoral politics of 1906 and 1910, possibly for age and health reasons, or perhaps because he was a more committed Home Ruler than were some of the local Liberals and, as his letters to his son, William, indicate, he was critical of the abilities of those, like local solicitor, Thomas Taggart, who were Glendinning's principal backers. However, following his championing of the Home Rule cause at the 1913 General Assembly of the Presbyterian Church in Ireland, he did play a behind-the-scenes role in the last act of the pre-1914 Home Rule political drama in the Route district – the meeting of Protestants in Ballymoney Town Hall on 24 October 1913 to protest against 'the lawless policy of Carsonism'.

The Ballymoney meeting of 1913

The meeting seems to have been originally the brainchild of Captain Jack White, DSO.[24] His autobiography certainly suggests this[25] and J.B. Armour's correspondence to his son William confirms it. However, almost simultaneously and independently, Sir Roger Casement appears to have had much the same idea,[26] possibly while staying with Joseph Bigger in Belfast. In their different ways both men were incurable romantics and they seem to have chosen Ballymoney as the venue for such a meeting largely because of its traditional reputation as a centre of radical, anti-unionist politics. White's foray into Irish affairs had begun on Saturday, 4 May 1912, when a letter written by him as a protest against unionist efforts to prevent Winston Churchill speaking in the Ulster Hall was printed in the *Ulster Guardian*.[27] He conceived of his role, as he always did, in grandiose terms. Although knowing little of Irish politics or Irish history, he confidently expected 'parties and personalities to respond to the predestined something I felt in myself … With my bible and my shillelagh, I went to the Route to chase the most elusive of all hares, the spirit of "98".' This republican spirit, he had been assured, still existed in north Antrim, 'waiting for discovery'.[28]

White was the son of Field Marshal Sir George White, VC, the 'hero of Ladysmith', whose family owned the Whitehall estate near Ballymena. As a boy he had always been a sore trial to his father and he attended a succession of schools, including Winchester, and was a success at none of them. A natural rebel and non-conformist, he nevertheless obtained a cadetship at Sandhurst where more adventures followed. He served with 1st Gordon Highlanders and 6th Mounted Infantry, and won a DSO under hilarious circumstances, according to his account, in South Africa in 1899. In 1902, he joined his father, now Governor of Gibraltar, as his ADC, and here he met his future wife, Mercedes (Dollie) Mosley, a half-Spanish Roman Catholic. Following army service in Peshawar and Aberdeen, he abandoned his military career and adopted an unconventional lifestyle. Working in a variety of unusual, unskilled jobs and a course of intensive reading of Bergson and Marx in the British Library persuaded him to join a Tolstoyan anarchist community in Gloucestershire. It was from 'Whiteway colony' that he made his first excursion into Irish politics in 1912.

So, the ex-soldier, ex-tramp, ex-lumberjack, a devotee of Bergson and Marx, fresh from a Tolstoyan community in Gloucestershire, accompanied by his half-Spanish wife, Dollie, descended on Ballymoney in his new two-seater Ford car. He found what he sought, or at least he thought he had. He obtained the support of Thomas Taggart and of J.B. Armour. Both were far from enthusiastic, however, especially about White himself, whom Armour subsequently described as 'peculiar'.[29] A committee was set up to organise a meeting which would demonstrate to the world that Carson did not enjoy the unanimous support of Protestant Ulster.

According to Armour's account, Casement had written to him about a week after White's visit suggesting a similar kind of meeting.[30] It is clear from Casement's correspondence with Alice Green, who at his suggestion was invited to speak, that he played a more active part than Casement's biographer Brian Inglis allows,[31] and also that his original conception of the meeting's function and purpose was rather different from that of the other organisers. He hoped, with the assistance 'of every drop of Fenian blood in my soul', to 'light a fire' which would 'set the Antrim hills ablaze' and would 'unite (for I think it is possible) Presbyterian and Catholic farmers and townsmen at Ballymoney in a clear message to Ireland ... I am now too deeply immersed in political intrigue to write further.'[32]

Armour and Captain White had to make it clear to Casement that an 'Irish-Ireland' meeting was out of the question, and that his suggestion of either Lord Ashbourne or F.J. Bigger as speakers would not be appropriate, since the former was a 'papish' and the latter 'a crank – a banner and pipe maniac', as Casement put it to Mrs Green.[33] They counselled instead that it would be better to limit the attendance to Protestants, since this would ensure that the meeting's essential message was underlined – namely that not all Protestants supported Carson. Having visited Ballymoney, lunched with Armour at Trinity manse and talked to some 15 local Liberals, Casement was convinced that a successful meeting was possible and that it would be the forerunner of similar meetings elsewhere in the province. These discussions settled the speakers and the resolutions but not who was to chair the meeting – an issue which was the subject of local rivalries and jealousies.[34]

White had not been present and characteristically objected violently to all the decisions taken and to Casement's role in particular. White was particularly unhappy about what he considered to be a change in the focus of the meeting from the theme of the 'lovelessness' to that of the 'lawlessness' of Carsonism. He believed that Casement was a wily, wrangling diplomat as well as a 'knight-errant'.[35] A stormy interview between the two men followed in Belfast, White accusing Casement of dishonesty and Casement feeling insulted. Casement had at first been well disposed towards him. 'Captain White is not a "lunatic" – but I am not very sure of his ability ... I don't think there is very much in him – save goodwill and a desire to knock Carsonism out, which is a good fighting instinct.'[36] However, after their disagreement Casement became convinced that White had, as Armour put it, 'a slate off'. Armour intervened and calmed White down by stressing that he would be the first major speaker. Casement refused to take the chair, as did John Baxter, who feared damage to his local business interests and felt that White was using the meeting as a stepping stone to contesting the North Antrim seat. Ultimately, the veteran Ballymoney businessman and Liberal, John McElderry, agreed to take on this task.[37]

It fell to Armour, through his friendship with Sir James Dougherty, the under-secretary of state at Dublin Castle and a Presbyterian native of Garvagh, County Londonderry, to thwart an alleged unionist plot to disrupt the meeting by importing 'a band of Orange rowdies with drums to drown the speakers'.[38] Armour, because of his influence with the Dublin Castle authorities, was able to secure the assistance of some 70 extra police to restrict entry to ticket holders only and to prevent drumming parties ensconcing themselves in the Protestant Hall, which lay just across the street from the Town Hall.[39] In the event the town was 'as quiet as on a Sabbath day',[40] and the only threat which the police had to deal with was that posed by two surveyors, whose car halted in the Diamond while the meeting was in progress. In the darkness the police mistook their theodolite and levelling staff for a dismantled Maxim Nordenfeldt gun, and were about to arrest both men when the mistake was realised.[41]

The Town Hall was bedecked with Union flags and a banner, hung above the platform, bore the legend: 'No provisional or provincial government for us'. Estimates of the attendance varied between 400 and 500, many of those present being farmers or businessmen.[42] The meeting passed two resolutions proposed by John McMaster and seconded by Robert Carson. The first rejected the claim of Sir Edward Carson's provisional government to speak for the Protestants of north-east Ulster and pledged lawful resistance to any decrees issued by this illegal and non-representative body. The second was Casement's work.[43] It was basically a call for the rejection of sectarianism as a divisive force amongst Irishmen and an invitation to the government to help bring all Irishmen together 'in one common field of national effort'. In addition to the resolutions, Captain White launched 'the new covenant', which was a pro-Home Rule pledge closely modelled on the unionist Covenant of 1912.[44]

The three principal speakers – White, Casement and Alice Green – all delivered stirring, if somewhat idealistic, appeals for love rather than hate amongst Irishmen. They all made references to the 'spirit of '98' and the need to revive it. Indeed, one of the supporting speakers, William Macafee, was so carried away by this spirit that he attributed the Dungannon convention of 1782 to the United Irishmen rather than to the Volunteers.[45] Since White, Casement and Green were all romantics, essentially out of touch with the realities of Ireland past or present, their emphasis was hardly surprising. It is significant that all three were not resident in Ulster and they had little experience of public speaking.

This was Casement's very first Irish political speech,[46] and both he and Mrs Green had declined Mrs Armour's invitation to have a meal at the manse before the meeting, because 'both of us wish to be quite to ourselves before the meeting – with no one to talk to, or talk to us'.[47] Sir Roger even suggested that Catholic nationalists sought not only the friendship and goodwill of Ulster Protestants but 'I believe even their leadership of Ulster'! Ulstermen (and presumably Ulsterwomen) had been led astray by sectarian animosity and imperialism. Casement urged them to take up a leadership role, as the old order was doomed to fall in Ireland.

It was left to Alec Wilson of Belfast and John Dinsmore of Ballymena to inject a note of realism into what Armour termed a 'high-toned' meeting.[48] Wilson stressed that he was anxious not just to protest against Carsonism, but to suggest a peaceful alternative. Many anti-unionist Ulster Protestants had reservations about Home Rule, he argued, but they would in the end do their best to make the new proposals work. Carsonism, he claimed, certainly did not reflect 'decent Ulster opinion' and it had led Ulster into a *cul-de-sac*, since Home Rule was inevitable. The proposed provisional government, he said, was unrepresentative and 'could not so much as collect the taxes', and at the end of the day Carson knew he would have to surrender since the UVF was designed only to be a useful bargaining counter.

Wilson deplored the vicious anti-Catholic propaganda put about by the unionists, born as it was out of unreasonable fears: 'If you cut the Pope out of Irish Unionism there is nothing left but a handful of rubbish'. He stressed that these fears of 'Rome Rule' were irrelevant since nationalism generally tended to reduce, not increase, clerical influence. Many Protestants, he suggested, had been coerced into signing the Covenant but, in a new Ireland, Irishmen would be able to work together for the welfare of all and a new and more normal party political system would emerge once the constitutional issue was taken out of politics. He concluded by asking that the meeting should be seen as the starting point of a movement for a peaceful settlement, which had to begin somewhere, sometime:

> Let Ballymoney have the great honour of starting a campaign which will show the world that Ulster Protestants are out for the welfare of all Ireland, no matter what the form of Irish government may be, and still more, that Ulster Protestants are Ulster Christians working for peace on earth and goodwill to [all] men.[49]

It is interesting to contrast the arguments of Wilson, an Anglican, with those of the Presbyterian Dinsmore. It was really left to him to state the Presbyterian case, since Armour did not speak at all. The familiar arguments about the evil influence of Belfast upon Ulster politics and upon the attitude of most Presbyterian clergy were once again deployed. The failure of Belfast to support the land campaign was put down to a desire on the part of Belfast mill owners for a continuing rural depression which would provide them with cheap labour. Once in the towns, the working class, Dinsmore argued, were distracted from their poverty through careful sectarian manipulation. 'When asked for bread they were given "The Boyne Water".'

The Pope, Dinsmore suggested, was worth 'at least half a million per annum to the linen lords of Ulster. It is not loyalty these men are out for, it is loot; and the true protagonists in the struggle are not the puppet Carsons and Londonderrys, but the great linen magnates of Belfast'.[50] The authors of *A Ripple in the Pond* noted that 'somewhat ironically, the meeting, bedecked with Union flags, where each speaker espoused the merits of Home Rule, ended with a rousing singing of the national anthem'.

However, given that most of the participants would have seen Home Rule very much within the context of the British Empire, this concluding action, along with the flags, was entirely logical and consistent.

The impact of the meeting was not as considerable as its organisers had hoped; indeed, Armour complained of the poor press coverage even in the nationalist *Irish News*.[51] At Casement's suggestion the speeches were printed in pamphlet form for local distribution.[52] Captain White's hopes of an Ulster Hall meeting came to nothing. Casement was at first delighted and wrote to Gertrude Bannister next day of 'a grand success'. 'Hall packed – smiling, good-faced farmers of the Route in hundreds and a magnificent table of reporters! I never saw so many in a small hall.' Friends such as Helen McNaghten and Erskine Childers liked Casement's speech and wrote to congratulate him.[53] But his attempt to organise a similar meeting in Coleraine foundered on local opposition,[54] and White and he soon found more exciting employment elsewhere – White in Dublin as the co-founder of the Irish Citizen Army and Casement as a gun-runner. The meeting did not even seem so numerically impressive to some observers, especially when the Ballymoney unionists were able to attract much greater numbers to a meeting which they held on 21 November. Both the Town Hall and the Protestant Hall had to be used to accommodate it.[55]

Unionist reaction was hostile but on the whole realistic. The *Ballymoney Free Press,* once a supporter of liberalism but by now a thoroughly unionist organ, argued that the organisers had failed to demonstrate that the majority of Protestants in the district were in favour of Home Rule,[56] and even had they been able to do so, as the Presbyterian weekly, *The Witness,* put it – 'the hum of a corner is not the buzz of a province'. *The Witness* also pointed out that some of those on the platform were individuals who had either been the recipients of posts from the Liberals, or were hopeful of such posts.[57] Very similar comments appeared in the Coleraine-based unionist newspaper, the *Northern Constitution*, which pointed out that the existence of a small body of Protestant Home Rulers had never been denied by unionists – they were 'merely the exception which proves the rule that at least ninety out of every hundred Ulster Protestants are Unionists'.[58]

But perhaps the most eloquent and objective assessment of all was that of the special correspondent of *The Times*. He drew attention to the fact that Ballymoney was the most favourable venue in the whole province for this kind of meeting:

> There is drilling here among the covenanters, but you see little sign of political enthusiasm in either camp. Every one seems to agree that all parties cultivate tolerance and an excessive amiability … The promoters of the meeting could say – what indeed elections had already made known – that there are a good number of radicals,

substantial people too,⁵⁹ about Ballymoney and district. Probably these men dislike the methods of the covenanters more than they like Home Rule, but that is another matter.⁶⁰

The editor of *The Times* of London was rather more scathing when he dismissed the meeting as representing,

> a small and isolated 'pocket' of dissident Protestants, the last few survivors of the Ulster Liberals of the old type. Ulster Liberalism is very like the Cheshire cat in 'Alice in Wonderland'. It has vanished till only its grin lingers furtively in a corner of County Antrim.⁶¹

This view was to be echoed by the 'official' historian of Ulster unionism, Ronald McNeill, when he asserted that the 'little handful of cranks' who had met in the 'village' [sic] of Ballymoney had simply emphasised the unanimity of Ulster behind Carson. ⁶²

From Armour's point of view, there was a rather unhappy postscript to the Ballymoney meeting in 1916. Following Casement's arrest and the failure of the Easter Rising, R.D. Megaw, the son of Armour's former boyhood friend and later political enemy, John Megaw, wrote to the *Northern Whig*, reminding its readers of Armour's connection with the 'traitor' Casement in 1913. But as Armour argued to his son: 'There was nothing said by Casement or anybody else at the meeting for which there is any need of apology. If Sir Roger has gone wrong in his mind, we cannot help that any more than we can help R.D.M.'s stupidities.'⁶³

Throughout the remainder of 1913 and 1914 Armour was simply a spectator of events both in Ulster and Europe. He was contemptuous of the Ballymoney unionist meeting of 21 November 1913, which was organised as a reply to the meeting of 24 October, attributing its success to the importation of large numbers of Orangemen from Ballycastle and Portrush by train and to the influence of 'John Barleycorn'. He alleged that the sitting member for North Antrim, Peter Kerr-Smiley, had, whilst drunk, delivered a speech written for him by W.J. Lynn, editor of the *Northern Whig*.⁶⁴ He was also concerned about the impact of Carson's tactics on dissident groups elsewhere in the world. 'Carsonism has something to answer for in regard to Larkinism, suffragetteism and Hindoo [sic] unrest.'⁶⁵

He still remained optimistic that a compromise settlement would be arrived at for Ireland, and he reacted sceptically to increasing discussion about the possible exclusion of Ulster from the Home Rule Bill – 'an idiotic proposal'⁶⁶ to which he was violently opposed:

> The Ulster counties are dependent commercially on their neighbours ... Derry would be in a nice position as a deal of its trade

is with Donegal ... 'The Tories' want Ulster to commit suicide. But they are not sincere... their whole design is to upset the parliament act. From a Protestant point of view, it would be calamitous as the Tories ... would give Catholics and Protestant home rulers no quarter and therefore... would stir up the Catholics in the south and west to harass ... the scattered Protestants.[67]

He continued to believe that a last-minute compromise was still possible and that if a plebiscite was to be held, the majority of the people of Ulster would vote against exclusion. He suggested that greater Protestant representation in the proposed Irish parliament could be the basis for such a compromise.[68] He stuck to his point of view right up to the outbreak of war. As late as 30 July, he was still convinced that 'if the bill was on the statute book, the excitement in Ulster would die down in a few weeks, as no sane person wants exclusion in any shape.'[69]

The Armour legacy

Prophetic visionary, courageous and consistent upholder of deeply and sincerely-held political views (despite personal abuse and threats of violence), enemy of the Church of Ireland and the landlord class, friend of the Roman Catholic community particularly in the educational field, a man who did not tolerate those whom he deemed to be fools gladly, a speaker and writer whose sense of anger and frustration led him to use quite violent and intemperate language at times, a 'thrawn Ulster Scot', a sportsman who, even in old age, played golf with the same single-minded determination with which he pursed his political goal of Home Rule, a broker who used his political influence after 1906 with the Liberal viceroy, Lord Aberdeen, to secure public appointments for his fellow Presbyterians – James Brown Armour was all of these things.

As I carefully noted even at the height of the historical revisionist fervour of the 1980s, Armour was 'a complex character in a complex situation'.[70] Perhaps the last words should be left to one of his sons – not the professional journalist William, who wrote a biography of his father by way of a memorial shortly after the latter's death,[71] but rather Max who followed in J.B.'s footsteps as a Presbyterian clergyman. The previously unpublished typescript notes which he compiled about his father to supplement his brother William's official biography are now available to the public for the first time, as part of the new deposit of J.B. Armour material in the Public Record Office of Northern Ireland.

> A home ruler and a Liberal he was till the day of his death, though it is true to say he was in no sense a revolutionary, and in many ways

he was more conservative than the Conservatives, but in the question of liberty of opinion and determination to uphold it he never drew back … The explanation of failure, if failure it was, was perhaps due to his force of character and a certain failure to suffer fools gladly… In the political situation in which he found himself he admitted that he spoke strongly, and he would add with a smile, 'A voice crying in the wilderness must be strident'.[72]

Notes

1. An earlier version of this essay appeared in *Familia: Ulster Genealogical Review*, 29 (2013), pp 20–43.
2. Ullans Speakers Association, *A Ripple in the Pond: The Home Rule Revolt in North Antrim* (Ballymoney, n.d.).
3. J.R.B. McMinn, *Against the Tide: A Calendar of the Papers of Rev. J.B. Armour, Irish Presbyterian Minister and Home Ruler 1869–1914* (Belfast, 1985).
4. J.R.B. McMinn, 'Armour, James Brown (1841–1928), Minister of the Presbyterian Church in Ireland' in *Oxford Dictionary of National Biography* (Oxford, 2004).
5. The additional J.B. Armour material has relatively recently been deposited in PRONI by J.B. Armour's grandson, J.S.S. Armour, a retired Presbyterian clergyman who lives in Canada. It has been separately catalogued by PRONI as D4515, while the more substantial J.B. Armour archive continues to be catalogued as D1792. The Alice Stopford Green Papers and the Roger Casement papers in the National Library of Ireland (NLI) are also relevant. Thanks are due to the Deputy Keeper of Records, PRONI, for permission to make use of the J.B. Armour papers.
6. J.B. Armour to J.B.M. Armour, 6 Apr. 1914 (PRONI, D4515/1/2).
7. J.B. Armour to J.B.M. Armour, 12 May 1914 (PRONI, D4515/1/2).
8. J.B. Armour to J.B.M. Armour, n.d. (PRONI, D4515/1/2).
9. J.B. Armour to J.B.M. Armour, 21 May 1915 (PRONI, D4515/1/2).
10. J.B. Armour to J.B.M. Armour, 4 Nov. 1915 (PRONI, D4515/1/2).
11. J.B. Armour to J.B.M. Armour, 6 Apr. 1916 (PRONI, D4515/1/2).
12. McMinn, *Against the Tide*, pp viii–lx.
13. J.S.S. Armour, 'It All Began with a Silver Spoon: a Family History Volume of the Armours, Stavelys and Annesleys' (PRONI, D4515/3/1).
14. Gordon Lucy, *Great Ulster Scots, People and Events in History: Armour of Ballymoney* (Belfast, n.d.); McMinn, *Against the Tide*.
15. W.S. Armour, *Armour of Ballymoney* (London, 1934); 'Notes on the Life of the Reverend J.B. Armour, M.A., by his son, the Reverend J.B.M. Armour, M.A., D.D.' (PRONI, D4515/3/2).

16. E.H. Carr, *What is History?* (London, 1961).
17. Arthur Marwick, *The Nature of History* (Basingstoke 1970 and 1981), p. 21.
18. Ibid.
19. This section of the essay and the two which follow it draw on both McMinn, *Against the Tide*, pp viii–lx and McMinn's more recent 2004 entry on Armour in the Oxford *DNB*. It also draws on Conor Morrissey, *Protestant Nationalists in Ireland, 1900–1923* (Cambridge, 2019), pp 177–8, for details of Irwin's career.
20. *Irish News*, 11 June 1921.
21. This section of the article is largely a summary of Richard McMinn, 'The myth of "Route" liberalism in County Antrim, 1869–1900', *Eire-Ireland*, 17:1 (Spring 1982), pp 137–49 and J.R.B. McMinn, 'Liberalism in North Antrim, 1900–14', *Irish Historical Studies*, 23:89 (May 1982), pp 17–29.
22. Brian Feeney, *Antrim: The Irish Revolution, 1912–23* (Dublin, 2021), p. 28. However, a much fuller analysis, based in part on the earlier work and publications by McMinn, can be found in Conor Morrissey's article, '"Rotten Protestants": Protestant home rulers and the Ulster Liberal Association, 1906–1918', *Historical Journal*, 61:3 (2018), which argues that 'this predominantly Protestant, pro-home rule organization, with its origins in nineteenth-century radicalism, complicates our understanding of the era' and demonstrates 'the existence of a significant group of Protestant Liberal activists in Ulster', who endured 'attacks and boycotting … and went into sharp decline after 1912'.
23. Feeney, *Antrim: The Irish Revolution*, p. 28.
24. For a full account of the controversial and colourful life of Captain Jack White (1879–1946) and also of his idiosyncratic political views, see Leo Keohane, *Captain Jack White: Imperialism, Anarchism and the Irish Citizen Army*, (Dublin, 2014). In reviewing the book in *Familia: Ulster Genealogical Review*, 34 (2018), this author noted (p. 230) that 'while White may remain something of an enigma, it can no longer be claimed that he is under-researched'.
25. J.R. White, *Misfit, an Autobiography* (London, 1930), p. 182.
26. J.B. Armour to W.S. Armour, n.d. (PRONI, D1792/A3/4/27). See also Michael Laffan, 'The making of a revolutionary: Casement and the Volunteers, 1913–14' in Mary E. Daly (ed.), *Roger Casement in Irish and World History* (Dublin, 2005), p. 66; Séamus Ó Síocháin, *Roger Casement: Imperialist, Rebel, Revolutionary* (Dublin, 2008), p. 361.
27. *Ulster Guardian*, 4 May 1912. The *Belfast Newsletter* had refused to publish it.
28. White, *Misfit*, p. 182.
29. J.B. Armour to W.S. Armour, n.d. (PRONI, D1792/A3/4/27).
30. Ibid.
31. Brian Inglis, *Roger Casement* (London, 1973), p. 235.
32. Roger Casement to Alice Stopford Green, 21 Sep. 1913 (NLI, A.S. Green papers, MS 10,464). The view that Casement played a direct

organisational role has been endorsed by recent biographers of Casement. See Laffan, 'The making of a revolutionary', p. 66 and Ó Síocháin, *Roger Casement*, p. 361. The latter refers in particular to Casement's lunch with Armour and to Sir Roger having arranged that Alice Green and 'probably' Alec Wilson would speak. 'He was responsible, too, for one of the two resolutions and for part of the second' (p. 361).

33. NLI, A.S. Green papers, MS 10,464.
34. J.B. Armour to W.S. Armour, n.d. (PRONI, D1792/A3/4/27).
35. White, *Misfit*, pp 183–5.
36. Roger Casement to Alice Stopford Green, 29 Sep. 1913 (NLI, A.S. Green papers, MS 10,464).
37. J.B. Armour to W.S. Armour, n.d. (PRONI, D1792/A3/4/28).
38. J.B. Armour to W.S. Armour, 16 Oct. 1913 (PRONI, D1792/A3/4/29).
39. J.B. Armour to W.S. Armour, 22 Oct. 1913 (PRONI, D1792/A3/4/30). The town commissioners had to meet the cost of the extra police.
40. J.B. Armour to J.B.M. Armour, n.d. (PRONI, D1792/A3/4/33).
41. *Ballymoney Free Press*, 30 Oct. 1913.
42. Ibid.; *The Times*, 25 Oct. 1913.
43. J.B. Armour to W.S. Armour, n.d. (PRONI, D1792/A3/4/28). Casement also seems to have considerably influenced the first resolution. White had originally wanted this resolution to register opposition to the 'lovelessness' rather than the 'lawlessness' of Carsonism and in his speech he dwelt on this theme at some length. See White, *Misfit*, pp 184–5.
44. All of the speeches delivered at the meeting, including the full text of the 'new covenant', were subsequently printed in pamphlet form. See *A Protestant Protest* (Ballymoney, 1913); copy in PRONI, T2362/2 and one also in Ballymoney Museum.
45. Ibid.
46. Inglis, Roger Casement, p. 238. Mrs. Green also found it difficult to prepare her speech. See R.B. McDowell, *Alice Stopford Green: a Passionate Historian* (Dublin, 1967), p. 94. See also Ó Síocháin, *Roger Casement*, pp 362–3.
47. Roger Casement to J.B. Armour, 23 Oct. 1913 (PRONI, D1792/A1/3/57).
48. J.B. Armour to J.B.M. Armour, n.d. (PRONI, D1792/A3/4/33).
49. *A Protestant Protest* (PRONI, T2362/2); Ullans Speakers Association, *A Ripple in the Pond*, p. 18.
50. Ibid.
51. J.B. Armour to J.B.M. Armour, n.d. (PRONI, D1792/A3/4/33). Ó Síocháin, on the other hand, refers to the meeting being well covered by the press, local and national (p. 363). More recently the late Alex Blair, a distinguished local historian of the Route, also argued that the meeting 'put Ballymoney into the press headlines across the United Kingdom.' (*Newsletter*, 17 Sep. 2013).

52. Roger Casement to J.B. Armour, n.d. (PRONI, D1792/A1/3/58).
53. B.L. Reid, *The Lives of Roger Casement* (New York and London, 1976), p. 179. See also letters to Casement in the Casement papers in NLI (MS 13,073) referred to by Ó Síocháin, *Roger Casement*, p. 363.
54. Ibid., p. 180. Despite the Coleraine set-back, the Ballymoney meeting was a significant landmark in Casement's career. As Reid points out, it drew him into the mainstream of Irish politics and was a link in a chain of events which led ultimately to his execution. Ó Síocháin suggests that the local council refused to rent Coleraine Town Hall and refers in endnote 69 (p. 587) to correspondence in the NLI Casement archive from Robert Hunter and Thomas Taggart which, along with a letter to the press by Hunter and Hugh Eccles, give full details of this.
55. *Ballymoney Free Press*, 30 Nov. 1913.
56. Ibid., 30 Oct. 1913.
57. *The Witness*, 31 Oct. 1913.
58. *Northern Constitution*, 1 Nov. 1913.
59. As regards the 'substantial' character of those at the meeting, it is interesting to note that the platform party contained ten magistrates, one county councillor, one rural district counsellor and three urban district counsellors.
60. *The Times*, 25 Oct. 1913.
61. Ibid. Angus Mitchell in *Casement* (London, 2003), p. 77, points out that these comments enraged Sir Roger and his reply was duly published on the paper's editorial page on 31 Oct. 'He argued that as someone born in Dublin and raised in Ulster, he was more representative of that province that any of the leaders behind Carsonism'.
62. Ronald McNeill, *Ulster's Stand for Union* (London, 1922), p. 158.
63. J.B. Armour to W.S. Armour, 17 May 1916 (PRONI, D1792/A3/7/14).
64. J.B. Armour to W.S. Armour, 27 Nov. 1913 (PRONI, D1792/A3/4/38).
65. J.B. Armour to W.S. Armour, n.d. (PRONI, D1792/A3/4/39).
66. J.B. Armour to W.S. Armour, 19 Feb. 1914 (PRONI, D1792/A3/5/9).
67. J.B. Armour to Jane MacMaster, 17 Mar. 1914 (PRONI, D1792/A3/13/14).
68. J.B. Armour to W.S. Armour, 11 Mar. 1914 (PRONI, D1792/A3/5/12).
69. J.B. Armour to W.S. Armour, 30 July 1914 (PRONI, D1792/A3/5/20).
70. McMinn, *Against the Tide*, p. lx.
71. W.S. Armour, *Armour of Ballymoney*.
72. 'Notes on the Life of The Reverend J.B. Armour' by J.B.M. Armour (PRONI, D4515/3/2).

2

Friends in Fleet Street

British press support for Ulster's anti-Home Rule campaign, 1912–14

ALAN F. PARKINSON

One of the early markers of this decade of anniversaries was the centenary of the ill-fated third Home Rule legislation of 1912–14. No other part of Ireland witnessed the same raw emotions which this impending legislation provoked amongst the Protestant community of its north-eastern corner. The legislation, proposing a single Dublin parliament which would retain its imperial connections, had been introduced at Westminster at the beginning of 1912, and community tension escalated across Ulster over the course of the next two years, resulting in political stalemate and the province of Ulster facing the outbreak of civil war. The north's religious and demographic divide had produced very different responses from Protestants and Catholics to the issue of Home Rule. After the highly fractious visit of Winston Churchill to address a pro-Home Rule rally organised by Joe Devlin's United Irish League at Celtic Park in February, politicians at Westminster were sharply 'reminded again that society in the north of Ireland was dangerously fractured [and] bitterly divided to a degree quite beyond the experience of any other part of the United Kingdom.'[1]

Unionists were led in their opposition campaign by their relatively new party leader, Sir Edward Carson, the Dublin-born barrister and parliamentarian.[2] The subsequent resistance campaign mounted by Carson and his able lieutenant, Sir James Craig, involved Irish unionists endeavouring to influence not only political parties at Westminster – where the Liberals, backed by John Redmond's Irish Nationalist Party, had a small majority over Andrew Bonar Law's Tory opposition, which by throwing its weight behind Ulster's unionists, was also prone to charges of political opportunism – and also in the recently reformed House of Lords. Arguably what mattered even more was the courting of public opinion. Apart from producing a colossal amount of propaganda material for the 'external' British and overseas market, unionists realised they would have to appeal directly to the wider British public.

Fortunately for them, sympathy for their perceived plight was strong. In an age of imperialistic and patriotic fervour, the resistance of 'loyal' Ulster had already garnered the attention of large sections of the British public, many of whom were prepared to identify with the loyal 'underdogs'. However, this sympathy for unionists' isolation – surrounded as they were by a majority of fellow countrymen determined to pursue a different political path and threatened by the rejection of the British political administration – needed to be accompanied by an orchestrated push to grab the attention, and most crucially of all, the support, of the bulk of the all-important British press.[3]

It is this widespread interest in and backing for the perceived fragile predicament of Ulster Protestants which is at the heart of this essay, though I investigated a raft of other resistance campaign strategies and backers in my book, *Friends in High Places*.[4] Whilst most of the British press during this Edwardian period were Tory-supporting journals (this also included most of the major provincial newspapers such as the *Birmingham Post, Yorkshire Post, Liverpool Post,* and *Glasgow Herald*), there was also a significant number of other, influential, papers and weekly journals strongly opposed to Ulster's unionists. As this is beyond the remit of this essay, I shall not delve too closely into their coverage of events in Ulster during these two years, but the position of most of them is encapsulated in the view of the liberal weekly, *The Nation* which airily pointed out that 'the position of Ulster seems to us to be essentially a question for Ireland herself.'[5]

'The greatest figure who ever strode down Fleet Street'

The early part of the twentieth century proved to be a halcyon period for the newspaper industry, and one which also proved to be beneficial for the cause of Ulster Unionists in their fight against impending Home Rule. In an age of ever-improving levels of literacy and greater involvement of ordinary people in the wider political process, journalists endeavoured to present the major topical stories in a less dry and more entertaining manner. The *Daily Mirror* had pioneered newspaper photography in 1905, and many new tabloids, including the best-selling *Daily Mail* – this had started operating in Fleet Street in 1896 and was soon boasting of a million plus daily sales – regularly printed emotion-pulling 'human' news stories, written in a dramatic style by on-the-spot reporters.

Unionists had benefitted from the relative decline of the radical press in the final years of the nineteenth century, whilst sympathetic editors and newspaper proprietors would aid the cause of Ulster's political resistance by the hard-hitting tone of their editorials; the lampooning of government ministers and nationalist leaders in regular cartoons; photographic accounts of the north's resolute leaders and defiant Ulster Volunteers; and also by affording newspaper space to a wide range of unionist backers in airing sympathetic views regarding the plight of loyalists in north-eastern Ireland. They were helped in this by the dramatic and militaristic nature of the ever-deepening Ulster crisis, with its overtly imperialistic undertones and the vastly increased audience of readers (this was believed to have quadrupled inside 20 years, between 1896 and 1914). Without question, this degree of press expansion had resulted in Edwardians becoming 'better informed and better entertained than any previous generation.'6

This was a golden period for newspaper 'barons' and editors, with the increased assertiveness of the latter a consequence of their greater independence. They included C.P. ('Great') Scott, the long-serving owner and editor of the *Manchester Guardian*; J.L. Garvin, the editor of both the *Observer* and the *Pall Mall Gazette*; H.A. Gwynne at the *Morning Post* (he succeeded W.T. Stead after the latter perished on the *Titanic* in April 1912); and the most influential of them all, Alfred Harmsworth.7 Described by another press magnate Lord Beaverbrook as 'the greatest figure who ever strode down Fleet Street', Harmsworth owned the most influential paper of the day, *The Times*, and also Britain's best-selling newspaper, the *Daily Mail*. Alfred Harmsworth was also a highly significant figure on account of his policy to distance himself, at least to a degree, from the main political parties.

Harmsworth had spent his childhood years in comparative poverty in Dublin, before making his fortune in London. His sympathy for the Ulster Unionists meant that he was an invaluable asset to their campaign, not least on account of the support provided in *The Times* and *Daily Mail*, but also because of the manner in which he could command the attention of senior politicians, particularly the opponents of Edward Carson's Ulster Unionist Party. In a letter to Winston Churchill during the spring of 1914, in which he espoused the case for Ulster's permanent exclusion from Irish Home Rule, Harmsworth turned down Churchill's offer of lunch – 'these are not lunching times' – and curtly reminded the First Lord of the Admiralty of his 'misguided' Home Rule policy:

> Any attempt to overcome the Ulster Protestants will mean Civil War. A tragic aspect of the situation is that the South of Ireland does not particularly want Home Rule. I went into the matter minutely on my last visit [to Ireland], and was surprised at the apathy existing.

> Your position seems completely out of touch with the real views of the English as well as the Irish peoples.[8]

Alfred Harmsworth's major contribution to the anti-Home Rule campaign was his broad, if conditional, support for the Ulster Unionist position. He was quick to realise the potential scale of the threat posed by Ulster resistance to the proposed legislation from its earliest phase, and one of the consequences of this was the detailed coverage in his newspapers of what he firmly believed was the most crucial domestic crisis during an era of crises. The editorials in Harmsworth's newspapers, often a mirror image of his own beliefs, were normally in broad agreement with the Irish policies of the Conservative Party. However, there were occasions when he disagreed with the virulent tone of language adopted by his editors, moaning on one occasion that they spent too much time 'leading with this gloomy Irish stuff'.[9]

Harmsworth was particularly concerned when his editors veered too closely to condoning potential civil disobedience and law-breaking, and communicated his misgivings to the new editor of *The Times*, Geoffrey Robinson, after his leading article backing Andrew Bonar Law's fiery speech in support of Carson's unionists at Blenheim Palace in July 1912. The result of this was that *The Times* withdrew its backing for Bonar Law's hard-line stance a fortnight later, now warning that the use of physical force would 'only invalidate Ulster's cause.' A pleased proprietor informed his editor that he had 'liked the leader better this morning' and that he had 'not cared for the violent Ulster language of Bonar Law, Carson and others.'[10]

Both Harmsworth and Robinson were anxious to raise the profile of the Ulster question in the British press, and were also committed to deploying some of their top writers to convey what it was like on the 'front line' to their readers. Shortly after taking up the editorship of *The Times*, Robinson wrote to John Healy, his counterpart at the *Irish Times*, to express his concern that the Ulster question was 'falling into the background in England' and that he was 'anxious to rescue it' from this 'obscurity'.[11] He soon appointed the experienced former *Times of India* editor, Lovat Fraser, to sound out how serious Belfast unionists were in their resistance to Home Rule. Fraser was asked to compile regular despatches that would help the paper's readers to better understand what the political temperature was like across the Irish Sea. Fraser's output in a relatively short period of time – some four or five months in 1913–14 – was considerable. He was purported to have drafted over 20 major articles on the Irish situation.

An analysis of Fraser's articles and correspondence with Robinson provides a fascinating insight into *The Times*' coverage of Irish events during this crucial spell in its history. Admitting to knowing 'nothing' about Irish affairs, Lovat Fraser expressed his view that 'solid Englishmen' were unlikely to 'back up serious rebellion in Ulster and [that] comic opera touches will kill it anyway.'[12] He was soon out and about, visiting the Belfast shipyards – 'masquerading as a tourist with a pair of field-glasses and a wife' – and watching a UVF demonstration in Armagh. Fraser was clearly impressed with this show of strength, claiming that the Volunteers' intentions were 'not bluff in that they mean to go as far as they are able.' Shortly after this Armagh demonstration, Fraser wrote about a UVF training exercise in the duke of Abercorn's grounds at Baronscourt in County Tyrone. He maintained that 'this is not a movement of aristocrats or landlords, [but] a movement of the people … who are at the backbone of Ulster.'[13]

Informed by Fraser's despatches and his research into the Irish political situation – he covered over 600 miles by road inside a few days – *The Times* increased its coverage of events in Ulster throughout the two years of the political crisis there. This is not to say that the newspaper was unsympathetic to the cause of Ulster's Protestant population at the start of the crisis in the spring of 1912. Opposing the Home Rule legislation, *The Times* pointed out that 'English Liberals may think that the attitude of this great community of Irishmen, composed of many churches and of different political schools, is unreasonable and unjustifiable, but no sane statesmanship can ignore it.'[14] Central to the thinking of the newspaper's editorial team, and indeed that of the Conservative Party's leadership, was the conviction that such a measure, which was likely to precipitate profound constitutional and political change, should first be rubber-stamped by the British electorate. This was clearly stated in an editorial half-way through the bill's parliamentary passage:

> A free community cannot justify, or even constitutionally be deprived of its privileges or its position in the realm by any measure, that is not stamped with the considered and unquestioned approval of the great body of electors in the United Kingdom.[15]

The Times' coverage of the key moments of the Ulster crisis

A striking feature of Edwardian journalism was the vivid, empathetic writing style and the on-the-ground nature of the reporting of key incidents. This was as true for 'quality' newspapers, like *The Times*, as it was for the more sensational tabloid press. One of the earliest meetings which gained considerable coverage in the British press was the massive unionist gathering at Belfast's Balmoral Showgrounds in April 1912. At this, Andrew Bonar Law, the Conservative Party leader, expressed his support for Ulster, reminding those assembled that 'once again you hold the pass for the Empire.'[16] *The Times* stressed the cross-community nature of the demonstration – 'one of the very greatest to be held in Britain' – where there was 'a mingling in their ranks [of] patrician and plebian, clergy and laity, masters and men.'[17] The newspaper's editorial that day also stressed the wider significance of the meeting which constituted 'the assemblage of a nation to defend its existence, [and] to plead against an attempt to suppress its identity, to plead and also to warn.'[18]

Later that month, *The Times* also had a team of reporters at the Blenheim Palace gathering in Oxfordshire, which had been called to illustrate the strength of support for Ulster's unionists within the Conservative Party and also at grass-roots level. Describing how the meeting had been 'framed in an incomparable setting', *The Times* advised its readers that the demonstration had been 'representative of the fighting strength of the Party throughout the length and breadth of the land'. The same edition of the paper also went into some detail on the multi-faceted experiences of the delegates that sunny day in Oxfordshire:

> They had come to the number of 3,000 in several trains to the quiet Oxfordshire stations which are nearest to the Palace of Blenheim; they were entertained to luncheon in a huge marquee; they were shown the treasures of the great mansion and finally, they marched in procession to the noble courtyards of Vanburgh's ornate pile to hear the speeches of Sir Edward Carson and Mr F.E. Smith.[19]

The Times was just one of many journals to retain staff in Ulster in order to cover the two-week long Covenant campaign in September 1912. The paper's correspondent once again stressed the cohesive nature of Protestant support for Carson, as the campaign of mass meetings commenced in Enniskillen. He observed that the Portora Gate Hotel began to 'fill with clergymen, landlords and ladies, while outside these aristocratic precincts, sauntered bearded Protestant peasants of extraordinary age, as if they had always remained faithful to the memory of King William.'[20]

Coverage of the other Covenant meetings was similarly detailed and sympathetic, and the paper's assessment of the tour's impact upon public opinion in England is a significant one. Noting how its English readers had 'followed in detail and with deepening interest the impressive series of meetings throughout the province', *The Times* believed that 'the same note of sincerity and enthusiasm ran through them all.' The editorial concluded:

> The impression left on the mind of every competent observer is that of a community absolutely united in its resistance to the act of separation with which it is threatened ... We believe that these Northern gatherings here have brought that conviction [the 'shipwrecking' of the Bill] home to many thousands of Englishmen.[21]

Another key incident during this anti Home Rule campaign was the Curragh 'mutiny' of March 1914 when several army officers expressed their opposition to participating in any military action designed to enforce the Home Rule legislation. *The Times*' 'special Irish' correspondent noted how 'the army has been brought into one sole band of brotherhood in its determination to refuse to coerce the loyalists of Ulster, and regiments which were indifferent to each other before are now sworn allies.'[22] A few days earlier, *The Times* had reflected on the end of the crisis at the Curragh camp. It concluded that the army had been 'saved from complete destruction by the timely retreat of the Government from a position which they should never had assumed.'[23]

Less than two weeks later *The Times* described the patriotic scene in the area around Hyde Park in central London. Thousands of pro-Ulster British loyalists and imperialists had congregated for a rally arranged by Lord Milner in support of Ulster's stand against the Home Rule legislation. Observing that the national flag was 'hanging from Piccadilly windows, omnibuses, cars, bicycles, barrows and even the dust-cart of a road-sweeper', the paper's reporter again emphasised the cross-class nature of support in Britain for the loyalist case, as 'Grosvenor Street rubbed shoulders with Whitechapel and peers struggled for places near the platforms with dockers from the East End'.[24]

As the crisis appeared to be heading towards its climax in the spring of 1914, the newspaper maintained its heavy presence of reporters in Belfast, where they filed their despatches on the latest events in Ulster. When news broke of gun-running along the Antrim and Down coasts, the tone of *The Times*' editorials did not turn on Edward Carson or his Ulster Volunteers for this aggressive and illegal action, but rather railed against the government for failing to grasp the 'real gravity' of the situation across the Irish Sea. The leading article dismissed the story of arms importation as being 'not new' and instead focused on the 'striking' solidarity of Ulster's unionists. The editorial suggested that the episode had instead sent a 'warning' to Asquith's administration, making it clear that 'a population so united and so determined cannot be dealt with by coercive measures.'[25]

The following month, *The Times* again called on its Belfast staff to assess the mood in Ulster as the Home Rule Bill prepared to enter its final parliamentary phase. In a detailed report, 'The war cloud: ominous quiet of the Covenanters', *The Times*' readers were warned against mistaking the 'quiet' response of Ulster's unionists for a weakening of resolve. Instead, the reporter emphasised the 'depth' of their commitment to the cause they shared with Sir Edward Carson:

> Let no one suppose that because Ulster is quiet she has weakened her resolve. The stillness which prevails is not indifference; it is the

stillness of water which runs deep. Deep is Ulster's mistrust of the Ministry; deep her resentment against it; deep is the feeling of danger which has bound all classes together in defensive preparation; and the deep determination that the whole of Ulster shall be left outside Home Rule.[26]

Apart from the invaluable contributions of staff reporters and editorial teams, the opinion columns and letter pages of *The Times* reverberated to strident and predominantly supportive noises, often emanating from leading politicians like Lord Milner and F.E. Smith (and even from political opponents such as Lord Loreburn). Leading Tory policy-makers, such as F.S. Oliver, a leading advocate of a federal solution to Ireland's political difficulties, were also involved in disseminating political propaganda within the pages of the influential *The Times*. Oliver was probably behind the writing of a series of letters in 1910 – he used the pseudonym 'Pacifus' – and other writers to have their work published in the paper's columns during this period included S. Weyman and the Ulster imperialist and writer, William Flavelle Monypenny. Rejecting the argument that Irish self-government based on the South African model would actually work, Monypenny maintained that dominion status for Ireland would fail to heal the ancient rift between its two distinct communities. He argued that Home Rule could 'not be applied to Ireland without at the same time violating those very principles to which its advocates appeal', and that 'self-government for either of Ireland's two peoples in the violated Home Rule sense means subjection for the other.'[27]

The *Daily Mail* and the 'New British Journalism'

Alfred Harmsworth's other major national newspaper, the *Daily Mail*, appealed to a socially different but more numerous audience. Founded by Harmsworth in 1896, the *Mail*'s style, presentation and type of readership contrasted sharply with that of the *The Times*, but the tabloid paper's focus on key Irish stories and its unremitting backing for Ulster's loyalists was similar to the approach of its more fashionable 'sister' paper. The million-a-day selling *Mail*, competitively priced at a halfpenny and enjoying a daily circulation five times greater than any other similarly-priced paper, was already encompassing several of the features of modern tabloid newspapers. Although relatively literary features articles, penned by the like of distinguished journalists like Charles E. Hands and H. Hamilton Fyfe were probably more common in the Edwardian version of the paper than in today's *Mail*, commercially motivated and 'human interest' factors were also very much to the fore, with considerable use of on-the-ground reporters, photographs and advertisements.[28] Yet defenders of Harmsworth have maintained that whilst he was clearly using commercial techniques to sell as many newspapers as he could, he was not deliberately endeavouring to trivialise the news. Tom Clarke argued that Alfred Harmsworth was rather a *vox populi*, non-compromising personality, who also possessed a surprisingly liberal streak on a number of issues. In suggesting that Harmsworth was the main driving-force behind a newspaper revolution in Britain, Clarke argued that he had battled all his life for 'the freedom of the printed word', not merely as a privilege of the press but as the fundamental right of the people, and as one of the safeguards against political misgovernment.'[29]

With its huge sales and circulation range, the *Mail* was a perfect illustration of what has been called the 'New Journalism in Britain'.[30] The paper provided copious coverage to Ulster's anti-Home Rule campaign. Throughout the period between the spring of 1912 and the start of the Great War in the late summer of 1914, there appeared within the *Mail's* pages, detailed reports of the latest political developments and crises, numerous opinion pieces or editorials and photographs of the leading personalities. Although the newspaper occasionally adopted low level coverage of Ulster events, this soon changed when there were major developments in the ongoing crisis. Examples of this occurred within weeks of one another in the spring of 1914. The *Mail*, with a penchant for covering dramatic events, had its reporters on the ground to cover key demonstrations both in England and in Ulster. It described in some detail the pageantry and pomp of the Conservative and Irish Unionist gathering in the grounds of Blenheim Palace in July 1912, comparing this to 'a peerless pearl of beauty set in a typical English landscape.' The main theme of the paper's coverage of this major demonstration – at which Andrew Bonar Law pledged that there would be 'no length of resistance to which Ulster can go in which I would not be prepared to support them' – was the wide-ranging support in Britain (and indeed, further afield) for the Ulster Unionist position:

> There was not an unrepresented county or city. Here were men from industrial centres such as Liverpool and Leeds fraternising with agriculturalists from Kent and Yorkshire; there Scotsmen holding out their hand to Ulstermen and Welshmen conversing with men from overseas. The same spirit imbued them – the spirit of the fight. [31]

Two examples of the *Mail's* detailed treatment of the Ulster crisis were the Curragh 'mutiny' and the gun-running expedition, brought to a successful conclusion by the UVF's Fred Crawford, in March/April 1914. For over a week in March, the *Mail* informed its readers about the 'sensational' developments at the Curragh military camp outside Dublin and London's

War Office. Sir Edward Carson was pictured leaving his home in London's fashionable Eaton Place at the height of this military crisis, and Harmsworth had telegraphed the editors of his newspapers from Paris, instructing them to expose the government's attempts to coerce Ulster. The *Mail* soon responded to its owner's directive, claiming that the Prime Minister would be unable to 'bully the Ulster Unionists without the whole-hearted support of the Army.'[32] The paper's editorial demanded the immediate dissolution of parliament, and if this resulted in Asquith's defeat, the editorial pointed out that the monarch would have to enforce his constitutional right and call on the leader of the opposition to form a new government, before either Ulster was 'goaded into insurrection' or 'the discipline of the Army [was] destroyed'.[33]

The sensational news of gun-running along Ulster's coastline the following month were tailor-made for a newspaper like the *Daily Mail* which was constantly looking out for 'scoops', to provide it with bragging rights over its rivals. One of its leading writers, H. Hamilton Fyfe, composed an article praising the 'discipline' of the Ulster Volunteers, and 'the precision of the whole gun-running operation'.[34] The central message of Fyfe's evocative article was the cohesion of Ulster's loyalist community, with whom he invited his readers to empathise. Detailing the 'normal, everyday lives of the Orangemen', Fyfe went on:

> I know perfectly well that the man who sells me collars was on picket duty. I know that the wealthy manufacturer who sits yawning in his office had no sleep last night. I know that almost every man I speak to was in some capacity or other contributing to the success of the manoeuvre ... but they make no boast of it. It has become part of their life. They are going about their ordinary occupations today just as if they had never handled anything more lethal than a ledger or taken part in any action more warlike than a football match on a Saturday excursion to the sea.[35]

In the same edition of the *Mail*, a leading article mocked the Prime Minister's earlier threat that he would take 'appropriate steps to vindicate the authority of the law' in Ulster by suggesting he was merely 'locking the stable door after the steed has been stolen.'[36]

During the early summer months of 1914, as the crisis appeared to be approaching a potentially bloody conclusion, the *Mail* devoted substantial sections of several editions to the deteriorating situation in Ireland. For instance, at a point when Alfred Harmsworth was himself 'observing' in Ulster, as many as 12 of his *Daily Mail* reporters were covering Edward Carson's address to the massed ranks of Orangemen and Ulster Volunteers in Belfast during the Twelfth of July celebrations. However, at least one of this large group of journalists held a rather different brief. The newspaper's travel correspondent, V.E. Ward, was there to assess the potential of the region as a tourist spot. In a bizarre invitation to readers to visit an area which was on the verge of civil war, Ward pointed at Ulster's 'scenic beauty' and the 'excellent motoring, golf and angling facilities', adding – perhaps with tongue in cheek – that the region was 'at the present unique as a holiday ground for the student of politics.' Much of the rest of his lengthy article was about the 'situation' in the north and the 'demeanour' of the Ulster Volunteers. He claimed that the Volunteer movement provided 'many interesting spectacles for the visitor', before concluding his piece with a reference to 'a friendly local' who had been 'wearing in his coat the badge of the Ulster Volunteers'.[37]

J.L. Garvin of *The Observer* and the *Pall Mall Gazette*

Another leading press figure and a constant friend of Ulster's unionists during this difficult period was J.L. Garvin, the editor of the longstanding, and at that time, right-wing, Sunday newspaper, *The Observer*, and later on, also the editor of the daily *Pall Mall Gazette*.[38] A leading figure in what was a golden generation of Fleet Street scribes, Garvin enjoyed a highly successful 40-year career at the heart of British journalism. Forthright and fearless, he was at times inclined to be controversial, and by going further than most Fleet Street journalists in his support for the Ulster Unionists, Garvin fell out with senior members of the Conservative Party (most notably with Bonar Law) largely on account of the extreme nature of his Ulster rhetoric. As early as mid-June 1912, J.L. Garvin was pressing the opposition leader and the wider Conservative Party to go one step further in its backing for Ulster's Protestant community. In an *Observer* editorial calling for public meetings to be organised on an 'unprecedented' scale across Great Britain, Garvin was anxious for a stepping up in such support for Ulster loyalists:

> The time is approaching, and in our view has almost arrived, when a great departure must be taken once and for all in the methods of Ulster resistance. Many respectable persons seem unwilling to contemplate ultimate bloodshed while deprecating any intermediate breach of the parliamentary conventions.[39]

Garvin was also of considerable importance for Carson and his colleagues, not only on account of his seemingly unqualified support for their campaign, but also because of his enthusiasm to directly challenge prevailing British apathy over the Home Rule issue. Garvin, firmly to the right in most of his political beliefs, was convinced that the electorate was relatively unsophisticated, and needed to have simple propaganda-style messages regularly conveyed to them in a straightforward but powerful manner. J.L. Garvin, like a few other writers (including F.S. Oliver), had been a former advocate of federalism but, as his influence over Tory party policy waned, his support for Ulster resistance deepened. A biographer maintained that Garvin's objective from 1912 onwards was to force the government into recognising that unionists would not countenance the third Home Rule Bill becoming law before an election had taken place on the issue.[40]

J.L. Garvin wrote most of his paper's editorials on Ulster and also visited the province to describe the mood of Carson's Volunteers. The most memorable of his despatches were those he penned for both his newspapers during the Covenant campaign of September 1912. Three issues of *The Observer* in late August and September were virtually devoted to Covenant proceedings. Garvin's justification for this was that apathy towards Irish Home Rule within Britain, whilst prevalent, was also superficial in its nature, and what was urgently needed was 'a great national awakening to the menace of the peril which draws slowly nearer.'[41] Garvin's report of events on Covenant Day in Belfast, composed whilst perching in a precarious position in the dome of its City Hall, just after Carson and his colleagues had signed the Covenant, spoke of the 'concentrated will and courage' of Ulster's loyalists. His assessment of the impact of the Covenant campaign was frank and unambiguous. He argued that Home Rule was 'dead, killed by the resistance of Sir Edward Carson and his followers', and concluded that it was up to 'the British electorate to see that it has no resurrection.'[42]

Although Garvin sustained unswerving support for Ulster's cause, he would radically reassess his hopes for the future governance of the region. The events during the build-up to the signing of the Covenant towards the end of September 1912 made him realise that 'Ulster too needed a place of its own', and he started to consider devolutionary options for the province. He wrote:

> We may think the causes for which the Scottish Covenanters or the French revolutionaries bonded themselves [to be] right or wrong. But the results of the Solemn League and Covenant and the Oath of the Tennis Court are written across the pages of history in letters of blood.[43]

Garvin also became editor of the *Pall Mall Gazette* in 1912. The *Gazette*, popular in London's clubland, had a relatively small, but influential, readership. Being an evening paper, it had distinct advantages over other daily newspapers, as far as covering breaking news stories were concerned.

An audit of editions of the *Pall Mall Gazette* during September and October 1912 reveal the extent of coverage and volume of support which Garvin's new paper afforded to what he regarded as the 'underdogs' in the Irish crisis, Ulster's unionist community. During quieter periods – like the first half of September – there were few Irish stories, but in the build-up to Covenant Day and its sequel (most especially Carson's subsequent visits to Liverpool and Glasgow), coverage of Ulster events was detailed and sympathy for the loyalist predicament was clearly evident. Over this two-month period, the *Gazette* carried Ulster stories on its front page for at least 12 issues. There were eight editorials on the crisis, as well as cartoons, enthusiastic letters of support, the printing of the text of Ulster's Covenant, and a poem by William Watson in celebration of the climax of the campaign.[44] The paper's correspondents, and of course its editor, reported from the various venues chosen as stages during the Covenant 'trail', frequently running out of superlatives as they filed their copy. At the start of the Covenant campaign, the *Gazette* observed that Ulster had 'planted her standard and it is for the Government to say whether they will try to uproot[it].'[45] The next day's editorial stressed the moral righteousness of Ulster's loyalists, dismissing their 'lampooners', who had simply dismissed them as 'a sordid, unimaginative, money-grabbing, self-centred race.' Rather the *Gazette* asserted, 'such men could never be prompted to stake their all for the Union unless the issue penetrated to the very roots of their being.'[46]

On the eve of 'Ulster Day', the *Gazette* reviewed the 'great campaign', which they estimated to have been 'the most remarkable political pilgrimage' since William Gladstone's renowned Midlothian campaign in 1880. The journal's assessment of the campaign was unambiguous. Above all else, the Irish unionist leader's tour had 'done more to unite and coalesce the elements of unionism' in the province than 'any other movement that has taken place during that period.'[47] In another editorial a few days later, the *Pall Mall Gazette* referred directly to the extensive coverage of Covenant Day in its columns, 'entirely without apology'. In a special article in the same edition of the paper, entitled 'Personal impressions', Garvin wrote at length and with unconcealed passion about the 'amazement' of the previous few days. He told his readers:

> Stronger in energy, determination, wealth, resources of every kind than any other city of equal size on earth, Belfast in this business is an Iron City, and those who talk of coercing it have their work cut out … I have come back as certain of that fact – Belfast would fight, would have universal sympathy and it would dominate Great Britain's politics – as of my own being. Belfast will not have Home Rule and the Nationalists will never have Belfast![48]

Other Fleet Street friends

Several other Conservative Party-leaning journals also provided considerable support for the Ulster Unionist position, though some of these – including the *Daily Telegraph* and the *Spectator* – remained anxious about becoming too deeply involved in the Irish political quagmire which would in turn stifle their coverage of other significant issues, and they were also concerned about the political right falling deeper into the trap of close association with Ulster paramilitary forces. Of all the respected, 'quality', newspapers, the *Daily Telegraph* offered the most reasoned endorsement of Ulster's arguments to be treated differently, with the newspaper emphasising the Liberal administration's 'unconstitutional' approach which had resulted in its 'clinging to power by means of a coalition which sticks at nothing and regards nothing but its own self-preservation'.[49] The *Telegraph* also maintained that Ulster had been 'goaded into an attitude which makes Home Rule a certain failure' and praised its leaders for conducting a Covenant campaign which illustrated 'a combination of wisdom, ability and restraint' that was clearly discernible in 'a great movement in defence of civil and religious liberty.'[50] The *Telegraph* also had its reporters on the spot covering the main 'pro-Ulster' events, including one of the earliest at the Balmoral Showgrounds in Belfast in April 1912. Hyperbole was the order of the day in its reporter's assessment of the day in south Belfast, which had 'constituted 'one of the greatest manifestos of the faith and determination of a people that the world has ever seen.'[51]

One of the most popular dailies at the time was the *Morning Post*, which also offered unconditional backing to Ulster's loyalists, much of it motivated by the journal's fundamental conservatism and its love of empire. Its editor, H.A. Gwynne, was a fervent admirer of Sir Edward Carson, writing regularly to the Ulster leader, and offering him words of encouragement. One such offer of assistance from Gwynne bordered on the irrational and probably embarrassed Carson. Writing to him on 18 February 1914, Gwynne emphasised his 'strong attitude to the Ulster question', declaring:

> if civil war arises or you or your friends think it inevitable, I would wish to place my services at the disposal of the [Ulster's] provisional government. I am not unacquainted with war and perhaps may be useful. Would you see that I am sent the proper form to fill up?[52]

Indeed, Gwynne would remind Carson of his pledge at the height of the Curragh crisis a few weeks later, reassuring Sir Edward that 'henceforth I am a private soldier and you are the general.'[53]

Gwynne's newspaper praised the steadfastness, orderliness and grim resolution of Ulster's Volunteers and condemned the actions of their various opponents, ranging from Asquith's administration to the small Labour parliamentary group at Westminster for 'betraying the interests of the industrial population of Ireland.'[54] The *Post* also contrasted Ulster's 'zeal for the Union' with what they dismissed as the apathy emanating from the ranks of Home Rulers towards Irish unity. An editorial in May 1913 argued that Carson's followers would 'freely and joyfully stake every thing for their liberty', pointing out that history was 'not made by Act of Parliament or the tramping of the division lobbies, but by the strength of purpose that is in the hearts of men.'[55] The *Post* was also effusive in its support for the formation and active role of pressure groups like the British League and the British Covenant movement. Acknowledging the 'plain and urgent need' for such organisations, the *Post* argued that English unionists were bound to give Ulster their fervent and unflinching support, since they realised 'not only the justice of their cause, but also the fact that she is in the forefront of a battle for the national strength and security.'[56]

Similar in style and presentation to its main competitor, Harmsworth's *Mail*, the *Daily Express* competed with its rivals for the latest 'scoop', or news story. The *Express* obviously won the day over its competitors at the time of the gun-running incident of April 1914, when one of its reporters showed considerable ingenuity by managing to talk his way into a UVF motor transport lorry which was setting off around nightfall for the Larne coast. The newspaper's cartoon the following day – in which sleepy coastguards Herbert Asquith and Winston Churchill missed an arms vessel as it steamed away on the horizon – illustrates wher the paper's sympathies lay. This cartoon, printed on the morning of the FA Cup Final, carried the title, 'The Coup Final!'[57] As the crisis deepened, the *Express* also backed fundraising campaigns within its pages, including one aimed at helping Ulster Protestants when the widely anticipated civil disturbances broke out across the Irish Sea. Appealing to 'The Women of England', the *Express* directly asked women readers in particular, 'what is to become of the women during the days of terror that threaten Ulster?' The campaign, which was eventually taken over by the Conservative Party's Primrose League group, raised in excess of £17,000 and received offers of accommodation for some 8,000 potential Ulster 'refugees'.[58]

The *Express* also devoted considerable space to the key events of Carson's resistance campaign, including the signing of the Covenant in Belfast during September 1912 and the massive Hyde Park demonstration in London during April 1914. Reflecting upon the true significance of the loyalists' two-week campaign, the *Express* insisted that there was now clarity over the intentions of the Ulster Unionists. An editorial concluded:

> Even the most obtuse and the least sincere can no longer pretend to misunderstand the mood of Ulster ... To call it bluff, or to deny the

desperate earnestness which inspires it is quite impossible. Ulster will not have Home Rule and all the world now knows it.[59]

Enthusiastically reporting on the 'overwhelming great demonstration' in London 18 months later, the *Express* maintained that it 'would have impressed the most cynical Fenian'. Comparing the likely size of the crowd with that attending the Scotland-England football match in Glasgow that day (around 120,000), the *Express*' reporter described how 'for an hour and a half a Niagara of men and women passed through Hyde Park's eight gates.'[60]

The Spectator, the weekly political magazine, was then edited by John St Loe Strachey, another confidant of the leadership of both the Conservative and Irish Unionist parties. Strachey was an early advocate of the provision of exclusion for Ulster which Edward Carson formally backed when he announced his exclusion amendment at Westminster early in 1913. A few days later, *The Spectator* articulated its view that 'if the Irish Nationalists have a right to Home Rule simply because they want it, then Ulster Unionists have an equal right to the form of government which they desire.'[61]

Another right-wing newspaper to promote Ulster's position was the *Daily Graphic*. The *Graphic* drew the maximum effect from its use of front page illustrations by artists depicting the key occasions during Ulster's anti-Home Rule campaign. The front page of one edition showed the crowd of enthusiastic unionists waiting outside the gates at Belfast's City Hall on Covenant Day – these had to be temporarily closed to 'stem the impetuous, incessant torrent that poured through' – and in other pages of the paper there were sketches of ordinary unionists later signing the Covenant and one of jubilant loyalists waving an old Orange banner which had reputedly led William III's army at the Battle of the Boyne in 1690.[62] Even cartoonists were sympathetic to the Ulster Unionists, thus respecting their 'underdog' status. A *Punch* cartoon of Sir Edward Carson during this Covenant campaign depicted him riding a horse and with a pen in his hand. Entitled 'Ulster will write!' the cartoon showed 'General' Carson announcing to his 'troops': 'The pen – for the moment – is mightier than the sword. Up nibs, and at 'em!'[63]

Final thoughts

It would be disingenuous to suggest that British right-of-centre newspapers were dominated on a daily basis by stories pertaining directly to the Irish crisis, or were overflowing with editorials sympathetic to the position of Ulster's unionists. Blanket coverage was restricted to major events during the Home Rule crisis, such as the Covenant campaign, the Curragh crisis and the gun-running into Ulster. During these times, the depth of sympathy for the loyal 'underdogs' was unrestrained in several journals. Many of these, ranging from the *Morning Post*, the *Daily Mail* and the *Daily Express* on the one hand, to *The Times*, the *Daily Telegraph*, *The Observer* and the *Pall Mall Gazette* on the other, encouraged their readers to empathise with UVF drilling squads and ordinary citizens signing the Ulster Covenant.

Most of the Conservative press, along with British mainland-based Irish unionist propaganda teams and pressure groups, used the appeal of a threatened loyal minority being pressurised by a bellicose nationalist majority on the island of Ireland and a bullying London administration with no clear electoral mandate on the issue, to drum up a patriotic response from the traditionally fair-minded English public. The other major chain which Ulster Unionists were pulling was the imperial one, so crucial during a period of dominance by the British Empire. Imperialists' great fear was the disintegration of this mighty, yet paradoxically vulnerable hegemony, and their dread was that its crumbling would start to occur in Ireland.

The cause of Ulster would have been a familiar one to the British public who were not only aware of political developments at Westminster, but also conscious of the extra-parliamentary campaign denouncing Home Rule which was brought directly to Great Britain, in the form of active 'pro-Ulster' canvassing in English and Scottish constituencies and the organisation of mass rallies across the British mainland. These direct encounters with the leading voices of Ulster unionism, aligned with the active backing of the Tory-leaning press, undoubtedly resulted in increased support for the anti-Home Rule movement in Great Britain and a gradual shift in British public opinion. This was probably the only occasion in its history that events in the north of Ireland would hold such electoral significance in Britain itself. Levels of apathy towards Irish Home Rule were noticeably reduced and the public was increasingly willing to empathise with Ulster Unionists, particularly during the final stages of the crisis. To a large extent, this was the result of 'the campaign for Ulster' conducted on a regular basis in many of Britain's most popular and respected newspapers and journals.[64]

Notes

1. Jonathan Bardon, '"Grotesque proceedings"? Localised responses to the Home Rule question in Ulster' in Gabriel Doherty (ed.) *The Home Rule Crisis 1912–14* (Cork, 2014), p. 277.
2. Sir Edward Carson (1854–1935) was a Dublin-born barrister who achieved fame and fortune in London. He entered politics as Irish unionist MP for Dublin University in 1892 and became leader of the Irish unionist parliamentary party in 1910. Carson spearheaded the resistance of Ulster to the proposed Home Rule legislation between 1912 and 1914 and held governmental posts during the Great War.
3. See Alan F. Parkinson, *Friends in High Places: Ulster's Resistance to Irish Home Rule, 1912–14* (Belfast, 2012).
4. Ulster Unionists had friends in other high places, including, of course, the Conservative Party, in the House of Lords, the army, the world of academia and the arts, the legal profession and influential pressure groups like Alfred Milner's British Covenant movement.
5. *The Nation*, 14 Feb. 1914. The *Manchester Guardian* was another thorn in the flesh of unionist propagandists. Reporting on Covenant Day, the *Guardian* (30 Sep. 1912) contrasted the 'anarchic hectoring of the ascendancy party and the loyal patient reliance of the Ulster Nationalists upon English justice and firmness.'
6. G.R. Wilkinson, *Depictions and Images of War in Edwardian Newspapers 1899–1914* (Basingstoke, 2003), p. 8.
7. Alfred C.W. Harmsworth (later Viscount Northcliffe), 1865–1922; newspaper and publishing magnate; established Amalgamated Press and was a pioneer of tabloid journalism. His newspaper group included *Evening News*, the *Daily Mail*, *The Times* and the *Daily Mirror*. He became director of war propaganda during the Great War. See my article 'Lord Northcliffe, Irish-born baron and his newspapers' coverage of Ulster's anti-Home Rule campaign 1912–14', *Familia: Ulster Genealogical Review*, 39 (2023), pp 47–61.
8. Harmsworth, quoted in J.L. Thompson, *Northcliffe: Press Baron in Politics 1865–1922* (London, 2000), p. 217.
9. Harmsworth, in Tom Clarke, *Northcliffe in History: An Intimate Portrait of Press Power* (London, 1950), p. 170.
10. Harmsworth, quoted in S.E. Koss, *The Rise and Fall of the Political Press in Britain* (2 vols, London 1981–4), vol. 2, p. 202.
11. Quoted in Belfast Historical & Educational Society, *Lovat Fraser's Tour of Ireland in 1913* (Belfast, 1992 edition), p. 6.
12. Ibid., p. 9.
13. Ibid., p. 12.
14. *The Times*, 5 Jan. 1912.
15. Ibid., 14 July 1913.
16. Andrew Bonar Law, quoted in *Manchester Guardian*, 10 Apr. 1912.

17 *The Times*, 10 Apr. 1912.
18 Ibid., 29 July 1912.
19 Ibid.
20 Ibid., 19 Sep. 1912.
21 Ibid., 30 Sep. 1912.
22 Ibid., 27 Mar. 1914.
23 Ibid., 24 Mar. 1914.
24 Ibid., 6 Apr. 1914.
25 Ibid., 28 Apr. 1914.
26 Ibid., 19 May 1914.
27 W.F. Monypenny, *The Two Irish Nations? An Essay on Home Rule* (London, 1913), p. 65.
28 For instance, during most of the second half of April 1912, the *Mail* led on the *Titanic* disaster, updating readers on the fate of both passengers and crew. Also, advertisements took up considerable space in the paper. Half or even whole page adverts were printed, promoting the attractions of products like Bird's cream custards, weight reduction aids and creams 'guaranteeing a beautiful bust in 30 days!'
29 Clarke, *Northcliffe in History*, p. 28.
30 Wilkinson, *Depictions and Images of War*, p. 7.
31 *Daily Mail*, 29 July 1912.
32 Ibid., 23 Mar. 1914.
33 Ibid.
34 Ibid., 28 Apr. 1914.
35 Ibid.
36 Ibid.
37 Ibid.
38 Of Irish parentage, James Louis Garvin (1868–1947) was born in Birkenhead and worked initially on the *Newcastle Chronicle* and *Daily Telegraph* before becoming editor of *The Observer* (1908) and the *Pall Mall Gazette* (1912). He was a confidant of Churchill and Lloyd George during the Great War, but an early proponent of appeasement in the 1930s.
39 *The Observer*, 16 June 1912.
40 A.M. Gollin, *The Observer and J.L. Garvin 1908–14: A Study in a Great Editorship* (Oxford, 1960).
41 *The Observer*, 29 Sep. 1912. Apart from this copy, the other editions of the *Observer* which devoted copious detail to the situation in Ulster were those of 22 and 29 September.
42 Ibid., 29 Sep. 1912.
43 Garvin, quoted in David Ayerst, *Garvin of The Observer* (London, 1985), pp 133–4.
44 *Pall Mall Gazette*, 10 and 14 Sep. 1912.
45 Ibid., 19 Sep. 1912.
46 Ibid., 20 Sep. 1912.

47 Ibid., 27 Sep. 1912.
48 Ibid., 1 Oct. 1912.
49 *Daily Telegraph*, 6 May, 1912.
50 Ibid., 3 Jan. 1913 and 25 Sep. 1912.
51 Ibid., 10 Apr. 1912.
52 H.A. Gwynne to Edward Carson, 18 Feb. 1914 (PRONI, Carson Papers, D1507/A/5/10).
53 H.A. Gwynne to Edward Carson, 20 Mar. 1914 (PRONI, Carson Papers, D1507/A/5/15).
54 *Morning Post*, 8 Jan. 1913.
55 Ibid., 17 May 1913.
56 Ibid., 29 Mar. 1914.
57 *Daily Express*, 28 Apr. 1914.
58 Ibid., 12 Aug. 1913.
59 *Daily Express*; quoted in Gordon Lucy *The Ulster Covenant: An Illustrated History of the Ulster Covenant* (Newtownards, 2012), p. 78.
60 *Daily Express*, 6 Apr. 1914.
61 *Spectator*, 4 Jan. 1913.
62 *Graphic*, 5 Oct. 1912, quoted in Lucy, *The Ulster Covenant*, p. 69.
63 *Punch*, 25 Sep. 1912.
64 This level of sympathy for the Unionist predicament would not be replicated in other times of crisis in the north of Ireland, both in the short and longer terms. Loyalists were seen to be the blockers of progress in the transformed political post-war world, as well as being primarily culpable for the violence on Belfast's streets in the early 1920s, whilst half a century later they were – at least until the clear emergence of the Provisional IRA threat in 1970/1– treated with suspicion and disdain by large sections of the British media.

3

Beyond the Somme

Northern Ireland's Great War ex-servicemen

RICHARD S. GRAYSON

'Memory' and commemoration of the First World War in Northern Ireland have for much of the past century been focused on the Somme. Or rather, they have focused not on a battle which lasted from 1 July to 18 November 1916, but on simply the 36th (Ulster) Division's actions on the devastating first day, the worst single day for fatalities in the British army's history. 1 July 1916 was the first day on which the 36th Division advanced into action, and, insofar as we have local breakdowns of fatalities, it was overwhelmingly the worst day of the war for Ulster's losses. Yet the same could be said for Dublin,[1] and the Somme has not been commemorated there in remotely the same way.

The reasons for Northern Ireland's focus are commonly held to be political: the Ulster Division was unionist-inspired and paid a price on the Somme which for some matched the blood sacrifice made three months earlier by Irish republicans during the Easter Rising. Just as the rebels' legacy paved the way for a later struggle against British rule, and became part of the new Irish state's foundation narrative, the Somme rapidly became central to ideas of loyalty to Britain, and commemoration of it became part of unionists' rituals in the new Northern Ireland.

However, narratives focused on the Somme are problematic and are very far from representing the overall war experience. They do not include those who never made it beyond 1914 or 1915, or served at sea or in the air, or saw action beyond Europe. Because so much more than the Somme took place during the First World War, so much else shaped the lives of Great War ex-servicemen as the new Northern Ireland state was founded and consolidated. This chapter examines the Somme's place in commemoration and ex-servicemen's lives, first by placing it in the context of the wider First World War, and then analyses the politics which followed the war.

The nature of service

As a result of the Cardwell reforms of the British army of the late 1860s and early 1870s, British army regiments became linked to specific localities with a home depot and a specific recruiting area. Of Ireland's eight infantry regiments, three were in Ulster: the Royal Irish Fusiliers, covering Armagh, Cavan and Monaghan, based in the city of Armagh; the Royal Inniskilling Fusiliers, based at Omagh and covering Donegal, Fermanagh, Londonderry and Tyrone; and the Royal Irish Rifles, covering Antrim and Down and based in Belfast. Ulster also contributed two cavalry regiments: the North Irish Horse and the 6th Inniskilling Dragoons.[2]

Each infantry regiment had two regular battalions, with (in peacetime) one based at 'home' and the other serving overseas around the British Empire. A third 'reserve' battalion supported the regulars, with reservists (part-time soldiers, who might be former full-time soldiers), ready to join the ranks at the outbreak of war. However, military service by Ulstermen was not limited to the three local battalions. If they joined up outside Ulster they might serve in that area's local unit, or they might opt for a more elite formation such as a Guards battalion, or they might have a family connection to a different regiment. There was also service in the Royal Navy: in parts of Ulster which routinely saw ships, most notably Belfast, that was a significant draw.[3]

When war began in August 1914, these pre-war patterns of service heavily influenced the units in which men served. However, that was also affected by the paramilitarisation of Ulster which took place over 1913 and 1914 due to the Home Rule crisis, first with the formation of the Ulster Volunteer Force and then the Irish Volunteers. The UVF was a practical manifestation of the pledge made by unionists in the Solemn League and Covenant of September 1912 to use 'all means which may be found necessary'[4] to resist Home Rule. By the end of February 1914, the UVF had around 90,000 members, armed and ready, ironically, to fight against law passed by the British Parliament so as to retain the connection with Britain.[5] The Irish Volunteers were formed from November 1913 to ensure that if the UVF fought against Home Rule, Irish nationalists' support for it would be equally militarily expressed.[6] By the summer of 1914, it looked like the two forces – with the Irish Volunteers numbering 170,000, including 2,000 in Belfast[7] – might clash in a civil war over Home Rule, but that was avoided with the outbreak of the Great War.

The existence of the UVF and Irish Volunteers had a significant impact on the shape of Ulster's recruitment into the British army. As war began, the Irish Parliamentary Party leader, John Redmond, declared that the Irish Volunteers could be used for home defence within Ireland. This was rapidly followed by the unionist leader, Edward Carson, negotiating with the War Office over the transfer of parts of the Ulster Volunteer Force into a single British army division. This resulted in the formation of the 36th (Ulster) Division in early September 1914. Following the standard structure of a British army division, it was comprised of three infantry brigades, which in turn each contained four battalions. Each battalion was based on a UVF unit with men from that unit joining together in pre-arranged slots (in Belfast, this was at the Old Town Hall recruiting office).[8] As Keith Jeffery wrote, this made the 36th Division the closest thing which Ulster had to a 'Pals' battalion, the units formed in England, especially in northern cities, consisting of groups of friends and neighbours who joined together.[9]

However, the 36th Division was not solely infantry: its 12,000 or so infantry were supplemented by another 4,000 support soldiers, especially the Royal Field Artillery, Army Service Corps, and Royal Engineers. In the Ulster Division, the artillery came from London.[10] Meanwhile, as the war progressed, the Ulster Division's UVF connections were greatly reduced. As losses were incurred on the battlefield new recruits came from far and wide, often from England and Scotland, and it is possible that by mid-1917 around half of soldiers in the Ulster Division were not the original cohort.[11] By 1918, following massive restructuring of the British army as a whole, the Ulster Division had lost many of its original battalions, which had been merged or wound up, and contained new ones, including those which were originally regular formations. A result was that this once Protestant and unionist formation included three to four thousand Catholics.[12] At the same time it is self-evident that with the Ulster Division initially numbering 16,000, and the UVF around 100,000, far from all of the UVF had joined it. Some were too old, or remained in industrial occupations, while others joined other units. Figures from west Belfast show that one-third of UVF men from there who served, never served in the Ulster Division.[13] Nevertheless, as we shall see, the fanfare which surrounded the formation of the Ulster Division, and the numbers involved in it, meant that it would come to dominate commemoration of the war.

Soon after the Ulster Division was formed, and with the passage of Home Rule in mid-September 1914 (though with implementation suspended due to the war), John Redmond enhanced his offer of the Irish Volunteers for home defence by calling on the ranks to serve 'wherever the firing line extends in defence of the right of freedom and religion in this war'.[14] This played on Irish sentiment in favour of defending plucky little Catholic Belgium against 'Hun' atrocities and led – though not without opposition from about 10 per cent of the Irish Volunteers who were against service in the British army – to drafts of Irish Volunteers going into 16th (Irish) Division's 47th Brigade. There was not quite the same link between battalions of that brigade as there was in the Ulster Division, but men did still join *en masse*. For example, from Belfast, men formed the core of what became the 6th Connaught Rangers and 7th battalion of The Prince of Wales's Leinster Regiment (Royal Canadians).[15]

Overshadowed by these political volunteer divisions was Ireland's first volunteer division, the 10th (Irish) Division. This was formed in mid-August 1914, prior to either the 16th or 36th, but it attracted far less publicity than the other two because it did not have political allegiances and recruitment to it was not accompanied by the same political and newspaper interest attached to the Carsonite and Redmondite volunteers. Yet supporters of both men joined it, not least because they were keen to join up as soon as possible: in mid-August 1914 around 500 members of the Tyrone UVF and 40 Belfast UVF members had joined the 10th (Irish) Division rather than await the formation of a UVF-linked division.[16] Meanwhile, any man serving in the UVF or the Irish Volunteers who was a British army reservist had no opportunity to join a volunteer division as they were immediately called up to serve in a regular battalion of whichever regiment they belonged to.

As a result, wartime service went very far beyond the Somme. It was not simply a story – as some loyalist murals would have it[17] – of men from the UVF first experiencing enemy fire on the Somme on 1 July 1916. More accurately, greater attention should be paid to the role played by regular battalions on the Western Front in 1914–15. Ulster men in Irish battalions were involved from almost the first engagements of the British army on the Western Front, with the 1st Irish Guards landing in France on 13 August 1914. Of the Ulster regiments, the 2nd Royal Irish Rifles arrived first on 14 August, with all except in France by Christmas except for the 1st Inniskilling who were first deployed at Gallipoli in April 1915.[18] These units took a significant part in the early stages of the war on the Western Front, for example at Le Cateau in late August 1914 and La Bassée in October. Of the regulars, the 1st Inniskillings took part in the early stages of the Gallipoli campaign before being deployed to the Western Front.

In the volunteer divisions, the 10th (Irish) Division, always overshadowed by the politically potent 16th and 36th Divisions, was the first in action, from 6 August 1915 when it took part in the landings at Suvla Bay and Anzac Cove, subsequently fighting at Chocolate Hill, Sari Bair and Hill 60 before withdrawing in September. It then moved to Salonika, where it fought at Kosturino in December 1915 before deployment to Macedonia in 1916–17 and the Middle East in late 1917 and early 1918, when it was then broken up with its battalions redeployed to the Western Front in a range of different divisions.[19]

The 16th and 36th Divisions were entirely on the Western Front. The 36th's first major action was on 1 July 1916 on the Somme. In part of its narrative, which became central to popular memory, it was initially successful in securing parts of the German lines at the Schwaben Redoubt, but divisions either side of it made less progress. As a result, it came under enfilade machine gun fire and the division lost over 5,000 men as casualties that day, of whom just over 2,000 were killed. Within the Ulster Division, four battalions each lost over 200 men dead on 1 and 2 July: 232 in the 11th Inniskillings (formed from the Donegal and Fermanagh UVF), 231 in the 13th Royal Irish Rifles (Down UVF), 228 in the 9th Royal Irish Fusiliers (Armagh, Cavan and Monaghan UVF), and 223 in the 9th Inniskillings (Tyrone UVF). However, the heaviest fatalities in any Ulster battalion came outside the 36th Division, in the 1st Inniskillings, who lost 235 men.[20]

Later in the battle, in early September 1916, the 16th (Irish) Division fought at Guillemont and Ginchy, in two successful advances. Post-Somme, the next major engagement for the 16th and 36th Divisions was at Messines on 7 June 1917. Because the two divisions fought alongside each other there, that battle has come to hold an important place in cross-community narratives of the war which emerged in the 1990s. After Messines, the 16th and 36th took part in the Third Battle of Ypres, specifically Langemarck, and then faced the German spring offensive in 1918.[21] Consequently, a narrative of service which focuses on only the Somme and sometimes Passchendaele, and more recently adding Messines, is problematic. It overlooks significant elements of service in the war. An accurate narrative of that might still prioritise the Somme, but it would also factor in Le Cateau, La Bassée, Gallipoli, Salonika, Macedonia, the Middle East, and the 1918 German spring offensive.

The shadow of the Somme

How then, did the Somme come to have such a dominant place in Northern Ireland's Great War commemoration? It partly reflects wider UK public 'memory' of the war which focuses on the two great focal points of Britain's war: the Somme and Ypres. With the political significance of the 16th and 36th Divisions, there was a further reason for focusing attention on their engagements at the expense of others. It also rightly reflects the heavy losses of 1 July 1916, and as Keith Jeffery wrote, 'The particularly concentrated nature of the Ulster Division, not just socially but also in terms of its religion and politics, meant that its losses on the first day of the Somme, grievous enough in themselves, had a disproportionately great impact back home.'[22] In addition, according to David Fitzpatrick, 'the advocates of Ulster's mobilisation in the Great War did their best to convert the First Day of the Somme into almost instant history, in the hope of bolstering home support for the war effort.'[23]

They could do that because of the presence in the battle of a specifically named 'Ulster' Division whose actions 'provided an irresistible loyalist narrative, with Thiepval as the latest instalment in Ulster's age-old struggle for civil and religious liberty.' This was informed by the coincidence of the date of the Somme's first day matching the date of the Battle of the Boyne in 1690 (under the Julian calendar then in use in Britain and Ireland, with 1 July later becoming 12 July). Fitzpatrick added that many of the Division of 1916 were UVF members or Covenant signatories, and plenty were in Orange lodges, while they had already 'been minutely chronicled by every unionist newspaper in Ulster'.[24]

So, the Somme became rapidly commemorated above all other events of the war since it contained all the elements required for promoting the unionist cause. Even if one can question how far Orange sentiments were visibly displayed at war in 1916, there is no doubt that the Orange Order speedily took on a special role in commemorating the Somme.[25] That manifested itself even in 1916 with special Orange Order services held in July and August, and then annually from July 1917.[26] That year also saw the public display and sale of reproductions of J.P. Beadle's painting of the Ulster Division's advance, with the painting presented to the lord mayor of Belfast on 1 July 1918, since when it has occupied a prominent position in Belfast City Hall and been much reproduced. Much later, Orange links to Somme commemoration were reinforced in the 1990s with the controversial annual commemoration in Drumcree, County Armagh, and the creation of Thiepval Memorial LOL 1916 in 1996.[27]

It was inevitable that when an Ulster memorial was built on the Western Front it would be on the Somme.[28] It was perhaps also inevitable that it was the first major British war memorial erected in France and Flanders since no other part of the UK has so revered its participation in one battle. Thus, Somme commemoration became a proxy for commemoration of the war as a whole with service there summarising Northern Ireland's contribution to the war effort.

I saw this in my own family. My father's parents were from Lurgan, County Armagh. Maud Powell, my grandmother, and Edward Grayson, my grandfather, both born in the 1890s, came of age during the tumultuous events of the Home Rule crisis and the Great War. Although my father was born and brought up in England, he was often 'home' at the Grayson family farm at Kinnego just outside the town, and soaked up much of the family narrative. He well knew of his father's own service in the Royal Flying Corps and Royal Air Force in 1917–18, and later Second World War service in the Home Guard after moving to England. But he also learned his mother's three brothers' service – one died – in what was said to be 'on the Somme'. That was how it passed down to me – always 'on the Somme'. Only in 1987, when I was 18 years old, did I discover that my dead great-uncle, James Powell, had been killed on 25 September 1915 near Hooge in Belgium, serving in the 2nd Royal Irish Rifles, far from the Somme and deployed in action before the Ulster Division had even arrived in France.

As I researched my book *Belfast Boys*, I started to be sceptical as to whether the other two brothers, Joseph and Charles, had ever served on the Somme. Contact from a relative in 2016 informed me that both had, both in the Ulster Division. Joseph served in the 9th Royal Irish Fusiliers, formed from the Armagh, Cavan and Monaghan UVF (he was in the Lurgan UVF). Charles enlisted under age, so joined up in Belfast where he would not be known, serving first in the 9th then the 15th Royal Irish Rifles. It was reassuring to learn that some part of that family narrative was true, though of my four Ulster relatives who served, two (and notably the one who was killed) had nothing to do with the Battle of the Somme. How many other Ulster families persist with Somme narratives which obscure the true breadth of their service and sacrifice?

EX-SERVICEMEN'S LIVES

Organisations

When post-war organisations were formed to speak for veterans, there was notionally a broad approach in some groups, theoretically taking no account of a veteran's unit of service or political views. However, divided allegiances were near the surface in post-war Ulster and some groups overtly reflected the divisions which had marked Ulster's politics since before the Great War. In part, this reflected a natural human tendency, seen in the way some wartime support for soldiers was organised, to aid one's 'own' community of neighbours.[29] A sign of how ex-servicemen's groups would develop was seen in the launch of the UVF Patriotic Fund in May 1916, solely to provide financial support for soldiers who had served in the Ulster Division or were UVF members pre-war.[30] There was a tendency for ex-servicemen's groups across the UK to have some political alignment, seen in the four groups which eventually came together to form the British Legion in 1921. The National Association of Discharged Sailors and Soldiers (known as the Association) had links with the Labour Party and trades unions, while the National Federation of Discharged and Demobilised Sailors and Soldiers (the Federation) was also egalitarian with links to radical Liberal MPs. In contrast, the Comrades of the Great War were seen as more to the right, while the Officers' Association was rather more establishment-based and simply charitable. Only the Federation and the

Comrades organised branches in Ireland, and the Comrades were especially active in Belfast.[31]

The Comrades formed in Belfast in June 1918 and much of the group's initial focus was on practical issues of employment and pensions. By March 1919, the Belfast Comrades had lobbied on 1,200 grievances and was in the process of tackling 500 more. Its membership was 2,000 and the Comrades also held social events.[32] The Comrades were not political enough for some: in 1920, the Ulster Ex-Servicemen's Association split from the Comrades to campaign for unionists in elections to the Northern Ireland parliament. However, the Comrades of the Great War overtly described themselves as 'a centre of loyalty and patriotism' and were unlikely to appeal to Irish nationalists for whom loyalty and patriotism were not directed towards Britain. They founded the Irish Nationalist Veterans' Association (INVA), which held its first general meeting in Dublin in May 1919, heavily influenced by Redmondite nationalism and declaring that it was a betrayal of promises to John Redmond and the men who went to France that Home Rule had not been implemented.[33] That view was also expressed when a Belfast branch was established in July 1919 stating that nationalist ex-soldiers had fought in the war explicitly to advance Home Rule. The organisation went on to hold social functions and charitable events, and support nationalist candidates in municipal elections. As nationalism radicalised and it became clear that many Catholics wanted a greater degree of independence from Britain than offered by Home Rule, the INVA began to work more with labour groups. It also represented its members to the local War Pensions Committee, even gaining formal representation on the committee in April 1920.

Daily life

That ex-servicemen's groups needed to support their members was because the war continued to impact the daily lives of so many.[34] A British government-funded Irish Sailors' and Soldiers' Land Trust provided some housing but it was a modest scheme with many delays. For example, in Lurgan and Portadown, building only happened after continuous pressure from ex-servicemen. From May 1920 to 1932, County Armagh saw 95 homes for ex-servicemen erected. But with only 19 complete by October 1922 the scheme hardly solved the problems faced by servicemen on their return. Across Northern Ireland, 733 were complete by mid-1926 and 1,217 by 1935, in contrast to 2,720 in the Irish Free State.[35]

Some ex-servicemen got on with life as best they could, rejecting help which might appear as charity. When John Dickson of Dover Street in the Shankill, who had been wounded in the war, was asked to jump over a chain as part of a pension test, his daughter recalled, 'My Dad ... told them he had been jumping over barbed wire fences for four years and flatly refused.'³⁶ Daniel McKeown, from west Belfast's Springfield Road area, secured a pension but believed that being a Catholic prevented him finding work. His wife said that he often lamented 'so much for the land fit for heroes'.³⁷

My own Lurgan relatives offer a snapshot of the war's varied impacts on those who served and the widowed. My grandfather, Edward Grayson, had moved to England to work as a civil servant (initially with the Post Office) before the war. We do not know exactly when but it was after September 1912 because he signed the Covenant in Lurgan. He was demobilised in 1919 by which time he had married Maud Powell (also from Lurgan) at Pimlico in London in August 1918. They brought up their six children initially in Ilford, Essex, before moving to Hemel Hempstead in Hertfordshire at the outbreak of Second World War to be away from the bombing of London (having considered sending their younger children back to Lurgan). My father recalled him listening to Neville Chamberlain's broadcast announcing the outbreak of a second war with Germany, head in hands and saying he could not believe it was happening again. Edward worked as a customs officer at Bovingdon airfield after the move, stationed there throughout the war including during its time as a United States Army Air Force base from 1942 onwards. He served in the Boxmoor unit of the Home Guard's Hertfordshire Regiment. Maud died in 1972 and Edward in 1973.³⁸

Annie Powell, the widow of my great-uncle James who was killed in 1915, had already faced tragedy when two of her children died young. Annie also lived for several years knowing that her husband's body had not been located. Indeed, as the panels for the Menin Gate were being prepared his name was added as one of those with no known grave. However, when the body was located in February 1926 he was given a burial and a headstone.³⁹ Perhaps it is no coincidence that in that year Annie and her three surviving children emigrated to Australia, where she remained until her death in 1965.

Another great-uncle, Joseph Powell, served through the war with the 9th Royal Irish Fusiliers. It is believed he was gassed but he survived to be part of the colour party which laid the battalion flag to rest at Armagh cathedral. He too emigrated to Australia and is believed to have died in the 1930s. The one brother to remain in Lurgan was the youngest, Charles. He worked as a driver for the local linen weavers, Johnston Allen. As a former member of the Ulster Division he was entitled to claim from the Patriotic Fund but did not do so until his retirement. He then made several claims from 1972, the last being in 1979. Annual payments began at £5 and rose to £30 in 1979, only partly reflecting the inflation then rampant in the UK.⁴⁰ The response to his last claim included the Fund's assessment that 'Charlie is "going down the hill" but still manages to get up town shopping with his wife.' He died in 1980 and his widow, Mary, then received similar support from 1980 until 1985 when she was described by the Fund as 'Another of our elderly widows. A very independent and active person.' Mary died in 1989 after suffering from dementia.[41]

The longest surviving ex-serviceman in Northern Ireland (and across the island of Ireland) was Thomas Shaw. He was born in Jameson Street in the Ormeau area of Belfast and lived variously just over the other side of the Lagan in Balfour Avenue, Rugby Avenue and Cromwell Road. He was born in 1899 and initially went to France as part of the draft replenishing the Ulster Division's 8th Royal Irish Rifles post-Somme. However, he was spotted in France by his brother who got him sent home for training until he was 18 due to being under age and ineligible to serve overseas. In 1918, after the 8th Battalion disbanded, he served in an entrenching battalion followed by the Ulster Division's pioneer battalion, the 16th Royal Irish Rifles, before serving in the 12th Battalion as part of the Army of Occupation in Germany.

Demobilisation in June 1919 was followed by work as a rent collector, but after being robbed twice he emigrated to Canada and worked there for a few years. Returning to Northern Ireland on his father's death he worked in the Ministry of Agriculture until retirement in 1964. During the Second World War, he was a rations agent for meat coupons. Shaw married Eleanor in 1942, and she survived him when he died on 2 March 2002, aged 102. They had no children.[42] The manager of the housing association whose accommodation the Shaws lived in from 1990 recalled:

> He was very reluctant to speak about the war, but two years ago I spoke to him in depth about the war for the first time and he told me about the horrors of what he experienced in the trenches. … The stories he told me about his comrades being blown to pieces and the bodies lying all over the place were horrific.' He added, 'Even on the day he turned 100, and we had a big do for him, he didn't want any fuss … And about the same time the French were going to honour him with their highest medal, but he even turned that down.[43]

On 4 August 2014, the centenary of the war's outbreak, a blue plaque commemorating Shaw was unveiled in Bangor.[44]

Politics and conflict

In addition to the challenges of surviving daily life, ex-servicemen also faced the tumultuous politics of the early 1920s.[45] Some were caught up as innocent bystanders, while others took a more active role. One prominent figure was Philip Woods, born in south Belfast's Norwood Street in 1880. Pre-war he was a UVF member who had been involved in gun-running, and then became an officer in the 9th Royal Irish Rifles, rising from lieutenant to being the battalion's commanding officer in 1917. From mid-1918 he fought against the Bolsheviks in the Russian civil war as part of the Allied intervention, organising and leading a local regiment in Karelia. After returning home he was elected to the Northern Ireland parliament in May 1923 as an independent unionist representing Belfast West. In 1925, he was re-elected (also winning in South Belfast, but opting to stay as MP for West), before he lost to an official unionist candidate in 1929 when he moved to England. He died in 1961. During this time as an MP he was seen as an ultra-loyalist and focused on working class concerns, as fitted his constituency.[46]

The sectarian tone of the times was indicated by the ejection of Catholic workers from Belfast shipyards in the summer of 1920 by militant Protestants returning from their Twelfth of July holiday. Violence spilled into the streets in the coming months, arising from grievances among Protestants about men who had gone to war returning to find their jobs were taken by others. At the time, this violence was widely seen to have involved ex-servicemen on both sides. They applied their wartime experiences to street fighting in Belfast.[47] On 30 July 1920, a meeting was held at the Deacon Memorial Hall in the Shankill's McTier Street, chaired by former 9th Royal Irish Rifles' Company Sergeant-Major Selby. There, it was said that in 1914 'the men who went' were told they 'would be reinstated in their jobs'. Selby said that instead 'men from other parts of the country, many of them Sinn Feiners' had taken the jobs and he said this was at the root of some of the violence in the city.[48]

Yet some ex-servicemen were on the receiving end of such violence when it broke out in the Falls on 21 July 1920. Bernard 'Bertie' Devlin was a resident of Alexander Street West and an INVA member. He was shot when soldiers fired on a rampaging crowd in the Falls Road. The next night, William Dunning of Bellevue Street had 'practically the left side of his head blown off 'and died instantly. The *Belfast Telegraph* said this was the result of 'intense firing ... by a Sinn Fein element' at the junction of Kashmir Road and Bombay Street. Dunning had served with the 9th Royal Irish Rifles but was discharged as unfit for further service in 1916.[49] Similar violence took place in Belfast later in 1920 and in the summers of 1921 and 1922, including on Armistice Day in 1920 as workers marched back to the shipyards from the two minutes' silence.[50] A notorious case was part of the 'Arnon Street massacre' on 1 April 1922. This took place when uniformed men in an armoured car, seeking revenge for the death of a policeman, drove round predominantly Catholic streets close to the Brown Square Barracks. Joseph Walshe, an ex-soldier, was killed and one of his young children died from wounds three days later.[51]

Even being a serving British soldier did not make guarantee safety. In June 1921, Patrick O'Hare was home on leave from the Connaught Rangers in west Belfast's Urney Street. The *Irish News* described how loyalist attackers 'told Mrs. O'Hare that they were going to shoot her husband.' The newspaper said that from the mob's point of view, despite his uniform, 'he was a Catholic, that was sufficient crime'. Patrick's grandson, Seán, said that in the family narrative, Patrick was saved by British regular soldiers from a peaceline. Seán went on to say, 'It's not something that would be made up because … they didn't have any love for the British army but they said that they had saved him'.[52]

Other men became formally involved as active participants in the ongoing conflict. Some did this in legal bodies in the form of the Royal Irish (and later Ulster) Constabulary and the Ulster Special Constabulary. But paramilitarism also resumed after the war: the UVF continued to exist, at least into 1921, while the Ulster Imperial Guards claimed 14,000 members in November 1921, said to be largely ex-servicemen. However, in that year, loyalist paramilitaries were effectively incorporated into the new Northern Ireland state through being drawn into the USC's C Specials. Some men were on the other side, as members of the Irish Republican Army, although for obvious reasons plenty of the latter, even some who were interned, kept that a secret.[53]

Someone who later became well known locally was Seán Cunningham. He first enlisted in the British army in 1904, claiming to be over 18, but he was probably only 15. After serving for eight years when he was discharged to the army reserve, he subsequently joined the Irish Volunteers. As a reservist at the outbreak of war, Cunningham was called up and served through to March 1920. On discharge he joined the east Belfast IRA, serving as a captain in 1920–21. Later, he served in the Irish Free State's army and in the Garda Síochána. In 1936, he joined Eoin O'Duffy's pro-Franco brigade in Spain. He served as captain of a machine-gun company, meeting Franco himself. He attended the opening of Franco's civil war memorial, Valle de los Caidos (Valley of the Fallen), after its completion in 1958, and died in 1963. The *Irish News* described how he had served in four armies: the British army, the IRA, the Free State army, and pro-Franco forces.[54]

Commemoration

Recent historiography has persuasively challenged the view that ex-servicemen were poorly received in parts of Catholic Ireland.[55] Brian Walker has pointed out that in the early to mid-1920s, in many local commemorations, 'there were efforts to keep these events open to all sections of the community.' Unveilings of war memorials included, for example, Protestant and Catholic war orphans at Enniskillen in 1922, and a wide mix of people (including a Catholic ex-NCO and a Catholic parish priest) at Portadown in 1925. At Ballymena in 1925, Sir Oliver Nugent, the former Ulster Division commander, proclaimed that Ulster's war service 'was not confined to one creed or one denomination; it was given by Ulstermen of all denominations and all classes'.[56] Catherine Switzer explains that Northern Ireland's 'national' politicians did not organise any kind of national commemoration and 'although it seems clear that commemoration did generally take on a broadly unionist complexion, this was not the result of an over-arching conspiracy on the part of the Ulster Unionist party or the Stormont government'. 'National' commemoration was done in London at the Cenotaph in Westminster and, in contrast, commemorations in Ulster were strongly local in their tone, without reference to Northern Ireland.

Memorial design was as much about 'cost, design and choice of site' as about 'political ideology'. Switzer argues that consequently, although 'politics clearly influenced the meanings which would be taken from the memory of the war', acts of commemoration were as much and perhaps more 'about people themselves and the places they lived in.'[57] The memorials people chose tended to be either an obelisk or a figurative sculpture. Figures tended to be ready for action rather than shown in action. In the one case where a soldier was shown striking towards an enemy – the city of Londonderry's memorial – this was controversial.[58] Revenge or aggression were not common sentiments in memorials erected by individuals and communities to mark the lost, nor were symbols of either Ulster or Ireland, or political messages: St Anne's cathedral in Belfast was a notable exception in paying tribute 'to the men of Ulster who fell in the Great War'. Crosses were put up at only Hillsborough and Cregagh (despite being very common in Britain), perhaps reflecting Ulster Protestant sensibilities about the Catholic connotations of crosses.[59]

However, a divide between Northern Ireland and the rest of Ireland was readily apparent with the former having already largely built its memorials while the Irish Free State still debated the creation of what would become Islandbridge.[60] Meanwhile, Great War commemoration in Northern Ireland in the interwar years came to be seen as Protestant, unionist and British, whatever people's intentions, because of the flag flown and the national anthem sung. As a consequence, it came to exclude much of the Catholic population.

This was foreshadowed in the way 'Peace Day' on 9 August 1919 – marking the signature of the Treaty of Versailles – was received in Belfast. Although the day was observed by Protestants and Catholics jointly in Enniskillen (despite a boycott by the nationalist local council),[61] the event took on sectarian tones in Belfast. Between 20,000 and 36,000 took part in an event which included a parade from the Antrim Road in north Belfast southwards to Ormeau Park. But many nationalists avoided Peace Day with the *Irish News* arguing that it celebrated militarism.[62]

This is not to say that nationalists began to avoid commemoration entirely (examples above demonstrate the contrary), but they were alienated from events which were deeply British in their tone. For example, the first Poppy Day was held on 11 November 1921. Organised by the British Legion (which added 'Royal' to its name in 1925), in Belfast it saw 20,000 people assemble around City Hall in Donegall Square and Donegall Place. There was a temporary Cenotaph in front of the Queen Victoria statue. Buglers announced the start, as did shipyard sirens, factory horns and church bells. At the end, the Union Flag was raised from half-mast to full on the city hall followed by singing of the 'God Save the King'. The Ulster Ex-servicemen's Association used the occasion to make a declaration of what they called their 'intense loyalty' to the throne.[63]

There was similar British and Protestant symbolism at Ulster Tower's opening on 19 November 1921. Fundraising for the project was through the Ulster Unionist Council, initiated by Edward Carson. The idea for the tower, replicating Helen's Tower at Clandeboye, County Down, where the Ulster Division had trained, came from Northern Ireland's first Prime Minister, James Craig. In front of a group of around 70, Craig and General Weygand unveiled the memorial (Carson was ill) with the Union Flag flying, and there was then a service led by the Anglican Primate of All Ireland, Charles D'Arcy, plus Presbyterian and Methodist leaders. The unofficial unionist anthem, 'O God, Our Help in Ages Past', was sung, and the Patriotic Fund took responsibility for running the Tower.[64] It should be no surprise then, that Belfast Cenotaph's unveiling in 1929 was notable for the absence of Catholic organisations. Two fascist groups laid wreaths in the formal ceremony, but ex-servicemen of the 16th (Irish) Division only did so after the official proceedings. They continued to organise their commemorations separately (although they did take place in the Belfast Cenotaph parade in 1930), such as by taking part in a September 1934 pilgrimage to Lourdes, organised by the French Association of former Priest-Combatants.[65]

Conclusion

As the Great War has receded in time, the way it has been remembered in Northern Ireland has changed significantly. The last year in which there was mass remembrance by ex-servicemen was 1966 marking the fiftieth anniversary of the Somme. In that year, about 200 veterans, many well into their seventies, marked the anniversary at the Ulster Tower on 1 July. On 4 July, Queen Elizabeth inspected 840 ex-servicemen at Balmoral Showgrounds in Belfast. Most ex-servicemen were dead by the sixtieth anniversary in 1976. In 1986, only three attended the Thiepval commemoration. Ten years on, a different two were there.[66] The very last ex-serviceman alive was Thomas Shaw, who died in 2002, discussed above.

Aside from being significant for the Somme's fiftieth anniversary, 1966 was also the year in which a loyalist paramilitary group carried out the first killings of the 'Troubles'. They revived the name 'Ulster Volunteer Force' and over time wrapped themselves in the narrative of the pre-1914 UVF whose men had joined the Ulster Division. The lineage they claimed could be seen in two Shankill murals photographed by the author in 2005. One, at the corner of the Shankill Road and Glenwood Street, depicted a 1914–18 soldier mourning his dead comrades alongside a contemporary masked UVF paramilitary. Poppies were included and the mural painters were implying some link between sacrifice in 1914–18 in the British army and UVF deaths post-1969. Another mural, on the corner of the Shankill Road and Canmore Street, showed that linkage even more starkly with the label 'The People's Army, 1912–2002: 90 years of resistance', picking out 1912, 1916 and 1969 as key moments in a continuous story of UVF organisation in the Shankill.[67]

That helps to explain why, during the Troubles, First World War commemoration was not a space which could be comfortably inhabited by nationalists, let alone republicans. However, after two decades of change, some led by academics and some by politicians, and much by the wider public, that has changed significantly. Even former IRA members have taken part in commemoration and take a deep interest in their forebears' service in the British army in 1914–18.[68] Although the wearing of poppies remains a profoundly unionist activity in Northern Ireland, historical research and community projects can and do now accommodate both 'sides' of political divides, just as the British military did in 1914–18. That offers some sign of how Great War commemoration, once so divisive, is playing a different role in the twenty-first century.

Notes

1. Richard S. Grayson, *Dublin's Great Wars: The First World War, the Easter Rising and the Irish Revolution* (Cambridge, 2018), p. 40.
2. H.E.D. Harris, *The Irish Regiments in the First World War* (Cork, 1968), pp 3–6; Gavin Hughes, *The Hounds of Ulster: A History of the Northern Irish Regiments in the Great War* (Oxford, 2021), p. 2.
3. Grayson, *Dublin's Great Wars*, p. 363.
4. 'Understanding the Ulster Covenant' (www.ulster-scots.com/uploads/USCNCovenant.pdf, accessed 7 Jan. 2022).

5. Timothy Bowman, 'The Ulster Volunteers 1913–14: force or farce?', *History Ireland*, 10:1 (2002), pp 43–7. See also Timothy Bowman, *Carson's Army: The Ulster Volunteer Force, 1910–22* (Manchester, 2007).
6. Grayson, *Dublin's Great Wars*, pp 19–20.
7. Richard S. Grayson, *Belfast Boys: How Unionists and Nationalists Fought and Died Together in the First World War* (London, 2009), p. 7.
8. Ibid., pp 11–12.
9. Keith Jeffery, *Ireland and the Great War* (Cambridge, 2000), p. 56.
10. Cyril Falls, *The History of the 36th (Ulster) Division* (Belfast, 1922), p. 8.
11. Richard S. Grayson, 'Ireland's new memory of the First World War: forgotten aspects of the Battle of Messines, June 1917', *British Journal for Military History*, 1:1 (Oct. 2014), pp 48–65 at p. 59.
12. Grayson, *Belfast Boys*, p. 129.
13. Richard S. Grayson, 'Beyond the Ulster Division: west Belfast members of the Ulster Volunteer Force and service in the First World War' in Richard S. Grayson and Fearghal McGarry (eds), *Remembering 1916: The Easter Rising, the Somme and the Politics of Memory in Ireland* (Cambridge, 2016), pp 112–37 at pp 125, 131–2.
14. *Irish News*, 21 Sep. 1914.
15. Terence Denman, *Ireland's Unknown Soldiers* (Dublin, 1992), p. 38.
16. Stephen Sandford, *Neither Unionist nor Nationalist: The 10th (Irish) Division in the Great War* (Sallins, 2015), p. 14.
17. Grayson, *Belfast Boys*, pp 174–5.
18. 'Royal Inniskilling Fusiliers' (www.longlongtrail.co.uk/army/regiments-and-corps/the-british-infantry-regiments-of-1914-1918/royal-inniskilling-fusiliers/), 'Princess Victoria's (Royal Irish Fusiliers' (www.longlongtrail.co.uk/army/regiments-and-corps/the-british-infantry-regiments-of-1914-1918/princess-victorias-royal-irish-fusiliers/) & 'Royal Irish Rifles' (www.longlongtrail.co.uk/army/regiments-and-corps/the-british-infantry-regiments-of-1914-1918/royal-irish-rifles/) (all accessed 5 Jan. 2022).
19. Sandford, *Neither Unionist nor Nationalist*, p. 191.
20. Download of data from 'Find War Dead' (www.cwgc.org/find-records/find-war-dead/, accessed 7 Jan. 2022).
21. Richard S. Grayson, 'Ireland' (encyclopedia.1914-1918-online.net/article/Ireland, accessed 5 Jan. 2022). On the spring offensive see Michael James Nugent, *A Long Week in March: The 36th (Ulster) Division in the German Spring Offensive, March 1918* (Warwick, 2019).
22. Jeffery, *Ireland and the Great War*, p. 57.
23. David Fitzpatrick, 'Instant History: 1912, 1916, 1918' in Grayson and McGarry (eds), *Remembering 1916*, pp 65–86 at p. 81.
24. Ibid., pp 82–3.
25. Philip Orr, *The Road to the Somme: Men of the Ulster Division Tell Their Story* (Belfast, 1987; 2008 edition), pp vii–ix, 282–96.

26 Grayson, *Belfast Boys*, p. 168.
27 Orr, *Road to the Somme*, pp 283–4; 'Thiepval Memorial LOL No. 1916' (www.goli.org.uk/post/thiepval-memorial-lol-no-1916, accessed 10 Jan. 2022).
28 Catherine Switzer, *Ulster, Ireland and the Somme: War Memorials and Battlefield Pilgrimages* (Dublin, 2013), pp 80–108.
29 Grayson, *Belfast Boys*, pp 3, 48.
30 Ibid., pp 48, 153. See also, Colin Cousins, *Armagh and the Great War* (Dublin, 2011), pp 193–4.
31 Mike Hally, 'The deep roots of the British Legion: the emergence of First World War British veterans' organisations' in David Swift and Oliver Wilkinson (eds), *Veterans of the First World War: Ex-Servicemen and Ex-Servicewomen in Post-War Britain and Ireland* (London, 2019), pp 17–33 at pp 17, 21–5); Paul Huddie, 'Ex-servicemen and the Soldiers', Sailors' and Airmen's Families Association, 1919–21' in Swift and Wilkinson (eds), *Veterans of the First World War*, pp 34–47 at pp 40–41; John Borgonovo, 'Revolution, ex-servicemen and the Cork Branch of the National Federation of Discharged and Demobilised Sailors and Soldiers, 1918–21', in Swift and Wilkinson (eds), *Veterans of the First World War*, pp 82–103 at pp 88–9.
32 Grayson, *Belfast Boys*, pp 155–6.
33 Ibid., p. 156.
34 On a range of ex-servicemen's lives, see Orr, *Road to the Somme*, pp 255–77.
35 Cousins, *Armagh and the Great War*, pp 197–200.
36 Grayson, *Belfast Boys*, pp 143, 151.
37 Ibid., pp 152–153.
38 Various family sources and knowledge, including marriage and death certificates.
39 'Serjeant James Powell' (www.cwgc.org/find-records/find-war-dead/casualty-details/480886/james-powell/, accessed 6 Jan. 2022).
40 1972's amount was equal to around £70 in 2017, and 1979's around £117. See, 'Calculate purchasing power' (www.nationalarchives.gov.uk/currency-converter/, accessed 21 Jan. 2022).
41 Tom Hayes, *The Powell Family and the Great War* (Milton Keynes, 2017); email to author from Maureen Lapthorne, 14 Dec. 2008; email to author from Doug Powell, 2 July 2016; email to author from Tom Hayes, 12 Dec. 2016; email to author from Tom Hayes, 8 Jan. 2022; Patriotic Fund claims 1972–1985 from Charles and Mary Powell, supplied by the Somme Heritage Centre; Nick Metcalfe, *Blacker's Boys: 9th (Service) Battalion, Princess Victoria's (Royal Irish Fusiliers) (County Armagh) & 9th (North Irish Horse) Battalion Princess Victoria's (Royal Irish Fusiliers) 1914–1919* (Woodstock, 2012), pp 256, 773.
42 Stuart N. White, *The Terrors: 16th (Pioneer) Battalion Royal Irish Rifles* (Belfast, 1996), pp 115, 204, 230 and 264; *News Letter*, 6 Mar. 2002; *County Down Spectator*, 7 Mar. 2002; birth certificate

43 'NI's last Great War veteran dies' (news.bbc.co.uk/1/hi/northern_ireland/1856403.stm, accessed 20 Jan. 2022).
44 'Northern Ireland's Last World War I Veteran Commemorated' (www.clanmil.org/newsdetail_front.php?id=283, accessed 27 Jan. 2022).
45 For a thorough account of this period, see Alan F. Parkinson, *Belfast's Unholy War: The Troubles of the 1920s* (Dublin, 2004).
46 'Woods, Philip James' (www.dib.ie/biography/woods-philip-james-a9117, accessed 27. Jan. 2022); birth certificate (civilrecords.irishgenealogy.ie/churchrecords/images/birth_returns/births_1880/02854/2045962.pdf, accessed 27 Jan. 2022).
47 T.K. Wilson, *Frontiers of Violence: Conflict and Identity in Ulster and Upper Silesia, 1918–1922* (Oxford, 2010), pp 128, 179.
48 Grayson, *Belfast Boys*, p. 157.
49 Ibid., pp 157–8.
50 Ibid., p. 158.
51 Ibid., p. 159.
52 Ibid., pp 159–60.
53 Steven O'Connor, '"It's up to you now to fight for your own country" Ireland's Great War veterans in the War of Independence, 1919–21' in Swift and Wilkinson (eds), *Veterans of the First World War*, pp 104–21; Bowman, *Carson's Army*, pp 195–201; Wilson, *Frontiers of Violence*, pp 84–6.
54 Grayson, *Belfast*, pp 164–5.
55 Niamh Gallagher, *Ireland and the Great War: A Social and Political History* (London, 2020), pp 177–8.
56 Brian M. Walker, *Irish History Matters: Politics, Identities and Commemoration* (Belfast, 2019), pp 85–6.
57 Catherine Switzer, *Unionists and Great War Commemoration in the North of Ireland: People, Places and Politics* (Dublin, 2007), pp 152, 156.
58 Ibid., p. 77.
59 Ibid., pp 80–81, 89; Nuala C. Johnson, *Ireland, the Great War and the Geography of Remembrance* (Cambridge, 2003), p. 107.
60 Johnson, *Ireland, the Great War and the Geography of Remembrance*, p. 108.
61 Ibid., p. 77.
62 *Irish News*, 21 July 1919.
63 *Irish Times*, 12 Nov. 1921.
64 Ibid., 6 Oct. 1921; 24 Oct. 1921; 18 Nov. 1921; 21 Nov. 1921.
65 Grayson, *Belfast Boys*, p. 171.
66 Ibid., p. 174.
67 Ibid., pp 174–5, 177.
68 Ibid., pp 183–4; Richard S. Grayson, 'The place of the First World War in contemporary Irish Republicanism in Northern Ireland', *Irish Political Studies*, 25:3 (2010), pp 325–45.

4

The Easter Rising and Belfast republicanism

JAMES McDERMOTT

Historical context

The purpose of this essay is to outline the fortunes of republicanism in Belfast from 1900 until 1920 with particular reference to the importance of the 1916 Easter Rising. It will examine the reasons for the development of republicanism in the northern capital despite the difficulties which marked Belfast. In 1901, Belfast and Dublin had similar populations of around 350,000. There were, however, major differences within those populations which made for differences in outlook. Dublin had a majority population which was Catholic and nationalist. Most of the Dublin electorate from 1900 until 1916 would have given their support to the Irish Parliamentary Party, which had reunited under the leadership of John Redmond and was pressing for Home Rule once again. Belfast was of much more recent growth than Dublin and the northern capital differed in its growth.[1]

In 1801, Belfast had a population of around 20,000 while Dublin had a population of 200,000. It had an exponential growth throughout the nineteenth century as a consequence of industrial development. The linen mills, shipyards and engineering works had drawn migrants from the surrounding counties. The migrants often brought with them attitudes which meant there would be intra-communal conflict, Belfast was marked by serious sectarian disturbances in 1843, 1857, 1864, 1872, 1880, 1884, 1898 and again in 1912. The later disturbances in the late nineteenth century had been sparked by unionist opposition to Home Rule. In 1901, over 75 per cent of Belfast's population was Protestant and unionist. They saw their future as tied to the British Empire. As George Boyce put it, to Ulster Unionists, Home Rule with a Dublin parliament, 'dominated by the agrarian interests of the South and West, would bring about the ruination of Ulster's prosperity'.[2]

Yet there was also behind this national argument a real and deep vein of dislike for the very notion of Catholic dominance. Ascendancy by a Catholic majority appeared 'all the more dangerous and unbearable'. The consequences of this fear by Ulster Unionists meant Belfast Catholics who comprised around 24.1 per cent of the population felt they were 'hemmed in by Protestants' and 'had long been held hostage for the good behaviour of their co-religionists elsewhere in Ireland'.[3] Tom McNally leaves a tongue in cheek memory of Belfast in the early years of the twentieth century:

> My early impressions of life in the city were influenced by riots, police baton charges, calling out the military – more charges – the reading of the Riot Act (a most vindictive element of British laws); some unfortunates, usually innocent people shot; Orange processions; Catholic counter-demonstrations with huge bonfires on each side'.[4]

In practice, a horror of partition among the nationalist minority in Belfast made them unwilling to provoke the unionist majority. Most nationalists were in favour of Home Rule, but the Irish Parliamentary Party MP for West Belfast, Joe Devlin, reflected his constituents' concerns in his circumspect approach. In 1906, Devlin had won his West Belfast seat by only 16 votes and had organised the Ancient Order of Hibernians (AOH) to get elected. They were seen by some as the alter-image of the Orange Order. As Brian Feeney puts it: 'Whereas Orangemen had to be born Protestant, AOH men had to be Catholic'. However, as Feeney continues, there was a strict limit to the provocation that the minority community could give:

> Even in West and North Belfast overt support for Home Rule was carefully managed, first by the Catholic Church and then after his election in 1906 by Devlin, the only Irish Parliamentary Party MP in Belfast or County Antrim. The certainty of instant violent retribution for overstepping the accepted position of Nationalism in Belfast was only too well embedded in recent local experience.[5]

It should not be surprising, therefore, that Belfast had not demonstrated as much support for militant separatism as Dublin. The views of most nationalists and even more profoundly unionists would have been opposed to the Irish Republican Brotherhood, with their belief in military force, their cell systems and their willingness to covertly enter any organisation which could fulfil or promote their ideals. While they believed in the unity of all Irish people irrespective of their religion, they had nothing to match the success of organised labour in the early years of the twentieth century. The dockers and carters strike of 1907 was the largest seen in Ireland up until that time and was functionally non-sectarian. The 1919 strike for a 44-hour week was of deep concern to the unionist establishment. In 1920, the Belfast Labour Party had won 12 local council seats. The party had been set up in 1917 by trade unionists of the Independent Labour Party, which had a presence in the city since 1893.[6]

Although there were ideological divisions in the Labour movement between the Independent Labour Party and Irish Labour Party on important issues such as separatism and partition, both organisations were non-sectarian and did have genuine outreach. The IRB and its ancillary groups such as the Dungannon Clubs, the Freedom Club and Sinn Féin had no such impact in Belfast in the first decade of the twentieth century. As Feeney points out: 'by 1908 there were eleven [Sinn Féin] councillors on Dublin Corporation out of a total of eighty members. In Belfast there were no Sinn Féin candidates let alone councillors'.[7] What events then changed the fortunes of Belfast republicanism so that in July 1921, as in the rest of Ireland, the IRA and Sinn Féin were taken as the accredited representatives of the minority population?[8]

Belfast republicanism 1900–14

To answer this, we must look at how republicanism developed in Belfast in the years 1900–14 and evaluate the success of those who were involved in it. For Austen Morgan, 'The topic of Belfast Republicanism remains microhistorical – big individuals in small organisations who leave for Dublin'.[9] There is considerable truth in this assertion, but it was written before the release of the Bureau of Military History (BMH) witness statements, which can now be accessed online. The opening of the O'Kane archive in the Cardinal Tomás Ó Fiaich Memorial Library and Archive in Armagh has also produced new and revealing details on Belfast republicanism. Together, the two new sets of sources give extra information about the early republican movement in Belfast. Certainly, the names most associated with the revival of Belfast republicanism are Denis McCullough, Bulmer Hobson and Sean McDermott.

According to McCullough, the IRB in the city had largely atrophied and its members were noted more for the singing of republican songs than for actual activity. McCullough showed he was quite ruthless in removing some older IRB members he did not consider were useful to the organisation. These included his own father.[10] He was not only from a republican family but was strongly influenced by the Gaelic revival in sport, culture and particularly language. McCullough realised that both Catholics and Protestants were attracted by the Gaelic League and some had begun to examine Ireland's relationship to England in the past and examine whether Ireland would be better as a republic.

Even before the McCullough purge there had been a small but significant presence of the IRB in Belfast. Seamus Dobbyn's BMH witness statement taken with his tapes in the O'Kane archive are very illuminating. His father Henry was born in Rocktown, County Derry, and he was one of the many migrants who came to late nineteenth-century Belfast. He had been a prominent member of the IRB before he and his family came to live in North Queen Street and later Clonard Gardens. In 1896, Henry Dobbyn with veteran IRB members Neal John O'Boyle and Robert Johnstone had worked with Martin Higgins, Dan McCullough (father of Denis), James Scullion, Joe Connolly and Dan O'Hagan to form the National Literary Club which met at Carrick Hill. It had strong links with the Gaelic League and also formed the John Mitchel hurling club. This GAA team were to use one of the several Willowbank huts on the Falls Road once used by cavalry units of the British army. Seamus Dobbyn's statements relates how he was able to obtain a quantity of Steyn rifles covertly stored in his north Belfast home. The primacy of armed revolt was then paramount. McCullough saw the Gaelic revival as a way to broaden support for the republican cause. Years later he recalled: 'The IRB in my time was not welded or pledged to actions in arms only; it was ready to back any man or movement that had separation from England as its final objective.'

Bulmer Hobson was probably the most active and in innovative republican in Belfast at the start of the twentieth century. He was a Quaker, born in 1883, and was educated at Friends' School in Lisburn. He became a convinced Irish separatist and helped form the Antrim County Board of Gaelic Athletic Association and was Secretary of the Gaelic League in Belfast. In 1902, Hobson had established the first branch of Na Fianna Éireann. This was revitalised in 1909 with the help of Countess Markievicz and obtained its own constitution by the Ard Fheis of 1913, which stated its object as to re-establish the independence of Ireland with 'The training of the youth of Ireland, mentally and physically. To attain this object by teaching scouting and military exercises. Irish history and the Irish language'.[11]

Eight years later, the Fianna was to produce some of the most important leaders of republicanism in Belfast such as Joe McKelvey, Roger and Felix McCorley and Joe Murray.[12] By this time Hobson had been involved in the Ulster Literary Theatre which attracted such free thinkers as the brothers Jack and George Morrow who were to produce the illustrations for the short-lived paper *The Republic* in 1906. In 1907, Hobson moved to Dublin where he became Secretary of the Irish Volunteers and a member of the supreme council of the IRB. The Fianna, arguably, was to have the greatest impact upon the development of republicanism in Belfast. There was a certain innocence in the re-formation of the republican scout movement. David McGuinness, later to be an important brigade intelligence officer with the IRB and IRA recalled how when the Fianna had been set up again in Dublin in 1909, Countess Markievicz contacted him through another IRB member, Joe Robinson, to look for recruits. Using GAA clubs, such as the Peter Crowley GAC, and with the help of Sean O'Sullivan, who was looked upon as the father of the Fianna, there were around 70 Fianna members, both boys and girls, by 1912. Significantly, Countess Markievicz was suspicious of clandestine Belfast republicanism. 'She expressed to me her disapproval of all secret societies and disapproved of the IRB using the Fianna as a recruiting ground for themselves'.[13]

In 1905, McCullough and Hobson formed the Dungannon Clubs as a debating forum on how to advance Irish separatism in language, culture and commerce. It was to attract some of the most important thinkers in Belfast at that time. The members of the Fianna probably exceeded the number of members of the Dungannon Clubs in 1910–14, but those who were there indicate a range of religious and political views on the left and on the right. Dungannon Clubs met originally above Finnegan's chemist shop in Royal Avenue. The Dungannon Clubs was used as a means to recruit IRB members. Thomas Wilson, later, as treasurer of the Clubs, remembered the early IRB:

> After being a short time in the Gaelic League I was approached by Henry Heaney to join the Irish Republican Brotherhood. The first meeting that I attended was in Denis McCullough's workshop. There were about eight or nine people at the meeting including Denis McCullough and Bulmer Hobson. To the best of my knowledge, this was the principal circle working in Belfast at that time. I think a few other circles were working in Belfast in 1909. One comprised the older boys of Fianna Éireann and another organised by Peter Burns.[14]

The early activities of the IRB were the collection of funds for weapons and anti-conscription campaigns. Their numbers were small and the cover of the Dungannon Clubs in 1905 and the later amalgamation with Sinn Féin in 1907 did not fool the authorities. A detective could be assigned to watch every individual. 'Our numbers were so small it was easy for the police to have a man on each of us'.[15] In 1912, the Freedom Club met to discuss matters of Irish history and politics and fulfilled the same function as the Dungannon Clubs. Not all of the members of the Freedom Club were in the IRB but all the members of the IRB were in the Freedom Club. Their numbers were still small and could be brought to mind years afterwards. Rory Haskins recalled:

> I was born into a Unionist family. In my early days I had no national ideals worth mentioning. I joined the Orange Order in 1912 (about the time the Ulster Volunteers were first organised). I met a man

> named Frank Wilson. He was a member of the Irish Republican Brotherhood. I did not know this at the time I first made his acquaintance. He brought me into the Freedom Club. I think the premises used by the Freedom Club was in Victoria Street. In the Freedom Club I met Denis McCullough, Frank Booth, Sean Lester, Ernest Blythe, Bulmer Hobson, Cathal O'Shannon and Joseph Connolly. Sean Kelly also attended and was then, I think, a member of Fianna Eireann.

The names given by Rory Haskins include three other non-Catholics out of eight people. They were: Blythe, Lester and Hobson. Other non-Catholics he could also have mentioned were: Sam and Archie Heron, the Morrow brothers, Alf Cotton and Herbert Moore Pim. The republicans of the time could claim a non-sectarian membership as well as a varied job profile. McCullough owned a musical instrument shop, Hobson was a journalist and printer, Joseph Connolly owned a furniture shop, Robert Lynd, Sean Lester and Ernest Blythe were journalists, and Cathal O'Shannon was a labour activist and writer. Pim was also a writer. Liam Gaynor, Tom Clear and Seamus Dobbyn were schoolteachers. As the biographer of Sean Lester comments: 'They were a bookish lot'.[16] Dobbyn believed that this could shade into snobbery with some members of the professions in the Freedom Club reluctant to admit members of the working class.[17]

By 1912, there was already some truth in Austen Morgan's eloquent comment that they were 'big individuals in little organisations leaving for Dublin'. Sean McDermott, who had been a paid organiser for the Dungannon Clubs (members gave one shilling each to supply him with a bicycle) was now a full-time organiser for the IRB and would do most to help Tom Clarke put together the military committee which would organise the Easter Rising of 1916.[18] Bulmer Hobson was central to the organisation of the Howth gun-running in 1914, yet he was ostracised from the IRB leadership by the time of the rising. As a man in his eighties, he felt it necessary to write *Ireland Yesterday and Tomorrow* in 1968 to explain the positions he took over 50 years before.

Yet although many Belfast republicans did end up going south, it is not true of all of them. At least until after the violence in Belfast in 1920–22 many remained, including Seamus Dobbyn who was an IRB organiser for east Ulster as his father Henry had once been. Liam Gaynor, whose brother Sean was killed by a reprisal gang in September 1920, remained in Belfast and was an IRB organiser for west Ulster. Sean Cusack and Peter Burns, both of whom had seen service as sergeants in the British army, stayed in Belfast. Peter Burns provided the invaluable service to historians of compiling lists of the members of the Irish Volunteers who were out at

Coalisland in 1916 and those IRA members who had known service in July 1921.[19] Despite the commitment of Belfast republicans from 1905 until 1914 they were small in number. Thomas Wilson commented, 'The majority of Nationalists in Belfast were indifferent if not hostile'.[20] When one considers the political developments at Westminster and in Ireland generally at this time this should not be surprising. From 1909 until 1911 the Irish Parliamentary Party supported Asquith's Liberal administration in the House of Commons.

The Liberals were locked in a tense struggle with the Conservative Party and the House of Lords to pass the 'People's Budget' and Parliament Act. Redmond and his phalanx of Irish MPs gave their support in exchange for Asquith's promise to place a Home Rule Bill on the statute book. To Irish nationalists, including those in Belfast, the long desired ideal of Home Rule looked as if it could now be delivered. The activities of Belfast republicans with their demand for complete Irish separatism could easily have led to an envenomed unionist majority in Belfast taking their anger out on the minority. On top of that, if republicans were to enter electoral politics, they could split the nationalist vote causing Joe Devlin to lose his seat.

By 1911, the Ulster Unionist Party was led by the redoubtable leadership of Sir Edward Carson and Sir James Craig who were not going to accept meekly a Home Rule settlement. As Éamon Phoenix explains, Carson hoped

> to use the resistance of almost 900,000 Ulster Protestants as a weapon in this battle, wrongly as it turned out – that Home Rule without Ulster would be impossible. Craig, the authentic representative of the Belfast business class had one idea, to preserve the character and integrity of the province he knew and loved. To this end he had been instrumental in setting up the Ulster Unionist Council (1905).

The unionist campaign was served by powerful interests in British society in the Conservative Party led by Bonar Law, a ruthless political antagonist, with support in the army, in the aristocracy and in big business. 'There are stronger things than Parliamentary majorities,' he declared at Blenheim Palace in 1912, underlining the extra-parliamentary nature of the Ulster campaign.[21] The signing of the Ulster Covenant in September 1912 and the setting up of the Ulster Volunteer Force in January 1913 left the minority population in no doubt that there was now a ramping-up of the armed threat of Ulster Unionists.

It was the formation of the Irish Volunteer Force in November 1913 which gave the Freedom Club an opportunity to influence a larger military organisation. Patrick Pearse wrote in 1913: 'Personally I think the

Orangeman with a rifle is a much less ridiculous figure than the Nationalist without a rifle.'[22] He was expressing the frustration of many nationalists who were becoming increasingly impatient of delays in the delivery of Home Rule. Surely Home Rule was but a very limited form of devolution which would keep Ireland firmly within the empire. Home Rule had the approval of the majority in Ireland and the majority of the elected representatives in the House of Commons; had the Ulster Unionists and their allies the right to stop it being implemented?

'The North Began' was the title given by Professor Eoin MacNeill for his article in the Gaelic League paper arguing for nationalists to organise and arm to fight for Home Rule as unionists had done to oppose it. By May 1914, MacNeill was in charge of 100,000 Irish Volunteers. The UVF were hardly in a position to criticise the Irish Volunteers who were now also openly drilling and shouldering weapons. To the IRB in Dublin, it was an opportunity to influence a body of armed men to stage a rising. In Belfast, 'the matter was discussed at the Freedom Club, and it was decided to issue a circular to all nationalist organisations in the city.

> Sean Cusack put his name to the circular as an Irish National Forester. Frank Booth signed as Ancient Order of Hibernians, American Alliance. Joe Connolly as Freedom Club and my name was on the circular as a member of the Gaelic League. There were names on the circular from the United Irish League, the Ancient Order of Hibernians, Board of Erin and the Gaelic Athletic Association.[23]

Thomas Wilson's BMH witness statement shows clearly that there was considerable broad-based support for the Irish Volunteers in Belfast. Problems arose, however, when a meeting was held in St Mary's Hall for delegates of those organisations which had signed the circular. McCullough chaired the meeting but business was not far progressed when:

> a Hibernian representative raised the question as to whether it was an opportune time to start the formation of the Volunteers. He read a letter addressed to him by Joe Devlin, MP expressing his approval of forming the Volunteers, but did not approve of the time and place of forming them.[24]

Wilson goes on to state that there was a strong support for the Irish Parliamentary Party at the meeting and if it were not for another Hibernian from a different branch who spoke strongly in favour of having a start made at once:

This man's action saved the situation at the meeting and gave us the necessary support to get a start made. I cannot remember the man's name. The organisation of the Volunteers was started that night. The majority of the men who joined the Volunteers at the start were men of good national backgrounds, who looked upon the Volunteer organisation as an essential safeguard for all Nationalists against the attentions of the Carsonite Volunteers. The welding of all the men who joined the Volunteers in the direction of extreme republicanism was the task undertaken by a small number of IRB men in Belfast.[25]

There was a governing committee to take control with the day-to-day functioning of the Volunteers left to two committees. The civil committee comprised the following: 'Denis McCullough (chairman) with members Joe Connolly, Dan Dempsey, Frank Booth, Tom Clear, Sean O'Kelly, Cathal O'Shannon. Another man whose name I think was O'Callaghan and myself.' Another committee, the military committee, was formed comprising at least the following: Peter Burns, Jim Burns and Rory Haskins.[26]

Frank Booth makes clear that not all those in senior positions in the Irish Volunteers were members of the IRB. On the civil committee, which had the functions of fundraising, booking halls, purchasing arms and equipment, only McCullough, O'Shannon and Thomas were members of the IRB. On the military committee at its formation, he recalled that only Sean Cusack and Peter Burns were members of the IRB. The key functions of the military committee were training Volunteers, selecting officers and all military and technical matters.[27] Booth's BMH witness statement gives an interesting profile of an IRB recruit. The driver of a bread van, Booth was 42 years old when he joined the IRB on 17 March 1914. About a month later he was head of his circle. He increased his circle with 'men of mature years but took in some younger men. In 1916, he had 17 members in his circle and had recruited Frank Crummey and Cathal McDowell.[28] What is interesting about these two BMH witness statements is that McCullough, although an IRB veteran, chose to be on the civil committee. Booth, seemingly, wanted to recruit steady, socially conservative recruits to the IRB rather than gung-ho militants. However, in 'Belfast before the split took place, the IRB had virtual control over the both Volunteer committees. From the start of the Volunteers up to July 1914 about 500 men joined the organisation.'[29]

To the RIC, the Irish Volunteers were controlled by 'Sinn Feiners and other extremists' while Joe Devlin held aloof from them with a directive to the local AOH 'forbidding them to drill with the Volunteers under pain of expulsion'.[30] The reasons for Joe Devlin's scepticism is given in a letter he wrote to John Redmond expressing his view that although Belfast was:

the headquarters of the Carsonite movement where the Catholic and Protestant Home Rulers would be among the first victims of any outbreak among the Orangemen, the Home Rulers regard the whole thing with absolute contempt and are astonished that anybody outside Belfast should take it seriously.

Certainly not all of the minority community shared Devlin's point of view. In March 1914 Bishop O'Donnell of Raphoe wrote 'The Orange faction is never done crying out intolerance and publishing what they might suffer under Home Rule, but not a word about what Catholics and Nationalists would suffer if the Orangemen got control.'[31] At Westminster, the Prime Minister was having difficulty with the Ulster Unionists and, in February 1914, asked Redmond to accept partition on the basis of the 'county option'. By this scheme there would be partition but a plebiscite would be put to each county in Ulster as to whether it would opt out of six-county partition. Fermanagh, Tyrone and Derry city all had nationalist majorities which would accept the 'county option' thereby making partition of a four-county area unviable. However, although Redmond was able to sell this scheme to his MPs, it was swiftly rejected by Carson, leaving the Irish Parliamentary Party leader looking weak for accepting the principle of partition. In the spring of 1914, the Curragh Mutiny and the Larne gun-running made the Ulster Unionists appear even more militant. Redmond decided the time had come to annexe the Irish Volunteers.[32]

On 9 June 1914, John Redmond placed an ultimatum in the press demanding that he be allowed to nominate 25 of his supporters to be members of the provisional committee of the Irish Volunteers in Dublin. Bulmer Hobson, then secretary of the Irish Volunteers, felt forced to accept but took pains to preserve the finances and rifles of the original governing body. Thomas Clarke of the IRB never spoke civilly to Hobson again.[33] In Belfast, Joe Devlin felt he had to follow the example of John Redmond and he too demanded that Denis McCullough give his nominees a majority on the Irish Volunteers executive committee while Thomas Wilson was opposed to this: 'Mr McCullough was in favour of their admission. Perhaps he had instructions from Headquarters in Dublin to admit them. He proposed their admission and it was agreed without a vote.'[34] Redmond's fortunes went into further decline with the Howth gun-running of 23 June 1914. Although the 'Howth Mausers' were landed successfully, three innocent people were shot dead by the military at Bachelors Walk in Dublin. It seemed to some Irish people that the authorities were showing more favour to Ulster unionism than Irish nationalism. No unionists were fired upon at the much greater Larne gun-running in April of that year.

World War and Ireland's Rising

The outbreak of the First World War in August 1914 was to prove a watershed. In September, Redmond decided to allow the Irish Volunteers to serve in the British army for the duration of the war. The third Home Rule Bill was put on the statute book, but it was a limited measure of self-government and there was an as yet unspecified special treatment for Ulster element in the Bill. However, Redmond calculated that support for the British forces would prove to be a good bargaining counter at the end of the hostilities.

At a famous speech at Woodenbridge, Redmond urged Irishmen to enlist and go 'as far as the firing extends'. This caused a split in the Volunteers. Those who did not wish to serve in what they saw as England's war stayed loyal to the Irish Volunteer command, which was in charge prior to Redmond's takeover. In Ulster, as in the rest of Ireland, the great majority of Volunteers were loyal to Redmond. In Belfast, a mere 120 out of 3,200 broke away to form a more extreme section led by Denis McCullough and the IRB. Thomas Wilson recalled: 'I felt particularly sore against Mr Devlin. His deliberate action in splitting the Volunteers was to place the unfortunate Catholic minority in most Orange districts at the mercy of Orange fanatics'. On top of this, 'Our efforts to increase our numbers after the split was about the same number and the same men as went to Tyrone on Easter Saturday, 1916'.[35]

In supporting recruitment of the renamed Irish National Volunteers, Redmond and Devlin were taking a risk. If the war was short and England was on the winning side, then the gamble might have paid off. In fact, after initial enthusiasm for the war, Irish casualties began to mount and a strong anti-war propaganda campaign developed.[36] James Connolly, for example, who was now a leader of the Irish Transport and General Workers' Union in Dublin, wrote an important pamphlet, *Slums and the Trenches*, in February 1916, pointing out that 'separation money' was very generous and a strong incentive for Irishmen to enlist. Even with separation money, Irish nationalist recruitment dipped in 1915 from 6,000 in April/May to 2,000 in September. Connolly had by this time become so convinced of the folly of a British connection that he planned to lead his small Irish Citizen Army in an armed revolt. Ben Novick argues that so large were the Irish casualties at Gallipoli that the Easter Rising of 1916 'was not so much transformative as the fulcrum upon which Nationalist opinion changed'.[37]

Connolly was persuaded to come on to the military strategic group in January to February of 1916. He would also offer the services of the Irish Citizen Army. Sean McDermott, who like Connolly had a thorough knowledge of Belfast, was already on the military committee. There were rumours of a rising in the late winter of 1915 and spring of 1916. Denis

McCullough was proposed as chairman of the supreme council by Sean McDermott and seconded by Tom Clarke at elections for the new IRB executive held in Clontarf in 1915. No doubt McCullough was flattered as he had only been released from Crumlin Road gaol under the Defence of the Realm Act. In fact, although no-one doubted McCullough's dedication to the IRB, it was 'a ruse by Clarke and McDermott' to further restrict the opportunity for dissension in the IRB. Under the 1873 IRB constitution the three-man executive could make policy for the entire organisation and, as McCullough correctly pointed out, he was too far away from events to have any influence. Clarke and McDermott of course were on the executive and had already decided on staging a rising in the near future.[38]

The part that Belfast had on the plans of the military committee is a different matter. The Irish Volunteers were weak in Belfast and there was always the fear that an antagonised unionist majority would attack exposed nationalist areas. It might create problems that would be difficult to solve. Connolly had given the Volunteers a lecture on street fighting in Belfast but had almost shouted 'You will fire no shots in Ulster'.[39] In 1966, McCullough wrote an account of the role of the Irish Volunteers who mobilised at Coalisland on Easter Saturday in 1916 in an attempt to take part in the rising.[40] He was kept in ignorance of the plans for the rising despite being head centre of the supreme council of the IRB. The small group that made up the military council of the IRB were determined to ensure that their efforts were not ruined by leaks or informers. Although McCullough had given his general consent for an insurrection rising, he was not told that a rising was imminent until the week before by IRB member Alf Cotton. McCullough went to Dublin to find out more. Tom Clarke and Sean McDermott were able to confirm that the 'Volunteers would be out on Sunday'.[41] The late confirmation of the rising goes some way to explain the chaos later when the Belfast Volunteers mobilised at Coalisland.

An Irish Volunteer from Belfast, Charlie Monaghan, was to lose his life on the Good Friday before the rising took place. He was one of three men who had been detailed to seize the wireless station at Valentia Island so that Roger Casement, another Antrim man, could safely land rifles for the rising. However, the car in which Monaghan was travelling on the way to Valentia Island took a wrong turn in a mountain and travelled over an unprotected ledge into the River Luane. Monaghan was drowned along with two Volunteers, Con Keating and Denis Lehane.[42]

The actual plans for the Coalisland mobilisation were delivered by Cathal O'Shannon. The plan was that the Belfast Volunteers should link up with other Volunteers from Tyrone, Derry, Armagh and Scotland. They should then march two hundred miles to Galway where they would link up with Liam Mellows's command. On the way to Galway, they were not to fire weapons at any time. To say the least, it was an improbable order. It is difficult even now to discern the reasoning behind it. There was obviously the fear that an overt action by the Irish Volunteers would spark a unionist backlash with the minority community being collateral damage. There may also have been a vague plan that British troops may have been moved to control the northern Volunteers, thereby taking pressure off the insurgents in other parts of Ireland. Whatever the intention, Connolly repeated Pearse's orders about marching west to his daughters, Ina and Nora, who were members of Cumann na mBan and along with Elizabeth and Nell Corr, Kathleen Murphy and Eilis Woods had travelled to the GPO in Easter week.[43]

Although Denis McCullough was able to mobilise the Belfast Volunteers at very short notice, buying tickets and supplies for Coalisland at his own expense, the mobilisation proved a comic opera. Thomas Wilson's BMH witness statement claims that three batches of men travelled by train on Saturday depending on what time they could get off work. Harry Osborne gives a corrective to this. He had to work late on the Saturday and the Sunday morning so he spoke to his brother Paddy, who was also a Volunteer. Harry gave Paddy a £5 note and told him that he would see him in Coalisland on Monday. This meant that although Thomas Wilson was probably correct in his estimation that 120 to 130 Volunteers had travelled to Coalisland on the Saturday, they would have been supplemented by more men on the Easter Sunday, which accounts for the figure of 156 names of Belfast Volunteers compiled by Peter Burns and others in 1936.[44]

Peter Burns and a few trusted Volunteers collected 42 rifles for the Volunteers. Some, like Harry Dobbyn who was told he was too old to mobilise, came anyway with his own personal weapon. He was to tell his son that he had waited for this rising all his life. In Coalisland itself, it seemed that everything Denis McCullough tried to do was marked by acrimony and confusion. Some Volunteers from Coalisland and Dungannon expressed a willingness to fight but found the military council's instructions to be unrealistic and they would have preferred to fight in their own area. Arguments prevailed and two local priests added to the confusion by insisting that the rising in Dublin was being controlled by the Irish Citizen Army, not the Irish Volunteers. The leader of the Tyrone contingent, Dr Pat McCartan, did not prove to be a firebrand leader and wrote later: 'Long before Easter I had not heart in it as it came and could not inspire others with courage as I had none myself.'[45]

On Easter Sunday, McCullough attempted to persuade the Tyrone Volunteers to embark for Galway. His arguments were not going anywhere and his problems became worse when he became the only casualty of the mobilisation. McCullough had not brought his own personal weapon with him and his attempts to unload a small automatic pistol he was given resulted in him shooting himself through the left hand. Dr McCartan bandaged McCullough's wound but already very emotional over his problems, he was now for a time delirious as a result of the bullet wound. Nonetheless, he and Herbert Moore Pim decided to check and see if they could get any support in other parts of Tyrone.[46]

Only in Beragh did the Tyrone Volunteers show any enthusiasm for leaving their area. Arriving back in Coalisland, McCullough found that local Volunteers were still arguing. Pat McCormick, a prominent IRB man from the Glens of Antrim, had arrived and he seemed to agree with McCullough's snap decision to bring the Belfast Volunteers home by train on the same Easter Sunday. After all, McCullough reasoned, they only had two days' rations with them. Thus, began what Seamus Dobbyn characterised as 'the retreat from Moscow'.[47]

McCullough held a meeting of section leaders and told them he would give the Volunteers the train fare from Cookstown and they should go home. Many of them demurred. Seamus Dobbyn recalled that one section leader, Liam Gaynor, was adamant that he and his men were willing to go to Galway to fight rather than go to Cookstown to catch the train. A staff captain, Cathal McDowell, refused to obey McCullough's order, pointing out that McCullough was essentially a civilian commander and that he was obeying Eoin MacNeill, the leader of the Irish Volunteers, rather than the military council of the IRB. This indicates that McDowell was not then aware of the MacNeill order to stop the rising. McDowell recalled that when he was acting up temporarily in McCullough's place, Patrick Pearse himself had insisted that in a rising all orders must be obeyed completely. McDowell's opposition to McCullough was only quelled when Peter Burns threatened to put McDowell on a charge if he did not follow orders.[48]

Back in Belfast, Frank Booth, who had used his bread van to transport the rifles for Coalisland, had waited in vain for the Glasgow boat. The Scottish Volunteers did not arrive. The Scottish contingent had gone straight to Dublin.

On Easter Monday, Peter Burns reviewed the returned Volunteers at 6.30 a.m. at Chapel Fields, near Broadway on the Falls Road. He warned them that they should be prepared to be called out at short notice for active service. After the rising the Volunteers went through a period of confusion and disillusionment. There was to be a further sting in the tail. Sean Cusack's BMH witness statement tells us that he approached Denis McCullough to express the disappointment of the Volunteers at the events in Coalisland. While Cusack personally liked and admired McCullough, the ex-training officer felt it was his duty to explain to his civilian commander that the Volunteers had lost confidence in him. To give McCullough his due, he accepted this well and he held no grudge against any of the Volunteers and continued to give good service to Belfast republicanism. This is indicated by the interview which a later republican leader, Seamus Woods, gave to Ernie O'Malley.

Woods recalled that the IRA in Belfast had learned the terms of the Treaty by Christmas 1921 but were worried about the possibility of partition. He noted that McCullough was 'fair and just. Although he still had importance within the IRB, he did not try to influence me. ... "You're the fellows that have borne the brunt of the fighting and I have been in gaol and have had a soft time of it".'[49] McCullough not only stayed up all night discussing the Treaty, but drove to Dublin on St Stephen's Day to discuss Belfast's view of it with Woods and Joe McKelvey also leaving a modest account of the meeting in a BMH witness statement.

In truth, McCullough's star was in decline since the Coalisland mobilisation. The period after the 1916 Rising was to bring a more realistic and more ruthless republicanism to the fore. Sinn Féin and the IRB were not the same so it would be inaccurate to generalise, but many of the leaders of the Volunteers out at Coalisland found that the centrality of their position to the republican movement in Belfast had waned. Twenty-four leading republicans from Belfast were arrested in the following weekend, but until their arrest the mobilisation was known to neither unionists nor nationalists in Belfast. The authorities, however, must have known who they were and the names of those arrested give an indication of who the most important figures in Belfast at the time of the Easter Rising. Their addresses are also given, indicating an upper working-class to middle-class profile.

They were: Jerry Barnes, 66 St James' Park; Frank Booth, Alexander Street West; Peter Burns, 7 Linden Street; Mick Carolon, 80 Chief Street; Thomas Clear, 57 Agincourt Avenue; Alex Connolly, Mulholland Terrace; Joseph Connolly, 38 Divis Street; Alfie Cotton, 40 Locan Street, Broadway; Henry Dobbyn, 21 Clonard Gardens; Seamus Dobbyn, 21 Clonard Gardens; Robert (Rory?) Haskins, c/o Coolfin Street, Donegall Road; Sam Heron, Divis Street; James Johnstone, Shandon Road, Knock; John Kelly, Iris Street; Denis McCullough, Grosvenor Road (Divis Street); Charles McDowell, 19 Locan Street; Pat Nash, 52 Gibson Street; Sean Neeson, 153 Falls Road; Harry Osborne, 16 Smithfield; Cathal O'Shannon, 27 Canning Street; James Smith, 3 Somerville Gardens, Andersonstown; Edward Tierney, Falls Road; Thomas Wilson, 248 Albertbridge Road'.[50]

The abovenamed were later placed in Frongoch internment camp in Wales where they were to meet republicans from other parts of Ireland. It must be kept in mind that the fighting in Easter week was largely confined to Dublin, and republicans in Cork, Kerry, Tipperary, etc were not out for the rising in 1916 any more than the Volunteers from Belfast. However, all of them were now aware of the scale of the insurrection in Dublin. What is interesting about the people interned from Belfast is the number of important individuals who were not apprehended. The senior intelligence personnel of Frank Crummey, David McGuinness and Owen McKiernan were not arrested. The acknowledged leaders of the IRA in 1921–2 – such as Joe McKelvey, Seamus Woods, Roger and Felix McCorley, Tom McNally, Sean O'Neill, Seamus McKenna, Thomas Fox, Rory Fitzpatrick, Sean Montgomery, Seán Cunningham and Joe Murray – were not seized. Nonetheless, from July 1921 until June 1922 they were the accredited representatives of the nationalist community in Belfast to a far greater extent individually than any of the Belfast republicans arrested in April 1916.

The reasons are various. Some, such as Roger and Felix McCorley and Joe Murray, were only Fianna boys in 1916, but later they were to exhibit a more militant outlook in the violent years of 1920–22 in Belfast. Roger McCorley probably expressed the view of all of them in his BMH witness statement when he wrote that his family leaned towards insurrection. He noted that large bodies of soldiers were going through Belfast in 1916 on their way to suppress the rebels in Dublin. He believed a few determined men could have given proper resistance and as a result he 'detested faint-heartedness in war'.[51] Seamus Woods had enlisted in the Irish Volunteers in 1914 when he himself was only 14.[52] Rory Fitzpatrick, Sean Montgomery and Sean McCartney had been British soldiers in the Great War. Tom Fox, Seamus McKenna and Thomas Flynn joined in 1917 as indeed did my grandfather.[53]

All of them were profoundly affected by the Easter Rising and the aftermath. There had been a growing resentment in nationalist Belfast against Joe Devlin and the IPP even before the 1916 Rising. As Éamon Phoenix explains: 'In Belfast, the National Volunteers tightly controlled by the Devlinite business and professional class had ceased route marches and military activity in the early months of 1916 in favour of whist drives.'[54] However, the Belfast National Volunteers' organisation remained in existence until October 1918 handing over its remaining arms – 210 weapons of 'old Italian pattern'.[55] At Westminster, John Redmond's influence waned further. While Redmond himself refused to take a cabinet post until a Home Rule Act was passed, the coalition government set up in May 1915 was to include Carson and several other ardent unionists.

The Easter Rising in Dublin made relations between this coalition and the Irish Parliamentary Party even worse. Pearse and the small cadre of revolutionaries knew that they could not win militarily but believed that their 'blood sacrifice' would encourage a new generation to fight for an Irish republic. The execution of 16 leaders in ten days after summary court-martials as well as the mass arrest of 3,400 Sinn Féin activists had caused a sea-change in Irish public opinion. Resentment turned to admiration and the commander of the National Volunteers, Colonel Maurice Moore, commented 'a few unknown men shot in a barrack yard had embittered a whole nation'.[56] There was a belief that Arthur Griffith's Sinn Féin party was behind the rising. In fact, Griffith knew nothing of the plans for the insurrection and was in Eoin MacNeill's house at Woodtown Park during it.[57] It was the proliferation of 'new' Sinn Féin clubs in 1917 which took advantage of the belief that the events of 1916 were a Sinn Féin rebellion. It is, however, fair to say that Sinn Féin did not make the Easter Rising but the Easter Rising made Sinn Féin.

In Belfast, after the rising David McGuinness was annoyed at how the mobilisation at Coalisland had worked out: 'After Easter Week 1916 a number of the important Volunteers and IRB members were arrested and deported. I was not arrested however'. After the release of the prisoners about early 1917 a move to reorganise the Volunteers was made. A notification by word of mouth was made that a meeting would be held at premises at the Foresters' Hall in Mill Street.

> It was agreed that a reorganisation would commence. This reorganisation had four companies in the Falls Road area: A, B, C and D. These companies were only in skeletal form at the start. 'A' Company was associated with O'Neill Crowley and Michael Davitt GAA Clubs; 'B' Company, John Mitchel GAA Club; 'C' the old Fianna companies again and the Clan Uladh band. 'D' Company had no association with outside clubs or bands.[58]

As Sinn Féin and the Irish Volunteers mushroomed in size in 1917–18 so did Belfast republicanism. Their growth was given further stimulation by the prospect of partition and the decision of the Irish Parliamentary Party to embrace a system of temporary exclusion of the six north-eastern counties during the rest of the First World War. The debate and votes on partition was to tear the IPP apart in the north and the debates of 'Black Friday' in June 1916 were long remembered.[59] By 1918, the Irish Volunteers were much more focused on military matters than their predecessors would have been before the 1916 rising. Tom Fox recalled how drilling had been central and frequently: 'rifle practice with small bore rifles'. This type of work continued until 1918 when the imposition of conscription was threatened which gave an impetus to Volunteer recruiting and succeeded in diverting the thoughts of the Volunteers to the possibility of another fight at no distant time.[60]

Conflict in Belfast, 1920–22

The prospect of partition and the expulsion of Catholics and socialists from their workplaces in July 1920 were to ensure that there was savage violence in Belfast. Andrew Boyd, the chronicler of Belfast's nineteenth-century sectarian conflicts, wrote: 'The Northern Ireland Government had made little effort to control the frequent outbreaks of fanaticism among its supporters. Far more terrifying than all the disturbances of the nineteenth century were in those years from 1920 to 1922.'61 The 'Young Turks' in the IRA at first found it difficult to persuade senior IRA officers to permit the IRA to protect the nationalist minority. Roger McCorley recalled:

> Some thought further IRA action would make the situation worse – most thought the IRA would have to hit back. Both battalion and brigade council agreed to this ... [It became] a fight between two disciplined bodies. The IRA posted pickets at entrances to Catholic districts and stayed all night.[62]

Kieran Glennon made a careful analysis of the deaths in Belfast from July 1920 until August 1922 in which he concluded that the death figure of 498 in the city was identical to the figure arrived at by Alan Parkinson in his meticulously researched study. Both writers agree that the smaller nationalist community suffered disproportionately.[63]

Alfred Cope, who brokered the truce between the British forces and the IRA in July 1921, had the terms of the truce applied to all 32 counties in Ireland. By those terms the IRA in Belfast was given quasi-legal status as representatives of the nationalist community in Belfast. The republicans set up their liaison office quite openly in St Mary's Hall in Bank Street. They could now contact the highest ranks of the British Army and the RIC. The situation was to effectively end by the spring of 1922 and the violence of the first half of 1922 was easily the worst and both communities suffered but especially the nationalists. In the last phase IRA activity in the north, it was largely confined to the burnings mainly of unionist commercial property in Belfast throughout June. Seamus Woods explained: 'The purpose of the campaign was to hit the authors and promoters of the pogrom'; he claimed it was having the effect of stopping the murder campaign and it gained the 'support and sympathy' of the nationalist population. This support, he stressed 'has been won not so much out of sympathy for our National aspirations but more on account of the part the IRA had played in defending the minority population against organised attacks by uniformed and non-uniformed Crown Forces'.[64] Soon after, the IRA split over the terms of the Treaty and republicans in Belfast found themselves overwhelmed by Crown forces. The terms of the truce of 1921 were now gone and support for an IRA campaign was on the decrease.

On 1 August 1922, a committee of the Provisional Government met to decide what their policy should be on the north-east of Ireland. They concluded that there should be a 'peace policy' whereby Catholics in the north should disarm and recognise the authority of the Northern Ireland government. One of the chief proponents of this policy was Ernest Blythe who claimed: 'Our boycott would not threaten the Northern shipbuilding industry any more than a summer shower would threaten Cave Hill. ... Pressure must be absolutely normal and constitutional'.[65] The Provisional Government was preoccupied with the civil war in the 26 counties. Michael Collins was now dead and northern nationalists had lost their champion. The IRA in the north had split, many of them going south to fight in the civil war. Partition now was a reality and support for the republican cause in Belfast had decreased. There was still celebration for the memory of the Easter Rising in Belfast but the nationalists there now felt betrayed by Westminster and abandoned by the south. Rebuilding a republican movement in Belfast was now even more difficult.

Notes

1. Sean J. Connolly (ed.), *Belfast 400: People, Place and History* (Liverpool, 2012), p. 17. See also the introduction to Raymond O'Regan and Arthur Magee, *The Little Book of Belfast* (Cheltenham, 2015).
2. George Boyce, 'Respectable rebels: Ulster Unionist resistance to the third Home Rule Bill, 1912–14' in Alan F. Parkinson and Éamon Phoenix (eds), *Conflicts in the North of Ireland, 1900–2000: Flashpoints and Fracture Zones* (Dublin, 2010), p. 29.
3. Jim McDermott, *Northern Divisions: The Old IRA and the Belfast Pogroms, 1920–22* (Belfast, 2001), p. 12. Quoted from Patrick Buckland, *Irish Unionism 1885–1923* (Belfast, 1973), p. 130.
4. Statement of Thomas McNally (BMH WS 410).
5. Brian Feeney, *Antrim: The Irish Revolution, 1912–23* (Dublin, 2021), pp 28–9.
6. Graham Walker and Aaron Edwards, 'The beleaguered left: the Northern Ireland Labour Party and its trials and dilemmas, 1924–79' in Parkinson and Phoenix (eds), *Conflicts in the North of Ireland*, p. 166.
7. Feeney, *Antrim: The Irish Revolution*, p. 32.
8. Éamon Phoenix, *Northern Nationalism: Nationalistic Politics, Partition and the Catholic Minority in Northern Ireland 1890–1940* (Belfast, 1994), p. 105.
9. Austen Morgan, *Labour and Partition* (London, 1991), p. 198.
10. *Northern Divisions*, p. 2; Denis McCullough 'The events in Belfast', *Capuchin Annual* (1966), pp 381–4
11. Bulmer Hobson, *Ireland, Yesterday and Tomorrow* (Belfast, 1968), pp 14–18.
12. Statements of Roger McCorley (BMH WS 389) and Joe Murray (BMH WS 412).
13. McDermott, *Northern Divisions*, pp 4–5; David McGuinness memoir (in the author's possession).
14. Statement of Thomas Wilson (BMH WS 176).

15 Statement of Rory Haskin(s) (BMH WS 223).
16 Douglas Gageby, *The Last Secretary General; Sean Lester and the League of Nations* (Dublin, 1999), p. 5.
17 Recording by Seamus Dobbyn in the O'Kane Collection, Cardinal Tomás Ó Fiaich Memorial Library and Archive, Armagh (COFMLA).
18 Gerard MacAtasney, *Seán Mac Diarmada: The Mind of the Revolution* (Drumlin Publications, 2004), Ch. 6.
19 These can be accessed on line on the Treasonable Felony Blog, https://treasonfelony.wordpress.com.
20 Statement of Thomas Wilson (BMH WS 176).
21 Éamon Phoenix, 'Northern nationalists in conflict: from the third Home Rule crisis to partition, 1900–21' in Parkinson and Phoenix (eds), *Conflicts in the North*, p. 48.
22 Jonathan Bardon, *A History of Ulster* (Belfast, 2005), p. 442.
23 Statement of Thomas Wilson (BMH WS 176).
24 Ibid.
25 Ibid.
26 Ibid.
27 Statement of Frank Booth (BMH WS 229).
28 Ibid.
29 Statement of Thomas Wilson (BMH WS 176).
30 Phoenix, *Northern Nationalism*, p. 10.
31 Ibid.
32 Ibid.
33 Morgan, *Labour and Partition*, pp 184–5.
34 Statement of Thomas Wilson (BMH WS 176).
35 Ibid.
36 *The 6th Irish Connaught Rangers, Belfast Nationalists and the Great War* (Belfast, 2011), pp 21–2.
37 Ben Novick, *Conceiving Revolution: Irish Nationalist Propaganda during the First World War* (Dublin, 2001), p. 18.
38 MacAtasney, *Seán Mac Diarmada*, pp 101–02.
39 Statement of Seamus Dobbyn (BMH WS 279).
40 McCullough, 'Events in Belfast', pp 381–4.
41 Ibid.; McDermott, *Northern Divisions*, pp 6–12.
42 McDermott, *Northern Divisions*, p. 10.
43 Statement of Mrs Kathleen O'Kelly (BMH WS 180); Feeney, *Antrim, The Irish Revolution*, pp 40–43; Jimmy McDermott, *Belfast Republicans and the Easter Rising* (Belfast, 2020) pp 3–7.
43 Ibid., p. 5.
44 Statement of Seamus Dobbyn (BMH WS 279).
45 Morgan, *Labour and Partition*, p. 206; McDermott, *Northern Divisions*, p. 10.
46 Statement of Denis McCullough (BMH WS 915).

47 Statement of Seamus Dobbyn (BMH WS 279).
48 Ibid.; O'Kane Collection, COFMLA.
49 McDermott, *Belfast and the Rising*, p. 8; statement of Cathal McDowell (BMH WS 173).
50 Síobhra Aiken, Fearghal Mac Bhloscaidh, Liam Ó Duibhir, Diarmuid Ó Tuama, *The Men Will Talk To Me: Ernie O'Malley's Interviews with the Northern Divisions* (Newbridge, Co. Kildare, 2018), p. 90.
51 Statement of Roger McCorley (BMH WS 389).
52 Aiken et al., *The Men Will Talk To Me*, pp 88–9.
53 Statements of Thomas Fox (BMH WS 365), Seamus McKenna (BMH WS 1016) and Thomas Flynn (BMH WS 429).
54 Phoenix, *Northern Nationalism*, p. 18.
55 Ibid.
56 Ibid, p. 20.
57 Hobson, *Ireland, Yesterday and Tomorrow*, p. 77.
58 David McGuinness memoir.
59 Feeney, *Antrim, the Irish Revolution*, pp 43–6.
60 Statement of Thomas Fox (BMH WS 365).
61 Andrew Boyd, *Holy War in Belfast* (Belfast, 1969), p. 176.
62 Statement of Roger McCorley (BMH WS 389).
63 Kieran Glennon, 'Facts and fallacies of the Belfast pogrom', *History Ireland*, 28:5 (Sep./Oct. 2020), pp 280–83; Alan F. Parkinson, *A Difficult Birth: The Early Years of Northern Ireland, 1920–1925* (Dublin, 2020), pp 272–3, 279.
64 McDermott, *Northern Divisions*, pp 253–4.
65 Ibid., p. 265.

5

Ulster unionism and the Irish Convention, 1917–18

NEIL C. FLEMING

The failure of the Irish Convention that met between 25 July 1917 and 5 April 1918 belies its significance to political developments across Ireland. As Alan O'Day has observed, it was 'the fifth attempt to implement Home Rule and marks [Patrick] Buckland's third step toward a solution of the Ulster question'.[1] The first step, the Buckingham Palace conference in 1914, revealed a narrow but unbridgeable gap between the respective positions of the Irish nationalists and the Ulster Unionists on the permanency of excluding the six north-east counties from Home Rule. The second, the settlement brokered by David Lloyd George in 1916 in the wake of the Easter Rising, adopted an ambiguous position on the duration of partition but was opposed by the Southern Unionists and undermined by their allies in the wartime coalition government. As such, it was inevitable that the special treatment of Ulster would feature prominently at the Irish Convention. The submission of a minority report by the Ulster Unionists at the convention's conclusion formally signalled that it too had failed to resolve the political impasse.

Three factors, individually and in combination, have typically been put forward to explain this outcome. First, the chairmanship of the onetime unionist turned home ruler, Sir Horace Plunkett, repeatedly dissipated the momentum towards an agreed settlement.[2] Second, Sinn Féin's boycott undermined the convention's legitimacy in the eyes of a growing number of nationalists, and at the same time limited the Nationalist Party's room for manoeuvre and divided its delegates on a number of sensitive questions.[3] Third, the obduracy of the Ulster Unionists rendered the purpose and methods of the convention unrealisable. As Cecil Harmsworth – a contemporary observer and member of the Prime Minister's secretariat – confided to his diary: 'The Ulstermen "lie low and say nuffin."'[4]

Harmsworth's pithy assessment is understandable. After the convention's demise it was seemingly substantiated by the Ulster Unionists' own efforts to play down, to the point of misrepresentation, the significance of their attendance and actions. This is examined below, along with its impact on historiographical assessments of the convention. The chapter then situates the Ulster Unionists' hesitancy and caution about the convention in the wake of the 1916 settlement that was thwarted by the Southern Unionists. The resulting limitations placed on the Ulster Unionist delegates by the Ulster Unionist Council (UUC) are scrutinised, and the chapter highlights the existence of differing opinions in their ranks about the positions to be adopted at Dublin, and the preparedness of some to test these at the convention and in dialogue with other Ulster Unionists.

Historical memory

The convention's proceedings were conducted in secret to 'encourage the utmost freedom of opinion.'[5] At the insistence of the Ulster Unionists, among others, Plunkett's official report, submitted to parliament in 1918, provided only a bare summary of its proceedings. Although the report hinted at tension between the Ulster Unionist delegates and the UUC, it was not this that preoccupied the former's dissenting report, but the implication in the official report that there had been 'a measure of agreement regarding Irish Self-Government'. 'The provisional conclusions on minor matters', the Ulster Unionists countered, 'were strictly contingent on agreement on the vital issues.'[6] That the convention sank almost without trace in the months that followed suited the Ulster Unionists, whatever their supporters might later suggest.[7]

Addressing the Ulster Unionist Labour Association on 13 July 1918, the Ulster Unionists' most flexible delegate, Lord Londonderry, declared that 'as a member of the Convention he was convinced that there was nothing between the maintenance of the union and separation.'[8] Such distortions did not go unchallenged. On 7 October 1919, the Liberal-Conservative government appointed a cabinet committee to consider Irish self-government. Against this backdrop, *The Times* soon after published 'An Untold Tale', a series of articles that expanded on Plunkett's report.[9] These provoked a defensive response from the Ulster Unionist and former convention delegate, Hugh MacDowell Pollock. He accused the newspaper of endeavouring to 'throw the responsibility for the failure of the Convention on the Ulster Unionist group', and, as a corollary, of seeking to justify the Southern Unionists' willingness to consider an all-Ireland settlement.

It was the nationalists' insistence on fiscal autonomy, Pollock claimed, that was the real obstacle to an agreement. As concessions to 'Ulster' were made on the basis of Ireland's separation from Great Britain, Pollock reasoned that these were not concessions at all. He also refuted the suggestion made in *The Times* that an advisory committee appointed by the UUC, to liaise with its delegates, had vetoed attempts by the latter to achieve a consensus at the convention. The advisory committee existed to represent 'all classes of Unionist opinion in Ulster' and 'to enable the delegates to keep in touch with their constituents in case proposals were submitted which in the opinion of the delegates were deserving of support.' The committee, Pollock went on, was 'kept *en rapport* with the general proceedings of the Convention from time to time', and at 'no time did the advisory council [*sic*] determine the policy of the delegates or interfere with their procedure'.[10]

In reply, *The Times*'s 'special correspondent' observed that Pollock had contradicted himself by refuting any suggestion that the Ulster Unionists were responsible for the convention's breakdown, and at the same time he challenged 'statements which imply that the Ulster delegates were less obdurate than Mr Pollock desired them to appear'. The latter, the special correspondent speculated, was a device to avoid stirring 'the resentment and suspicion of a large number of Unionists in Ireland who have hitherto heard only a partial story of the Convention.'[11] Elsewhere in the same issue, *The Times* again averred that the picture drawn by Pollock was 'for the benefit of readers of the Belfast Press', which as a result presented the Ulster Unionist delegation 'in a light which we can only regard as highly unbecoming, and in the truth of which we find it very difficult to believe.'[12]

Stephen Gwynn's account of Redmond's final years, also published in 1919, essentially concurred with the interpretation advanced by *The Times*. Gwynn, a nationalist delegate to the convention, recalled that the Ulster Unionist delegation, 'though we did not know it at first, was dictated by the conditions of their attendance' to 'submit every question of importance to an Advisory Committee in Belfast – behind which again was the Ulster Unionist Council. They had therefore no freedom of action and were of necessity extremely guarded in speech.'[13] William O'Brien's memoirs, published the following year, are considerably less flattering to the Ulster Unionists, though he too concurred with the interpretation put forward in *The Times*.

> The 'Ulster' Partitionists ... were the mere puppets of an invisible power behind the throne – 'The Ulster Unionist Council' in Belfast – who were not even present at the Convention but put an instant extinguisher upon their delegates the moment there was a whisper of any agreement other than the Partition agreement.[14]

The former MP for Cork had been the leading nationalist proponent of conciliation with Irish unionism.[15] O'Brien was nevertheless a staunch opponent of partition, and, like a number of leading nationalists, he had been absent from the convention.

Pollock's contrasting interpretation was subsequently embellished in Ronald McNeill's *Ulster's Stand for the Union*, published shortly after the establishment of Northern Ireland. McNeill was the Conservative MP for the Kent constituency of St Augustine's, and a member of the UUC's standing committee, but he had not been a delegate to the convention or a member of the advisory committee. McNeill nevertheless advanced a cynical and seemingly authoritative interpretation of the Ulster Unionists' behaviour by claiming that at the convention they sought only to preserve the status quo, and that their delegation had raised 'no objection' to the convention's 'expenditure of time and energy' because it distracted nationalist MPs from criticising the wartime government.[16]

Select paragraphs of *Ulster's Stand* were reproduced in Denis Gwynn's 1932 biography of the Nationalist Party leader, John Redmond. Gwynn was less sympathetic to the Ulster Unionists than his father Stephen, but like *The Times*, he questioned the Pollock-McNeill interpretation. 'It may be doubted whether the veto of the Orangemen [*sic*] was as securely established as [McNeill] believed', Gwynn remarked before quoting his correspondence with the leading Southern Unionist delegate, Lord Midleton. The Ulster Unionists had entered the convention, Midleton recalled to Gwynn, 'without any limitations' and their 'most prominent ... members expressed themselves as determined to come to terms for an All-Ireland settlement.' Referring to his compromise scheme, proposed in December 1917 and debated through to January 1918, Midleton asserted that the Ulster Unionists were likely to have thrown their weight behind such a settlement only for Plunkett's decision to move proceedings in a different direction.[17]

Midleton expanded on these remarks in *Ireland – Dupe or Heroine* and later again in his memoirs. He detailed how Hugh Thom Barrie, the chairman of the Ulster Unionist delegation, along with his party leader, Sir Edward Carson, and the Church of Ireland archbishop of Armagh, John Crozier, were all willing to consider an all-Ireland settlement. Midleton again attributed the loss of momentum towards an agreement to Plunkett's chairmanship. Midleton's evident bitterness about the failure of his proposals extended to the Ulster Unionists, but unable to join those attacking them for intransigence throughout the convention, he found a more peculiar method. At the outset of the convention, the Ulster Unionists had in effect vetoed the Southern Unionists' preferred candidate for its chairmanship. It was this, Midleton recalled, that helped to pave the way for Plunkett's appointment.[18] Equally questionable is his barbed observation that the Ulster Unionists had combined with the Catholic bishops, 'the men they most distrusted in Ireland'. It was, in fact, the fundamental disagreement between these two delegations on customs, not Ulster, that undermined Midleton's scheme, and far from combining each produced separate dissenting minority reports.[19]

It might be expected that the unionist-partitionist historiography of the inter-war years would follow the line taken by Pollock and McNeill.[20] However, Henry Maxwell's *Ulster was Right*, published not long after Gwynn and Midleton's accounts, depicts the 'attitude' of the Ulster Unionist delegation as 'strictly compatible with the notions of compromise embodied in the conception of the Irish Convention'. Maxwell offered little to substantiate the assertion and failed to address Midleton's claims directly. He instead preferred to dwell on the 'corresponding attitude of mind with which the [Catholic] Hierarchy approached the question'.[21] Likewise, the third volume of *Carson*, by Ian Colvin, published in 1937, foregrounded the pragmatism of its subject in contrast to the actions of the nationalist delegates – including bishops ostensibly representing the Catholic Church – and their republican critics.[22] Five years later, Hugh Shearman's *Not an Inch* was so preoccupied with the latter task that it had nothing at all to say about the Ulster Unionists.[23] St John Ervine's biography of James Craig, published in 1949, offers a little more by reiterating the Pollock-McNeill line albeit in the playwright's more colourful language. Comparing the expectation that the Ulster Unionists reach a settlement at the convention to urging someone to commit suicide, Ervine declared that 'I should not be acting in a negative manner if I rejected his poison or his razor. I should be affirming my belief in life'.[24]

The most significant and comprehensive scholarly work on the convention remains R.B. McDowell's *The Irish Convention 1917–18*.[25] Unlike earlier accounts, McDowell had the benefit of Plunkett's confidential report, a document, he observed, that was influenced by its author's 'determination to achieve a settlement, his amusement at the idiosyncrasies of some members and his impatience at the obstinacy of others – especially the Ulster unionists.'[26] McDowell nonetheless arrived at a similar judgment about the latter, describing them in his conclusion as obdurate and obstinate.[27] His findings have inevitably shaped subsequent historiographical assessments of Ulster unionism and the convention.[28] Alongside the corroborating output of the Ulster Unionists and their sympathisers, the result is that the rival, partial and misleading theses established in the convention's wake remain largely unchallenged, a problem compounded by the tendency of most accounts to telescope eight months of deliberations into a relatively brief overarching summary.[29] Yet, like Plunkett, McDowell's assessment of the Ulster Unionists' conduct at the convention is more nuanced than is suggested by his concluding description of them as obstinate. He acknowledged, in particular, differences of opinion within the Ulster Unionist delegation, and that their attitude to the convention, whilst markedly cautious, even suspicious, compared with the other groups represented, was more dynamic than is often supposed.[30]

Hesitancy and acceptance

Those sceptical of the sincerity of the Ulster Unionists' participation in the convention highlight the fact that its most senior figures did not attend.[31] Carson, and his eventual successor as party leader, James Craig, were preoccupied with their duties in the wartime coalition government through to their resignations in January 1918. Carson, however, was consulted throughout the convention's existence by Barrie, much to the frustration of Carson's wife, and the Ulster Unionist delegates met periodically to discuss the convention with the party's MPs.[32] The acting leader of the Ulster Unionists, Sir John Lonsdale, also elected not to attend, but he played a significant role in securing the party's backing for entering the convention. Like Redmond, Lonsdale opted for it rather than Lloyd George's alternative of immediate Home Rule and six-county exclusion when these were put to the Irish party leaders on 16 May 1917.[33] And like Redmond, Lonsdale needed to secure the approval of his party, in his case by convening the UUC.

The creation of the UUC in 1904–05 represented, according to Jackson, 'even if only in principle … a check on the freedom of Irish Unionist members of parliament.'[34] Still, as Timothy McMahon has argued, scholarly attention tends to focus on the actions of the leading Ulster Unionists and not the dynamic relationship that existed between them and their supporters.[35] Like many political movements, periods of high mobilisation meant that the enhanced engagement of ordinary members could not be ignored by the leadership.[36] As with any large body, of course, the UUC was overseen by a smaller group, its standing committee, which was assisted by a permanent staff. But the council was intended, according to Buckland, to be 'democratic and wholly representative of Ulster unionism', with most of its members nominated by local constituency associations and Orange county grand lodges.[37] To this already sizable assembly, 12 representatives of the Ulster Women's Unionist Council were added following an 'uncharacteristically vehement appeal' in 1918.[38]

The UUC meeting to approve sending a delegation to the convention was summoned for 8 June 1917. It was held almost exactly a year after the UUC had been convened to give its backing to the settlement reached between Lloyd George, Carson and Redmond in the wake of the rising. On that occasion, it took Carson two hours to persuade the UUC's executive, on 6 June 1916, before he addressed the full council on 12 June. The latter gave its formal approval after a 'highly charged and emotional' meeting.[39] Even so, the divisions then exposed – about abandoning to immediate Home Rule the Ulster Unionists in counties Cavan, Donegal and Monaghan – rumbled on afterwards, on both sides of the Irish Sea, with critics arguing that Lloyd George had misled Carson and by implication the UUC.[40]

It was a bruising episode for Ulster unionism and Carson in particular. The latter, nevertheless, was able to return to government in December 1916, and in the months that followed he and his ministerial colleagues actively considered alternative settlements. This was made easier by Lloyd George's – now Prime Minister – assurance to the House of Commons on 7 March 1917 that the Ulster Unionists would not be coerced by the government into an all-Ireland settlement.[41] The following month, Carson circulated among his cabinet colleagues a memorandum in support of a national consultative assembly. It would be composed of Ulster's MPs to Westminster and a delegation from the Home Rule parliament, and it would be empowered to frame legislative measures for the entire island that would be brought into operation in Ulster through orders in council.[42] For Redmond, the convention was a means of countering this and other partitionist schemes.[43]

Carson was won over to the convention idea by the support given to it by several highly placed figures in the government, but this did not guarantee the assent of his party.[44] Its acting leader, Lonsdale, was evidently not satisfied by the Prime Minister's earlier assurance, as he sought Lloyd George's further assurance that if legislation resulted from the convention which provided for exclusion, it would not be amended with regard to the area to be excluded.[45] The UUC duly met at the Ulster Hall, Belfast, on 8 June 1917, to consider sending delegates to the convention. *The Times* reported that the meeting was attended by 'about 500'. The resulting resolution in favour made it plain that the UUC relied

> upon the assurances of the Government that every form of proposal will be open for consideration ... that in the event of no agreement being come to no party will be bound or committed in any way ... and that no scheme will be forced upon the Ulster Unionists with which their representatives are not in agreement.[46]

Carson played an important part in securing the result. Ulster remained included under the Home Rule Act passed in 1914, he argued before the UUC, just as he had in June 1916, until a compromise was agreed and passed by parliament.[47] Another similarity with the previous year's council meeting was the catalyst provided by the Great War, in particular, the need for some movement on the constitutional question for the sake of Great Britain's relations with its allies and potential allies. In 1917, the entry of the United States supplied the rationale for holding a convention of

Irishmen on Irish soil, and the British government's need to placate American opinion extended to the Ulster Unionists.[48]

As the UUC made plain in its resolution, it had been 'largely influenced by the representations which have been made to us by the Government that an agreement on the Irish question would materially help in the prosecution of the war to the victorious conclusion.'[49] But there was still an important difference between the UUC's resolutions of June 1916 and June 1917. Whereas the former committed the council to support a specific settlement, the latter merely committed it to sending a delegation to the convention. And the war that compelled both decisions also limited how far the UUC was prepared to move in the direction of a new settlement in 1917 given the heavy losses experienced by the 36th (Ulster) Division the previous summer.[50] Indeed, the UUC's support for the Lloyd George settlement in 1916, which had provoked dissension within its ranks only for it to be undermined by the opposition of the Southern Unionists, rendered the movement considerably more cautious the following year in response to the Prime Minister's latest initiative.

Beset by his own internal party divisions, Redmond's desperate pleas during the course of the convention, that Lloyd George press Carson to force a settlement on the UUC, demonstrate his ignorance of or indifference to the internal dynamics of Ulster unionism and the shifting distribution of power in the movement.[51] Lonsdale alluded to these when he addressed the House of Commons on 21 May 1917, in response to Lloyd George's convention proposal.

> The new proposals of the Government would involve still further concessions from us, and the House will understand that I am not in a position to pledge the people of Ulster to agree to them without their consent. The people of Ulster are a democratic community, and they possess in the Ulster Unionist Council a thoroughly representative organisation.[52]

Lonsdale's invocation of democracy was, of course, a useful means of divesting the party leadership of responsibility for any unwelcome proposals at the convention, and his public commitment to seeking the UUC's approval for his actions, and those of delegates sent to the convention, no doubt helped to secure the reluctant complicity of doubters when it met in June 1917. But it should not be seen merely as an exercise in cynical expediency. Not only were senior Ulster Unionists periodically given cause to doubt their influence over supporters, but Ulster unionism had for almost a decade countered nationalist arguments about Irish self-determination by articulating the case for Ulster Protestant self-determination.[53] This drew on and fed into concerted efforts to cultivate solidarity within the regional movement as it embarked on increasingly militant strategies and practised high-risk brinkmanship.[54] A by-product was that differences of opinion within Ulster unionism were actively curbed, especially during periods of political crisis, to the disadvantage of those advocating flexible and moderate approaches to the movement's strategy and tactics.[55] In the case of the convention, it served ultimately to reinforce what Graham Walker has described as the Ulster Unionists' 'self-preservationist and exclusive outlook.'[56]

Delegates and advisors

Like the other major parties, the UUC was permitted to nominate five delegates to attend the convention on its behalf. The large size of the convention – initially 95 delegates – is explained by the government's appointment of representatives of local government, the churches, the peerage, chambers of commerce, and labour. In practice, many of these delegates were representatives of the main political parties. Still, the UUC could not take the loyalty of the larger cohort of Ulster Unionists for granted. A whip was duly appointed as well as an 'executive committee' made up of the UUC's nominated delegates and other Ulster Unionist delegates.[57] And the UUC's secretary, Richard Dawson Bates, although not a delegate to the convention, was appointed secretary to the regular meetings of the Ulster Unionist delegates, and at joint meetings between the delegates, the advisory committee, and MPs. The UUC acquired premises at 20 Merrion Square to serve as their headquarters, though the minutes indicate that many of the delegates' meetings in Dublin occurred at the Shelbourne Hotel and at the convention venue, Trinity College.

The UUC's five-man delegation might not have included Carson or Lonsdale, but it contained two parliamentarians. Its chairman, Barrie, had been the MP for North Londonderry since 1906. Originally from Glasgow, he was a successful merchant based in County Londonderry. The delegation's honorary secretary, Lord Londonderry, hailed from one of the wealthiest families in the United Kingdom. He had been the Conservative MP for Maidstone from 1906 until inheriting his father's peerage in 1915, after which he sat in the House of Lords.[58] The delegation contained two lawyers: Robert Hugh Wallace, a senior County Down Orangeman and veteran of the South African War, and Michael Knight, the grand master of County Monaghan's Orangemen. As Monaghan fell outside the excluded area agreed by the UUC in 1916, Knight's inclusion is noteworthy, especially as he was appointed the party's whip at the convention.[59] The fifth member of the UUC delegation was the Scottish-born Belfast shipbuilder and former MP, Sir George Clark.[60]

The wider cohort of the Ulster Unionist delegates included the lord mayor of Belfast, James Johnston, and the mayor of Derry, R.N. Anderson, along with a handful of county councillors – the duke of Abercorn, Colonel Robert Sharman-Crawford, Lieutenant-Colonel Clark, H.B. Armstrong, and Stouppe McCance – and the urban councillor, John McMeekin. Crozier, the Anglican primate, and John Irwin, the moderator of the General Assembly of the Presbyterian Church in Ireland, also sat and acted with the Ulster Unionists. So too did Hugh Pollock, officially a representative of Belfast's Chamber of Commerce. In addition, four senior figures within Ulster unionism were nominated by the government: the Monaghan-born physician and university professor, Sir William Whitla; the former lord mayor of Belfast, Sir Crawford McCullagh; the Belfast solicitor, Sir Alexander McDowell; and the shipyard worker and trade unionist, John Hanna. In the case of McDowell, and to a lesser extent Hanna, nomination by the government and not the UUC made it easier for them on occasion to challenge Ulster Unionist colleagues at the convention.[61]

The advisory committee that is reputed to have vetoed the above group of delegates was comparatively lightweight. Its most significant members were the two elderly and veteran unionists, Sir James Stronge and Hugh de Fellenberg Montgomery, both landlords.[62] The remainder of the first appointments to the advisory committee were relatively junior in comparison. These included another representative of the landed elite, John Porter Porter, né Archdale; John Glendinning, an activist in Derry city; and the industrialists Lloyd Campbell, John Miller Andrews, and John Milne Barbour.[63] The three remaining members of the original advisory committee are more obscure: T. Chambers, Rev. John Johnston, and Edward Leatham. The advisory committee, however, appears to have been a nebulous body. Early on, the 'monotype editor', Dealtry Thompson, was added to represent 'Labour'; he is described later in the same minute book as a 'farmer'.[64] The minutes also claim that the advisory committee further expanded, shortly after its creation, to include six 'farmer representatives' and three from the trade unions.[65] The creation of a separate Labour Advisory Committee, referred to elsewhere as a Working Men's Advisory Committee, is recorded in the minutes, with Andrews, a large employer, in the chair, though what role it played in the delegation's deliberations is not altogether certain.[66]

The same might be said of the advisory committee itself. The contrast between the profile of its members and the Ulster Unionist delegates gives a sense of the task that the former faced if it, alone, sought to veto or otherwise cajole those actively engaged in the convention. Pollock, as noted above, suggested that the advisory committee existed 'to enable the delegates to keep in touch with their constituents.' As the convention's proceedings were subjected to repeated delays, there was ample time for the delegates to consult with party colleagues in Ulster. What Pollock's opaque phrasing probably alludes to is the advisory committee's role as a sounding board: it provided a foretaste of what the delegates might face in bringing a proposed settlement reached at Dublin before the UUC. In this sense the status of its members, or the uncertainty over their number, is not that relevant. It also helps to explain why vocal sceptics of the convention, such as Montgomery, were appointed to the advisory committee. In this sense, it had the additional utility of involving them without sending them to Dublin. The supposed status and influence of the advisory committee is further confused by an important feature overlooked by its critics at the time and ever since. At many of its meetings with the Ulster Unionist delegates, especially on the critical occasions detailed below, it was joined by the party's MPs. This adds an ironic twist to the double criticism that the advisory committee vetoed the Ulster Unionist delegates and that the party's MPs had no role in the convention. Pollock's response to *The Times* did nothing to make anyone the wiser.

The Convention

O'Day has divided the progress of the Irish Convention into four phases.[67] The first, the presentation stage, lasted 18 sittings between July and September 1917. Twelve were held in Dublin and the remaining six were divided equally between Belfast City Hall and the Crawford Technical Institute, Cork. The second phase is marked by the establishment of a sub-committee of nine. The new arrangement was a device to exclude the chairman, concentrate deliberations to nine senior representative delegates, and actively explore the possibilities of a settlement. The difficulties that it encountered led to a third phase characterised by the greater involvement of Lloyd George, between December 1917 and March 1918. The fourth phase was inaugurated on 12 March when the Ulster Unionists presented their only formal proposal: nine-county exclusion.

The convention opened on 25 July at Trinity College. After initial delays necessitated by the need to agree and install its officers, secretariat, and procedure, Plunkett's presentation stage got underway on 21 August. Despite his later misgivings, the convention's secretary, Lord Southborough, hoped that wide-ranging and non-committal debate would wear down the Ulster Unionist delegates.[68] Similarly, the Ulster Unionists' participation in 'entertainments' held out the hope that the resulting sociability would permeate into the convention's proceedings.[69] The Ulster Unionists' opening speech to the presentation stage, delivered by Londonderry, was therefore 'listened to with the closest attention, there being, naturally, much anxiety as to the line the Ulster Unionist group would take.' Londonderry claimed that his party had come to the convention in 'friendliness' and with an 'open mind' to reach 'some general kind of agreement of what is the best for the government of this country ... Unionists can be won if they can be persuaded that self-government is better than the Union.' Like Barrie and Pollock, when they afterwards addressed the convention, Londonderry emphasised his party's belief that Ulster's prosperity was attributable to the union.[70]

Plunkett was fulsome in his praise for the speech, and as such appears to have misunderstood the significance of some of its phrasing.[71] Londonderry had effectively disavowed his party's responsibility for actively reaching an agreement by calling on others to *persuade* the Ulster Unionists to support the case for self-government. It was more upbeat than what Carson had apparently said to the UUC when he addressed it in June 1917, 'Let every man have his fling; let them all go for one another ... Then we shall know where we are.'[72] But in practice the underlying message was the same. Plunkett also appears to have missed the potential significance of the Ulster Unionists' early emphasis on economics – an issue that they took seriously enough to appoint an expert advisor.[73] He preferred instead to depict it as a welcome departure from the sectarian arguments that he had expected to hear.[74]

Even when, later on, Barrie and Wallace conformed to Plunkett's preconceptions, raising their concerns about *Ne Temere* and *Quantavis Diligentia* – the papal decrees that had aroused great controversy in Ulster and mobilised many of its women unionists – he was evidently satisfied by the apparent ease with which these were countered by the Catholic bishop of Raphoe, Patrick O'Donnell.[75] In these early months, it is likely that Plunkett felt that the Ulster Unionists' economic case might be similarly despatched. For although it confirmed the hard-headed stereotype cultivated by northern unionists, Clare O'Halloran has argued that it was a stereotype accepted among southern nationalists on the basis that it meant that the former were an uncomplicated and unsophisticated people who could be persuaded to accept the case for self-government.[76]

As these contributions to the convention demonstrate, the Ulster Unionists did not stand aloof from its proceedings. Harmsworth's accusation that they said 'nuffin', uttered with far greater force on the floor of the convention by Lord MacDonnell, the former Under-Secretary for Ireland and government nominee, criticised something more specific, the Ulster Unionists' disinclination to engage with the various proposals – described by John D. Fair as 'strongly nationalist' – put forward during the presentation stage let alone come up with a proposal of their own.[77] Barrie rejected MacDonnell's criticism by explaining that his delegation wished to arrive at an agreement that they could bring back to their supporters.[78] For Barrie, therefore, the 'silence' of his delegation was not negative in so far as they did not oppose outright the self-government schemes discussed at the convention, let alone derail its proceedings early on with a partitionist proposal. The delegation's silence, moreover, was not as unique as is often suggested. Redmond, Stephen Gwynn acknowledged, 'absolutely declined to put forward a plan' because as the leader of his party he was 'pledged not to bind it without its consent.'[79]

In spite of that, Redmond actively encouraged nationalists and others to advance schemes, whereas the Ulster Unionists, during the convention's first phase, did the very opposite by insisting on the withdrawal of an anonymous proposal from the Southern Unionist camp for separate legislatures and executives for the six north-east counties and the remainder of Ireland, and an all-Ireland senate with its own executive.[80] As such, it is not hard to understand why the posture adopted by the Ulster Unionists during the convention's first phase – often criticised as *non possumus* – dashed nationalist expectations and even provoked anger. Edward Lysaght, like George Russell, nominated by the government to represent advanced nationalism, later recalled of Barrie, 'it was his air of looking on at a lot of chatterboxes wasting time and the unctuous platitudes he uttered when he did speak that got me.'[81]

The behaviour of the Ulster Unionists during the first phase appears to have satisfied Montgomery: 'they are proposing nothing, but obstructing everything which would tend to commit the Convention to any form of Home Rule.'[82] He and other Ulster Unionists ill-disposed to the convention were at the same time increasingly questioning the need to appease opinion in the United States on the basis that the American people had become too entangled in the war.[83] The currency of such attitudes, however naïve, would increase in the longer run, but the minutes of the Ulster Unionist delegation suggest that its members had little interest in meeting with the advisory committee during the first phase of the convention, consulting Carson was just as if not more important, and that they were more open minded than their critics suggested.[84] On 6 September, for example, the Ulster Unionist delegates responded positively to Redmond's request for 'a conference' as long as it was 'of a private and non-commital [*sic*] character.'[85]

A few weeks later Londonderry confided to his mother, the president of the Ulster Women's Unionist Council, 'We could govern Ireland from Belfast but I am not sure the stalwarts want to do that; they would much prefer to remain behind a six county [border] and make faces at the rest of Ireland.'[86] At a hitherto rare meeting with the advisory committee on 10 October, at the Old Town Hall, Belfast, the Ulster Unionists agreed to do nothing 'without consultation with the Ulster people.'[87] Yet, far from encouraging them to lie low, the following day witnessed Alexander McDowell push 'Barrie and Londonderry aside', in Plunkett's words, and propose the creation of a subcommittee of nine intended put the convention's chances of success onto a stronger footing.[88] Plunkett's phrasing must be treated with caution given Londonderry's disposition, noted above, and Midleton's later recollection that Barrie at this time was strongly in favour of reaching a settlement.[89] If McDowell did surprise them with his suggestion, Barrie and Londonderry subsequently took advantage of the opportunity it offered to move the convention beyond the failure of its first phase and inaugurate its second and more constructive phase.

The Ulster Unionists were represented on the subcommittee of nine by Barrie, Londonderry and McDowell. The latter's declining health meant that he was soon after replaced by Pollock, 'an able but somewhat uncompromising exponent of the Ulster business objections to Home Rule', Plunkett recorded, 'and not, therefore, an ideal understudy to the great negotiator.'[90] Midleton represented the Southern Unionists, and the remaining five places were given to the nationalist MPs, Redmond and Joseph Devlin, the businessman and former nationalist MP, William Martin Murphy, Bishop O'Donnell, and Russell.[91] After some initial hesitation, the Ulster Unionists agreed to discuss a hypothetical Irish parliament on the basis that the subcommittee's deliberations would be non-binding.[92] Progress thereafter was surprisingly swift on the parliament's composition. The senate would be appointed not elected and contain representatives from the churches, peerage, privy council, and organised commerce, with four seats allotted to the representatives of labour.[93] The disproportionate number of seats that this would give to Unionists was harder to justify in the lower house. Having initially demanded 50 per cent of the seats, Barrie was prepared to settle for 40 per cent.[94] Midleton and the Ulster Unionists also succeeded in securing continued Irish representation at Westminster.[95]

Having largely settled the question of composition, the sub-committee of nine turned to the powers to be transferred to the parliament and executive. This quickly encountered a serious difficulty when the Ulster Unionists opposed O'Donnell's demand that Ireland should have fiscal autonomy from Great Britain, in particular, control of customs and excise. The bishop was prepared to support a British Isles free trade area and an imperial contribution from Dublin to London, but it was not enough to ameliorate the Ulster Unionists' economic concerns about home rule.[96] Attempts by Plunkett to broker a resolution only brought into sharper relief the nationalists' position that nationhood required fiscal autonomy and the inevitable opposition of Midleton and the Ulster Unionists to this justification. On 12 November, Barrie, Londonderry and other Ulster Unionist delegates held a meeting at Belfast with MPs and members of the advisory committee. Barrie relayed how the subcommittee of nine 'had gone into [O'Donnell's] scheme, and had considered the same without prejudice.' He then 'submitted various points of view as presented to him in connection with the scheme, and subsequently a discussion followed.'[97] As the preceding excerpt suggests, Bates's minutes betray little of what was actually said, but it appears that having expressed his opposition to the O'Donnell scheme at Dublin, Barrie was still prepared to discuss it with party colleagues back in Belfast. What resulted from the meeting is much clearer, for the Ulster Unionist delegation wrote to Plunkett two days later confirming their opposition to fiscal autonomy, declaring pointedly that it would achieve the goals of Sinn Féin.[98]

The sub-committee of nine met on 15 November to prepare a negative report for the convention's 20-man grand committee scheduled to meet a week later. During the intervening period, it became known that Londonderry intended to table a motion proposing Irish Home Rule within a federal United Kingdom.[99] Plunkett was delighted: 'Now an Ulster leader suddenly announces his intention of not only making, on behalf of his party, a constructive proposal, but of offering at any rate a certain measure of self-government, presumably for the whole of Ireland.'[100] Once again, Plunkett's assessment of Londonderry's intentions was an exercise in wishful thinking. Federalism necessarily ruled out Ireland's fiscal autonomy, so it was unlikely on its own to break the deadlock. Other than this, Londonderry offered few details about his proposal. This was not unusual. Although a federal solution to the Irish question was increasingly popular among Conservative MPs, and it had the support of Carson, there was little consensus about what it meant in practice outside the small circle of its most committed proponents, and considerable doubt existed about public support for the constitutional transformation that it would entail across the United Kingdom.[101]

Bates's minutes are conspicuously silent in the week following news of Londonderry's intention. The latter, however, received a letter from Adam Duffin, an elderly linen merchant and prominent member of the UUC. After expressing his admiration for 'the view held by you and Mr Barrie on the desirability of the Ulster Unionists on the convention showing readiness to consider if not to initiate some alternative constructive policy while breaking with the Nationalists on the demand for fiscal autonomy', Duffin went on to warn that 'you may be launched upon a sea of fresh controversy if they are even tentatively accepted as a basis for discussion by the other side, especially as you would have to make large reservations for Ulster, including probably education and judiciary.'[102]

When the sub-committee of nine met on 21 November, Barrie informed them that Londonderry would not propose a federal scheme as the Ulster Unionists 'did not think that such a course would ease the situation.' Plunkett recorded that 'There was nothing for it but to take Lord Londonderry's will for somebody else's deed'.[103] Duffin afterwards confided to his wife that 'I think I am of use if only in supporting Pollock and keeping some check on L[ondonderry].'[104] That he singled out Pollock, in juxtaposition to Londonderry, suggests not only that he was aware of significant differences within the Ulster Unionist delegation, but that Duffin identified his own view with an individual, Pollock, rather than a subset of the delegation. As for his letter to Londonderry, it served to remind its recipient of what had to be overcome in advocating a settlement that could command widespread support in the UUC. Federalism, ill-defined and contingent on many factors, was not up to the task. Duffin's intervention, therefore, was not so much a veto as a warning, though in practice the difference was minimal.

As the federal proposal was never formally presented to the subcommittee of nine, Barrie was able to attribute the latter's failure to the fiscal question when he addressed the grand committee on 22 November; there was, he argued, no 'half-way house' on this sensitive question. Afterwards, however, Barrie moderated his stance following the energetic intervention of the Church of Ireland archbishop of Dublin, John Bernard. Like other Southern Unionists, Bernard was anxious to salvage the thwarted progress of the subcommittee of nine. In reply, on 26 November, Pollock remained unyielding, but Barrie, in contrast, now admitted, 'for the first time', in Plunkett's words, 'that an Irish parliament must have some taxing power, and that there must be a responsible financial authority in Ireland', but that 'Customs and excise must be left absolutely to the Imperial Government.'[105]

Alarmed by the faltering progress of the subcommittee of nine, Redmond urged the Prime Minister to apply pressure on Carson and the Ulster Unionists.[106] At first, Lloyd George responded by relaying his cabinet colleague's belief that he 'cannot persuade his people to go to the length of the proposals put forward by the Nationalists', as well as Carson's reassurance that he 'promised to do his best' in finding 'some compromise which would represent a substantial advance on the part of his friends.' Then the Prime Minister arranged to meet with Barrie, Londonderry and Pollock, on 6 December, but on that occasion the Ulster Unionists stuck to their position on customs and excise, arguing that O'Donnell's proposal would effectively end free trade between Ireland and Great Britain and be the ruin of Ulster industry.[107] This marked the beginning of the convention's third and penultimate phase.

With the Ulster Unionists refusing to budge, Redmond, Midleton and Lloyd George were disposed to exert pressure on them by arranging a settlement between the nationalists and the Southern Unionists. Midleton made the decisive move on 18 December, at the last full meeting of the convention before it adjourned for Christmas. He gave notice of his intention to propose a scheme that gave an Irish parliament powers over all domestic affairs, including excise, with customs remaining under the control of Westminster. In addition, Irish representation to Westminster would continue.[108] The Ulster Unionist delegates met that afternoon to discuss 'the attitude taken up by Lord Midleton … and it was agreed that for the present there appeared to be no necessity for [Barrie] to make any reply thereto.' Several hours later they met again, and on this occasion a more constructive posture was adopted. Now they resolved to move an amendment that would explicitly reserve excise to Westminster, as well as the 'right to impose Military Service'. The minutes also record that 'A discussion took place in regard to the various schemes for safeguarding the interests of Ulster.' It was agreed that they would meet with the advisory committee in the new year.[109]

On the morning of 1 January 1918 the Ulster Unionist delegates assembled at Belfast's Old Town Hall, ahead of their scheduled meeting in the afternoon with MPs and the advisory committee. They agreed that the amendments previously discussed should be put before the convention. In addition, they resolved that 'a scheme for exclusion should also be put in; this latter matter being left in the hands of the Chairman as to a suitable time for putting such a scheme in.'[110] At the afternoon meeting, the minutes record only that a 'discussion' was held, the position already adopted in the morning seems to have assuaged those MPs and advisory committee members wary of what was happening in Dublin. But this should not disguise the fact that Barrie had been given a free hand, and whatever had been the intention of those meetings on new year's day, it seems clear from his subsequent behaviour that the delegation chairman would use that discretion to tread carefully.

The convention reconvened on 2 January with Midleton pressing for the adoption of his scheme. Barrie, according to Plunkett, indicated that 'he had already laid the proposals … before his Advisory Committee in Belfast, and that they had rejected them.' The Ulster Unionists, Barrie declared, 'had come to the Convention to find a compromise between the Act of 1914, which had been accepted as a final settlement of the nationalists demand, and the partition proposals of 1916.' It was the Nationalist Party, 'entirely owing to outside influences', that had enlarged its demand and submitted proposals which 'headed for separation and nothing else'. Barrie's message, however, was contradictory and maybe deliberately so. He 'hoped that it was not even now too late to find a mean between the two extremes of the Home Rule Act on the one hand and the partition of Ireland on the other.'

> If the Convention wanted the support of Ulster … the proposals now before them must be jettisoned. His suggestion was that they should agree upon some modest scheme which would induce the Ulstermen to come in. Once they were satisfied that it was wise and in the interests of the Empire that further powers should be given to

an Irish Parliament, he believed that Ulstermen would be willing to join in 'securing a larger amount of elbow room for a Parliament that had proved itself worthy of trust and confidence.'[111]

Barrie's balancing act continued into the following day. On the afternoon of 3 January, the Ulster Unionist delegates met and discussed when partition should be addressed. As before, discretion was given to the chairman 'as to the time that this should be done'. Notably, on this occasion, Barrie was to do this along with Londonderry. The meeting also decided that the shipbuilder, Clark, 'should take charge of the scheme' – an indication, perhaps, that it had not yet been fully worked out for presentation to the convention.[112] That evening, following one of the convention's entertainments, Barrie is said to have confided to Midleton that 'I think you may count on us. We shall certainly not be against you.'[113] If true, Barrie is likely to have welcomed the pressure that was brought to bear on the Ulster Unionists in the days that followed. Regardless of Lloyd George's previous assurances to them, the increasing likelihood of a historic agreement between unionism and nationalism would bring forth significant pressure – domestic, dominion and international – on the government to give it legislative effect.

The Prime Minister, for one, appears to have felt the strain and prevailed upon his coalition partner and Conservative leader, Andrew Bonar Law, to exert pressure on Barrie.[114] A week later, Barrie met with W.G.S. Adams of the cabinet secretariat and discussed – without committing himself – the possibility of a home rule parliament with an Ulster committee that could veto and initiate legislation affecting the north.[115] At this critical juncture, two factors combined to ensure that the Ulster Unionists were relieved from the pressure to agree a settlement. First, Plunkett's decision to switch debate at the convention for ten days to less contentious subjects more likely to secure agreement. Second, Redmond's decision to withdraw – temporarily as it turned out – his support for the Midleton scheme following a revolt within his own party.[116]

The convention's disarray delighted its critics and doubters among the Ulster Unionists.[117] Londonderry, in contrast, informed his mother that 'the Ulster men have a great opportunity … a great deal will depend on what comes out of the next few weeks.' But his outlook was gloomy: 'it certainly looks as if they would come out of the Convention as being quite non-possumus.'[118] On 2 February, Carson met with the delegates, the advisory committee and the party's MPs. Inevitably, he discussed his recent departure from the government; the resignation letter that appeared in the press had explicitly referred to 'the strains' of his 'dual position as Member of the Government and as leader of the Ulster Unionist Party'.[119] Carson now appeared to endorse the narrow vision of Ulster unionism articulated by Montgomery. The latter, after all, had been exercised about Carson's 'dual position' in June 1917, and now Carson shared with colleagues his belief that there was no pressing need for them to appease American opinion.[120] On the other hand, Carson encouraged those in attendance to continue to consider proposals at the convention.[121] Like Barrie, Carson had also met previously with Professor Adams and discussed an Ulster committee, as well as a proposal for two lower houses, one representing Ulster and the other the remainder of Ireland.[122] But Carson's preferred solution now increasingly lay with something along federal lines, and he wrote to Lloyd George to this effect on 14 February: 'If such a policy was adopted it is easy to see that a settlement of the Ulster difficulty could be found either by making Ulster a unit or by providing for its particular needs within another unit.'[123]

The day before Carson's missive, on 13 February, the Prime Minister had met with a combined delegation from the convention. Addressing them all, Lloyd George suggested a number of practical safeguards intended to reassure and entice the Ulster Unionists into agreeing an all-Ireland settlement. He met with an Ulster Unionist deputation the following day and was informed that they would meet with Carson and then their advisory committee.[124] At the first, Carson endorsed the delegates' right to propose Ulster's exclusion from a Home Rule settlement. He also suggested federalism as an alternative solution, which, though he thought impractical during the war, had the virtue of allowing the Ulster Unionists to rebut the charge of being *non possumus*.[125] After the meeting, Barrie called off the planned meeting between the Ulster Unionist delegates and the advisory committee. As he informed Londonderry, Carson's response had amounted to 'an absolute refusal of the P.M's suggestions, and no doubt this is a correct interpretation of the feeling of most of our delegates.'[126]

At Plunkett's behest, Lloyd George signalled on 25 February his support for a series of recommendations that could form the basis of an agreed settlement at the convention. These included an all-Ireland parliament that provided for the greater representation of Ulster and an Ulster committee with the power to veto relevant legislation, and the reservation of customs and excise to Westminster until a new arrangement could be agreed after the war's conclusion.[127] The Prime Minister had previously written to Barrie, on 21 February, urging him to accept the proposals for the sake of the convention and American opinion.[128] Having learnt that Carson would not support the proposals, Londonderry complained directly to the party leader about the delegation's 'procrastinating':

> I believe ... that you are satisfied that the offers suggested to be made to Ulster now eliminate those dangers which induced us in 1914 to take up arms in our own defence. But even holding these

views ... you feel that because Ulster opinion appears to be so strong, we should not even make an effort to induce our constituents not only to consider the desperate position of the Empire, but also to realise that from the tactical point of view we can brand the R.C. Church [O'Donnell and his supporters] as really opponents to a settlement of the question.[129]

On the same day that Lloyd George's recommendations were made known to the convention delegates, representatives of the Ulster Unionist delegation assembled in Belfast. Barrie discussed with them his interviews with the Prime Minister, after which 'Lord Londonderry and Mr Pollock also made statements' – it is not difficult to discern in Bates's terse minutes the airing of two opposing views.[130] Later in the afternoon, the delegation met with MPs and the advisory committee. Londonderry 'made a statement' and read Lloyd George's letter to Barrie. The delegation's chairman spoke next, and the minutes list the names of those who spoke in response. Barrie is recorded as having concluded the meeting with the reassurance that 'if any definite proposals were made to him, he would submit them to the meeting for consideration.'[131] Montgomery also addressed the meeting, and his letter to Londonderry the following day provides the context and tone missing from Bates's minutes.

> It may have appeared unnecessary and perhaps offensive to insist so strongly on your bringing L[loyd]G[eorge]'s proposal before us again before giving any sort of consent to it, but what I felt was that your statement was to the effect that Lloyd George had asked you to bring the suggestion before us, and that you had done so, therefore, merely to give you a free hand.

That, he went on, 'would have implied that you were at liberty to consent to this proposal if you liked.' Montgomery dismissed the Prime Minister's 'reasons for urging you virtually to come to some agreement' as 'absolute bunkum', designed to extricate him from 'promises to the Home Rulers and possibly to the Americans and other sentimental sympathisers and finds he cannot deliver goods, and wants us to enable him to do so.' The war was not a reason for reaching a settlement that would hand 'over the administration of a great part of this country to the friends of the enemy.' He concluded that the previous day's meeting resolved that the delegates should refuse 'to consider the suggestions in Lloyd George's letter, till they are put in a clearer and more detailed form'.[132]

When the convention reconvened shortly afterwards, Barrie placed responsibility for the deadlock at the feet of the other parties and called for the fiscal issue to be solved so that the Ulster Unionists might declare their views.[133] Londonderry, according to Plunkett, 'evidently feeling that Mr

Barrie had not placed Ulster in an altogether favourable light, restated his position in less uncompromising terms.' Revisiting his opening remarks to the convention, the marquess said that the nationalists 'had never tried to win Ulster, and he asked whether even now it was not possible for the various elements in the Convention to combine and agree on a plan for the government of Ireland.' Again, he raised the possibility of a federal solution but on the understanding that it ruled out fiscal autonomy.[134] Londonderry's addendum to Barrie's speech could not disguise the fact that the Ulster Unionists were isolated at the convention, but divisions within the ranks of both the nationalists – to say nothing of Redmond's death on 6 March – and the Southern Unionists – encouraged by Montgomery and other Ulster Unionists – prevented the possibility of their combining to outflank the men from the north.[135]

The convention's fourth and final phase began on 12 March with a series of votes on an extensive list of proposals. That day, the Ulster Unionists presented their proposal for nine-county exclusion.[136] Having charged Clark in early January with drawing up the exclusion proposal, the delegation discussed it regularly from 5 March. The scheme placed before the convention represented a departure in two important respects: the appointment of a secretary of state for the excluded area, Clark possibly influenced by the practice in his native Scotland; and the extent of the area to be excluded. The latter was larger than what had been agreed by the UUC in 1916, though it is unclear if, as in 1916, and as they would again in 1919–20, the Ulster Unionists gave any serious consideration to the precarious majority that nine-county exclusion would give their party. It may be, after all, as some have argued, that the proposal was merely a 'wrecking device.'[137] Given that it was unlikely to succeed – it was defeated 51 to 19 – proposing nine-county exclusion was certainly a means of avoiding the internal acrimony that Ulster unionism experienced in 1916, once the convention's conclusions became more widely known.

In any case, the growing conscription crisis almost completely overshadowed the convention's final days, but it limped on with the Ulster Unionists opposing the transfer of various powers to a Home Rule parliament, even gaining a little support on defence questions, and ignoring the various attempts to woo them with safeguards. Among the latter was the suggestion of disproportionate representation in an all-Ireland parliament – an idea considered favourably by the Ulster Unionists in November 1917 but now dismissed by them as undemocratic and untenable.[138] Likewise, on 13 March, they resolved to 'prevent any misdescription of the alleged agreements' by voting against 'everything that could have been alleged to have been agreed upon'.[139] On 5 April a combined majority of Southern Unionists and Redmondite nationalists supported the final report, 44 to 29. The latter figure was made up of

11 O'Donnell nationalists – including the leading northern nationalist, Joseph Devlin – and 18 Ulster Unionists.[140]

Damage limitation

In advance of the convention's conclusion, the Ulster Unionists had met with 'representatives of the press' at the Shelbourne and arranged for 'documents' to be supplied to them.[141] The minority report subsequently produced by the Ulster Unionists likewise had an eye on managing their reputation. It outlined their preparedness to do what was best for the empire at its time of need and restated Barrie's claim that they had hoped to find common ground between the 1914 Act and 'the views of Ulster'. In accounting for the convention's failure, the report expressed misgivings about undertaking constitutional change in wartime, as well as during 'a great renewal of lawlessness, and crime bordering on anarchy'. It nevertheless attributed the convention's breakdown to the disagreement over fiscal autonomy, arguing that 'Ulster takes a firm stand on the people's common prosperity, and maintains that the fiscal unity of the United Kingdom must be preserved intact.' The examples of the United States and the federation of Australia and Tasmania were given to shore up this position.[142]

The defensive tone of the report was no doubt influenced by the need to address the growing unease among Conservatives, and the accompanying shift in English opinion, that left the Ulster Unionists feeling politically isolated by 1918.[143] In the years that followed, however, the need to rally supporters in Ulster tended to exert a greater force on how the Ulster Unionists chose to recollect their attendance and actions at the convention. It helped that the Ulster Unionists were the only party to emerge from it outwardly united, and, after 1921, occupying government office. The resulting distortions and incomplete recollections presented a simplified and reassuring narrative that cast the convention as a sideshow on the path towards partition and devolution. A number of their opponents, of course, highlighted the divisions within Ulster unionism, but they tended to frame these as a simplistic binary, between the delegates and the advisory committee.

The evidence, however, highlights that the former contained a range of views, and nothing definite can be said about those of the latter except for the opinions of a very small number. Moreover, the composition of the advisory committee is unclear, and its periodic encounters with the Ulster Unionist delegates were made more significant when they were joined by MPs. Carson's role throughout was equivocal, uncertain and shifting. The outcome of the convention, therefore, was not preordained, as the internal dynamics of Ulster unionism responded to those of the Redmondites, the O'Donnellites, the Southern Unionists, and the coalition government. As the Ulster-born George Russell cautioned in August 1917, 'None could do without the others; all must co-operate.'[144]

This is not to downplay structural factors. The significant and dramatic shifts in Irish nationalism that accompanied the convention need not be rehearsed here. The Southern Unionist delegates were clearly much weaker than their northern counterparts and as a result prepared to reach an accommodation with the Redmondites on Home Rule. And to the frustration of both nationalist and Southern Unionist delegates alike, the Ulster Unionists had the assurance from Lloyd George, delivered to the Commons in March 1917, that they would not be coerced by the government. The Ulster Unionists certainly valued that parliamentary intervention, as indicated by the wording of the UUC's resolution to enter the convention and the Ulster Unionists' minority report. Yet, the utterances of that wily politician were unlikely to actually reassure – during the course of the convention the Ulster Unionists were acutely aware of their vulnerability not only to Liberals in the coalition government, but to the desire of an increasing number of Conservatives to recast Great Britain's relationship with Ireland.

J.J. Lee has observed that 'the convention has been unjustly neglected in nationalist historiography.' It had 'confronted at a high level of civility and intelligence, most of the issues that would baffle later generations of Irishmen, not only in terms of unionist-nationalist relations, but in terms of the nature of a nationalist state.'[145] A significant assessment when it was written, it is all the more remarkable that it still pertained in the 2010s, during the 'decade of centenaries.' Inevitably, perhaps, the convention did not attract the type of intense and sustained interest that was given to commemorating events such as the Easter Rising and the establishment of Northern Ireland.[146] This was reinforced rather than challenged by the Irish and British governments' efforts to reflect and shore up the Northern Ireland peace process through broadening sympathies without abandoning loyalties.[147] But in the context of the United Kingdom's withdrawal from the European Union, the accompanying debates about Irish unification, and the attendant calls on Ulster unionism – Democratic Unionist, Ulster Unionist and others – to prepare for this end, it is striking that nationalism and Ulster unionism alike remained largely indifferent to that assembly of Irishmen on Irish soil discussing a hypothetical Irish parliament.

Acknowledgements

The author acknowledges the support of the T.W. Moody Memorial Fund, Trinity College Dublin; and the advice and assistance of Dr Anne Dolan, Dr Timothy G. McMahon, and Professor Eunan O'Halpin.

Notes

1. Alan O'Day, *Irish Home Rule 1867–1921* (Manchester, 1998), p. 280; Patrick Buckland, *Irish Unionism: Two: Ulster Unionism and the Origins of Northern Ireland 1886–1922* (Dublin, 1973), pp 95–6.
2. Trevor West, *Horace Plunkett, Co-operation and Politics: An Irish Biography* (Gerrards Cross, 1986), pp 157–76; Carla King, 'Defenders of the union: Sir Horace Plunkett' in D. George Boyce and Alan O'Day (eds), *Defenders of the Union: A Survey of British and Irish Unionism since 1801* (London, 2001), pp 137–54.
3. Diarmaid Ferriter, *The Transformation of Ireland* (Woodstock, 2004), p. 179.
4. Cecil Harmsworth, diary, 20 Nov. 1917, in Andrew Thorpe and Richard Toye (eds), *Parliament and Politics in the Age of Asquith and Lloyd George: The Diaries of Cecil Harmsworth MP, 1909–22* (Cambridge, 2016), p. 260.
5. Horace Plunkett, *The Irish Convention: Confidential Report to His Majesty the King by the Chairman* (s.l., 1918); R.B. McDowell, *The Irish Convention, 1917–18* (London, 1970), p. 98.
6. Horace Plunkett, *Report of the Proceedings of the Irish Convention Presented to Parliament by Command of His Majesty* (Dublin, 1918), pp 5, 30.
7. See, for example, Marchioness of Londonderry, *Retrospect* (London, 1938), p. 163.
8. *The Times*, 15 July 1918, p. 8.
9. Ibid., 24 Oct. 1919, p. 13, 25 Oct. 1919, p. 13, 27 Oct. 1919, p. 13.
10. Ibid., 28 Oct. 1919, p. 18, 5 Nov. 1919, p. 8.
11. Ibid., 7 Nov. 1919, p. 8.
12. Ibid., 7 Nov. 1919, p. 13.
13. Gwynn's recollections of Pollock are particularly striking given the latter's concern about readers of the Belfast press. Pollock had 'outlined two essentials of the Ulster demand. The United Kingdom must remain a fiscal unit; and Ireland must be represented at Westminster. If these points were conceded, agreement, he thought, should be possible.' Gwynn also recalled an occasion when Pollock had been taunted, how he 'refused to reply … because … "I have made friendships here which I never expected to make, and I value them too much to risk the loss of them."' Stephen Gwynn, *John Redmond's Last Years* (London, 1919), pp 281, 299, 308. See Colin Reid, *The Lost Ireland of Stephen Gwynn: Irish Constitutional Nationalism and Cultural Politics, 1864–1950* (Manchester, 2011), pp 151–8.
14. William O'Brien, *Evening Memories* (London, 1920), p. 496.
15. Sally Warwick-Haller, 'Seeking Conciliation: William O'Brien and the Ulster Crisis, 1911–14' in D. George Boyce and Alan O'Day (eds), *The Ulster Crisis* (Basingstoke, 2006), pp 146–64. See also N.C. Fleming and Alan O'Day, 'Accommodation, Conciliation and Cooperation: A Gladstonian Legacy' in D. George Boyce and Alan O'Day (eds), *Gladstone and Ireland: Politics, Religion and Nationality in the Victorian Age* (Basingstoke, 2010), pp 233–55.

16 Ronald McNeill, *Ulster's Stand for Union* (London, 1922), chapter 22.
17 Denis Gwynn, *The Life of John Redmond* (London, 1932), pp 567–9.
18 Midleton had nothing to say about Gwynn's claim, see *Redmond*, p. 559, that 'the Ulstermen had signified their consent' to Redmond being offered the chairmanship. Earl of Midleton, *Ireland – Dupe or Heroine* (London, 1932), pp 110–21; Earl of Midleton, *Records and Reactions, 1856–1939* (London, 1939), pp 235–46.
19 Midleton, *Ireland*, p. 120. Like other unionist writers, Midleton questioned the Catholic bishops' commitment to reaching an agreed settlement.
20 Alvin Jackson, 'Irish unionism' in D. George Boyce and Alan O'Day (eds), *The Making of Modern Irish History: Revisionism and the Revisionist Controversy* (London, 1996), pp 120–40.
21 Henry Maxwell, *Ulster was Right* (London, 1934), p. 194.
22 Ian Colvin, *The Life of Lord Carson, Vol. III* (New York, 1937), p. 313.
23 Hugh Shearman, *Not an Inch: A Study of Northern Ireland and Craigavon* (London, 1942), pp 151–3.
24 St John Ervine, *Craigavon: Ulsterman* (London, 1949), pp 330–52. Ervine's metaphor can be contrasted to that of the Ulster Women's Unionist Council, which in 1914 declared with regard to home rule that 'prevention is better than cure', see Diane Urquhart (ed.), *The Minutes of the Ulster Women's Unionist Council and Executive Committee 1911–40* (Dublin, 2001), p. xvii.
25 McDowell, *The Irish Convention*.
26 Plunkett, *Confidential Report*, p. 98.
27 McDowell, *Irish Convention*, pp 213, 217.
28 F.S.L. Lyons, *Ireland since the Famine* ([1971] London, 1973), p. 386; F.S.L. Lyons, *Culture and Anarchy in Ireland 1890–1939* (Oxford, 1979), p. 107; John D. Fair, *British Interparty Conferences: A Study in the Procedure of Conciliation in British Politics, 1867–1921* (Oxford, 1980), p. 223; J.C. Beckett, *The Making of Modern Ireland 1603–1923* (London, 1981), p. 443; R.F. Foster, *Modern Ireland 1600–1972* (London, 1988), p. 486; D. George Boyce, *Nineteenth-Century Ireland: The Search for Stability* (Dublin, 1990), pp 254, 259; F.S.L. Lyons, 'The new nationalism, 1916–18' in W.E. Vaughan (ed.), *A New History of Ireland, Vol. VI: Ireland under the Union, II 1870–1921* (Oxford, 1996), pp 224–59 at p. 229. Lyons did not depend on McDowell's *Irish Convention* for his assessment, having earlier described them as 'unyielding' in his biography of John Dillon, see F.S.L. Lyons, *John Dillon: A Biography* (London, 1968), p. 427.
29 For *The Times*'s proposition – that the Ulster Unionist delegates were flexible but were held in check by their advisory committee – see, for example, Buckland, *Ulster Unionism*, pp 108–109, 111; Jonathan Bardon, *A History of Ulster* (Belfast, 1992), pp 458–9. For the contrasting Pollock-McNeill line of argument see, for example, Michael Laffan, *The Partition of Ireland 1911–1925* (Dundalk, 1983), p. 56; George Dangerfield, *The Damnable*

Question: A Study in Anglo-Irish Relations (London, 1977), pp 266–7; Nicholas Mansergh, *The Unresolved Question: The Anglo-Irish Settlement and its Undoing 1912–72* (London, 1991), p. 104; David Harkness, *Ireland in the Twentieth Century: Divided Island* (London, 1996), p. 30; Graham Walker, *A History of the Ulster Unionist Party: Protest, Pragmatism and Pessimism* (Manchester, 2004), p. 41; Brendan O'Leary, *A Treatise on Northern Ireland, Vol. I: Colonialism: The Shackles of the State and Hereditary Animosities* (Oxford, 2019), p. 332. For variant, see Lawrence J. McCaffrey, *The Irish Question 1800–1922* (Lexington, 1968), p. 168.

30 Among the few that have repeated or expanded on these particular observations are Buckland, *Ulster Unionism*, pp 108, 112; Thomas Hennessey, *Dividing Ireland: World War I and Partition* (London, 1998), pp 203, 218; Alvin Jackson, *Home Rule: An Irish History, 1800–2000* (London, 2003), pp 178–80, 182–3.

31 See, for example, Gwynn, *Redmond*, p. 560.

32 Colvin, *Carson*, pp 296, 320–21.

33 Brian M. Walker, 'Actions and views: John Brownlee Lonsdale, unionist MP, 1900–18 and party leader, 1916–18' in D. George Boyce and Alan O'Day, *The Ulster Crisis* (Basingstoke, 2006), pp 128–145 at pp 140–41.

34 Alvin Jackson, *Colonel Edward Saunderson: Land and Loyalty in Victorian Ireland* (Oxford, 1995), p. 156.

35 Timothy G. McMahon, '"It does not matter what the authors meant": covenanters in conflict, 1916–1920' in N.C. Fleming and James H. Murphy (eds), *Ireland and Partition: Contexts and Consequences* (Clemson, 2021), pp 267–82 at pp 268–70.

36 Susan E. Scarrow, 'Political activism and party members' in Russell J. Dalton and Hans-Dieter Klingemann (eds), *The Oxford Handbook of Political Behaviour* (Oxford, 2007), pp 636–54.

37 Buckland, *Ulster Unionism*, p. 21. See also F.S.L. Lyons, 'The Irish Unionist Party and the devolution crisis of 1904–5', *Irish Historical Studies*, 6:21 (1948), pp 1–22.

38 Urquhart, *Ulster Women's Unionist Council*, p. xx. The Ulster Unionist delegation resolved to oppose any attempt to co-opt women to the convention, see 'Minutes of the Ulster Unionist delegation to the Irish convention', 17 Aug. 1917 (PRONI, Ulster Unionist Papers, D1327/3/17).

39 McMahon, 'Covenanters in conflict', pp 272–3.

40 See correspondence between Lady Londonderry and Ronald McNeill in N.C. Fleming (ed.), *Aristocracy, Democracy, and Dictatorship: The Political Papers of the Seventh Marquess of Londonderry* (Cambridge, 2022), pp 23–8; N.C. Fleming, *Britannia's Zealots, Volume I: Tradition, Empire and the Forging of the Conservative Right* (London, 2019), pp 83–5.

41 See *House of Commons Debates*, 7 Mar. 1917, vol. 91, cols 425–528.

42 Colvin, *Carson*, pp 243–6.

43 Gwynn, *Redmond*, pp 542–1. See Pauric Travers, *Settlements and Divisions: Ireland 1870–1922* (Walkinstown, 1988), p. 139.
44 Colvin, *Carson*, pp 239–40.
45 John Lonsdale to David Lloyd George, 17 May 1917 in Fair, *Interparty Conferences*, p. 201.
46 *The Times*, 9 June 1917, p. 6.
47 O'Day, *Home Rule*, p. 280.
48 Alan J. Ward, *Ireland and Anglo-American Relations 1899–1921* (London, 1969), pp 149–50; Stephen Hartley, *The Irish Question as a Problem in British Foreign Policy, 1914–18* (Basingstoke, 1987), pp 151–73; Lindsey J. Flewelling, *Two Irelands Beyond the Sea: Ulster Unionism and America* (Liverpool, 2021), p. 70.
49 *The Times*, 9 June 1917, p. 6.
50 Colvin, *Carson*, p. 326; Alvin Jackson, *Ireland 1798–1998: War, Peace and Beyond* (2nd edition, Oxford, 2010), p. 207.
51 N.C. Fleming, 'The landed elite, power and Ulster unionism' in D. George Boyce and Alan O'Day (eds), *The Ulster Crisis* (Basingstoke, 2006), pp 86–104; N.C. Fleming, 'Leadership, the middle-classes and Ulster unionism since the late nineteenth century' in Fintan Lane (ed.), *Politics, Society and the Middle Class in Modern Ireland* (Basingstoke, 2009), pp 212–29. It is noteworthy that long before the convention the Ulster Unionists had reason to believe that Redmond 'could not fully deliver Irish nationalism', see Alvin Jackson, *Judging Redmond and Carson: Comparative Irish Lives* (Dublin, 2018), pp 44, 48.
52 *House of Commons Debates*, 21 May 1917, vol. 93, cols 2005–2008.
53 Jackson, *Judging Redmond and Carson*, pp 156, 158.
54 Paul Bew, *Ideology and the Irish Question: Ulster Unionism and Irish Nationalism 1912–1916* (Oxford, 1994), pp 46–49; Colin Reid, 'Democracy, sovereignty and unionist political thought during the revolutionary period in Ireland, c. 1912–1922', *Transactions of the Royal Historical Society*, 27, 6th series (2017), pp 211–32 at p. 213. See also Robert Saunders, 'Tory rebels and Tory democracy: the Ulster crisis, 1900–14' in Richard Carr and Bradley W. Hart (eds), *The Foundations of the British Conservative Party: Essays on Conservatism from Lord Salisbury to David Cameron* (London, 2013), pp 65–83.
55 Buckland, *Ulster Unionism*, p. 66; Paul Bew, Peter Gibbon and Henry Patterson, *Northern Ireland 1921/2001: Political Forces and Social Classes* (London, 2002), p. 60; Jennifer Todd, 'Two traditions in unionist political culture', *Irish Political Studies*, 2 (1987), pp 1–26; Jennifer Todd, 'Unionist political thought, 1920–72' in D. George Boyce, Robert Eccleshall and Vincent Geoghegan (eds), *Political Thought in Ireland since the Seventeenth Century* (London: Routledge, 1993), p. 191; Andrew Gailey, 'The destructiveness of constructive unionism: theories and practice,

56 Walker, *Ulster Unionist Party*, p. 41.
57 Ulster Unionist delegation, minutes, 21 July 1917; 26 July 1917 (PRONI, Ulster Unionist Papers, D1327/3/17).
58 N.C. Fleming, *The Marquess of Londonderry: Aristocracy, Power and Politics in Britain and Ireland* (London, 2005), pp 19–44.
59 McMahon, 'Covenanters in conflict', pp 273–5.
60 Graham Walker has noted the delegation's 'strong Presbyterian and Ulster-Scot flavour', see Walker, *Ulster Unionist Party*, p. 41.
61 Jackson, *Home Rule*, p. 180; Austen Morgan, *Labour and Partition: The Belfast Working Class, 1905–23* (London, 1991), pp 217–18. It is likely that Lord Londonderry delayed accepting the UUC's nomination to the convention in the hope that he might be appointed instead by the government, see Fleming, *Marquess of Londonderry*, p. 51.
62 See Brian M. Walker, *Ulster Politics: The Formative Years 1868–86* (Belfast, 1989), pp 193–4; Fair, *Interparty Conferences*, p. 206.
63 Admittedly, several members of the advisory committee went on to occupy more senior positions in Ulster unionism. Porter became a senator in the devolved parliament established at Belfast in 1921. Campbell, Barbour and Andrews were all later elected to it as MPs, with Barbour succeeding Andrews as Minister of Finance in 1941 as a consequence of Andrews' appointment as Prime Minister. But in 1917 they had no such status in the movement. Even applying this measure, the subsequent record of the UUC's delegation is just as impressive, at least in the years immediately following the convention. Having retired from Westminster in 1918, Barrie was again returned for North Londonderry in 1919 and sat until he died in 1922. He was also appointed to the senate, as were Clark and Londonderry. Clark was deputy speaker of the senate between 1932 and 1934, and Londonderry the leader of the senate, and Minister of Education, between 1921 and 1926. Londonderry went on to serve in the British cabinet in 1928–29 and 1931–35.
64 Ulster Unionist delegation, minutes, 7 Aug. 1917, 22 Aug. 1917 (PRONI, Ulster Unionist Papers, D1327/3/17).
65 Ulster Unionist delegation, minutes, 17 Aug. 1917 (ibid.).
66 Ulster Unionist delegation, minutes, 18 Aug. 1917, 26 Sep. 1917 (ibid.).
67 O'Day, *Home Rule*, pp 282–4.
68 McDowell, *Irish Convention*, p. 106.
69 Ibid., p. 112.
70 Plunkett, *Confidential Report*, p. 18.
71 Ibid., pp 11–12.
72 Colvin, *Carson*, p. 294.

73 Ulster Unionist delegation, minutes, 8 Aug. 1917 (PRONI, Ulster Unionist Papers, D1327/3/17).
74 Plunkett, *Confidential Report*, pp 13, 15.
75 McDowell, *Irish Convention*, p. 114; D.A.J. MacPherson, '"Exploited with fury on a thousand platforms": women, unionism and the *Ne Temere* decree in Ireland, 1908–1913' in Joan Allen and Richard Allen (eds), *Faith of Our Fathers: Popular Culture and Belief in Post-Reformation England, Ireland and Wales* (Newcastle, 2009), pp 157–75. Stephen Gwynn recalled that the Ulster Unionists had applauded O'Donnell's reply to their concerns, see Gwynn, *Redmond's Last Years*, pp 299–300.
76 Clare O'Halloran, *Partition and the Limits of Irish Nationalism: An Ideology under Stress* (Atlantic Highlands NJ, 1987), p. 41.
77 Fair, *Interparty Conferences*, p. 207.
78 McDowell, *Irish Convention*, p. 116.
79 Gwynn, *Redmond's Last Years*, p. 280.
80 Ulster Unionist delegation, minutes, 22 Aug. 1917 (PRONI, Ulster Unionist Papers, D1327/3/17); McDowell, *Irish Convention*, pp 114–15.
81 Edward MacLysaght, 'Some memories of the Irish Convention 1917–1918', *Capuchin Annual*, 35 (1968), pp 345–50 at p. 349. See Brideen Hickey, 'Edward MacLysaght and the Irish Convention 1917–18', *Studia Hibernica*, 44 (2018), pp 103–28; Nicholas Allen, 'National reconstruction: George Russell (AE) and the Irish Convention' in D. George Boyce and Alan O'Day (eds), *Ireland in Transition, 1867–1921* (London, 2004), pp 128–41.
82 Hugh de Fellenberg Montgomery to A.V. Dicey, 23 Aug. 1917 in Fair, *Interparty Conferences*, p. 208.
83 McDowell, *Irish Convention*, p. 115; Hartley, *Irish Question*, pp 159, 164–5.
84 Ulster Unionist delegation, minutes, 20 Sep. 1917, 26 Sep. 1917, 10 Oct. 1917 (PRONI, Ulster Unionist Papers, D1327/3/17).
85 Ulster Unionist delegation, minutes, 6 Sep. 1917, 12 Sep. 1917 (ibid.).
86 Londonderry to Theresa, Lady Londonderry, 23 Sep. 1917, Durham County Record Office, D/Lo/C/682 (245); see Diane Urquhart, *The Ladies of Londonderry: Women and Political Patronage* (London, 2007), pp 75–135.
87 Ulster Unionist delegation, minutes, 10 Oct. 1917 (PRONI, Ulster Unionist Papers, D1327/3/17).
88 McDowell, *Irish Convention*, p. 119.
89 Midleton, *Records and Reactions*, p. 238.
90 Plunkett, *Confidential Report*, p. 41.
91 Ibid., pp 7–8.
92 McDowell, *Irish Convention*, pp 120–21.
93 Plunkett, *Confidential Report*, p. 42.
94 Midleton to Londonderry, 25 Oct. 1917 (PRONI, Londonderry Papers, D3099/2/7/14).

95 McDowell, *Irish Convention*, pp 121–2.
96 Plunkett, *Report of the Proceedings*, p. 16.
97 Ulster Unionist delegation, minutes, 12 Nov. 1917 (PRONI, Ulster Unionist Papers, D1327/3/17).
98 Hugh T. Barrie and Lord Londonderry to Horace Plunkett, 14 Nov. 1917 in Plunkett, *Report of the Proceedings*, pp 68–9; Plunkett, *Confidential Report*, p. 47.
99 Plunkett, *Confidential Report*, p. 51.
100 Ibid., p. 51.
101 John Kendle, *Ireland and the Federal Solution: The Debate over the United Kingdom Constitution, 1870–1921* (Kingston and Montreal, 1989); Nigel Keohane, *The Party of Patriotism: The Conservative Party and the First World War* (Farnham, 2010), pp 89–92; Jeremy Smith, 'Federalism, devolution and partition: Sir Edward Carson and the search for a compromise on the third Home Rule Bill', *Irish Historical Studies*, 35:140 (2016), pp 496–518; Jeremy Smith, 'Sir Edward Carson and the myth of partition' in Roger Swift and Christine Kinealy (eds), *Politics and Power in Victorian Ireland* (Dublin, 2006), pp 178–91.
102 Duffin to Lord Londonderry, 16 Nov. 1917 in Patrick Buckland (ed.), *Irish Unionism 1885–1923: A Documentary History* (Belfast, 1973), pp 422–3.
103 Plunkett, *Confidential Report*, p. 52.
104 Adam Duffin to Mrs Duffin, 28 Nov. 1917 in Buckland (ed.), *Irish Unionism*, p. 423.
105 Plunkett, *Confidential Report*, p. 55.
106 Gwynn, *Redmond*, pp 570–72.
107 Colvin, *Carson*, pp 302–03.
108 Plunkett, *Report of the Proceedings*, p. 18.
109 Ulster Unionist delegation, minutes, 18 Dec. 1917 (PRONI, Ulster Unionist Papers, D1327/3/17).
110 Ulster Unionist delegation, minutes, 1 Jan. 1918 (ibid.).
111 Plunkett, *Confidential Report*, p. 62. Redmond replied that it was the Ulster Unionist delegates who were 'pledge-bound to consult an outside body', see McDowell, *Irish Convention*, p. 146.
112 Ulster Unionist delegation, minutes, 3 Jan. 1918 (PRONI, Ulster Unionist Papers, D1327/3/17).
113 Midleton, *Records and Reactions*, p. 242.
114 Fair, *Interparty Conferences*, p. 215.
115 McDowell, *Irish Convention*, p. 156.
116 Plunkett, *Confidential Report*, p. 67.
117 See, for example, J.R. Fisher to Hugh de Fellenberg Montgomery, 25 Jan. 1918 in Buckland (ed.), *Irish Unionism*, pp 424–5.
118 Lord Londonderry to Theresa, Lady Londonderry, 21 Jan. 1918 (Durham County Record Office, D/Lo/C/682 (258)).

119 Carson to Lloyd George, 21 Jan. 1918 in Colvin, *Carson*, p. 310.
120 Jackson, *Judging*, p. 229.
121 Colvin, *Carson*, p. 314.
122 McDowell, *Irish Convention*, p. 156.
123 Edward Carson to David Lloyd George, 14 Feb. 1918 in Colvin, *Carson*, pp 325–7.
124 McDowell, *Irish Convention*, p. 161.
125 Ibid., p. 162.
126 Hugh T. Barrie to Lord Londonderry, 16 Feb. 1918 (PRONI, Londonderry Papers, D3099/8/3).
127 David Lloyd George to Horace Plunkett, 25 Feb. 1918 in Plunkett, *Report of the Proceedings*, pp 20–22.
128 David Lloyd George to Hugh T. Barrie, 21 Feb. 1918 in McDowell, *Irish Convention*, p. 163.
129 Lord Londonderry to Edward Carson, 21 Feb. 1918 (PRONI, Londonderry Papers, D3099/8/3).
130 Ulster Unionist delegation, minutes, 25 Feb. 1918 (PRONI, Ulster Unionist Papers, D1327/3/17).
131 Ulster Unionist delegation, minutes, 25 Feb. 1918 (ibid.).
132 Hugh de Fellenberg Montgomery to Lord Londonderry, 26 Feb. 1918 in Buckland, *Irish Unionism*, pp 425–6. Given Montgomery's views on American opinion, it is worth noting that nationalists at this time were angered by the efforts of British propagandists in the United States to explain the Ulster Unionists' case, see Hartley, *Irish Question*, p. 169.
133 McDowell, *Irish Convention*, p. 167.
134 Plunkett, *Confidential Report*, p. 91.
135 Patrick Buckland, *Irish Unionism: One: The Anglo-Irish and the New Ireland 1885–1922* (Dublin, 1972), pp 146–85; Hennessey, *Dividing Ireland*, p. 213.
136 Plunkett, *Report of the Proceedings*, p. 116
137 Mansergh, *Unresolved Question*, p. 104.
138 Fair, *Interparty Conferences*, pp 219–21.
139 Ulster Unionist delegation, minutes, 13 Mar. 1918 (PRONI, Ulster Unionist Papers, D1327/3/17).
140 Plunkett, *Report of the Proceedings*, pp 30–34; Plunkett, *Confidential Report*, pp 134–7; A.C. Hepburn, *Catholic Belfast and Nationalist Ireland in the Era of Joe Devlin 1871–1934* (Oxford, 2008), pp 184–92.
141 Ulster Unionist delegation, minutes, 20 Mar. 1918 (PRONI, Ulster Unionist Papers, D1327/3/17).
142 Plunkett, *Report of the Proceedings*, pp 31–32. See Jason Knirck, 'Confederates, Boers or Silesians? Analogies to world history in arguments about partition during the Irish Revolution' in Fleming and Murphy (eds), *Ireland and Partition*, pp 15–32.

143 D. George Boyce, *Englishmen and Irish Troubles: British Public Opinion and the Making of Irish Policy 1918–22* (Cambridge MA, 1972), pp 36–9.
144 Plunkett, *Confidential Report*, p. 16.
145 J.J. Lee, *Ireland 1912–1985: Politics and Society* (Cambridge, 1989), p. 39.
146 The most significant event was a symposium held at Trinity College Dublin in July 2017, at which speakers from academia and politics reflected on the convention's legacy to contemporary Ireland. Like the convention itself, though for very different reasons, the proceedings have not been published.
147 Diarmaid Ferriter, '1916 in 2016: personal reflections of an Irish historian', *Irish Historical Studies*, 42:61 (2018), pp 161–74.

6

Combating the 'flu'

Regional responses to the 1918–19 influenza pandemic in Ulster

PATRICIA MARSH

On 12 June 1918, tucked away on the back pages of the *Northern Whig* and the *Belfast Newsletter*, under the heading 'Influenza Epidemic', were three lines notifying the female workers of James Mackie & Sons Ltd to return to work after an outbreak of influenza.[1] This was the first indication that the mysterious malady that had caused so much havoc in Spain had reached Ireland.[2] Although this was the first article, many more would appear over the following 12 months as influenza impacted on Irish life in many different ways. The 1918–19 influenza pandemic, commonly known as 'Spanish influenza' struck in three concurrent waves throughout the world and the Irish experience was no exception. In Ireland, the first wave occurred during June and July of 1918, the second most virulent wave during the autumn of 1918 and the final wave in the spring of 1919.

The recorded Irish influenza death toll was 20,057.[3] However, pneumonia was the most common complication associated with the disease and if excess pneumonia figures for both 1918 and 1919 are added to the recorded mortality figures, the death toll rises to 23,288.[4] However, the true death toll may never be known as not all Irish influenza deaths were registered and also some were registered incorrectly, meaning the mortality from the disease in Ireland could have been much higher. According to Ida Milne, as many as 800,000 Irish people could have been infected with influenza.[5] In the province of Ulster at least 7,582 people were recorded as dying from influenza, and 303,000 people in the province could have been infected.[6]

In Ulster, as elsewhere in Ireland and Great Britain, the local authorities and their Medical Officers of Health (MOH) were responsible for public health in their respective towns and cities. The MOHs, in particular, were tasked with the production of an influenza policy for the management of the disease within their jurisdiction. The main medical care was provided through the poor law medical system of the union infirmary and dispensary districts and this was administered by the respective board of guardians. The Local Government Board for Ireland (LGBI) controlled the activities of the boards of guardians with respect to the administration of the dispensary medical system, union infirmaries and fever hospitals. Added to this the LGBI also controlled the administration of the Public Health Acts by the rural, urban and county councils.[7] This chapter will discuss how the combined forces of the local authorities and poor law medical system responded to the public health crisis of epidemic influenza in the province of Ulster. It will show how the lack of a cohesive medical and welfare response to influenza at central government level in both London and Dublin impacted on the local response to the pandemic and explore what more could have been done to alleviate the plight of the sick poor at this time.

The first reported outbreak of influenza in Ireland was in May 1918, on the USS *Dixie*, which was docked in the naval base in Queenstown (now Cobh), County Cork. It is likely that this outbreak was confined to the ship as there were no contemporary reports of influenza in the town.[8] Despite this, according to the LGBI, the first wave of influenza during June 1918 was principally in Belfast and other districts of the north of Ireland.[9] The first influenza death in Belfast was recorded on 7 June 1918, indicating that the disease probably started in the city.[10] From Belfast, influenza spread westwards to Lisburn, Lurgan and Portadown by mid-June, probably via the rail network and eastward to Holywood, Bangor and Newtownards by the end of the month. There were also outbreaks in Londonderry, Enniskillen and Strabane in the north-west of the province. Sporadic outbreaks occurred elsewhere in Ireland such as Dublin, Ballinasloe, Tipperary town and Athlone. It is notable that many of these towns were situated near army bases or military hospitals as the general consensus especially during this first wave was that influenza was spread by troops returning home to Ireland from the Western Front.[11]

The second wave started in the province of Leinster, specifically in the Howth district of Dublin, where influenza was first reported on 1 October 1918. It spread to Dublin and the rest of Leinster during October and then throughout the rest of Ireland. In Ulster, early reports of influenza were in towns as far apart as, Newry, Dungannon and Londonderry. However, the first report of the second wave in Ulster was in Larne, County Antrim, on 9 October 1918. As there was a port with a Royal Navy base situated in Larne, it is probable that influenza entered here independently.[12] First newspaper reports of the disease in Belfast appeared on 30 October 1918 and advised that 100 Sinn Féin prisoners in Belfast gaol were suffering from influenza. However, influenza deaths were reported in the Belfast union infirmary on 21 October, indicating that the disease had taken hold in the city earlier in the month.[13]

The second wave spread throughout Ulster and was considered to be the most virulent of the three. Maybe surprisingly, due to the rural nature of the county, Donegal, especially the Inishowen peninsula, had a very high death rate during this wave. However, other areas in the west of Ireland, such as County Mayo, were not affected to the same extent. The lack of influenza in the rural parts of Connaught has been attributed to an absence of an extensive rail network in this part of the country.[14] In contrast, Donegal was serviced by the Londonderry & Lough Swilly Railway, which travelled from the city of Londonderry throughout County Donegal, and the prevalence of influenza in the county helps corroborate the theory that the virus was spread through the rail network.

First reports of the third wave of influenza in early February 1919 were again in Leinster, in County Kildare, and from there it spread to Dublin by 12 February.[15] In Ulster, influenza first appeared in Holywood, County Down, on 6 February, spreading to Belfast by 12 February.[16] Influenza visited most Irish towns during this wave but in Belfast, Lurgan, Larne, Newry and Dungannon this was a milder wave than those in 1918, which may be explained by immunity that was gained from previous waves in 1918.[17] There was a recurrence of influenza in County Donegal, with a severe outbreak along the north-east seaboard of the county.[18] Again, there was a very high death rate in the county. Donegal poor law union had the highest death rate per thousand of population in Ulster during 1919. The poor law unions of Dunfanaghy, Stranorlar, Glenties, Ballyshannon and Letterkenny also had high death rates during this wave.[19]

Local authority response

During June 1918, the first outbreak of influenza in the towns and cities of Belfast, Lurgan, Portadown and Londonderry, caused havoc to businesses and factories which were forced to close or function on reduced staff. By 1 July 1918, 100 tramway system staff were absent with influenza, which caused operational problems.[20] As influenza spread through Belfast during the first wave, the Medical Superintendent Officer of Health (MSOH) for Belfast Corporation, Dr Hugh Bailie, ordered school closures and recommended the thorough disinfection of cinemas once or twice a day.[21] Influenza was rife in the neighbouring towns of Lurgan and Portadown in County Armagh. It is worth noting that during the first wave hundreds of people were absent with the flu from the Lurgan factories. Added to this, 31 influenza deaths were recorded in the Lurgan town area alone from the middle of June until the end of July 1918.[22] Nevertheless, there was no evidence that any preventative measures were recommended by the MOH in either Lurgan or Portadown. Meanwhile in Londonderry, school closure was the main preventative recommendation offered by the city's corporation. It was not unusual for schools to be closed during outbreaks of infectious disease. The Londonderry schools had already been shut due to an outbreak of measles and were re-opened on 24 June 1918, only to be closed again on 25 June because of the outbreak of influenza in the city.[23]

During the first wave, the response from these local authorities was apathetic to say the least. Despite the high death rates in these industrial towns, few preventative steps were taken apart from school closures. It should be noted that just prior to the outbreak of influenza in the summer of 1918, measles had been rife in all of these towns and this may have led to the consensus that this wave of influenza was nothing more than a seasonal 'flu'. This is illustrated by the approach of Dr Samuel Agnew, MOH for Lurgan who was of the opinion that influenza would die out as rapidly as it had started and this attitude may explain why he and the local authority did not take any preventative measures.[24]

During the more virulent second wave of influenza in the autumn of 1918, the local authority response in Ulster's towns and cities was more proactive as many of the councils took preventative measures. A widespread recommendation by local authorities throughout Ireland was the closure of National day schools, Sunday schools and technical schools to stop the spread of influenza. This was a decision that the central government in Britain and Ireland left to individual local authorities.[25] Generally, the managers of the National schools throughout Ireland adhered to this recommendation, but secondary and grammar schools remained open, sometimes with tragic results. The virulent second wave of influenza hit Belfast Methodist College at the end of October 1918, infecting students who were boarders at the school. Many members of staff also caught influenza with the exception of the school Medical Officer, matron and headmaster. Tragically, between 17 and 23 November 1918, two members of staff, George Manning, aged 22, and Rev. Patrick O'Sullivan, aged 44, as well as one of the boarders, Oliver Crawford, aged 15, died from influenza.[26]

In Lisburn, the Friends School also remained open during the second wave. By the end of October 1918 only 17 of the boarders, as well as two members of staff had not contracted the disease. On 31 October, a pupil, Helen Clarke died from influenza, followed on 3 November by a second pupil, Anna Magowan, and it was at this time that the decision was made to close the school. A third pupil, Sadie Walsh died on 8 November but the tragedy did not end there. The housekeeper, Emma McCullough, aged 35, and the headmaster's daughter, Frances Ridges, aged 21, nursed the remaining students suffering from influenza. Unfortunately, they too lost their lives to the disease on 10 and 15 November 1918, respectively.[27]

The closure of schools would have helped to curtail the spread of influenza among children, but the congregation of adults together in other confined spaces would have led to the rapid spread of the disease through the community. Therefore, unsurprisingly, many local authorities were concerned about the diffusion of the virus in crowded venues, such as places of entertainment especially cinemas. Several local authorities tried to enforce the closure and ventilation of cinemas to curtail the spread of influenza. Councillors in Belfast, Portadown, Newry and Newtownards recommended the closure of cinemas in the interest of public health. In Belfast the cinema owners refused to close their premises, which prompted the MSOH, Dr Bailie, to request permission from the LGBI to enforce the closure of cinemas in the city to stop the spread of the disease. However, the LGBI advised that they had no powers to force the closure of cinema premises, as this action was not approved in any part of the United Kingdom. Although the LGBI did not authorise cinema closures, they did sanction their ventilation and disinfection and exclusion of children under age 14 from the premises. As many National schools were closed due to influenza, children found other places to congregate during school time, one of which was the cinema. Consequently, to avoid the spread of influenza it was thought that children should be excluded from these premises and the LGBI was happy to recommend this action.[28]

In Ulster, as with the rest of the United Kingdom, several councils singled out cinemas for closure and ventilation under the pretext that people gathered there and there is no doubt that the closure of these premises would have curtailed the spread of the disease. Nevertheless, people congregated in many venues apart from cinemas, in places such as theatres, trams and churches. Although it was never suggested that people should not attend church services or that they should be abandoned, attendance at wakes was a cause of concern. The Irish tradition of waking the dead was controversial and came in for much criticism as it was feared that the custom would aid in the spread of infectious disease. In Dublin, during the second wave, an editorial in the *Irish Times* criticised as an objectionable practice the attendance of people at wakes of those who had died from influenza believing it to be a significant factor in spreading the disease. It was stated that this custom more than anything else thwarted the public health authorities in their efforts to eliminate influenza.

Sir Charles Cameron, MSOH for Dublin also voiced his objections to the custom, stating 'that persons who disregarded the injunctions and advice, which had been publicly circulated in the interests of the health of the citizens wilfully made themselves disseminators of infection, and risked their own lives.' Rather than be 'waked', he believed that bodies of persons who died from influenza should be isolated.[29] There were also objections to bringing corpses of influenza victims to the church before burial. A correspondent to the *Freeman's Journal* could not 'imagine any more fruitful method of spreading disease,' adding that it was 'very wrong to expose healthy persons to the danger of contagion in this manner.'[30]

The custom of waking the dead was largely associated with the Roman Catholic faith and its critics argued that the wake was little more than an excuse for excessive drinking of alcohol and general revelry in the presence of the corpse.[31] In Ulster, the Church of Ireland archdeacon of Armagh was of the opinion that 'crowded houses at the solemn time of death were a contradiction of everything that was desired in a time of sorrow. It was a most undesirable custom and a most fruitful source of spreading the disease.'[32] Some Ulster councils also voiced their concerns. In December, members of the Dungannon Rural District Council, disapproved of waking victims of influenza and thought that their corpses should be interred immediately. However, the council did not take any official action to prohibit wakes with the clerk remarking that 'the doctors should see to that.'[33] In Cookstown, the MOH, Dr Charles Graves, recommended prompt burial after death in order to protect the living and as wakes were a definite way of spreading the infection, that they should be abolished.[34]

During the December Public Health Committee meeting in Belfast, Councillor Thomas English emphasised the importance of avoiding visiting people who were suffering from septic pneumonia, as well as not attending wakes of those who had died from influenza.[35] However, Belfast Corporation did not make any recommendation to stop the practice. The town clerk for Larne asked the LGBI if any order had been made regarding persons attending wakes, but was given no guidance in the matter.[36] Although several local authorities objected to the practice, it appears that central government did not sanction the prohibition of holding or attendance at wakes. Instead the LGBI shifted the responsibility onto individual local authorities to make the decision and recommendation on this issue.

Seasonal migration of young adults from Donegal to Scotland for work was a strategy which helped to bolster the income in the poorer parts of the county.[37] Young people travelled annually to Scotland from Donegal for work and did so during 1918 and 1919 as well. Unfortunately, numerous young adults contracted influenza in Scotland and did not recover from it. The death rate of young people was very high and the *Belfast Newsletter* reported in March 1919 that over 50 natives of Donegal employed in Scotland had died from influenza.[38] In many instances, the corpses of the dead were transported home to Donegal for burial. On 1 March 1919, the *Ulster Herald* voiced concern about 'a reprehensible custom' in the westerly portion of Donegal of

> Bringing home for burial of persons dying of the epidemic in Scotland It is undoubtedly true that the coffins containing remains

of victims of the disease, three or perhaps four days ahead, are for a night 'waked' in the home, the coffin lid being taken off. The gravity and far-reaching effect of this dangerous procedure can be understood when it is stated that on Saturday there passed through Letterkenny on motorcars six coffined dead from Scotland. This danger should at once be dealt with.[39]

It is clear that there were moral objections to holding wakes in Ulster and indeed the practice was one that would have facilitated the spread of influenza. During 1918, it was thought that the infection remained in the corpse and, therefore, could be spread to the living especially at a wake with an open coffin. However, there is no evidence that this was the case with the influenza virus.[40] Therefore, waking the body in an open coffin would not have spread influenza through the corpse, but, by their nature, wakes involved many people congregating in a confined space such as a cottage. Anyone who had contracted influenza could bring the infection to a wake. Traditionally a person attending a wake would shake the hands of all the bereaved in the house and not only pass on their sympathies but maybe the influenza virus as well. Therefore, all members of the household as well as other attendees of the wake could have contracted the virus and spread it throughout the wider local community.

There has been much speculation why there was such a high death rate in County Donegal in both 1918 and 1919, especially as it was such rural part of the country. Could it be that it was the high incidence of influenza deaths in Scotland of young adults from Donegal due to seasonal migration along with them being waked back home that was instrumental in disseminating the disease in rural districts?[41] More recent events during the early stages of the Covid-19 pandemic help illustrates the danger of infection from attending crowded events such as funerals or wakes. In Hara in northern Spain in March 2020 over 60 people were thought to have caught Covid-19 which was traced back to their attendance at a funeral that took place at Vitoria-gastreiz in the Basque country.[42]

The high death rate of young people from Donegal in Scotland illustrates one of the global peculiarities of the pandemic, which was how it targeted young adults. Normally influenza kills the very young or the very old, but the 1918–19 influenza pandemic showed an unusual age distribution of deaths. Although there was still high mortality for the very young and very old, there was also an extreme departure from the norm with a high mortality for the 15–44 age group.[43] In England and Wales the mortality seemed to be concentrated among those aged 20–40 and especially those aged 25–35.[44] Ireland followed the global trend of targeting young adults as well as the very old and the very young. In 1918, 55 per cent of all deaths from influenza were of people aged between 15 and 45.[45] In 1919, more than 58 per cent of the total influenza mortality was between the ages of 20 and 65.[46] The Irish figures also show that infants under one year were at particular risk from influenza. This was hardly surprising as, even without epidemic disease, the urban areas of Ireland such as Dublin and Belfast suffered from one of the highest infant mortality rates in the United Kingdom due to infection and poor diet.[47]

It was not only the gathering of people in crowded indoor venues that was a cause of concern. An article in the *Irish News* on 13 November 1918 raised concerns about the huge crowds of people congregating on the streets during the armistice celebrations in case this would further spread influenza.[48] It has been suggested that extra infections and deaths occurred as a result of the armistice celebrations, as these gatherings became the foci of new or recurring outbreaks of influenza.[49] The armistice celebrations in Belfast took place during the peak of the most virulent wave of the disease in the city. Lasting a few days, musical bands and crowds of people congregated on the streets, singing and dancing in celebration of the end of the war.[50] Therefore, is not surprising that the pneumonia and influenza mortality in Belfast peaked on 23 November 1918 not long after these celebrations took place.[51] Not all towns had a celebration and the decision was made in Clones, County Monaghan, that due to the high influenza death rate, no armistice event should take place in the town in order to stop the spread of the disease.[52]

Other measures taken by local authorities included the production of public notices. These notices listed preventative measures and were produced by local authorities in Belfast, Larne and Cookstown. In late October 1918, towards the end of the war, a memorandum was produced by the Imperial Local Government Board (LGB) based in London and this was issued to the LGBI. This memorandum contained advice and preventative measures for influenza and the LGBI in turn issued it to all the MOHs in Ireland. The public notices produced by the local authorities were derived from the advice contained within the memorandum.[53] These public notices were displayed in public places and published in the local newspapers. The public notice issued by Dr Bailie, the MSOH for Belfast, included the following recommendations:

> Avoid all crowded gatherings.
>
> Secure good ventilation and cleanliness in the home and bedroom.
>
> Delicate people should take good plain nourishing food and avoid cold and fatigue as far as possible. Warm clothing should be worn as a precaution against pneumonia.
>
> If a tonic is required, take quinine in doses of from 2 to 5 grains night and morning.

> All rooms used as Workshops, Factories etc, should be sprayed morning and afternoon with a dilution of Jeyes Fluid, or other disinfectant, in the strength of a small cupful to 3 gallons of water and thorough ventilation secured.
>
> A small pellet of permanganate of potash, about the size of a pickle or rice, dissolved in a wine glassful of warm water should be used for gargling the throat or sniffing up the nose twice daily.
>
> When a person has actually sickened, he should be isolated at once.
>
> Special care should be taken to destroy the sputum by burning, as the spit is very infectious.
>
> When coughing or sneezing the mouth and nose should be covered with a handkerchief.
>
> Persons must not spit in streets, tramcars, or any public place or vehicle.
>
> If attacked go to bed at once and remain there until allowed up by the doctor.
>
> When the doctor is required send for him as early in the day as possible.
>
> If medical aid is called in immediately and the foregoing precautions followed, the disease need not necessarily be particularly dangerous.[54]

Although the above advice was issued by the Belfast MSOH, the public notices produced by Dr Graves, MOH in Cookstown, and the MOH in Larne contained similar recommendations. The advice normally placed responsibility for prevention of influenza on to the individual rather than recommend what actions the local authorities were to take during the pandemic to prevent the spread of the disease.

In 1897, the introduction of *the Infectious Disease (Notification) Act of 1890* made it easier to trace infectious diseases such as typhoid and typhus. Under this act there were clear instructions for public health departments on how to trace and thus stop the spread of infectious diseases. The LGBI did not recommend placing influenza on the list of notifiable diseases under the act since they thought, probably correctly, that it would be difficult to trace in a similar manner to other infectious diseases and thus its spread would not be curtailed.[55] However, septic pneumonia was a common complication of influenza and the local authorities of both Larne and Belfast made this disease notifiable during the virulent second wave. This meant that certain procedures could be put into place with respect to notification, isolation and treatment of septic pneumonia patients.[56]

Central government was not proactive during the influenza pandemic. The LGB in London and its head Sir Arthur Newsholme came in for criticism for its lack of action during this medical crisis. Newsholme acknowledged that during the first wave more could have been done. Measures such as prevention of mass migrations and overcrowding, as well as the isolation of the sick from the healthy should have been taken but he believed that, due to the demands of war, this was not an option as 'it was necessary to carry on and the relentless needs of warfare justified incurring the risk of spreading infections.'[57] In Ireland, the LGBI took its lead from the LGB in London so if there was a lack of action in London the same inaction was also seen in Ireland. The LGBI provided little advice to local authorities with respect to influenza, often shifting the onus back onto the local authority when queried about which course of action to take. This resulted in a lack of a coherent policy or official guidance on influenza and left individual local authorities to decide on the policy within their jurisdiction. Some local authorities rose to the challenge while other did not.

Medical response

There was much confusion and scepticism about the disease and the *Derry Journal* in October 1918 asked 'Is it influenza at all?[58] Tom Quinn argued that many of the world's top scientists were convinced that it was not influenza due to both the ferocity of the disease and the speed at which it incapacitated and killed its victims.[59] There was an overwhelming number of influenza patients and doctors found their task to cure the sick an impossible one. As there is still no known cure for influenza, it was hardly surprising that there was little agreement among the Irish medical profession on the best treatment for, or prevention against the disease. This resulted in many cures and treatments being suggested. Gargling with a solution of permanganate of potash was recommended by both the MOH for Cookstown, Dr Graves, and MSOH for Belfast, Dr Bailie. They also recommended taking quinine tablets of between two and five grains twice a day as a tonic and preventative.[60]

Quinine was a popular treatment choice. Irish Sinn Féin leader, Arthur Griffith, who had contracted influenza at Gloucester gaol in 1919, was reported to have consumed a full bottle of quinine one night, which he claimed had successfully cured his influenza attack. Fellow prisoner Denis McCullough was not so sure how successful quinine was as a cure for when he saw Griffith the next day he was alarmed at his appearance. He feared that Griffith would 'collapse as much from the remedy as from the disease.[61] In Dungannon, Dr Mathew Marmion tried turpentine capsules, which he claimed to have marvellous effects. He had tried the capsule in the cases of a patient in the infirmary one evening and had found that in the morning the patient was much better.'[62]

The use of alcohol as a treatment was also popular but controversial.[63] Alcohol was widely endorsed by some doctors in cases of influenza to relieve pain and bolster strength.[64] The Assistant Director of Medical Services at the Curragh army camp in County Kildare advised: 'we do not stint alcohol, for we are convinced of its stimulating properties, it is also a food. Good whiskey is better than bad brandy. Port wine and hot soda water is perhaps preferred by ladies.'[65] He was not alone in recommending alcohol and it was such a popular treatment the Ministry of Food regarded the shortage of spirits in some districts as a health problem.[66] During December 1918 the Ministry of Food arranged to direct special supplies of spirits for influenza patients to districts where there was a shortage, and where medical opinion showed the need existed. Bottles of spirits supplied for this purpose would only be sold against a doctor's certificate.[67] In February 1919, the Dublin Public Health Committee requested the War Cabinet to call for the immediate release of supplies of whiskey in the interests of public health.[68] Alcohol was a popular treatment in workhouse infirmaries but this did not always sit well with the guardians who held temperance values such as those in Lisnaskea who queried the use of 24 glasses of whiskey and ten of brandy for the workhouse during a week in March 1919, remarking, 'You would not get more outside a public house.'[69]

Vaccines were available during the pandemic but the organism that caused influenza was unknown. It was believed at the time to be a bacterial disease and the streptococcus of *Pfeiffer's Bacillus* was thought to be cause. Therefore, when developing a vaccine many were based on *Pfeiffer's Bacillus*.[70] During 1918, the LGBI did not advocate the use of vaccination or supply vaccines to boards of guardians for inoculation against influenza as they were not confident that a vaccine would confer immunity from an influenza attack.[71] Vaccines were expensive and this stance may have had more to do with their cost rather than their effectiveness as a treatment.[72] Nevertheless, MOHs in Dungannon, Ballyshannon and Keady unions used vaccines on their patients and sought reimbursement in retrospect.[73] Unfortunately, it is not known how successful these vaccines were. Vaccines were used by the military but not always successfully. The military hospitals in Cork found that vaccines were of value in treatment in the early stage of influenza.[74] However the treatment of patients with vaccines was discontinued at the Curragh military camp, as those so treated appeared to become worse.[75] Since the organism that produced influenza was not known, the effectiveness of these vaccines would have been limited, except possibly against secondary bacterial infections such as pneumonia.[76]

The main medical response in Irish towns was provided by the poor law medical system through union infirmaries and the dispensary districts. However, these institutions were unprepared for the number of influenza patients needing treatment and were under severe pressure. Workhouse infirmaries were extremely busy. During the first wave in Belfast the number of influenza patients admitted to the union infirmary was so large that it prompted the Visiting Medical Officer, Dr Gardner Robb, to remark: 'Never in my recollection has the strain on the staff been so great as during the past few weeks.'[77] In Lurgan, the union infirmary had not been so full in over 30 years due to an influx of influenza patients. Also, within the Lurgan union district, the dispensaries in Aghalee, Portadown and Lurgan suffered great delays in obtaining medicines supplies for influenza patients. This resulted in Dr James Rowlett, the MOH for Portadown, having to turn away 40 patients from the dispensary due to the lack of medicines.[78] During 1918, the impact of influenza on Irish workhouses and infirmaries was enormous as the number of deaths in these institutions increased by 3,329 on the previous year with influenza and pneumonia deaths rising by 2,551.[79]

Traditional nursing care provided the best and only effective treatment for influenza.[80] However, nurses were in short supply as many professional nurses volunteered for both the army and naval medical corps during the war.[81] This situation was further exacerbated when the remaining nurses started to contract influenza themselves. During the first and second waves, numerous nurses in the Belfast union infirmary contracted influenza. Unfortunately, during June 1918, one probationary nurse died, and four more ladies succumbed to the disease between 5 November and 3 December 1918.[82] In Londonderry union infirmary, two nurses died from influenza during November 1918.[83] In the same month eight nurses in the Lurgan union infirmary contracted influenza; subsequently two nurses died from the disease.[84] The lack of healthy nurses put a strain on the workhouse infirmaries throughout Ireland. Added to this, there was also a scarcity of temporary doctors throughout the country again due to large number of practitioners serving on the Western Front.[85] As a result, union infirmaries suffered staff shortages during the influenza outbreaks. Dispensary doctors worked long hours to treat their patients, paying 100,000 more home visits during this period than in the previous year, indicating not only the virulence of the disease throughout Ireland but also the work pressure that these physicians were under during the pandemic.[86]

The medical response during the second and third waves was similar to that of the first. Influenza sufferers continued to avail of treatment and medicines through the dispensary system and the workhouse infirmaries, which were full to capacity, if not overcrowded. In Clones, the union infirmary was fully occupied and medical staff were scarce due to illness, meaning the remaining doctors and nurses were working to full capacity. Extra medical assistance was needed and during December 1918, the board of guardians persuaded eight members of the 343rd Field Ambulance of the Royal Army Medical Corps (RAMC) to assist them in the Clones union infirmary as well as making home visits to patients.[87] The members of the RAMC remained on duty day and night for two or three weeks and their assistance was much appreciated by the guardians who thought that their nursing saved many lives in the infirmary during the outbreak.[88]

In Ulster the demands of war impacted on institutions such as workhouse infirmaries. There were many cases where wards or entire workhouse hospitals were requisitioned for military patients. In Strabane, the military acquired the workhouse for treatment of troops just prior to the outbreak of influenza in October 1918 and most of the inmates were sent to the Londonderry workhouse.[89] This not only impacted on the sick poor from Strabane, who were left without a local infirmary during the beginning of virulent second wave, but it also put extra strain on the Londonderry infirmary which was already suffering from overcrowding due to the high influx of influenza patients from the local area.[90] The care of military patients was vital to the war effort but it appeared to be more important to some boards of guardians than the welfare of the poor. This could have been due to patriotic fervour on behalf of the gurdians or alternatively the guaranteed fees they received for accommodating military was a welcome source of income.[91]

Charitable response

The shortcomings of both the local authorities and poor law meant that it was up to the residents of individual towns to step up and help the sick poor, especially during the more virulent second wave. In Newry, the local authority was aware that the poor needed more substantial charitable help during this medical crisis. They arranged for two Newry creameries to supply pasteurised milk to be distributed free to those who needed it.[92] The provision of nourishing food was also deemed important. As the Newry Technical School was closed due to the pandemic, the staff of the domestic department worked all through day and night to make wholesome foodstuffs for the sick. However, this work was discontinued on 25 November 1918 when the school re-opened.[93]

Despite this aid, the situation in Newry was so serious that a Relief of Distress Fund Committee was formed to 'consider the best means of meeting the exceptional expenditure that has been and is being incurred by the various charitable organisations in the relief of distress arising out of the influenza epidemic.' Prior to the formation of the committee, the local St Vincent de Paul Society rose to the challenge to help the sick poor in the area, spending several hundred pounds providing clothing, coal, groceries, butter, milk and other necessities for the poor of all denominations in Newry. The committee sent out a circular inviting subscriptions for the fund, which was closed on to 31 December 1918. A total of £734 4s. 2d. was raised and three-quarters of this sum was allocated to Catholic charitable organisations, such as the St Vincent de Paul Society, to reimburse them for expenditure they had already incurred in helping the poor in Newry. One quarter went to the local Protestant clergymen for distribution among their congregations.[94]

In Cookstown, there was also an awareness that the local poor needed help. A subscription list was opened and a committee formed to look after the sick poor in the town and dispensary district. Many local trained ladies volunteered to act as nurses in the district and offered their services for no payment. The MOH for the Cookstown union, Dr Graves was full of praise for these ladies who under the command of Nurse Milliken of the District Nursing Society took charge of different sections of the district, visiting the sick and distributing food and nourishment to those unable to provide it for themselves. Dr Graves stated that if it had not been for this organisation the death rate in Cookstown would have been appalling and he expressed his appreciation of the devotion and self-sacrifice shown by these ladies as many contracted influenza in the discharge of their 'self-appointed duties.'[95] As well as caring for the sick, the Sick Nursing Society made use of the Technical School kitchen to provide nourishing food not only for the sick poor but also for those who were too ill to physically provide food and nurture for other family members. Food was given free of charge to those in need, but if people could afford to pay for it, they were encouraged to do so. This service proved to be very popular with up to 170 families in the town and district receiving this aid.[96]

In Clones, as previously stated, the workhouse infirmary was overcrowded and there was a shortage of medical personnel. As in Newry and Cookstown, a relief committee was formed to assist families incapacitated by influenza with both nursing and nourishment. A kitchen was set up in the town hall where food was prepared and distributed to those people who required it. Although the St Vincent de Paul Society placed their funds at the disposal of the relief committee, the committee did not raise a public subscription in the town as had occurred in Cookstown and Newry. Instead they took action first and provided food, medicine, fuel and clothing to the poor and needy in the town and then presented the bill to the board of guardians for the expenses incurred. The guardians raised objections to paying this bill. However, the chairman pointed out that if the guardians had been able to both accommodate and treat all the influenza patients in the local hospitals that the cost to them would have been considerably more than the £95 requested by the committee.[97]

The pandemic highlighted the failings of the poor law system, which was overstretched due to a lack of suitable accommodation and medical personnel. The boards of guardians actively tried to obtain sufficient medical personnel to help during the pandemic and in general adhered to the requests of their MOHs with respect to treatment of the disease. However, Fred Van Hartesveldt argued that the provision of public aid with food, fuel and nursing during the 1918 pandemic was of much more value to the poor than treatment by local doctors.[98] However, the boards of guardians or the local authorities in Ulster did not help the poor by providing food or other necessities, so it was left to the philanthropy of the middle-class population to rise to the challenge to help their less well-off neighbours. Although they differed in approach, the middle class citizens of Cookstown, Newry and Clones were happy to help their less well-off neighbours in a tangible way.

These towns were among the few in Ulster that organised relief committees and helped the sick poor during the pandemic. They opened subscription lists and the ladies volunteered their services to provide nutritious food. They also nursed the local poor to alleviate the suffering of their sick neighbours, often at risk to their own health. This meant that the boards of guardians in some cases abdicated their responsibility for the poor in the union to the volunteers who were willing to help. It is telling that in the bigger industrial towns like Belfast, Londonderry, Lurgan and Portadown there is no evidence of any philanthropic enterprise to help the needy in those districts, which maybe was due to a lack of connection between the middle classes and their working class neighbours. Perhaps, this lack of charitable action on the part of citizens of the industrial towns could account for the high death tolls during the pandemic – if they had helped in a more tangible way the mortality in these towns may not have been so high.[99]

Notes

1   *Northern Whig*, 12 June 1918; *Belfast Newsletter*, 12 June 1918.
2   *The Times*, 3 June 1918.
3   *Fifty-fifth Detailed Annual Report of the Registrar-General (Ireland) … During the Year 1918*, HC 1919 [Cmd 450] x.849, p. v; *Fifty-sixth Detailed Annual Report of the Registrar-General (Ireland) … During the Year 1919*, HC 1920 [Cmd 997] xi.629, pp v, xxv.
4   Patricia Marsh, 'The effect of the 1918–19 influenza pandemic on Belfast' (MA thesis, Queen's University Belfast, 2006).
5   Ida Milne, 'Epidemic or myth? The 1918 flu in Ireland' (MA thesis, National University of Ireland Maynooth, 2005), p. 35.
6   Patricia Marsh, *The Spanish Flu in Ireland: A Socio-Economic Shock to Ireland, 1918–1919* (Basingstoke, 2021), p. 58.

7 *Report of the Irish Public Health Council on the Public Health and Medical Services in Ireland*, HC 1920 [Cmd 761], xvii.1075, p. 4.
8 Marsh, *The Spanish Flu in Ireland*, pp 19–20.
9 *Annual Report of the Local Government Board for Ireland for the Year Ended 31st March 1919*, HC 1920 [Cmd 1432], p. xxxvii.
10 Marsh, *The Spanish Flu in Ireland*, p. 22,
11 Ibid., pp 20–21.
12 Ibid., pp 22–23.
13 Ibid., p. 24; *Belfast Newsletter*, 30 Oct. 1918.
14 Ida Milne, *Stacking the Coffins: Influenza, War and Revolution in Ireland, 1918–19* (Manchester, 2018), p. 63.
15 *Irish Independent*, 5 Feb. 1919; *Irish Times*, 12 Feb. 1919.
16 Belfast Board of Guardians minutes, 18 Feb. 1919 (PRONI, BG/7/A/101).
17 Marsh, *The Spanish Flu in Ireland*, p. 48.
18 *Irish Independent*, 17 Feb. 1919, p. 2.
19 Marsh, *The Spanish Flu in Ireland*, p. 49.
20 *Irish News*, 2 July 1918.
21 Marsh, *The Spanish Fu in Ireland*, pp 164–5.
22 Lurgan Medical Officer of Health Report, 5 Aug. 1918 (PRONI, LA/51/9/D/6); *Lurgan Mail*, 10 Aug. 1918.
23 *Irish News*, 25 June 1918; *Derry Journal*, 26 June 1918; *Dungannon Democrat*, 26 June 1918.
24 *Lurgan Mail*, 6 July 1918.
25 Marsh, *The Spanish Flu in Ireland*, p. 232.
26 John Watson Henderson, *Methodist College, Belfast, 1868–1938: A Survey and Retrospect*, vol. 1 (Belfast, 1939), p. 271.
27 Neville H. Newhouse, *A History of the Friends School, Lisburn* (Lisburn, 1974), pp 90–91.
28 Marsh, *The Spanish Flu in Ireland*, pp 172–3
29 *Freeman's Journal*, 2 Nov. 1918; *Irish Independent*, 2 Nov. 1918; *Irish Times*, 4 Nov. 1918.
30 *Freeman's Journal*, 20 Nov. 1918.
31 Julie-Marie Strange, *Death, Grief and Poverty in Britain, 1870–1914* (Cambridge, 2005), p. 87.
32 *Armagh Guardian*, 6 Dec. 1918.
33 *Tyrone Courier*, 19 Dec. 1918.
34 *Mid-Ulster Mail*, 30 Nov. 1918.
35 *Belfast Newsletter*, 9 Dec. 1918; *Irish News*, 9 Dec. 1918.
36 Proceedings of the Larne Urban Sanitary Authority and Urban District Council, 11 Nov. 1918 (PRONI, LA/43/27/A/4).
37 T.W. Freeman, 'The changing distribution of population in Donegal, with special reference to the congested areas', *Journal of Statistical and Social Inquiry Society of Ireland*, 16 (1940–41), p. 40.
38 *Belfast Newsletter*, 13 Mar. 1919.

39 *Ulster Herald*, 1 Mar. 1919; *Down Recorder*, 8 Mar. 1919.
40 S.S. Bakhshi, 'Code of practice for funeral workers: managing infection risk and body bagging', *Communicable Disease and Public Health*, 4:4 (Dec. 2001), pp 283–7.
41 Marsh, *The Spanish Flu in Ireland*, p. 56.
42 *The Guardian*, 7 Mar. 2020.
43 Andrew Noymer and Michel Garenne, 'The 1918 influenza epidemic's effects on sex differentials in mortality in the United States', *Population and Development Review*, 26:3 (2000), pp 566–7.
44 Herbert French, 'The clinical features of the influenza epidemic 1918–19', *Ministry of Health, Report on the Pandemic of Influenza, 1918–19* (London, 1920), pp 90–91.
45 William J. Thompson, 'Mortality from influenza in Ireland', *Journal of the Statistical and Social Inquiry Society of Ireland*, 14:1 (1920), pp 1–14.
46 *Fifty-sixth Detailed Annual Report of the Registrar-General (Ireland)*, p. xvi.
47 Ruth Barrington, *Health, Medicine and Politics in Ireland, 1900–1970* (Dublin, 1987), p. 75.
48 *Irish News*, 13 Nov. 1918.
49 Niall Johnson, *Britain and the 1918–19 Influenza Pandemic: A Dark Epilogue*, (London and New York, 2006), p. 193.
50 Typescript history compiled by John Baxter of the Baxter family of Dunadry, County Antrim, and Belfast, and related families, *c.* 1780–1980 (PRONI, T3582/1, pp 105–07).
51 Marsh, *The Spanish Flu in Ireland*, p. 174.
52 *Belfast Newsletter*, 13 Nov. 1918.
53 Marsh, *The Spanish Flu in Ireland*, pp 251–2
54 *Irish News*, 31 Oct. 1918; *Belfast Newsletter*, 31 Oct. 1918
55 *Annual Report of the Local Government Board for Ireland for Year Ended 31st March 1919*, pp xxxvii–xxxviii.
56 Marsh, *The Spanish Flu in Ireland*, p. 252
57 John M. Elyer, *Sir Arthur Newsholme and State Medicine, 1885–1935* (Cambridge, 1997), pp 268–9.
58 *Derry Journal*, 28 Oct. 1918.
59 Tom Quinn, *Flu: A Social History of Influenza* (London, 2008), p. 45.
60 *Mid-Ulster Mail*, 1 Mar. 1919.
61 Padraic Colum, *Arthur Griffith* (Dublin, 1959), pp 187–91.
62 *Tyrone Courier*, 5 Dec. 1918.
63 Charles Graves, *Invasion by Virus: Can it Happen Again* (London, 1969), p. 27.
64 Lori Loeb, 'Beating the flu: orthodox and commercial responses to influenza in Britain, 1889–1919', *Social History of Medicine*, 18:2 (2005), p. 220.
65 Returns: historical review of medical and sanitary work in the Irish Command during the war; Report of the medical and sanitary work of the Dublin and Curragh Brigade, sanitary work during the war, Curragh (TNA, WO 35/179/4, p. 3).

66 Loeb, 'Beating the flu', p. 209.
67 *Northern Whig*, 10 Dec. 1918, *Irish Times*, 17 Dec. 1918.
68 *Irish Independent*, 22 Feb. 1919.
69 Marsh, *The Spanish Flu in Ireland*, p. 144.
70 Johnson, *Britain and the 1918-19 Influenza Pandemic*, p. 145.
71 *Annual Report of the Local Government Board for Ireland for the year ended 31st March 1919*, p. xxviii.
72 Martin Gorsky, Bernard Harris, Patricia Marsh and Ida Milne, 'The 1918/19 influenza pandemic and COVID-19 in Ireland and the UK', *Journal Historical Social Research, Supplement*, 33 (2021), p. 210.
73 Marsh, *The Spanish Flu in Ireland*, p. 147.
74 Returns: historical review of the medical and sanitary work of the Cork district during the war period (TNA, WO 35/179/4, p. 4).
75 Returns: historical review of the medical and sanitary work of the Dublin and Curragh Brigades, sanitary work during the war, Curragh (TNA, WO 35/179/4, p. 2).
76 Gorsky, Harris, Marsh and Milne, 'The 1918/19 influenza pandemic', p. 210.
77 Belfast Board of Guardians meeting, 9 July 1918 (PRONI, BG/7/A/100); *Irish News*, 10 July 1918; *Belfast Newsletter*, 10 July 1918.
78 *Belfast Evening Telegraph*, 19 July 1918, *Belfast Newsletter*, 20 July 1918, *Armagh Guardian*, 26 July 1918.
79 *Annual Report of the Local Government Board for Ireland for the Year Ended 31st March 1919*, p. xxiii.
80 Carol R. Byerly, *Fever of War: The Influenza Epidemic in the U.S. Army During World War 1* (New York and London, 2005), p. 144.
81 Barrington, *Health, Medicine and Politics in Ireland*, p. 73.
82 Belfast Board of Guardians minutes, 25 June 1918 (PRONI, BG/7/A/99); *Irish News*, 26 June 1918; Belfast Board of Guardians minutes, 2 July 1918, 5 Nov. 1918, 26 Nov. 1918 and 3 Dec. 1918 (PRONI, BG/7/A/100); *Irish News*, 2 July 1918.
83 Londonderry Board of Guardians minutes, 9 Nov. 1918 (PRONI, BG/21/A/33); *Derry Journal*, 11 Nov. 1918.
84 Lurgan Board of Guardians minutes, 21 Nov. 1918 and 5 Dec. 1918 (PRONI, BG/22/A/114).
85 *Annual Report of the Local Government Board for Ireland for the Year Ended 31st March 1919*, p. xxvii.
86 Ibid., p. xxvi.
87 *Anglo-Celt*, 30 Nov. 1918; *Belfast Newsletter*, 14 Dec. 1918.
88 *Anglo-Celt*, 14 Dec. 1918.
89 Strabane Board of Guardians minutes, 27 Sep. 1918 and 8 Oct. 1918 (PRONI, BG/27/A/50).
90 Patricia Marsh, '"An enormous amount of distress among the poor": aid for the poor in Ulster during the influenza pandemic of 1918–19' in Virginia

Crossman and Peter Gray (eds), *Poverty and Welfare in Ireland, 1838-1948*, (Dublin, 2011), pp 213–17.
91 Marsh, *The Spanish Flu in Ireland*, p. 197.
92 Newry Urban District Council minutes, 4 Nov. 1918 (PRONI, LA/58/2/CA/6).
93 *Newry Reporter*, 29 Oct. 1918; *Newry Reporter*, 28 Nov. 1918.
94 *Newry Reporter*, 16 Nov. 1918, 11 Jan. 1919; *Belfast Newsletter*, 13 Jan. 1919.
95 *Irish News*, 23 Dec. 1918.
96 *Irish News*, 18 Nov 1918; *Belfast Newsletter*, 18 Nov. 1918; *Mid Ulster Mail*, 17 Nov. 1918, 30 Nov. 1918 and 7 Dec. 1918.
97 *Belfast Newsletter*, 21 Nov. 1918, *Anglo-Celt*, 30 Nov. 1918, 1 Feb. 1919, 15 Feb. 1919.
98 Fred R. Van Hartesveldt, 'Manchester' in Fred R. Van Hartesveldt (ed.), *The 1918–1919 Pandemic of Influenza: The Urban Impact in the Western World* (Lampeter, 1992), pp 91–103.
99 Marsh, *The Spanish Flu in Ireland*, pp 245–7.

7

Rev. John Redmond, vicar of Ballymacarrett
Army chaplain, peace maker and temperance advocate

BRIAN M. WALKER

On 25 November 1929, the *Belfast Newsletter* described Rev. John Redmond as 'one of the best known ministers in the Church of Ireland'. It recorded how from 1920 until his recent resignation he had served as vicar of St Patrick's church and parish, Ballymacarrett, east Belfast, home to more members of the Church of Ireland than any other parish in the country. The paper noted how he had done 'a vast amount of organizing work in his parish', described him as 'one of the keenest temperance reformers of modern times' and referred to his wartime service as a chaplain. No mention was made of his sterling efforts to end rioting and restore peace in the years 1920–22, perhaps reflecting a desire to forget and to move on from that deeply troubled period. In 1960, however, Redmond published a history of Ballymacarrett parish, which included 'vivid records of social and political upheavals in the nineteen-twenties'.[1] About his wartime experiences, like many others, he chose not to speak or publish. But he wrote diaries during his service as a chaplain, and these, along with other papers from the war, have recently been deposited by his family in the Somme Museum at Newtownards, County Down. His writings, published and unpublished, along with press reports of his activities, give a special view of events at this time.

John Redmond spent nearly 40 years in the full-time ministry of the Church of Ireland. At the beginning of 1912, however, he was neither a member of the Church of Ireland nor even resident in Ireland. Redmond was not the original family name. His parents were Johnston and Elizabeth Redmond of Grange House, Annaghmore, north County Armagh. The family name originally had been Redman but it was changed to Redmond in the late nineteenth century. Even today some family relatives in County

Armagh still carry the name Redman. John Redmond was born on 5 February 1876. The 1901 family census return records his father as a Methodist and his mother as a member of the Church of Ireland, while two siblings are Methodist and the other two Church of Ireland. In the 1911 census both Johnston and Elizabeth are recorded as Methodist while all four siblings are listed as Church of Ireland.[2] John was not at home on either of these census nights (he was in Kilkenny in 1901), but we know that he followed the faith of his father. In 1896 he entered Methodist College Belfast (theological department).[3] In 1899, he gained his Bachelor of Arts degree in philosophy from the Royal University of Ireland and subsequently was ordained in the Methodist ministry.

After some time on various Methodist circuits, he left in 1904 for India, After a year in Hassan, Redmond spent seven years as a Methodist missionary in Mysore, southern India, especially among the tea planters. After he left in 1912, the superintendent of the Wesleyan Mission in Bangalore wrote of him that his work had 'demanded long journeys, exposure to heat and rain, much horse riding and a good deal of "roughing" while his dealing with the planters required great patience, tact and perseverance'. An extract from the Mysore District Methodist report for 1911 noted: 'We will greatly miss Mr Redmond's bright and breezy personality'.[4] However, as an obituary observed many years later, during his stay in India 'he was redrawn to the Church of Ireland'.[5] He returned to Ireland in early 1912, served briefly in Cork and then resigned from the Methodist ministry. He was ordained in the Church of Ireland as a deacon in December 1912 and as a priest in December 1913 in St Anne's cathedral, Belfast. He served as a curate in St Aidan's, Belfast, 1912–15, and Holywood, County Down, 1915–16.

Military service

John Redmond was interviewed for military service on 16 December 1915, and was commissioned as a temporary chaplain in the forces, 4th class (ranking as a captain) from 1 January 1916.[6] In late January he was appointed a chaplain with the Mediterranean Expeditionary Force and sent to Egypt where he served with the King's Own Yorkshires. He was posted to the 31st Division in France in May 1916 and then, on 16 June, to Doullens at the Somme, although not with the Ulster Division. He was based at a casualty clearing station 15 miles from the frontline. He visited and comforted the wounded, wrote letters for patients and to family relations of those who had died, and conducted funerals. In his diary on 12 July 1916 he recorded:

> On the 1st inst. the 'big' advance began and since then I have had very little time for anything beyond my work as chaplain to this casualty clearing station. For the first three days we worked two of the nights as well as throughout the days. It was very fatiguing but we were all glad to do all we could for the poor wounded men they were sending our way. ... During these first three days we must have taken in about 1,000 wounded.[7]

In his diary at this time he wrote:

> War is a barbarous thing and cruel and atrocious beyond words. This comes home to a man with a shock as one sees young men coming in from the battlefield with the most terrible gashes and wounds – faces broken and swollen into all shapes and into no shape, limbs blown off and bones stripped of their flesh for many square inches.[8]

Redmond then applied to go to the frontline and to join the 36th (Ulster) Division. Eventually, after serving with the 6th Brigade, on 12 May 1917 he arrived with the 9th and 10th Royal Inniskilling Fusiliers, part of the Ulster Division. By June 1917, at the Battle of Messines, he was based at an advanced aid post at Dranoutre, near Locre in Belgium. The battle plan involved men of the Ulster Division fighting alongside men of the 16th (Irish) Division. Early on the morning of 7 June a badly wounded officer from the Irish Division was brought to the post. He was 56-year-old Major Willie Redmond, the nationalist MP for East Clare, and brother of John Redmond, leader of the Irish Parliamentary Party. He had been rescued by Private John Meeke, a stretcher-bearer of the 11th Royal Inniskilling Fusiliers. Rev. Redmond recorded his first meeting with Major Redmond:

> I said, 'Are you Major Willie Redmond?' and he said yes. I said, 'I am John Redmond'. He was amused for a moment and seeing my uniform that I was a chaplain he said 'Padre, I am dying' and he asked me a question which showed clearly that he wanted spiritual consolation. Before saying anything more I wanted to put things straight between us. Knowing he was a Roman Catholic I explained that I was Church of Ireland and he said that he always had a great respect for the Church of Ireland ... I gave him the guidance he asked for.[9]

Rev. Redmond stayed with Major Redmond throughout the day. He died from the shock of his wounds at around 6.30 pm. Before the end, two Catholic chaplains gave him Extreme Unction. After his death, Rev. Redmond wrote to his widow, Eleanor:

When he was brought in he said he was going to die. I helped the doctors dress his wounds. The doctor did everything possible to ease his pain and I did what I could to sooth him and cheer him up. He bore his pain most patiently. He asked me to write to you and give you the following messages. He sent you his love and said 'please thank her for all that she has done for me and tell her that if we do not meet again in this world I hope we shall meet in the next.'[10]

Eleanor Redmond replied to John Redmond on 21 June:

I am indeed grateful to you for your kind letter and especially for your kindness to my dear husband in his hour of need. How glad I am that you were able to be with him and I am sure he was pleased to find himself so tenderly cared for by the 36th Division. It was always to him a source of joy that there was such a friendly feeling between the two Irish Divisions.

She went on: 'I wish you would please thank for me all your friends who helped him in his last hours. Is the soldier who first carried him alive and where is he, also the stretcher-bearers? I would especially like to thank them'.[11]

Major Redmond was buried in the graveyard of a nearby convent at Locre. Unusually, after the war his body was not moved to one of the major Commonwealth cemeteries but remained at Locre. In succeeding decades, the grave fell into disrepair and Redmond was largely forgotten. All this changed with the publication in 1995 of Terence Denman's book, *A Lonely Grave: The Life and Death of William Redmond*, which included Rev. John Redmond's correspondence with Eleanor Redmond. His grave was restored and his story became widely known and appreciated. Private Meeke, about whom Eleanor Redmond had enquired, was awarded the Military Medal for his bravery on the day. Meeke survived the war and was discharged in June 1919, due to wounds. He returned home to Benvarden, Ballymoney, County Antrim, but died of tuberculosis in 1923. He was buried in an unmarked grave at nearby Derrykeighan Old Graveyard. New interest in the 1990s in the fate of local soldiers led to the organisation of a public subscription which resulted in the erection of a headstone to Meeke in 2004.

In June 2017 there were major events at Messines to mark the centenary of the battle. A ceremony was held at Wytschaete to unveil a memorial depicting John Meeke carrying Willie Redmond off the battlefield. This action was seen as symbolising unity between unionist and nationalist soldiers at the battle. The unveiling was attended by members of the families of Willie Redmond and John Meeke. Present also were His Royal Highness Prince William of the United Kingdom, Her Royal Highness Princess Astrid of Belgium and Taoiseach Enda Kenny of Ireland.[12]

During his time as a chaplain, Rev. John Redmond wrote many letters to families about their deceased sons or husbands. A letter from him notifying the mother of cadet Jasper McCleery Warke, Royal Fusiliers (Tyrone Volunteers), of his death from wounds received in action was published in the *Londonderry Sentinel* on 20 September 1917:

> Your gallant son was a great friend of mine and I cannot tell you how much I was grieved of his death. I prepared him for confirmation ... and gave him his first communion. He was a good boy and very fine soldier. He was a thorough master of the Lewis gun. I constantly miss him as I move about the battalion. He was so cheery.

He received back letters from grateful families which he kept and 70 of these are now deposited at the Somme Museum. One was from Jeannie McCarter from Derry, dated 27 December 1917:

> It was only a short time that I said goodbye to my boy on his way to the front and I little thought I should have to say goodbye for ever in this world. I am a widow of less than a year and that makes the loss of my eldest son all the harder to bear.

In her final words she acknowledged the tough job that Redmond had: 'You must have many sad letters to write and much sadness and pain all around you.'[13]

Parish concerns

In late 1918, John Redmond returned to Belfast where he served as a curate at St Anne's cathedral until January 1920 when he was appointed vicar of St Patrick's church and parish, Ballymacarrett. The Church of Ireland faced special challenges in Belfast at this time. In 1861, members of the church numbered 30,080, or 24.6 per cent of the town's population, but by 1926 members numbered 133,100 or 32.1 per cent of the population.[14] They included many of the poorest inhabitants in the city. St Patrick's parish, in the shadow of the shipyards, contained a very large number of working class members of the church, many of whom suffered social and economic deprivation. From a census he conducted in 1920 Redmond reckoned that there were some 18,000 nominal Church of Ireland people in the parish, but only about 5,000 had any connection with the church.[15]

To meet this challenge, he engaged new clerical and lay staff, including female workers, and volunteers. They established Sunday schools and young people's organisations. He recorded how: 'There was widespread unemployment in the parish and poverty that in those days accompanied unemployment. Many of our lapsed people, for want of decent clothes, or for other reasons, never came to the parish church'. To reach out to these members of his congregation he organised the erection of a number of mission halls in the parish, the first one opening in June 1922. They served designated districts in the parish. At the dedication of this first hall, Charles Grierson, bishop of Down, Connor and Dromore, spoke of how he and Redmond had discussed the 'crying need' for these halls where 'men and women in the surrounding streets could come as they were, without any special clothing, and feel at home'.[16]

Poverty and unemployment were deep concerns for Redmond and his staff. In the economic depression of 1921 and 1922 help from various funds was directed by them to assist those affected by unemployment, including 342 families between May and October 1922.[17] Conditions were worst during the general strike and coal strike of 1926. A *Belfast Telegraph* report of 18 December 1926 described how important relief work was being carried out among the poorer families of St Patrick's parish: 'Orders for groceries are being given weekly to over 300 families, while at the soup kitchens voluntarily carried on in St Patrick's school by ladies from Strandtown and Knock, 3000 meals of hot and nourishing food are distributed weekly'. It continued: 'Further, the suffering of the poor is mitigated in the parish through the same agency, the Canadian Flour Fund, and the Lord Mayor's Relief Fund'. The coal strike caused a severe shortage of fuel. To provide firewood for his parishioners Redmond bought the wooden cargo ship the *Argenta*, the former internment ship.[18] Some of his out-of-work parishioners then stripped the ship of all its wood which they used for their fires. Redmond later calculated that by the end of his ministry at Ballymacarrett more than £5,000 worth had been distributed for relief.[19]

Riots in Belfast, 1920

On 21 July 1920, following the funeral of policeman Lt Col. G.B. Smyth in Banbridge after his murder in Cork by the IRA, violence broke out in Belfast. In the shipyards, Protestant workers expelled known or suspected Sinn Féin supporters, followed by all Catholic workers and some Protestant labour supporters. Riots followed, including in Ballymacarrett. Protestant rioters went onto the Newtownards Road to attack and loot public houses and spirit grocery stores (stores which sold groceries and alcohol), which were mainly Catholic-owned. Redmond pushed through the crowd and sought to prevent these attacks. A report in the *Scotsman* recorded: 'Rev. John Redmond, a local Church of Ireland clergyman, pluckily got up in the frame of one of the broken windows of a spirit grocery and addressed the crowd, advising them to go home'. His words had little effect. 'His speech was followed by orations from half-drunken rioters who spoke of outrages which had recently been perpetrated by Sinn Feiners throughout Ireland'.[20]

The following afternoon Redmond returned to the Newtownards Road and overheard plans to loot Burke's large drapery business not far from St Patrick's. He hastened to Burke's to warn the proprietor. Then as he recorded in his book: 'The crowd soon came up opposite to the shop, and I walked up and down between the crowd and the shop. They looked unpleasant, but made no attempt to rush me and the shop was saved'.[21] On 30 November 1955, in a newspaper letter, C.E. Burke of 213–23 Newtownards Road recalled this event from 1920: 'I would personally like to thank the Rev. John Redmond then Vicar of Ballymacarrett for the assistance and help he gave me during the crisis, and for his outstanding courage which I believe saved my premises from being looted'.[22]

In his later account of events on this day, Redmond described how after the confrontation outside Burke's store dangerous crowds still remained on the Newtownards Road. He explained that there were relatively few police in Belfast because many had been drafted south, so he decided to take action. He sent a messenger to the Albert Bridge Orange Hall asking for help. About 60 men arrived, mostly ex-servicemen, including a drill sergeant. He put the sergeant in charge and the men 'formed fours'. Then, as he recorded: 'I asked them to march up and down the Newtownards Road and if they found a building threatened, to form up between it and the crowd. This they did for the rest of the evening till the crowds dispersed and no further breaches of the law took place'.[23] A report in the *Northern Whig*, 26 July 1920, observed that 'the greater peace [which] prevailed over the last two nights has been largely due to Redmond's volunteer patrols who have been able to do by persuasion what could not be done by other means'. The paper declared that Belfast owed 'a distinct debt to these public-minded citizens whose numbers, we trust, will be reinforced by others'.[24]

Given the success of these actions, Redmond decided to organise a volunteer force to patrol the parish. After getting the approval of the lord mayor and the police deputy commissioner, he placed advertisements in the press looking for volunteers. A large number came forward and he selected some 100, many of them ex-servicemen. In a newspaper article in 1960 he recalled: 'Some of the men wanted arms but I said there would be none of that. All they got was armlets. But their presence as they marched up and down in military formation put an end to a lot of looting which was going on at that time'.[25] His curate, Major Rev. Frederick Chestnutt-Chesney, took charge of the volunteers. Originally from England, Chestnutt-Chesney entered Trinity College Dublin in 1910. He enlisted in 1914 before completing his degree. At the Battle of Passchendaele, he took command of his battalion following the death of the commanding officer.

In 1919, he was awarded his BA by Trinity. He was appointed a curate in Ballymacarrett parish in early 1920.

Riots broke out again in Belfast after the murder of District Inspector Oswald Swanzy in Lisburn on 21 August 1920. The violence was extreme in Ballymacarrett and Redmond's original volunteer force was unable to cope with the crisis. Redmond personally intervened on a number of occasions to try to stop the rioting. On 25 August 1920, the *Belfast Newsletter* reported how the 'Rev. John Redmond, rector of St Patrick's, Ballymacarrett, accompanied by his church warden, Mr Toomath, spent a considerable time in appealing to members of the crowd to return to their homes, and this had a decidedly good effect'. The following day the paper stated that 'a serious situation was avoided through the timely intervention of the Vicar of Ballymacarrett' in a stone throwing incident between shipyard workers and Sinn Féin supporters.

That same day the *Irish News* recorded how Redmond and his curate, Major Rev. Chestnutt-Chesney, had worked throughout the night to calm things and declared that 'These gentlemen, at considerable risk, succeeded in saving Catholic property which was about to be destroyed'.[26] By Saturday night, 28 August, there was appreciable improvement in the Ballymacarrett district except for an incident of stone throwing between unionist and Sinn Féin mobs. With a headline, 'Mr Redmond's plucky conduct', the *Belfast Newsletter* reported: 'matters were assuming a grave complexion when the Vicar, at great personal risk, boldly walked in between the contending parties and by voice and gesture brought about a cessation of hostilities'.[27] The report continued:

> Before the engagement ended, the Clonallon Street mob captured a member of the Sinn Féin mob. This individual would have suffered serious injury but for the prompt manner in which he was rescued by Mr Redmond, who also escorted him across the main thoroughfare to his own territory.

An important factor in the reduction of violence in the Ballymacarrett district was a revival of John Redmond's idea of a volunteer force. On 26 August, an advertisement in the local press stated that, with the approval of the lord mayor and the commissioner of police, Redmond requested ex-servicemen of Ballymacarrett to meet him and Chestnutt-Chesney that evening at St Patrick's School, beside the church, for the formation of patrols 'to prevent further looting and destruction of property in Ballymacarrett'.[28] Many volunteers, including some of those who had served in July, came forward and were sworn in as special constables by two magistrates at the school. Patrols, organised by Redmond, Chestnutt-Chesney and another curate, J.E.K. Haddick, now operated along the Newtownards Road.

Their main duty was to protect property. They were allowed to carry batons and to make arrests. On 28 August, the *Belfast Newsletter* reported that 'The patrols were ... frequently instrumental in allaying excitement, and preventing the destruction and looting of shops'. At the end of 1920 the work of these special constables was superseded by the newly formed Ulster Special Constabulary (USC). Later, in one of John Redmond's obituaries, it was stated that his constables were forerunners of the USC.[29] We should note, however, that in his 1960 book Redmond emphasised that at the same time as his volunteers operated in Belfast, other loyalist volunteer groups sprang up in rural areas in response to the deteriorating security situation and raids by republicans on homes of loyalists for arms.[30]

On 26 August, a public appeal for peace from Ballymacarrett clergy, invited by Redmond, was published in the local press. It was signed by Redmond and three other Protestant clergy. They appealed to all their parishioners to exercise the utmost restraint and to use all their influence on behalf of law and order. They declared: 'Let us reflect that if we counter wrong doing on the part of others by wrong doing on our part we make ourselves as bad as they are, and profit nothing'.[31] Later, in his 1960 book, Redmond stated that he had written to Father George Crolly of St Matthew's Catholic church, Ballymacarrett, on this subject but he did not answer his letter. He wrote: 'Owing to the extremely disturbed conditions of the district, my letter may not have reached him'.[32] On the evening of Sunday, 29 August Redmond preached in St Patrick's church on the situation. In his sermon, reported in the press, he expressed his grief for all the acts of looting, burning and lawlessness that had taken place in the Ballymacarrett area. He pointed out 'the sin and folly of such work' and strongly condemned 'the doctrine of an eye for an eye, a tooth for a tooth'. He warned how reprisals led to counter reprisals. He urged parents to keep young people indoors and asked for 'every respectable man' to sign up as a 'special constable'.[33]

'Strong drink' and riots, 1920–22

In his sermon in St Patrick's on 29 August, John Redmond denounced the part that 'strong drink' had played in the riots. In sermons in following months Redmond returned to this theme of the damage done by alcohol, not just in the riots but among families in the parish, leading to poverty and domestic 'quarrels'.[34] He argued that the recently wrecked spirit groceries, which he had sought to protect, should not reopen. He reckoned that before the riots there were 54 spirit groceries in the parish. The owners of the wrecked stores were compensated and he believed that they should remained closed. He was conscious that most of the stores were Catholic-owned, but he pointed out that there was a strong temperance movement in the Catholic Church.[35]

In October 1920, he inaugurated a 'crusade' against the reopening of spirit groceries in the Ballymacarrett district.[36] Opposition to spirit groceries not only in east Belfast but elsewhere in Northern Ireland was now backed by other temperance supporters and organisations. In November, Redmond was co-opted as a member of the executive committee of the Ulster Temperance Council.[37] On 4 February 1921, a deputation from the council, including Redmond, was received by the standing committee of the Ulster Unionist Council. They were addressed by Sir Edward Carson, on his last morning as Unionist Party leader. He expressed support for temperance reform, but urged 'moderation', and warned that the temperance movement could cause dangerous political division.[38] Redmond took this advice to heart and at the 1921 general election declared his support for his local Unionist Party candidate.[39] Later, however, he and others would take on the unionist establishment over temperance issues.

During 1921, Redmond continued with his parish work and his temperance advocacy, especially his campaign against spirit groceries.[40] He also continued to comment on the broader situation in his parish magazine and in sermons which were reported in the press. In the March magazine he welcomed the incoming Northern Ireland government and urged that they should provide better housing, raise the school leaving age to 16 and free 'our beloved Ulster from the deadly vampire of the Liquor Traffic which is sucking our life blood'.[41] On Sunday, 26 June, Redmond, who was a keen Orangeman, preached in the Grosvenor Hall, Belfast, at a special, well-attended memorial service, organised by the Orange Order, to mark the anniversary of the Battle of the Somme. He said that the sacrifices of the Ulster Division had earned for Ulster the position it now held, and referred to the opening a few days earlier of the parliament by the king. He declared that they had a duty to maintain this position, and also to ensure, as Orangemen, that 'no political or religious minority in Ulster could justly complain of bigotry or intolerance'.[42]

In a sermon in St Patrick's church on 17 July 1921, he spoke about recent riots in Belfast.[43] He stated that attacks by Sinn Féin gunmen on Crown forces and Orange parades had started the violence, but he then denounced strongly the rioting by loyalists in retaliation, fuelled in part, he believed, by 'strong drink'. He also expressed concern that young people were being drawn into the riots. He declared that the churches had failed in their responsibility to influence these people against violence. Subsequently, Redmond established a number of social clubs for young men in his parish to keep them off the streets. Succeeding months in 1921 witnessed considerable violence in Belfast, including the Ballymacarrett district.

The first months of 1922 saw matters deteriorate even further. The parish magazine in January recorded that due to rioting and shooting: 'it was necessary to give up our Sunday School and service for the time being'.[44] The violence continued with many deaths, including the murder on 24 March of six members of the Catholic McMahon family in north Belfast following the murder of two members of the USC in central Belfast. In response to this heightened violence, in late March the four church leaders, Church of Ireland bishop, Dr Charles Grierson, Catholic bishop, Dr Joseph McRory, Presbyterian moderator, Dr W.J. Lowe and Methodist president, Dr W.H. Smyth, issued a joint manifesto. They denounced the taking of life and urged Christian citizens to refrain from 'lawlessness and disorder' and to 'recognise the rights of others who differ in creed and politics to live in peace'.[45] On 8 April, the churches in Belfast ran a 'Good-will Sunday', when the church leaders' manifesto was read out in most of the city's churches.

That afternoon a public meeting at the Custom House steps in central Belfast, attended by some 3,000 people, was addressed by a number of Protestant clergy, including John Redmond. He said that he wanted to speak to the gunmen. He declared:

> Why are Roman Catholic gunmen killing their Protestant fellow citizens: what did they hope to accomplish by it? And he would ask the Protestant gunmen, who had been committing horrible crimes in the city, were they going to promote happiness for themselves or for anybody by lawlessness and outrage.[46]

He warned of the danger of reprisals. The violence continued, but was mostly over by the end of June. The parish magazine in late May recorded the murder of two Ballymacarrett residents.[47] Ten-year-old Georgina Campbell was killed on 26 May on the Newtownards Road by a sniper's bullet, and William Patterson was one of three Protestants killed at a cooper's yard in Little Patrick Street in central Belfast on 19 May.

Temperance and controversy

The year 1923 saw considerable success for Redmond's ambitions for temperance reform, but also an acrimonious and much publicised incident with one of his curates over the temperance issue (which was not mentioned in his book). The Intoxicating Liquor Act (Northern Ireland), passed in June 1923, wiped out all spirit groceries, not just in the Ballymacarrett district but throughout Northern Ireland.[48] Spirit grocers had to give up their spirits licence or their grocery business and if the licence was given up compensation was paid. Other reforms included Sunday closing of licensed premises and the raising of the age limit for the purchase of alcohol from 14 to 18 years of age. On Sunday morning, 9 March 1923, however, his curate, Major Rev. Frederick Chestnutt-Chesney, preached a controversial sermon.[49] He spoke on the subject of sin and vice. He declared that 'sin is a wrong against God', and that drinking and gambling are vices, not sins. This greatly upset Redmond, and at the end of the sermon he flatly contradicted his curate to say that certainly they were sins.

Afterwards, Chestnutt-Chesney insisted on a public apology from Redmond for his rebuke. When Redmond refused, the curate appealed to Bishop Grierson who declined to order such an apology. Consequently, Chestnutt-Chesney resigned and moved to a parish in London. On 13 June, an event was held in his honour in St Patrick's parish hall, involving many parishioners, but not the vicar.[50] He was presented with an illuminated address which has been recently donated to St Patrick's by his family. The address thanked him for his 'faithful ministration during these three strenuous years' and declared: 'Your practical work of organizing patrols during the riots of 1920 to prevent looting, in which your military experience was of inestimable value, will not be forgotten.'

This was not the end of the matter. Chestnutt-Chesney then petitioned a Church of Ireland diocesan court in an appeal against the refusal of the bishop to order a public apology. The court, under Lord Justice Moore, along with two church representatives, met in open session in Clarence Place Hall in Belfast on 1 October 1923.[51] Grierson and Redmond were the respondents. The *Belfast Newsletter* recorded; 'When Mr Redmond entered the hall he was greeted with applause, and there was an enthusiastic demonstration when Mr Chesney made his appearance'.[52] In his evidence Chestnutt-Chesney said 'he could accept no private apology for a public insult'. Redmond explained that he had spoken out for fear that some recently reformed young church members would feel 'they were free to go back to the drinking and gambling they had given up'. The bishop explained that he believed that Redmond should have raised his objections privately after the service. He had been willing to order a public apology by Redmond but he felt that if he had done so he would also have had to state that the view expounded in the sermon was erroneous, two clergy would have been discredited. So he decided not to act.

There was great interest in the case, local and national. The London *Times* of 12 October had a headline: 'Sin and vice: an Irish clerical dispute'. In its verdict, delivered on 11 October, the court dismissed the petition.[53] They backed the bishop on the grounds that he had offered to the petitioner a private apology from the vicar, not for his criticism (which the bishop agreed with) of the sermon but for where and how it was delivered. This offer was rejected by Chestnutt-Chesney. The court accepted that the bishop had used fairly his discretion to decide that it would not be in the public or church interest to order a public apology. The bishop's costs were made payable by the petitioner. At the same time, they stated that 'while prompted by the best motives' Redmond should not have reproved his curate in front of the congregation before speaking to him in private, and ordered him to meet his own costs.

Undaunted by this incident, John Redmond continued with his temperance advocacy. Temperance supporters in Northern Ireland were greatly encouraged by the 1923 Licensing Act and the rise of the prohibition movement in America. Redmond and others now focused on the idea of local option, that is the right of local districts to close licensed premises. On 11 November 1926, however, Sir James Craig in a speech at Newry stated that the Northern Ireland cabinet had decided there would be no further temperance legislation, except some minor improvements to the 1923 Act. This caused a considerable reaction, including a speech by Redmond in the Belfast City YMCA hall on 20 November, leading to a newspaper headline: 'Local option. Vicar of Ballymacarrett and Sir James Craig – a great moral question'.[54] Redmond thanked the Prime Minister for the 1923 Act and then declared that 'it was a painful thing to them to find it necessary to express publicly their great dissatisfaction with his Newry statement'. He ended with a promise of an 'extensive campaign for educating public opinion on the question of local option', so that by the next general election it would not be possible to deny this reform.[55]

The following year 1927 saw continued, widespread public controversy over temperance issues. At the end of the year, on 23 December, the *Belfast Newsletter* recorded: 'The question of local option loomed large on the political horizon during the year'. With a parliamentary majority of only 14 due to losses to labour and independent unionists at the 1925 general election, the Unionist Party now found itself faced with division and potential serious losses over temperance matters. In reaction, on 12 July 1927, at his first attendance at a Twelfth of July demonstration in five years, Craig (now Lord Craigavon) spoke to stress the need for unionist unity and to announce plans to end proportional representation (PR) in local parliamentary elections – a move intended to help curtail both independents and small parties.[56] Redmond and other temperance advocates continued to challenge government policies over temperance matters.[57] At the 1929 general election three local option candidates came forward but were unsuccessful, due partly to the abolition of PR and also to divisions among temperance supporters. Labour and independent unionists lost seats while both the unionist and nationalist parties gained seats.[58] The removal of PR in parliamentary elections was not directed against nationalists but did damage their political prospects because it restricted potential allies in the form of independents and labour MPs.

Parish affairs

During Redmond's ministry Ballymacarrett parish witnessed great organisational growth. In late 1928 the Dublin-based *Church of Ireland Gazette* published an article about the problems facing the church in Belfast.[59] This led to a response from Redmond. On 22 February 1929, the *Gazette* carried a statement from him with an appeal, plus a page listing the parish activities. Staff consisted of Redmond, two curates, three Church Army members and two female workers, plus 179 Sunday School teachers and 157 members of choirs. On a Sunday there was a morning service at St Patrick's, followed by another six evening services, one in St Patrick's and five in mission halls. There were ten young men's Bible classes, 20 Sunday schools, 23 scout, boys' brigade and guide companies, and six young men's clubs, as well the Mothers' Union and the Girls' Friendly Society.

Redmond appealed for financial support of £1,000 to cover parish debts including some £600 for the building of one of the mission halls. He also expressed a wish that other members of the church might 'adopt' one of the mission districts. This appeal quickly brought in subscriptions from all over Ireland. On 15 May 1929, a conference presided over by the bishop of Meath, Dr John Orr, was held in the Gregg Hall, Dublin, to discuss Ballymacarrett parish and its needs. The outcome was the appointment of a committee to establish the Southern Church Mission to Ballymacarrett.[60] Money was raised from southern sources which led to the building of St Martin's church, off the Lower Newtownards Road, which opened in 1933, with the appointment of the incumbent residing with the bishop of Meath, an arrangement unique in the Church of Ireland.

By 1933, however, John Redmond was no longer vicar of St Patrick's. He took ill during 1929. In the July magazine he reported that his doctors had said that 'nothing worse was the matter with me than over-fatigue of brain and body as the result of a long period of over-work and strain'.[61] He failed to recover and in late November he resigned. In a farewell letter in December to his parishioners he explained that he had been 'feeling the strain and pressure of the work so much that I felt compelled to ask the bishop if he could find me a parish where I could get relief from the present strain and yet do useful work for the Church'.[62] He was appointed curate-in-charge of the small rural parish of Kilbride, County Antrim, comprising some 130 families. He remained there until his retirement in 1951 when he moved back to the family home at Tartaraghan, County Armagh.

In 1958, however, 82-year-old John Redmond went on one final 'peace mission', at the request of the archbishop of Armagh, Dr J.A.F. Gregg. The archbishop had a problem with Tullaniskin (Newmills) parish, County Tyrone. Several meetings between him and parochial nominators to select a new rector had failed to reach an agreement. In protest the nominators left the church, followed by the vestry members, the organist and the sexton. With other parishioners they decamped to worship in a nearby Orange hall. The keys and books of the church were handed over to the archbishop. The controversy attracted considerable attention in both the local and Belfast press. Redmond was asked to intervene by the archbishop who appointed him rector *in loco*. He and his wife Margaret visited every parishioner, usually on foot, as neither could drive a car. After nine months of patient work they succeeded in restoring parish harmony and the appointment of a new rector. He then wrote a pamphlet describing the 'revolt' of Tullaniskin parish.[63] He sent the first copy to the new archbishop, Dr James McCann, who, worried that it would bring back tensions, asked for it to be withdrawn. Redmond agreed. A few copies, marked 'not for publication', have survived. One copy owned by Armagh church historian, Canon Ted Fleming, who officiated at John Redmond's funeral, is the source of the above information and has now been deposited in the RCB library for consultation.

Rev. John Redmond died on 17 July 1967, aged 91, and he was buried in the graveyard at Tartaraghan parish church. His death came after 16 years of a peaceful retirement and 21 years of service in a small rural parish. These quiet years came after a very different 13 years in the eye of the storm, first on the battlefields of Western Europe and secondly on the troubled streets of east Belfast. There is no memorial to John Redmond. But he left us his war diaries and other documents, and his parish history. These sources, along with the press coverage of his activities, serve to give a unique insight into the human cost of the war in Europe and of the 'Troubles' in Ireland which followed. They also enable us to appreciate the bravery and special qualities of John Redmond.

Notes

1. John Redmond, *Church, State, Industry, 1827–1929, in East Belfast* (Belfast, 1960), hereafter Redmond, *Church and State*.
2. The returns of the 1901 and 1911 census are held in the National Archives of Ireland and are available online (https://census.nationalarchives.ie).
3. Record of Rev. John Redmond (Methodist Historical Society, Edgehill College, Belfast).
4. D.A. Rees, 11 Oct. 1912; Mysore District Methodist Report 1911 (Somme Museum, Newtownards, County Down, Redmond Papers).
5. *Belfast Telegraph*, 18 July 1967.
6. www.kilbrideparishchurch.org.redmond-rev-john.

7 John Redmond's diary for 1915–16, pp 110–11 (Somme Museum, Redmond Papers, E1774).
8 Ibid, p. 118.
9 John Redmond's diary for 1917, pp 79–80 (Somme Museum, Redmond Papers, E1774).
10 Terence Denman, *A Lonely Grave: The Life and Death of William Redmond* (Dublin, 1995), p. 120.
11 Eleanor Redmond to Rev. John Redmond, 21 June 1917; John Redmond's diary for 1917, pp 80–81 (Somme Museum, Redmond Papers, E1774).
12 'Willie Redmond and the commemoration of the centenary of the Battle of Messines' (https://www.westernfrontassociation.com/latest-news/2018/january-2018/willie-redmond-and-the-commemoration-of-the-centenary-of-the-battle-of-messines); *Irish Times*, 7 June 2017. Also, article by Ronan McGreevy in *Irish Times*, 22 July 2017.
13 Jeannie McCarter to Rev. John Redmond, 27 Dec. 1917 (Somme Museum, Redmond Papers, E1774).
14 W.E. Vaughan and A.J. Fitzpatrick, *Irish Historical Statistics, Population, 1821–1971* (Dublin, 1978), pp 52, 70.
15 Redmond, *Church and State*, p. 34.
16 Ibid., p. 56.
17 Ibid., p. 59.
18 Ibid., pp 84–6.
19 Ibid., p. 86.
20 *Scotsman*, 23 July 1920.
21 Redmond, *Church and State*, pp 12-3
22 *Belfast Newsletter*, 30 Nov. 1952.
23 Redmond, *Church and state*, p.13.
24 Alan F. Parkinson, *A Difficult Birth: The Early Years of Northern Ireland, 1920–25* (Dublin, 2020), p. 41.
25 *Belfast Telegraph*, 7 Dec. 1960.
26 *Irish News*, 26 Aug. 1920.
27 *Belfast Newsletter*, 30 Aug. 1920.
28 Ibid, 26 Aug. 1920.
29 *Belfast Telegraph*, 18 July 1967.
30 Redmond, *Church and state*, pp 23–4.
31 Ibid., p. 29.
32 Ibid., pp 28–9.
33 *Belfast Newsletter*, 30 Aug. 1920
34 Ibid., 27 Sept. 1920, 25 Oct. 1920.
35 *Church of Ireland Gazette*, 8 Oct. 1920.
36 Redmond, *Church and State*, pp 36–8; *Belfast Newsletter*, 1 Nov. 1920.
37 *Belfast Newsletter*, 4 Nov. 1920.
38 Ibid., 6 Feb. 1921.
39 *Northern Whig*, 30 Apr. 1921.

40 *Belfast Newsletter*, 6 Jan. 1921, 21 March 1921; Redmond, *Church and State*, p. 37.
41 Redmond, *Church and State*, p. 43.
42 *Belfast Newsletter*, 27 June 1921.
43 Ibid., 18 July 1921.
44 Redmond, *Church and State*, p. 48.
45 *Ballymoney Free Press*, 13 Apr. 1922.
46 *Northern Whig*, 10 Apr. 1922.
47 Redmond, *Church and State*, p. 54.
48 Ibid., p. 38.
49 See letter in *Church of Ireland Gazette*, 31 Mar. 1923.
50 *Belfast Telegraph*, 14 June 1923.
51 *Belfast Newsletter*, 2 Oct. 1923; *The Times*, 2 Oct. 1923.
52 Ibid.
53 *Belfast Newsletter*, 12 Oct. 1923; *The Times*, 12 Oct. 1923.
54 *Belfast Newsletter*, 22 Nov. 1923.
55 Ibid.
56 Ibid., 13 July 1927; Brian M. Walker, *A Political History of the Two Irelands: From Partition to Peace* (Basingstoke, 2012), p. 21.
57 Meeting in Portadown, *Portadown Times,* 28 Sep. 1928.
58 Brian M. Walker (ed.), *Parliamentary Election Results, 1918–92* (Dublin, 1992), pp 49–51.
59 *Church of Ireland Gazette*, 16 Nov. 1928.
60 Redmond, *Church and State*, pp 100–03.
61 Ibid., p. 104.
62 Ibid., p. 105.
63 John Redmond, *The Tullaniskin (Newmills) Clonoe Parish Revolt, 1958–9* (1962).

8

The USC and the formation of the Northern Ireland state, 1920–22

BRIAN BARTON

From its formation in November 1920 to its disbandment in March 1970, the Ulster Special Constabulary (USC) has attracted much controversy and criticism. This chapter traces the origins of the force, and asks whether it was really the pre-war 'UVF in all but name.'[1] It reviews the debate over whether the term 'pogrom' is applicable to the 'Troubles' in Belfast (1920–22), evaluates the role and record of the USC then, and sets this in the context of the creation of, and challenges to, the six-county state. It also considers how events in Southern Ireland, and the policies adopted by its leaders, impacted on Northern Ireland, and discusses the British government's response to developments in Ireland during the revolutionary period. The legacy of these years is also briefly appraised.

Levels of tension in the north-east rose sharply from mid-1920. This was related to: the looming prospect of partition which added significance to the Sinn Féin/nationalist parties' successes in the local government elections that year; deepening recession; the region's tradition of 'holy war' and, above all, the impact of the Anglo-Irish War which spilled over into Ulster. The murder of Divisional Commissioner, Colonel Gerald Smyth, in Cork by the IRA (17 July 1920) resulted in sectarian disorder in Banbridge, his native town, and in Dromore, Lisburn, Newtownards and Bangor. It also 'roused ... great anger'[2] in Belfast where there were 21 deaths in four days. Already labour relations were a 'powder keg',[3] partly because of the belief that Catholics had taken servicemen's jobs in wartime, and presumption, 'generally speaking', that they 'were approving the outrages'[4] in Ireland. Catholic property was attacked, hostile crowds of up to 10,000 clashed on the streets and 'disloyal elements' – 5,500 Catholics and 1,850 'rotten Prods' – were expelled from the shipyards and engineering works. This prompted the Dáil in Dublin to instigate a boycott of goods produced in the city. The murder of DI Oswald Swanzy in Lisburn (22 August 1920) by an IRA unit from Cork resulted in many Catholics living there being expelled during two days of rioting. The violence spread; in Belfast, 33 people lost their lives in one week. Already a pattern was emerging, IRA action precipitating loyalist reprisals and sectarian confrontation.

Establishment of the Ulster Special Constabulary

The Ulster Volunteer Force (UVF), an antecedent of the USC, originated in 1912. It had emerged spontaneously amongst grassroots unionists in opposition to the third Home Rule Bill. The Unionist Party's leadership began recruiting the force in December 1912, in part, 'to deter … indiscriminate violence'[5] by its supporters. By 1914 almost 100,000 had joined, roughly one-third of whom enlisted in the 36th (Ulster) Division after the outbreak of war. It numbered 50,000 in May 1918, and the RIC Inspector General warned that it was ready to resume its activities if required by political circumstances.[6]

In mid-1920, the UVF revived and various paramilitary groupings mushroomed up throughout the North. Their formation was rooted in: fears that the IRA campaign would spread to Ulster; evidence that support for Sinn Féin was increasing; doubts regarding the capacity of Dublin Castle to preserve order; suspicions regarding the reliability of the RIC and concern that British troops deployed regionally would be transferred south as the Anglo-Irish War intensified. By August they had been established in all six north-eastern counties, bar County Down.[7] Their distribution was largely determined by the initiative of local leaders, the traditions of the area and the degree of concern felt by citizens about the imminence of any breakdown in order. Where conducive circumstances pertained, various organisations sprang up. In June, Basil Brooke established one of the earliest. Though 'using the material of the UVF', he called it 'Fermanagh Vigilance' as he hoped to attract Catholic recruits but, he wrote, 'owing to distrust it failed'[8] to do so. In east Belfast, Rev. John Redmond, rector of St Patrick's church, Ballymacarrett, 'conceived the idea of organizing a volunteer force … for the protection of human life and property … regardless of creed, class or political affiliation.' One hundred, 'mostly ex-servicemen not long demobilized,'[9] were enrolled. In east Ulster, 'the last bastion of constitutional nationalism in Ireland',[10] such vigilante groups emerged more slowly.

On 25 June 1920, the Ulster Unionist Council decided to revive the UVF as the 'best and safest way' to avoid 'serious trouble'.[11] In September, when James Craig addressed British ministers in London, he pleaded for the formation of an armed, state-sponsored special constabulary using the reinvigorated UVF as its nucleus. He claimed that his supporters were 'losing faith' in the government, and 'threatening an immediate recourse to arms which would precipitate'[12] serious inter-communal conflict. He also pressed Westminster politicians to appoint a senior civil servant to the north-east to expedite preparations for partition. Distrustful of Westminster and Dublin Castle, unionist leaders were anxious to consolidate the putative state of 'Northern Ireland', as a means of frustrating any attempt to force the region under the jurisdiction of any future Dublin parliament.

Some British politicians and officials opposed the initiation of an auxiliary police force. But Lloyd George was more pragmatic. He was influenced by the need to release more troops for service elsewhere in Ireland, a concern to avoid the collapse of order in Ulster and a readiness to exploit the willingness of loyalists to protect themselves. He was also anxious to project the region's tensions as merely a policing matter, rather than one requiring military intervention. On 8 September 1920, Westminster agreed to recruit a 'Special Constabulary.' But it was not until 22 October that the legislative procedure for launching the scheme was initiated by Dublin Castle and, as Alan Parkinson points out, the 'contentious issue of utilizing existing UVF structures in [its] … creation … was conspicuously ignored.'[13] Patrick Buckland notes that when the UVF had been 'revived' in July, it had not been regarded as 'a success … partly because the work [of preserving order] was too arduous for a volunteer force.'[14]

On 1 November 1920, an official appeal was made for 'all law abiding citizens', aged 21–45, to join the Special Constabulary. Its purpose was the 'maintenance of law and order' and the 'prevention of crime.'[15] It was to be comprised of three classes: 'A' Specials who were full-time, lived in quarters and served alongside the RIC; 'B' Specials, by far the largest element, who were part-time, and performed one evening patrol weekly within their own neighbourhood, and 'C' Specials who were an unpaid reserve, to be called out in emergency. Unlike the UVF, it was decentralised. County, district and townland leaders of the 'B' Specials ran their own areas; their 'local knowledge' was valued, to help ensure that the 'right men'[16] were enrolled and could be contacted quickly.

The force's primary purpose was to supplement the security forces in defending the local community against the incipient IRA campaign and, ultimately, to preserve the union. Its members considered that their national identity was under threat; enlistment enabled them to express their loyalty and sense of duty to king and country. There was an elaborate vetting procedure. Selection committees were established, composed of retired officers and JPs, and were instructed to enlist 'only men of … unquestionable fidelity and efficiency.' It is evident from the oath taken by recruits that the 'emphasis [was] on loyalty.' Each swore to 'truly serve our Sovereign Lord the King', that they would 'cause the Peace to be kept … and prevent all offences against the persons and property of His Majesty's subjects.'[17] Despite the hopes and intentions of Ernest Clark, the newly appointed Assistant Under-Secretary in Belfast, the Special Constabulary emerged as an unrepresentative, largely Protestant and loyalist force.

Clark was instructed to make the formation of the Special Constabulary his first priority. By March 1921, counties Fermanagh and Tyrone had fulfilled their recruitment quotas. But in Belfast, where it had been intended to raise 4,000 'B' Specials, just 1,480 had joined by May 1921. Initially at least, half of these were ex-servicemen, suggesting that a significant number had served in the UVF.[18] Michael Farrell claims that there was continuity in personnel between the UVF and the new force, citing the recruitment pattern in Armagh, Derry city and elsewhere. It has been described as being 'originally recruited from the Ulster Volunteer Force', and as the UVF 'in police uniform ... rebranded.'[19] But the evidence suggests otherwise. Under the Westminster scheme there was no direct link between the UVF and USC; this may account for its slow progress in Belfast. There were not enough ex-UVF members to fill the ranks of the USC, and there was competition from loyalist paramilitaries. Some UVF units joined and were integrated into the USC but this, it seems, was 'not representative of general recruitment trends.'[20]

A comprehensive analysis by Christopher Magill of 1,191 successful 'B' Special applicants in County Down reveals that 42 per cent were less than 16 years old in 1914 – too young to have been involved in the pre-war UVF – and just 17 per cent had served in the armed forces. There was a strong sentiment that ex-soldiers had 'done their bit'; a new, younger generation of loyalists joined, equally committed to maintaining the union and countering the nationalist threat.[21] Likewise, a study of USC fatalities, 1920–22, indicates that roughly 43 per cent were under the age of 16 in 1914 and that approximately 24 per cent had any earlier military experience.[22] Most USC recruits in County Down were single men, and farmers, farmers' sons, workers or labourers. This pattern of appears to have been replicated elsewhere; members of the professions and shopkeepers were under-represented. During the 'Troubles' they were to assume a vastly more pre-eminent security role than the unionist leadership had envisaged in 1920.

The beginnings of the 'Troubles'

Under the Government of Ireland Act (23 December 1920) responsibility for 'peace, order and good government', including policing, was to be transferred to the Belfast administration. Clark's diligent preparatory work made it possible to hold a parliamentary election on 24 May 1921, and it provided evidence of the region's deep political divisions. All 40 unionist candidates were successful, but its 'most obvious feature' was the 'rise in popularity of Sinn Féin',[23] an indication of how much loyalties within the northern minority had changed since 1918. Its primary objective was a Gaelic, Catholic republic. It regarded partition as reversible, a consequence of England's duplicity and colonialism. It refused to accept the right of unionists to their own political identity, regarding them as misguided dupes who would eventually recognise that they were Irish or as an Anglicised, alien element who might have to be 'coerced [into unity] if they stood in the way.'[24]

Constitutional nationalism's hold in east Ulster was chiefly due to Joe Devlin's personal appeal, the strength of the Ancient Order of Hibernians (AOH) and influence of the Catholic Church. Partition was, of course, anathema to all members of the minority. Their level of engagement with the new state was largely determined by Southern Ireland's Sinn Féin leadership. In 1921–22, they expressed their hostility to the partitioned state by constitutional means, including abstention from the Belfast parliament, some public bodies they controlled pledging allegiance to Dáil Éireann and schools not recognising the education department. Michael Collins encouraged and helped organise these responses, and was acknowledged by Britain, as their spokesperson.

When opening the Northern Ireland parliament (22 June 1921), George V appealed for Irishmen 'to forgive and to forget' and, soon afterwards, the truce was signed (11 July) which ended the Anglo-Irish War. It was applied to the six counties without Craig being consulted; because of its security implications, he considered that it 'gravely imperiled the position of Ulster.'[25] Under its terms: the Special Constabulary was suspended, the army reduced to a peripheral peacekeeping role, and the operations of the RIC curtailed. Most controversially the IRA was given official recognition and consequently was at liberty to organise, drill, train and recruit, so boosting its prestige and membership. Seamus Woods (OC Northern Division) claimed, with perhaps some exaggeration, that before the truce just 25 per cent of the Catholic population supported it but, afterwards, 'believing … we had been victorious and that the Specials and UVF were beaten, practically all flocked to our standard.'[26]

The truce increased party feeling in the six counties. On 14 July, 20 people died during riots in Belfast. Most unionists regarded it as a surrender to Sinn Féin; their feelings of optimism after the May election were replaced by a sense of disillusionment, isolation and vulnerability. They anticipated that the IRA would launch a full-scale campaign against Northern Ireland, and distrusted the British government in its negotiations with Sinn Féin. As these proceeded Craig came under acute pressure from all Westminster parties to accept all-Ireland institutions. Moreover, so as not to prejudice their outcome, the transfer of powers to the government in Belfast, legislated for in the 1920 Act, was delayed; consequently, it was reduced to the role of a 'glorified pressure group'.[27] Leading businessmen derided the Conservative Party for having been a 'false friend' that had 'assassinated Ulster.'[28] In Fermanagh 10 per cent of 'B' Specials resigned from the force during August/September. The membership of Protestant paramilitary organisations had reached 21,000 by November.[29]

Meanwhile the IRA's northern units had been reorganised and formed into divisions (February 1921) on the initiative of its Dublin HQ. Robert Lynch describes this restructuring as the 'birth of the Northern IRA itself';[30] it became more professional and aggressive and linked more closely to its southern leadership. Its subsequent actions raised republican morale, but unleashed a ferocious backlash against the Catholic minority. There were outbreaks of violence in Belfast in July, late August and late September, but November was the worst month yet; between the 20th and 30th, 35 people lost their lives. Rev. John Redmond referred to the murders occurring daily as 'deeds ... abhorred by practically the whole community.'[31] No identifiable IRA members were killed or injured in the riots in the city (1920–22). The AOH was the 'principal group' to assume the role of defending the minority; it was aggressive, armed, regarded by most nationalists as their 'natural defenders'[32] and therefore targeted by the IRA. Already, between July 1920 and November 1921, 165 persons had died in Northern Ireland's 'Troubles.'

After law and order powers were transferred to the Northern Ireland government (22 November 1921), the 3,450 'A' and 16,000 'B' Specials were placed under the Ministry of Home Affairs and unionists demanded that their leaders deal with the republican threat. The Anglo-Irish Treaty (6 December 1921), however, prolonged the political uncertainty. Under Article 12, a Boundary Commission was to be established to review and revise the boundary between Northern and Southern Ireland if Craig's government refused to accept all-Ireland institutions. He described it as the 'predominant danger'[33] his party faced. It also raised the hopes of nationalists that its adjudication would so reduce Northern Ireland territorially as to leave it no longer viable. It encouraged their strategy of non-recognition and efforts to destabilise the putative state.

Political violence peaks

In early 1922, the intensity of the 'Troubles' reached unprecedented levels. Political uncertainty fomented sectarian tensions, whilst the IRA launched an increasingly determined campaign. It had been revitalised by the truce, and its numbers were augmented by Westminster's decision to release republican internees (14 January 1922) and by deepening recession. Lynch states that three-quarters of its new recruits in Belfast joined for 'sectarian reasons only', but that it was its radical, pre-1920 elite who was 'responsible for almost all major IRA attacks', and 'transformed' it from an 'irrelevant and disorganized body ... into a vicious guerrilla force.'[34] An additional reason for the accelerating descent into violence was the deterioration in north/south relations. On Churchill's initiative, Collins and Craig met on 21 January 1922; Craig stated that he was anxious to ascertain if Sinn Féin 'intended to declare peace or war with Northern Ireland.'[35] During this engagement and subsequent discussions, their differences proved to be irreconcilable. Collins genuinely sympathised with the position of northern nationalists, but an increasingly important motive for his intervention was his determination to use the partition issue to bridge Sinn Féin's deepening divisions over the Treaty. He adopted various strategies to undermine the northern state. Amongst these, as the Northern Ireland authorities were fully aware, he covertly sponsored and orchestrated the IRA's escalating campaign.

Initially this was a 'largely Belfast and border affair.'[36] On 14 January 1922, after an IRA squad from Monaghan, ostensibly *en route* to a Gaelic football match in Londonderry, was arrested by police, Collins ordered the kidnapping of over 40 unionist notables in Fermanagh and Tyrone; over half were members of the USC. Craig responded by fully mobilising the Special Constabulary for the first time since the truce. One month later (11 February), 19 'A' Specials were dispatched to Enniskillen by rail as security reinforcements. Their journey from Newtownards entailed crossing the border at Clones and, while there, they were attacked by the IRA; four were killed. After the blood-stained train arrived at Lisbellaw, loyalists drove the 'Sinn Feiners' out of the village. In Belfast, sectarian riots and reprisals between 12 and 16 February resulted in 31 deaths.[37]

The Catholic Church and Protestant denominations issued a 'united appeal for peace', but to little effect. In March, 59 persons lost their lives; it was the most brutal month of the 'Troubles' so far. IRA attacks on police barracks and personnel and on property again provoked confrontation and retaliation, and occasioned some of the most infamous incidents of these years: on 23/24 March six members of the Catholic McMahon family were murdered; on 31 March a bomb was thrown into the Protestant Donnellys' home, and two children died and, hours later, five Catholics were killed in Arnon Street. Overall, between 1 January and 14 March, there were 83 murders in Belfast and 'no one brought to justice.'[38]

When responding to this growing level of violence, the Northern Ireland cabinet's agreed priorities were: to ensure 'the safety of Ulster'; 'to maintain the confidence of our people' and 'to bring the British government along with us.'[39] Its objective was to assure itself that, independently of London, it could cope with any disorder short of southern invasion or border raids in force. In March 1922, the size of the USC was increased, and Field Marshall Sir Henry Wilson appointed as its 'security advisor' and, on 7 April, the Civil Authorities (Special Powers) Act became law. It empowered the Ministry of Home Affairs 'to take all such steps ... as may be necessary for preserving the peace and maintaining order.'[40] It could impose the death penalty for specified offences, imprison without trial, prohibit inquests and convene non-jury courts. However, unlike Southern Ireland, Craig's government rejected suggestions that capital punishment should be introduced 'for all cases of persons found carrying firearms.'[41] Though he did not immediately invoke these additional powers, Craig described them as a vital weapon in 'breaking the power of the IRA.'[42]

Once again, the deteriorating security position in the north prompted Churchill to arrange a meeting between Collins and Craig, and they signed a pact (30 March) which began: 'Peace is today declared.' But the level of violence continued to rise and peaked in May 1922, by which point the two Irish states were 'to all intents and purposes at open war.'[43] After anti-Treaty forces had seized the Four Courts in Dublin (14 April), and desperate to avoid civil war, Collins launched a 'shared crusade' aimed at ending partition. An 'Army of the North' was formed, a composite force which included input from both the pro- and anti-Treaty IRA who combined with its northern divisions in an all-out offensive, a 'virtual full-scale invasion of Northern Ireland.'[44]

In Belfast, the IRA's actions were 'crude in the extreme', and were accompanied by inter-communal conflict and retaliation by loyalist mobs. In May a 'war of intimidation' was conducted against Protestant civilians which ranged from expulsions from 'mixed areas' to the sectarian murder of workers travelling to work or being selectively shot at work places.[45] Arson continued to be 'the basic strategy of all militant republicans',[46] and was directed at a variety of economic targets with the aim of destroying the city's industrial and commercial heart and destabilising the state. From 10–25 May there were 45 fires, mainly Protestant businesses in Catholic areas. That month alone claims for compensation arising from malicious injuries totalled almost £800,000 and there were 75 murders, 42 of them of Catholics.[47]

Over 600 violent incidents were recorded in Northern Ireland during May and, by then, almost £3m worth of damage had been done to property since January 1922. Outside Belfast, 'big houses' and other buildings were subjected to arson attack, RIC barracks and police personnel were targeted, especially the 'B' Specials, and there were guerrilla attacks and smaller incursions along the border. On 27 May, roughly 600 IRA members occupied a salient in Fermanagh (including Belleek and Pettigo). A 60-strong USC contingent tasked with expelling them, failed. On the 31st Craig, therefore, requested that troops be deployed 'otherwise … people [would] take things into their own hands.'[48] Lloyd George reluctantly acceded and, by 8 June, the republican force had been driven out. It had been the first direct confrontation between British troops and IRA since the truce, and had generated fears of a renewal of the Anglo-Irish War.

Meanwhile Collins had been protesting that an anti-Catholic 'pogrom' was taking place within the six counties, with the USC implicated, and urging Britain to impose martial law or institute a judicial investigation. Lloyd George was responsive. He was concerned at the continuing level of violence in Northern Ireland, and regarded it as the 'weakest part of the British case ... The first murders were of Catholics', he said, '[yet] no one had been punished ... We had made no enquiry.'[49] A declaration of martial law, however, risked renewed confrontation with the IRA and Craig opposed it, stating that it would imply 'one side was as bad as the other.'[50] It was also feared that a judicial enquiry might undermine the authority of the unionist government. Instead, in late June, Stephen Tallents, the Lord Lieutenant's private secretary, was dispatched to conduct a preliminary investigation. By the time he was writing his report the violence had subsided, and he therefore counselled against initiating any further review of the recent past mainly on the grounds that it would revive nationalist 'propaganda about matters best forgotten',[51] and encourage the minority in its non-recognition of the state.

During June 1922 the number of fatalities fell sharply, and thereafter order was gradually restored. This was partly a result of the security measures taken by Craig's government. In late May it had invoked its emergency powers in response to a sharp upsurge in violence, which had included the murder of William Twaddell, a unionist MP (22 May). In addition, the Unionist Party's leadership feared that the de Valera/Collins electoral pact (20 May) presaged an intensification of the IRA campaign. Consequently, on 22 May, republican organisations including the IRA were proscribed, and internment was introduced; between May 1922 and December 1924 728 persons were imprisoned, virtually all of them Catholics and suspected republicans. Also heavier USC patrols were deployed; by mid-1922 there were 32,000 'A', 'B' and 'C' Specials. Follis claims that these steps '[broke] the IRA terror offensive', which had ended in 'dismal failure.'[52]

However, the outbreak of civil war in Southern Ireland also contributed to the restoration of order. When Collins' forces began bombarding the Four Courts (28 June) it could be said to have officially begun. Subsequently the IRA was ordered to cease all operations in the six counties. The morale of its northern divisions was shattered by the Dublin government's abrupt reversal of policy, the incipient conflagration in the south which led to men and arms flowing across the border, and internment. To Lynch the 'most telling point' was that the northern minority 'turned against the IRA [which] ... sealed its collapse.' He describes its entire campaign as having been 'almost wholly counter-productive.' Its arson attack on business interests had been 'hugely detrimental to ... already poverty-stricken' Catholics. But 'above all', he writes, its actions had provoked 'the most brutal response from loyalist extremists', yet it had persisted 'even when the link was glaringly obvious.'[53] By mid-1922 northern nationalists had come to 'regard republicans as attempting the impossible'; their war-weariness was reflected in the increasing flow of information being passed to the security forces. Seamus Woods, IRA OC, acknowledged that, if they were to continue, his volunteers would be 'compelled to mete out capital punishment amongst the Catholic civilian population.' Lynch asserts that, by 1923, 'to all intents and purposes [the IRA] … no longer existed.'[54]

The 'Troubles' perceived as being a 'pogrom'

Antithetical views have been expressed regarding the role of the USC during the 'Troubles.' It was universally detested by northern Catholics. Their perception of the violence in 1920–22 was of it having been a premeditated anti-Catholic 'pogrom', orchestrated by the Northern Ireland government which colluded with loyalists, and encouraged systematic indiscipline and bias on the part of the Special Constabulary. To unionists, the USC was virtually beyond reproach and criticism of it tantamount to disloyalty. Clark spoke proudly of its members as being his 'own children'.[55] Craig would 'hear nothing to … [its] detriment'. Likewise Basil Brooke, its Commandant in Fermanagh, depicted the 'B' Specials as being dedicated, courageous in sacrificially volunteering to defend their community and the Union in perilous border areas and, ultimately, triumphant in defeating those 'intent on arson and murder.'[56] The Westminster politicians, who had constituted, funded and equipped the force, and transferred policing powers to Craig's government, generally felt profound reservations about it – its almost exclusively Protestant membership, dubious disciplinary record and effectiveness, given the persistence of political disorder. They also discerned that in future it might clash violently with crown forces over boundary revision.

It is indisputable that members of the northern Catholic community were the 'losers and principal victims'[57] during the 'Troubles.' Lynch calculates that, between June 1920 and June 1922, 366 of them lost their lives, compared with 278 Protestants; thus they accounted for 57 per cent of the total though they comprised just one-third of the population of the six counties.[58] In Belfast, there were 498 deaths between July 1920 and June 1922, mostly civilians, 15 per cent women, and a high proportion died during urban rioting. Kieran Glennon writes that the violence was 'perpetrated against the minority to a hugely disproportionate degree.' Fifty-six per cent of the killings in the city were of Catholics, though they made up just 24 per cent of its population. Between October 1921 and October 1922, Glennon claims that Protestant aggression was less reactive, 'more constant' and 'seemed … aimed at suppressing Nationalism entirely.'[59] Northern Ireland Catholics also suffered from a high level of intimidation:

from 1920–22, 8,500 were expelled from their workplaces, 23,000 from their homes and, between 1911 and 1926, their number shrank by 10,000.[60]

The minority therefore felt justified in classifying this experience as a 'pogrom.' The word is derived from the Russian verb *gromit*,[61] meaning to smash or destroy. It was first used to describe the spontaneous eruptions of mob violence in Russia, beginning in the 1880s, perpetrated by the majority population against the small, defenceless Jewish community. As a consequence, two million of its members fled abroad between 1890 and 1920 (it numbered 5.2 million in 1897). There is now a consensus that the Russian state was not involved.[62] There is no consensus among historians, however, on whether the designation 'pogrom' can legitimately be applied to Northern Ireland, 1920–22. Glennon uses it and justifies doing so on the grounds that it was 'widely used' by nationalists themselves. Lynch argues that the violence during the 'Troubles' 'lacked … key characteristics that are inherent in' the term. Parkinson concludes that it had 'some common characteristics of a pogrom' as evidenced by the 'disproportionately high number of Catholics killed and injured, and the raw sectarian nature of many of these killings', while Christopher Magill describes the riots in east Ulster as constituting a 'pogrom',[63] though not as nationalists defined it.

Certainly, the minority's sense of 'alienation' from the state was 'confirmed by the belief that many of the outrages' they had experienced 'had been perpetrated … particularly [by] the USC.'[64] The Tallents Report was especially critical of the 'B' Specials, stating that: 'there can never be any possibility of establishing confidence and security so long as [they are] … supplied with arms and clothing by [their] … government … Even the … constitutional nationalist gets more bitter as the record of raids and abuses by the uncontrollable elements pile up and … innocent people suffer.'[65] Some of the USC's County Commandants expressed similar sentiments. Brigadier-General Ambrose St Quintin Ricardo (Tyrone) alleged that the 'B' Specials carried out reprisals, drew up 'sectarian death lists' and willfully destroyed property. Basil Brooke (Fermanagh) described the 'A' Specials as a 'wild crowd' with 'many ex-soldiers … More trouble than they were worth.'[66]

It has been argued that a 'disproportionate number of fatal attacks' in Northern Ireland were 'executed by the Specials',[67] and that 'gross excesses were carried out by some [of them].' Many of the sectarian assaults on Catholics initiated by 'partisan police' occurred in Belfast (McMahons, Arnon Street), but not all. Magill cites instances of reprisals in Rosslea, Rathfriland, and Manorhamilton. The death of three young Catholic men in Cushendall (23 June 1922) has been described as the most 'notorious example' and 'best documented case'[68] of USC indiscipline. It has been claimed and broadly confirmed by a British judicial enquiry (9 September) that 'A' Specials went into the town, shot into a crowd and then dragged the youths up an alley and shot them as a reprisal for the murder of Sir Henry Wilson (22 June). A later Northern Ireland government investigation exonerated the 'A' patrol, claimed that an unlawful assembly had taken place and it had been fired on. In Parkinson's opinion, it is 'difficult to come to a firm conclusion', but he points out that there is no evidence that the 'A' patrol had been shot at. Magill concludes that 'most likely ... the 'A' Specials carried out a triple punishment killing.'[69]

Incidents of USC indiscipline can readily be accounted for: the 'B' Specials were particularly easy targets – living at home, uniformed, isolated and therefore anxious and under stress; they lacked adequate training and proficient leadership; they were burdened with, perhaps unrealistic, expectations regarding their ability to neutralise the IRA; they developed a group solidarity, and thus a strong impulse to avenge stricken comrades and they shared a presumption that Catholics were disloyal and supported the IRA. Moreover, the investigative and punitive procedures within the force were perfunctory and deficient.[70]

The 'Troubles'; the role of the Northern Ireland government and security forces

But the incidence of USC indiscipline can easily be overstated. Follis states that despite 'great provocation ... the vast majority' of its members 'displayed surprising restraint.'[71] In total, 93 members of the RIC and USC lost their lives during the 'Troubles.' Of the 39 RIC victims, over half were killed in Belfast, 21 in the course of IRA attack and most of the remainder were off-duty at the time. Fifty-four Special Constables died, some in horrific circumstances; 36 when on patrol and fired on by the IRA or republican snipers, and 12 when not in uniform. Thirty-seven of their fatalities occurred outside Belfast, evidence of their security role in border areas. They increasingly bore the brunt of IRA aggression; 41 of them perished in 1922.[72] Yet, arguably, their discipline did hold up well. Parkinson estimates that approximately 25 Catholic deaths were 'carried out predominantly by uniformed assassins', while Glennon attributes some of the most brutal reprisals by the security forces to an RIC 'murder gang',[73] rather than USC members.

The Northern Ireland government has been criticised for helping 'create a permissive environment'[74] by its failure adequately to investigate USC reprisals or strengthen the force's disciplinary procedures. Parkinson described its response to the Cushendall incident, after which there were no prosecutions, as 'lethargic ... [It] compromised any possibility that Catholics would trust either the police or the justice system' and they resigned themselves to 'further unnecessary slaughter.'[75] The Ministry of Home Affairs consistently exhibited a distinct bias, dealing severely with IRA and suspected republicans while treating Protestant offenders with leniency. Patrick Buckland cites its response to the Belfast Protestant Association. Belatedly it interned 16 members of this brutal, sectarian organisation and he notes that: 'lives [would have been] saved had the government been willing to use its powers as fully against loyalists as it [did] against nationalists.'[76] Craig and his ministers prioritised unionist solidarity over social justice and did too little to prevent the violence of its grassroots supporters apart from expanding the ranks of the USC. Vetting procedures for applicants were compromised by their strategy of trying to discipline Protestant paramilitaries through enrolment into the force. As a consequence, 'too many unsuitable people were allowed to join.'[77]

Nonetheless in recent studies there is much agreement that Northern Ireland ministers neither condoned nor encouraged USC reprisals or retaliation. While accepting that the force committed 'outrages', Follis argues that these were 'unauthorized … localized … not part of a comprehensive policy of sectarian repression.'[78] Other historians have stated that there is 'no evidence of a systemic plan' to dominate Catholics or enforce ethnic cleansing, that the intimidation was in all 'likelihood … not orchestrated' by the regional government and that loyalist riots erupted spontaneously, with no unionist leadership involvement. Parkinson states that assaults on the minority were 'random … reactive … temporary', and the 'Troubles' therefore 'cannot be perceived as a fully fledged pogrom.'[79] Lynch, in contrast, considers that the term is inapplicable precisely because anti-Catholic violence was not indiscriminate. He points out that 80 per cent of its victims in Belfast were men, many involved in rioting, mostly aged 20–50. He also calculates that just 35 IRA members died in the 'Troubles', 12 of these at most in the city.[80] It seems probable that loyalists targeted those who they thought likely to be involved in the republican campaign, or who they assumed were giving it their support, because it was so difficult to identify those who were actually responsible. The USC's effectiveness was constrained by its 'inability to penetrate republican territory.'[81]

A Northern Ireland cabinet priority was the retention of Westminster's support; it was the repository of sovereign power, of troops and of finance. Consequently, it had a powerful motivation to prevent police reprisals and sectarian violence which it regarded as 'very adverse to the loyalist cause.'[82] In February 1922 Craig expressed his fear that British politicians might 'wash their hands of the whole affair [Northern Ireland].'[83] He was aware that the state on its own could not survive a 'campaign of atrocity'[84] with the south. In April 1922 he therefore rejected advice to introduce internment as he was anxious not to alienate the UK government or English opinion. For this reason, he willingly entered into dialogue with

Collins, agreed to hold an enquiry into the Clones incident, and offered £1,000 reward for information on the McMahon murders.[85] He also strove to pre-empt outbreaks of lawlessness. In February 1922, fearing retaliation after recent events in Fermanagh, he immediately toured the county, appealed for 'discipline and restraint', announced additional security measures and in a press statement relating to the Boundary Commission reassured supporters that 'what Ulster has she holds'.[86] In attempting to assuage his party's grassroots, he was also narrowing his policy options. Imputations of bias and weakness on the part of Craig and his ministers should be set in the context of the 'wider conciliatory polic[ies]'.[87] adopted in Ireland by both the British and southern Irish governments during the revolutionary period. For example, on 14 January 1922, Westminster granted an amnesty to republican prisoners. Magill has described this decision as having been 'aimed pragmatically at easing the overall security situation.'[88] According to Rev. John Redmond, it resulted in an 'orgy of riot and bloodshed'[89] being unleashed in east Belfast.

Southern perspectives

The new government in Southern Ireland also faced immense challenges to the existence of the state and took strong measures, many of which were harsher than those adopted in Northern Ireland. Richard Mulcahy (Minister of Defence) opposed imposing 'rigorous discipline' on the National Army, and was prepared to disregard its excesses in the interests of its 'internal stability.' He also justified state executions of anti-Treaty IRA members partly in order to prevent the force from carrying out 'unofficial killings.'[90] The Dublin authorities used their extensive emergency powers ruthlessly; 77 executions were authorised by the Provisional and Free State governments between 17 November 1922 and 30 May 1923 (53 more than by Britain during the War of Independence) and, 'by February 1924, there were in the region of 13,000 republican prisoners and internees.'[91] Though Northern Ireland's Special Powers Act has been described as 'draconian',[92] just 545 were arrested without trial in 1922, and no death sentences were ratified in the region during the 'Troubles.'[93]

Moreover, southern Irish governments exercised a policy of authorised reprisals. A National Council order (February 1923) stated that 'in any case of an outrage in a [National Army] battalion area three men will be executed.'[94] A controversial application of this approach occurred on 8 December 1922 when, the day after Seán Hales, TD, was murdered by the anti-Treaty IRA, four of its prisoners were shot, none of whom had been implicated in the crime. This measure was taken not just as an act of state retribution, but 'as a solemn warning to those associated with you'[95] regarding the brutal consequences of political assassination. Numerous unauthorised reprisals were carried out as well. Amongst these was the slaying of Seán Lemass' brother, Noel, after the civil war. The most infamous such incident was the Ballyseedy massacre, when nine republican prisoners were tied to a landmine which was then detonated. As Magill observed, 'unlawful killings were not uncommon in revolutionary Ireland.'[96]

Fatality levels in Northern Ireland have been portrayed as being the highest in Ireland during the post war period. But it is evident that the 'Troubles' peaked at a time of comparative peace in the south. Between 1917 and 1921, there were 2,346 deaths in the 32 counties caused by political violence; just 353 (15 per cent) of these occurred in the six counties, though 28 per cent of the island's population lived there (Fermanagh, with nine, had the lowest number).[97] Between January and June 1922, 300–350 people lost their lives in the North while, in the 26 counties, 1,500–2,000 killings took place during the Civil War; again, proportionately, this represents a higher level of violence. In Belfast 450–480 fatalities occurred in 1920–22; Dublin city/county and Cork city/county experienced a much greater number when those during 1922–23 are included.[98]

The role of the IRA during the 'Troubles'

Clearly the 'suffering' in Northern Ireland was 'far from being restricted to one religious group.'[99] Twenty per cent of those expelled from their homes (1920–22) were Protestants fleeing from republican intimidation. Between July 1920 and October 1921 more Protestants lost their lives in Belfast than members of the minority, and in total 160 during the 'Troubles'; this represented one-third of all murder victims, all at the hands of Catholics (mainly the IRA), who caused one-third of fatalities in the city though Catholics comprised one-quarter of its population.[100] Unionists generally blamed the IRA for all violent deaths, arguing that they were either perpetrated or provoked by it. Follis asserts that, though the 'B' Specials 'contributed to the tension and violence', they were 'reacting to ... IRA outrages.' Likewise, Parkinson concludes that 'the usual catalyst' for security force retaliation was 'the IRA's murder of police personnel.' He states unequivocally that, during 1921–22, 'republican activism [was] ... very much the driver of sectarian violence ... the single most significant factor,'[101] a conclusion also reached by Tallents.

Lynch, therefore, observes that the term 'pogrom' cannot legitimately be applied to the disorder in Belfast because it was largely a 'response to perceived provocations ... result[ing] from the activities of the IRA', which 'ensured that the violence continued.' He cites instances including: the reprisals provoked by DI Swanzy's murder; the violence in November 1921 which was a 'direct response to the IRA bombing ... shipyard trams' and the McMahon murders which were preceded by the shooting of a police officer.

That May 1922 was the 'bloodiest month' was 'no coincidence', he writes, because it was then that the IRA 'launched its ... offensive ... It is a telling statistic that almost 75 per cent of all people killed in [the city] ... died within a few days of a major IRA attack.'[102] It is also the case that the 'Troubles' ended after the republican campaign was abandoned in June 1922.

Overall, the statistics of the violence do not justify the application of the term 'pogrom', 1920–22. Though the minority suffered disproportionately, it was a 'small proportion' of its members who 'experienced ... horrific ... personal suffering.' The number who died, some at the IRA's hands, represented 'barely 0.1%'[103] of its population. Furthermore, the Catholic population in Northern Ireland fell by just two per cent, 1911–26 and, as Lynch points out, it actually grew in Belfast during the revolutionary period (from 93,243 in 1911 to 95,682 in 1926). The most significant demographic impact of the disorder was increased religious segregation as minority enclaves were driven from 'mixed areas' in cities and towns. The mass exodus of population, a defining characteristic of the Russian 'pogrom', was absent.[104] The only comparable decline in the size of any group in Ireland was of the Protestant population in the 26 counties which fell by one-third between 1911 and 1926. Forced migration contributed to this contraction, and was caused by the physical assaults, boycott, intimidation and arson attacks its members experienced; Peter Hart states that the 'motive' for this 'was sectarianism and ethnic cleansing.'[105] Estimates of the number of Protestants who fled involuntarily range from 39,000 to 48,000.[106]

Craig's reliance on the Ulster Special Constabulary

The USC played a 'crucial part in suppressing violence.'[107] It placated loyalists, largely satisfying their impulse to confront the republican threat, whilst helping bridge the gap between the Unionist Party's leadership and its grassroots. In east Ulster it was 'the key to the IRA's inability to effectively challenge British authority.'[108] Lynch regards it as having been the most effective opposition the IRA faced.[109] Certainly, Craig and his ministers had no choice but to rely on the force. Though critical of the 'B' Specials, Brigadier-General Ricardo considered that they did 'magnificent work' and were a 'necessity' as the 'troops had taken no hand in subduing the present rebellion.'[110] The 22 battalions based in Northern Ireland in mid-1922 were under British government control, and were reluctant to use their far-reaching emergency powers under the Restoration of Order in Ireland Act. After the July 1921 truce Lloyd George was concerned that Sinn Féin might regard their deployment as a breach of its terms, and it would have risked confrontation with the IRA and a renewal of war. After the Treaty he wished to avoid taking any action that might undermine Collins' resolve to implement it, and upset the delicate talks regarding the formulation of a new Irish constitution. Britain still harboured fears that the Irish leaders might 'break on Ulster.'

Reliance on the RIC was not an option for Craig either. It was a Westminster responsibility, and British politicians had unilaterally decided to disband it with effect from 31 May 1921. It was under-strength (there had been no recruitment since the truce), demoralised, and distrusted by unionists partly because some members were suspected of having Sinn Féin sympathies and colluding with the IRA. As policing was a 'transferred' service, the regional government was at liberty to institute a replacement, the Royal Ulster Constabulary. But it was not operational until 1 June 1922 by which time the 'Troubles' were almost over, and it had then just 1,100 members (one-third of its establishment) and no adequate system of intelligence. The USC therefore 'bore the brunt of security work'[111] in Northern Ireland, 1921–22; Churchill stated that even the 'watching of the frontier must be undertaken by police.'[112] This was not the role that Craig had envisaged for the Special Constabulary in September 1920. He had envisioned it then as being a 'reserve force' to support troops and RIC, 'only [to] be called out … in case of emergency.'[113]

Follis described the USC as a 'symptom of the divisions [in the six counties], and not the cause.'[114] Thus, when it was being established, the *Irish News* had confidently predicted that 'not a nationalist'[115] would apply. It was almost exclusively Protestant; in County Down 1.3 per cent of 'B' Specials were Catholic, and Brooke stated that there were none in Fermanagh's 'B' class.[116] It was never likely to attract many recruits from the minority. Its oath, and the publicity for the force, stressed loyalty to the Crown and, by implication, to the Northern Ireland state whose existence most Catholics bitterly opposed. Moreover, they were discouraged from joining by the Church, and any that did would have faced social ostracism within their community and likely IRA retribution, while compromising the nationalist position before the Boundary Commission. Fearing republican infiltration Craig's government did little or nothing to encourage their enrolment; some USC commandants rejected Catholic recruits, while others welcomed them. These same issues arose in relation to the RUC. By the late 1920s the proportion of its personnel who were Catholic was, and it remained, around 17 per cent.[117]

The legacy of the 'Troubles'

When considering the legacy of the 'Troubles', Follis writes that the 'sectarian attacks' made on the minority, including those by 'elements' within the USC, 'scarred [its] collective consciousness.'[118] Likewise Magill comments that 'more than any other factor, it was the sectarian nature of security policy and the state's response to police and military violence that alienated Catholics from the Northern government.' But, he also emphasises that Special Constables committed 'few atrocities.' He stresses that, 'in contrast, the IRA activities that often provided the basis for police reprisals were forgotten, leaving only pure distilled Catholic victimhood.'[119] The hopes of northern nationalists that the Boundary Commission's findings might result in Irish unity proved illusory; an intergovernmental agreement (3 December 1925) reaffirmed the border enshrined in the 1920 Act. Meanwhile their 'failure to engage' in the public life of the six counties had 'robbed them of any say in the future shape of its institutions or political culture',[120] including police reform. As unionists failed to offer them 'greater participation' it is evident that 'problems were being stored up for the future.'[121]

Ulster Unionists have been described as the 'only clear winners'[122] to emerge in Ireland, 1886–1925. Their achievement was to form a functioning Northern Ireland state, which survived the 'Troubles' with its 1920 powers and boundaries intact. However, in 1922, they were not a 'confident and generous majority',[123] but felt beleaguered and misunderstood, and exhibited a siege mentality even after the siege was over. Their sense of insecurity was rooted in: the recurrence of IRA campaigns; apprehension regarding the existence of an alienated and growing minority; uncertainty as to the reliability of Westminster's support and the persistence of Dublin irredentism. After the Treaty southern Irish leaders continued to claim jurisdiction over the entire island, while making no attempt to attract the pro-union majority in the north-east: Irish was declared the 'national language' (1922); the Catholic Church was accorded a 'special position' (1937) and Eire's remaining ties with Britain were severed (1948). One consequence of these policy priorities was a 'widening gulf' between Northern Ireland and the Irish Free State. Another was that the Protestant population within the 26 counties dwindled by 60 per cent between 1911 and 1991.[124] In contrast, during these years, the size of the minority in Northern Ireland rose from 34.4 to 38.4 per cent of the population.[125]

Notes

1. Christopher Magill, *Political Conflict in East Ulster: Revolution and Reprisal* (Woodbridge, 2020), p. 83. The 'Special Constabulary' was given the name 'Ulster Special Constabulary' under the terms of the Constabulary (Northern Ireland) Act, 1922.
2. John Redmond, *Church, State, Industry, 1827–1929, in East Belfast: Vivid Records of Social and Political Upheavals in the Nineteen-twenties* (Belfast, 1960), p. 12.

3   Henry Patterson, 'The Belfast shipyard expulsions of 1920', posted 3 Sep. 2020, p. 6 in https://thebrokenelbow.com. See also Patterson's article, '"Infamous attacks on Women": sectarian violence in Bangor in July 1920' in Caoimhe Nic Dháibhéid, Marie Coleman and Paul Bew (eds), *1921–2021: Northern Ireland Centenary Historical Perspectives* (Belfast, 2022), pp 22–9.
4   Redmond, *Church, State, Industry*, p. 12; Patterson, 'Belfast shipyard expulsions', p. 8; also, Kieran Glennon, 'The dead of the Belfast pogrom – counting the cost of the revolutionary period, 1920–22', posted online 27 Oct. 2020 (https://www.theirishstory.com).
5   Wilfrid Spender, 'The Origin of the Division' (PRONI, Spender Papers, D1295/2/1A).
6   Inspector General, Monthly Report, May 1918 (TNA, CO 904/106).
7   Ibid., June–Aug. 1920 (TNA, CO 904/112).
8   Brooke to Clark, undated [Sep. 1920] (PRONI, Clark Papers, D1022/2/9).
9   Redmond, *Church, State, Industry*, pp iii, 13, 17, 23–4. Redmond lists other units and the approximate date of their formation: the Diamond, autumn 1919; Milford, March 1920; and Magherafelt, late summer 1920.
10 Magill, *Political Conflict in East Ulster*, p. 182.
11 Lady Spender diary, July 1920 entry (PRONI, D1633/2/23); Inspector General, Monthly Report, June 1920 (TNA, CO 904/112).
12 Alan Parkinson, *A Difficult Birth: The Early Years of Northern Ireland, 1920–25* (Dublin, 2020), p. 63.
13 Ibid., p. 64. When forming the USC, Dublin Castle used existing legislation – the Special Constabulary Acts of 1832 and 1914; no new legislation was required. See Alan Parkinson, *Belfast's Unholy War* (Dublin, 2004), pp 84–5.
14 Patrick Buckland, *The Factory of Grievances: Devolved Government in Northern Ireland, 1921–39* (Dublin, 1979), p. 181.
15 Quoted in Redmond, *Church, State, Industry*, p. 25.
16 Brooke to Clark, Sep. 1920 (PRONI, Clark Papers, D1022/2/9).
17 Parkinson, *A Difficult Birth*, p. 65. See also Magill, *Political Conflict in East Ulster*, p. 113.
18 Clark to Brooke, 30 Apr. 1921 (PRONI, FIN/18/1/54); also Parkinson, *Difficult Birth*, pp 65–6.
19 Michael Farrell, *Arming the Protestants: The Formation of the Ulster Special Constabulary and the Royal Ulster Constabulary, 1920–27* (London, 1983), pp 7–30. The quotations are from articles written by Brendan O'Leary in the *Irish Times*, 7 Aug. 2022, and by Seán Bernard Newman in *History Ireland*, Mar.–Apr. 2021, respectively.
20 Magill, *Political Conflict in East Ulster*, pp 87–8.
21 Ibid., pp 82–3, 90–91, 93, 95. See also Brian Barton, *Brookeborough: The Making of a Prime Minister* (Belfast, 1988), p. 39.

22 Richard Abbott, *Police Casualties in Ireland, 1919–22* (Dublin, 2000) and local newspapers.
23 Magill, *Political Conflict in East Ulster*, p. 143; also 10 & 11 Geo. V, c. 67 (23 Dec. 1920).
24 Robert Lynch, *Revolutionary Ireland, 1912–25* (London, 2015), p. 58.
25 Cabinet Conclusion File, 16 Aug. 1921 (PRONI CAB/4/14); 'His Majesty's Message' in Hansard, NI (Commons), 23 June 1921, vol. 1, col. 21.
26 Robert Lynch, *The Northern IRA and the Early Years of Partition, 1920–1922* (Newbridge, 2006), p. 79.
27 Brian Follis, *A State Under Siege: The Establishment of Northern Ireland, 1920–1925* (Oxford, 1995), p. 57.
28 Brian Barton, 'The Dáil cabinet's mission to Belfast' in Nic Dháibhéid et al., *Northern Ireland, 1921–2021*, p. 39.
29 Barton, *Brookeborough*, p. 44; also Barton, 'Northern Ireland, 1920–25' in J.R. Hill (ed.), *A New History of Ireland: Ireland 1921–1984, Vol. VII* (Oxford, 2003), p. 169.
30 Lynch, *Northern IRA*, p. 47.
31 Redmond, *Church, State, Industry*, p. 31, quoting from a sermon delivered by Bishop Charles Grierson; also Follis, *State Under Siege*, p. 84.
32 Robert Lynch, 'The People's Protectors? The Irish Republican Army and the "Belfast Pogrom", 1920–1922', *Journal of British Studies*, 7:2 (April 2008), pp 381–3; also Glennon, 'The dead of the Belfast pogrom'.
33 Speech by James Craig, Hansard, NI (Commons), 14 Mar. 1922, vol. 2, col. 9.
34 Lynch, 'People's Protectors', pp 384–5.
35 Cabinet Conclusion File, 26 Jan. 1922 (PRONI, CAB4/30).
36 Lynch, *Northern IRA*, p. 125.
37 Follis, *State Under Siege*, p. 89; Parkinson, *Difficult Birth*, p. 96; Barton, *Brookeborough*, pp 46–7; Glennon, 'The dead of the Belfast pogrom'; Redmond, *Church, State, Industry*, p. 31.
38 Speech by R.J. Lynn, Hansard, NI (Commons), 14 Mar. 1922, vol. 2, col. 10; also Redmond, *Church, State, Industry*, pp 31–2. The church appeal was made on 22 Feb. 1922.
39 Cabinet Conclusion File, 12 May 1922 (PRONI, CAB4/41). This was the cabinet's most detailed consideration of its priorities.
40 12 & 13 Geo. V Civil Authorities (Special Powers) Act (Northern Ireland), 1922, Sect. 1 (1).
41 Parkinson, *Difficult Birth*, p. 234. Erskine Childers was executed by the southern authorities on 24 Nov. 1922 for possession of arms (a pistol that had been gifted to him by Michael Collins). The Special Powers Act did not empower the Northern Ireland government to impose the death sentence for such an offence.
42 Hansard, NI (Commons), 14 Mar. 1922, vol. 2, col. 10.

43 Patrick Buckland, *Ulster Unionism and the Origins of Northern Ireland 1886–1922* (Dublin, 1973), p. 154.
44 Lynch, *Northern IRA*, p. 140.
45 Lynch, 'People's Protectors?', pp 286–8.
46 Ibid., p. 288.
47 Barton, 'Partition: origins and implementation' in Patrick Roche and Brian Barton (eds), *The Northern Ireland Question: Nationalism, Unionism and Partition* (Tunbridge Wells, 2013), p. 84; Follis, *State Under Siege*, pp 81, 98.
48 Cabinet Conclusion File, 31 May 1922 (PRONI, CAB4/46); Follis, *State Under Siege*, p. 103.
49 Quoted in Thomas Jones, *Whitehall Diary, Volume III, 1918–25*, edited by Keith Middlemas (Oxford, 1971), p. 204.
50 Cabinet Conclusion File, 14 Feb. 1922 (PRONI, CAB4/32).
51 Tallents to Masterson-Smith, 4 July 1922, and Tallents Report, 6 July 1922, and diary (TNA, CO 906/30, 24).
52 Follis, *State Under Siege*, p. 108. See also Buckland, *Ulster Unionism*, p. 173, which states: 'firm measures … gradually brought peace.'
53 Lynch, 'People's Protectors?', pp 388–90.
54 Ibid., p. 390; Lynch, *Northern IRA*, p. 208.
55 Tallents' comment on Craig in Tallents Report, 4 July 1922 (TNA, CO 906/30); also Clark's letter to Charles Wickham, 16 Nov. 1920 (PRONI, Clark Papers, D1022/2/9).
56 Brooke in submission to Boundary Commission (PRONI CAB61/64).
57 Lynch, 'People's Protectors?', pp 378–9.
58 Lynch, *Northern IRA*, Appendix 1, p. 227.
59 Glennon, 'The dead of the Belfast pogrom'.
60 Statistics given in Follis, *State Under Siege*, pp 93–4, and Lynch, *Northern IRA*, p. 227.
61 See David Aaronovitch's article in *The Times*, 20 Nov. 2021. Aaronovitch was reviewing Jeffrey Veidlinger's book, *In the Midst of Civilized Europe: The Pogroms of 1918–1921 and the Onset of the Holocaust* (London, 2021).
62 See Irena Grosfeld, et al., 'Middleman minorities and ethnic violence; anti-Jewish pogroms in the Russian Empire', *The Review of Economic Studies*, 87:1 (Jan. 2020), pp 289–342.
63 Glennon, 'The dead of the Belfast pogrom'; Lynch, 'People's Protectors?', p. 377; Parkinson, *Difficult Birth*, p. 280; Magill, *Political Conflict in East Ulster*, p. 57.
64 Patrick Buckland, *A History of Northern Ireland* (Dublin, 1981), p. 50.
65 Quoted in Magill, *Political Conflict in East Ulster*, pp 174–5.
66 Barton, *Brookeborough*, pp 55, 53.
67 Follis, *State Under Siege*, pp 111-12; Parkinson, *Difficult Birth*, p. 71.
68 Buckland, *History of Northern Ireland*, p. 51; Follis, *State Under Siege*, p. 112.

69 Parkinson, *Difficult Birth*, pp 183, 185–6; Magill, *Political Conflict in East Ulster*, p. 111.
70 See Magill, *Political Conflict in East Ulster*, pp 119–27.
71 Follis, *State Under Siege*, p. 94.
72 These figures have been extrapolated from Richard Abbot, *Police Casualties in Ireland, 1919–1922* (Cork, 2019).
73 Parkinson, *Difficult Birth*, pp 279, 243; Glennon, 'The dead of the Belfast pogrom'.
74 Magill, *Political Conflict in East Ulster*, p. 79.
75 Parkinson, *Difficult Birth*, pp 181, 186.
76 Buckland, *Factory of Grievances*, p. 218.
77 Buckland, *History of Northern Ireland*, pp 41–2.
78 Follis, *State Under Siege*, p. 115.
79 Magill, *Political Conflict in East Ulster*, p. 180; Parkinson, *Difficult Birth*, p. 280.
80 Lynch, 'People's Protectors?', pp 377–8, 386; Lynch, *Northern IRA*, p. 227.
81 Magill, *Political Conflict in East Ulster*, p. 130.
82 Cabinet conclusions, 14 Feb. 1922 (PRONI, CAB4/32).
83 Ibid.
84 Ibid. See also Hansard, NI (Commons), 14 Mar. 1922, vol. 2, col. 15.
85 Barton, *Brookeborough*, p. 48; Follis, *State Under Siege*, p. 95.
86 Barton, *Brookeborough*, pp 47–8, *passim*.
87 Magill, *Political Conflict in East Ulster*, p. 180.
88 Ibid.
89 Redmond, *Church, State, Industry*, p. 32.
90 Diarmaid Ferriter, *A Nation and Not a Rabble: The Irish Revolution* (London, 2015), pp 287–8.
91 Diarmaid Ferriter, *The Transformation of Ireland, 1900–2000* (London, 2005), p. 300.
92 See Magill, *Political Conflict in East Ulster*, p. 34; Parkinson, *Difficult Birth*, p. 281.
93 Tom Williams was the only republican executed in the history of the Northern Ireland state. He was hanged on 2 Sep. 1942 for the murder of RUC Constable Patrick Murphy on 5 Apr. 1942. See James McVeigh, *Executed: Tom Williams and the IRA* (Belfast, 1999).
94 Ferriter, *Nation and not a Rabble*, p. 286.
95 *Irish Times*, 10 May 2022, quoted by Gerard Shannon in *Special Supplement*, p. 42.
96 Magill, *Political Conflict in East Ulster*, p. 114.
97 See Eunan O'Halpin and Daithí Ó Corráin, *The Dead of the Irish Revolution* (New Haven and London, 2020), p. 543.
98 Lynch in 'People's Protectors?', p. 375, describes the 'conflict' in Belfast as 'by far the most violent in Ireland during the whole revolutionary period.' The Irish counties with the lowest number of fatalities per 10,000

population, between 1916–21, were Tyrone, Cavan, Fermanagh and Down; see O'Halpin and Ó Corráin, *Dead of the Irish Revolution*, pp 543, 545.

99 Parkinson, *Difficult Birth*, p. 280.
100 Lynch, 'People's Protectors?', pp 378, 385–6; Glennon, 'The dead of the Belfast pogrom'.
101 Follis, *State Under Siege*, p. 94; Parkinson, *Difficult Birth*, pp 162, 192; Tallents papers, July 1922 (TNA, CO 906/30).
102 Lynch, 'People's Protectors?', pp 378, 388–9.
103 Parkinson, *Difficult Birth*, p. 280.
104 David McKittrick, et al., *Lost Lives: The Stories of the Men, Women and Children who died as a result of the Northern Ireland Troubles* (Edinburgh and London, 1999), Tables 1, 6, 16, pp 1,473–82; Lynch, 'People's Protectors?', p. 378; Magill, *Political Conflict in East Ulster*, pp 170, 167–74. See also, W.E. Vaughan and A.J. Fitzpatrick (eds), *Irish Historical Statistics: Population, 1921–1971* (Dublin, 1978).
105 Ferriter, *Nation and not a Rabble*, p. 289.
106 Ibid., p. 290; Robin Bury, 'Buried lives: the Protestants of southern Ireland' in Roche and Barton (eds), *The Northern Ireland Question: Perspectives on Nationalism and Unionism* (Tunbridge Wells, 2020), p. 318.
107 David Fitzpatrick, *The Two Irelands, 1912-1939* (Oxford, 1998), p. 119. See also Follis, *op. cit.*, p. 94.
108 Magill, *op. cit.*, p. 97, 129.
109 Lynch, *Northern IRA*, *op. cit.*, p. 35.
110 Barton, *Brookeborough*, *op. cit.*, pp 55-6; also Tallents papers, 'Notes on police force' (TNA, CO906/27).
111 Buckland, *History of Northern Ireland*, p. 42.
112 Follis, *State Under Siege*, p. 90, citing a letter from Churchill to Craig dated 14 Feb. 1922.
113 Parkinson, *Difficult Birth*, pp 63–4; also Barton, *Brookeborough*, p. 49.
114 Follis, *State Under Siege*, p. 16.
115 Quoted in Parkinson, *Difficult Birth*, p. 68.
116 Magill, *Political Conflict in East Ulster*, p. 85; Barton, *Brookeborough*, p. 57.
117 Magill, *Political Conflict in East Ulster*, p. 85.
118 Follis, *State Under Siege*, pp 190, 193.
119 Magill, *Political Conflict in East Ulster*, pp 175–6, 181.
120 Lynch, *Northern IRA*, *op. cit.*, p. 210.
121 Follis, *State Under Siege*, pp 193-4.
122 Michael Laffan, *The Partition of Ireland, 1911–1925* (Dundalk, 1983), p. 106.
123 Buckland, *History of Northern Ireland*, p. 50.
124 Bury, 'Buried lives', p. 325.
125 See Yaojun Li and Richard O'Leary, 'Progress in reducing Catholic disadvantage in Northern Ireland', *Proceedings of the British Academy*, 137 (Oct. 2007), Table 13.1.

9

The life and career of Denis Henry (1864–1925)

An Irish political misfit: Catholic unionist politician and first Lord Chief Justice of Northern Ireland

ÉAMON PHOENIX

Denis Henry – a man of the law

In the quiet Catholic churchyard at Straw, near Draperstown, County Londonderry, a plain rectangular stone marks the grave of the Right Honourable Sir Denis Henry, Bart., the only Roman Catholic ever to have become an Ulster Unionist MP and the first Lord Chief Justice of Northern Ireland.

Denis Stanislaus Henry was born on 7 March 1864, in the townland of Cahore, Draperstown, the sixth son of James Henry, a prosperous merchant and landowner, and his second wife, Ellen (née Kelly). Of his 15 siblings (he was one of nine brothers and seven sisters), two brothers and two sisters were to enter religious life; one brother was a Marist priest while another, Rev. William Henry SJ became rector of the Jesuit Novitiate at Tullamore in King's County (now County Offaly). Two other brothers became solicitors.[1]

The Henrys were a well-established, wealthy family in a largely Catholic farming district which had been planted by the Drapers' Company of London during the seventeenth-century Plantation of Ulster. The village in the foothills of the Sperrins had been laid out in 1845 by the Drapers' Company. The district suffered considerably during the Great Famine but, thanks to the establishment of a railway connection in the 1850s, Draperstown was a successful market town by the time of Denis's birth. In 1862, a deputation from the Drapers' Company recorded that the village was 'flourishing'. Henry's father, James is not mentioned by name but he was undoubtedly the unnamed 'owner of the townland of Cahore' who, the report noted, 'had rebuilt ... his part of the town ... giving it a most respectable appearance.' The Henrys lived in a substantial Georgian villa known as 'The Rath' with a coach-house and servants' quarters attached. In a memoir his Jesuit older brother, William recalled that their father was 'a landlord'.[2]

The young Denis Henry received his early education at the local boys' National school where he was enrolled as a Catholic pupil in a school which had some Protestants as well. He proceeded to the Marist College in Dundalk, transferring, in 1878, along with his brother Patrick to the Jesuit college of Mount St Mary's in Chesterfield. The choice of an English, rather than an Irish, Catholic public school was probably due to the fact that Denis's late uncle, Father William Henry SJ, had been a pupil there – further evidence of the family's status. Denis would appear to have been an average student. Interestingly, his period at Chesterfield overlapped with the teaching career there of the poet Gerard Manley Hopkins. Henry proceeded to Queen's College, Belfast, where he read law. This was an unusual choice for an Ulster Catholic in the 1880s when the hierarchy was railing against the so-called 'godless colleges.' After a glittering academic career, in which he achieved the distinction of winning every available law scholarship possible, he was called to the Irish Bar in 1885 at the early age of 21.[3]

A keen legal mind – attested to by his contemporaries – together with a 'captivating appearance' and 'a fine musical voice' assisted his rapid progress at the late Victorian Bar. Henry quickly established himself on the North-West Circuit, extending from Westmeath to Derry, Tyrone and Donegal, eventually taking silk in 1896 when he was only 32. Two years later he was elected a Bencher of King's Inns. Thereafter, he was much in demand as a prosecutor and in 1898 he appeared for the Crown in three murder cases in Belfast, securing convictions in each case.

It was not until he had already established himself as a successful advocate that Henry began to consider the attractions of a career in politics. However, when he finally entered political life, he aligned himself not with the Irish Home Rule Party – soon to be reunited under John Redmond after the bitterness of the Parnell split – but with the Conservative and Unionist Party. Indeed, his family background, though intensely Catholic, was strongly conservative and pro-union. As his political adversary, T.P. O'Connor, the celebrated Home Rule MP for Liverpool, later observed:

> He was of a somewhat unique type in Irish life, Catholic by descent and personally ... yet he was entirely at variance with the politics of his co-religionists. His family had always belonged to the prosperous middle classes of Ulster. They shared none of the enthusiasms of his co-religionists and it was in this realistic atmosphere that he was brought up.[4]

Denis Henry – a political career

The Henry family, as landlords in mid-Ulster, were remembered as opponents of the Land League in the 1880s. Like many middle class Ulster Catholics and Presbyterians, they had been liberals but, according to Denis Henry in a 1906 speech, had shown 'a reluctance to go with Mr Gladstone when he took up Home Rule'. Thus, while the bulk of Catholics in the north of Ireland rallied to the revitalised Home Rule Party under Parnell in the so-called 'invasion of Ulster' of 1885, the Henrys gravitated to liberal unionism, placing themselves in the same camp as the great mass of former Presbyterian liberals.[5]

As early as the 1895 general election Henry publicly endorsed the unionist nominee in South Londonderry. In the 1895 election, the rising advocate spoke on unionist platforms in East Donegal on behalf of the local industrialist, E.T. Herdman, earning him a scornful rebuke from the nationalist *Derry Journal*. It noted with some disdain how: 'A star of North-West circuit magnitude ... has appeared over the hills of Dark Donegal. Mr Denis S. Henry, Barrister, has found time in the midst of his brief ... to rush from the Derry Assizes to East Donegal to save his country.'[6] Speaking to an exclusively Protestant audience, Henry dealt frankly with the issue of his religion:

> While a member of another Church, he was not afraid to stand there and say that he was not ashamed of his religion (applause) and that he felt, as an Irishman who had the welfare of his country at heart, he could sink religious differences and support the candidature of Mr Herdman.[7]

Henry's remarks show that at this early stage in his career he subscribed to the broader, more inclusive Irish unionism of the Anglo-Irish Southern Unionists rather than the narrower sectarian-based unionism of the north.

Significantly, Henry attended the inaugural meeting of the Ulster Unionist Council on 3 March 1905 as a delegate – one of the very few Catholics to identify with the Orange-dominated movement. Apart from his family background it would seem that Henry's educational experience had played a role in shaping his political outlook. Unlike most nationalists and the future Ulster Unionist leader Sir Edward Carson, Henry rejected his church's demand for a Catholic denominational university, declaring: 'Mixing was good for everyone as it broadened their views and let them see that other people held as honest opinions as themselves.'[8]

Henry's first attempt to enter parliament came in the 1906 general election when he was selected as the unionist candidate for the highly marginal seat of North Tyrone. The 1906 contest and the by-election which arose there the following year, provide useful insight not only into Henry's personality and outlook, but also into the manner with which Ulster politics was conducted at a local level. The Catholic unionist's nomination for North Tyrone was significant. The constituency was one of the most peculiar in Ireland at the time. Despite a slender Catholic majority in population terms, the nationalist strength on the register was several hundred votes below that of the unionists. The fate of the seat turned on the votes of some 200 Presbyterian farmers who adhered to the old liberal faith: they would support a Liberal Home Ruler but could not be relied upon to vote for a full-blooded Irish nationalist. As a result, the nationalists had tended to allow the Liberal Party a clear run and in 1906 William Dodd KC, a lawyer and Protestant Home Ruler, was the outgoing member and candidate. Thus Henry, the Catholic unionist lawyer, was pitted against Dodd, the Protestant Home Ruler. In an exciting contest Dodd managed to hold the seat by the narrow margin of just nine votes.

The nationalist press showed little sympathy for the Catholic lawyer. The *Irish News* described Henry as 'one of that weird class of creatures known as an Irish Catholic Unionist' whose stance would be anathema to Catholics and whose religion would arouse the worst sectarian feeling among Protestants. Orangeism remained the bedrock of Ulster unionism and Henry's meetings in Orange halls riled the nationalists, while the unionist *Londonderry Sentinel* riposted that Henry's attitude reflected his belief that 'the Orangemen of Ireland are a highly constant factor in defending the Union ...'.[9] Henry deftly ignored the sectarian issue, but reiterated his belief in a pluralist, non-sectarian unionism:

> I am opposed to the establishment of any separate legislature for this country or to any legislature which may in any way tend to weaken the Union between this country and the rest of the United Kingdom. Whether this change is sought to be effected by a Home Rule Bill or under the guise of devolution, it shall have my strongest opposition.[10]

During the 1906 campaign, the rising senior counsel elaborated on his views on the union. At Strabane, he stated that it was the finality of Home Rule which made the measure particularly dangerous and warned that a Home Rule Act could not be repealed or amended. At Castlederg, he declared that Ireland was already free enough, with full religious equality. At Plumbridge, he stressed that a Dublin government would have little sympathy for Ulster or its industries.

The Dublin-based lawyer added that he could see little in common between the north and the rest of Ireland, saying that the south represented 'quite a different community altogether.' This speech marks a clear hardening of Henry's unionism and an overt partitionism, reflecting the more 'Ulstercentric' outlook of James Craig and the Ulster Unionist Council. In 1895, Henry had addressed Donegal unionists as an 'Irishman', yet now he seemed keen to emphasis 'the distinctiveness of Ulster'.[11] The election result showed that while Henry attracted few Catholic votes, he enjoyed the overwhelming endorsement of the Conservative leadership, including Joseph Chamberlain and the Irish Chief Secretary, Walter Long, as well as local Orangemen.

Henry's reliance on the Orange Order aroused a mixture of anger and bewilderment among his co-religionists. One leading nationalist cleric, Rev. Philip O'Doherty, referred to the 'incredible state of affairs' in North Tyrone, commenting that while Judge William Kenny, a former Dublin MP, had merely been a Catholic unionist, Henry had embraced the Orange faction too. In the annals of Irish elections, he added, 'it was a thing unknown to have a Catholic supported by the Orange lodges.' In the *Irish News*, a correspondent poked fun at 'Brother Dinish [Denis]' in doggerel verse:

> A Papist beating the Orange drum!
> Surely no slavery could be 'maner'?
> To what base uses you have come
> In the hope of a North Tyrone retainer![12]

In an election generally devoid of rancour, 5,954 voted out of a total electorate of 6,174 – 'a remarkable testament to the organisational flair and perhaps the personating ability of both parties'. When the result was announced, Henry rejected the advice of his agent to demand a recount. He congratulated the victorious Home Ruler and promised to continue their amicable relationship. The election, he observed, had shown that the north of Ireland was a tolerant as anywhere else in the United Kingdom although he had been 'technically beaten for the time being'.

Henry again fought North Tyrone in 1907 when a by-election arose following Dodd's elevation to the Bench. Unionist suspicions of the new Liberal government were stoked by the introduction of the (ill-fated) Irish Council Bill which promised a measure of devolution. This time Henry lost to another Liberal Home Ruler, the Catholic Redmond Barry by seven votes. As in the previous year, over 90 per cent of votes were cast as the opposing sides spared no effort to maximise their respective turn-outs. One man died in the arms of friends while being lifted out of bed while a Catholic student for the priesthood made a 400-mile round trip from Maynooth seminary to register his vote against Henry. One voter arrived from Buenos Aires, while brandy was administered to one man who managed to vote for Henry before expiring. The defeated unionist candidate once more suppressed his disappointment, enjoining his supporters to desist from violence: 'if you keep the peace you will please me as much as if you had returned me'. Henry could return to the Four Courts in Dublin secure in the knowledge that his unionist credentials had been firmly established for the future.[13]

The Catholic unionist's political ambitions were destined to remain in abeyance for the next decade as he concentrated on his legal career. He declined a nomination in North Tyrone in the 1910 general elections 'owing to increasing professional duties' and took little public part in the anti-Home Rule struggle of 1912–14. His unionism remained solid, however, despite the apparent inevitability of Home Rule, speaking on anti-Home Rule platforms in England and Scotland 'with great effect' according to the *London Times*, to refute the impression that unionism was a sectarian cause.[14]

Henry did not sign the Ulster Covenant in 1912 which was not merely a self-consciously 'Protestant' protest against the third Home Rule Bill, but invoked the right of Ulster unionism to resort to violence to thwart Irish self-government. However, speaking in Dublin in November 1912, he argued that an Irish parliament would do little to protect the rights of minorities and that in the 30 years since he had come to Dublin, no unionist had held public office under the corporation. This was a bad augury for a future Home Rule parliament. If Home Rule were passed, he said, displaying his characteristic court-room wit, the loyal minority would be at the mercy of 'metropolitan misfits and provincial pirates'. In a speech which echoed the Tory rhetoric of the 1880s, Henry expressed the hope that the British public 'would decline to hand them over to a party of disorder and ... disloyalists'.[15]

Henry's legal and establishment connections were strengthened in October 1910 by his marriage to Violet Holmes, the daughter of Hugh Holmes, an Irish Lord Justice of Appeal from County Tyrone. Despite the fact that his bride was a member of the Church of Ireland, the couple were married quietly according to the rites of the Catholic Church at St Ethelbert's, Leominster, Herefordshire. The decision to marry outside Ireland may have been politic at a time when the implications of the *Ne Temere* decree and the acrimonious McCann mixed marriage case of 1910 was exercising Ulster unionism. The marriage was solemnised by Denis's older brother, Rev. William Henry, who was then working among the Dublin poor at the Jesuit mission in Gardiner Street. Denis was now 46, his wife 31. They would have five children: James, born in 1911, Denise, Alice, Denis and Lorna. They were brought up as Catholics while Violet adhered to her Protestant faith.[16]

Henry was now at the top of his profession with a Georgian townhouse in Dublin's fashionable Fitzwilliam Square. In a will dated November 1910, he was able to bequeath to his wife the substantial sum of £16,000. W.E.

Wylie, later a law advisor to the British government in Ireland, recalled him as 'the quickest thinker and most brilliant advocate' he ever knew, a view shared by A.M. Sullivan, who defended Roger Casement in 1916. Sullivan felt that Henry was 'the best man the Irish bar produced' in his time. Henry remained on cordial terms with political opponents such as Tim Healy KC, the maverick nationalist MP, and T.P. O'Connor. One nationalist legal colleague recalled the lack of rancour at the pre-partition Irish Bar: 'To listen to the circle often formed around Tim Healy or Denis Henry ... was to enjoy a feast of reason...The [Law] Library was a microcosm of the life of Ireland ... political foes sat cheek by jowl ... good companions all.'[17] Henry's legal standing was recognised in January 1914 when he was one of two counsel appointed to head an inquiry into the famous Dublin lock-out of 1913 when a clash between police and strikers resulted in two deaths. His final report exonerated the police though some 20 members were found to have committed unjustifiable assaults.

Victory at last

An unexpected opportunity for Henry to redress his earlier political disappointments came in April 1916 when the South Londonderry seat became vacant. With a wartime political truce in force, Henry's selection and return for his native constituency seemed a foregone conclusion. This was not the case, however. He won the nomination only after a third ballot against Colonel Robert Chichester, the local squire, and D.D. Reid, a fellow barrister, and had to face a contest against a maverick independent candidate from Scotland, Dr Arthur Turnbull, a critic of the government's handling of the war.

While Henry once more enjoyed the support of the Orange Order, the brief campaign which followed suggested a softening of nationalist asperities towards him. A local Catholic curate, Father P. McGeown of Kilrea, went so far as to welcome Henry's election:

> At present it matters not whether a man is a Nationalist, a Unionist, or a Liberal, but to us it does matter very much that he should be a Catholic. And Mr Denis Henry, KC, is a Catholic. We feel that when our interests, or the interests of our religion are at stake we shall have a supporter in our future MP.

Interestingly, this was the first by-election in Ireland following the Easter Rising, with the poll coming a mere 11 days after the final executions and in an atmosphere of martial law.[18] Henry's early parliamentary career was low-key though he served on the royal commission into the deaths of three innocent civilians, including the pacifist Francis Sheehy-Skeffington, during the rebellion. In November 1918, he was appointed Solicitor-General for Ireland in the Lloyd George coalition.

In the run-up to the post-war general election – the first test of public opinion to be held since 1910 – Henry appeared for the unionists at the Tyrone revision sessions in Omagh in November 1918. When his nationalist opponent, the local Sinn Féin leader and solicitor, George Murnaghan, claimed that the 'greater part of the Unionist objections dealt with religion', a question the court was not competent to deal with, Henry was quick to emphasise the overlap of religious and political allegiances in Ulster:

> They all knew that in Northern counties religious and political fears coincided. ... The Unionist population of Tyrone was 45 per cent and the Nationalists 55 per cent and, on those grounds, they [the unionist minority] were at least entitled to some consideration.

His efforts ensured that one of the county's three designated seats – South Tyrone – would return a unionist candidate in the subsequent general election.[19]

In that general election, which saw Sinn Féin sweep the polls in nationalist Ireland, he successfully defended his South Londonderry seat against Louis J. Walsh of Sinn Féin (who was, ironically, a distant cousin) and a Home Rule candidate. Selected in Kilrea Orange hall, Henry was publicly endorsed by Carson as 'a most loyal and devoted colleague', while the Orange grandmaster in the constituency called on every member of the Order to support him.

Henry warned his supporters that his Sinn Fein opponent represented 'everything that was abominable to their loyalty and allegiance.' With Sinn Féin and the nationalists focusing on the growing threat of partition, Henry showed no enthusiasm for it. He told a meeting in Magherafelt that he felt deeply for his fellow unionists in the south and west and stated that he would prefer to see the present constitutional arrangements unchanged so that both unionists and nationalists could 'enjoy the blessings and benefits of ... the Union.' Unionists, he declared, would never submit to a Dublin legislature. A young nationalist who heard Henry speak recalled him as 'an accomplished and convincing orator' who spoke with 'a refined, cultured Dublin accent.'[20] The fatal split in the Catholic vote combined to give Henry a comfortable majority of nearly 5,000 votes over his nearest opponent, the constitutional nationalist, Professor John Conway. Yet the South Londonderry election of December 1918 would represent the last occasion in which a Catholic won a unionist seat in Ulster.

The return of the Tory-dominated Lloyd George coalition in 1919, with its explicit commitment to partition, enabled James Craig and the Ulster Unionists to accept four junior ministries. These included Henry, now promoted to the post of Attorney-General for Ireland, a position he held throughout the violence of the Irish War of Independence. The first meeting of Dáil Éireann in January 1919 coincided with the opening shots in the independence struggle. In the House of Commons, Henry, the superb advocate whose mastery of his brief had been his hallmark, now found himself in the invidious position of having to defend the British government's controversial policy in Ireland against a background of mounting insurgency and increasing militarism and organised 'reprisals' by Crown forces.

Henry served two Irish chief secretaries: Ian Macpherson and, following the latter's resignation in April 1920, Sir Hamar Greenwood. Throughout this tempestuous period, Henry had to respond to persistent allegations of misconduct by Crown forces; evidence of orchestrated British reprisals for IRA attacks; the introduction of coercive legislation; and the activities of new irregular forces, namely, the Black and Tans, the Auxiliaries and the Ulster Special Constabulary – all introduced in 1920 to strengthen the collapsing Royal Irish Constabulary. His discomfiture was not eased by Greenwood's frequent absences from the Commons and the mounting indictment of the government by the British press, the Labour Party, the former Prime Minister, Herbert Asquith and the rump of the nationalists under their formidable leader, 'Wee Joe' Devlin.[21]

One of Henry's first major challenges was a hunger-strike by Sinn Féin prisoners in Mountjoy jail in April 1920. The Attorney-General's palpable lack of reliable information on the condition of the hunger-strikers left him struggling at the despatch box. With *The Times* calling for decisive action (the prisoners were eventually released), Henry admitted in cabinet that the whole affair had been 'badly managed'. In his sensitive position as chief Irish law officer at this critical juncture Henry was closely involved in the formulation of the British government's controversial Irish strategy spanning partition and the ending of the Anglo-Irish War. As the IRA campaign escalated and a system of republican courts displaced the Crown courts, he remained unrepentant in his vindication of government policy, telling the Commons in February 1920 that Ireland was virtually in a state of war: 'It was not an attack on one party, it is not an attack on the Coalition government, it is an attack on your nation. It is an attempt to drive your nation out of Ireland.'

Henry was responsible for introducing the draconian Restoration of Order in Ireland (ROIA) legislation which became law in August 1920 and enabled legalised internment and the suppression of inquests. The *Irish News* condemned the proposal to establish military courts-martial with the power to impose the death penalty while Devlin's bitter attack on the measure result in his suspension from the House of Commons. In a heated exchange with T.P. O'Connor, Henry denied any ill-treatment of prisoners by military authorities. The government, said Henry, had striven 'for a better state of affairs' and the ROIA was a last resort. He regarded those engaged in violence as 'rebels' and 'traitors' and declared that the government was entitled to deal with them on that basis.[22]

Such stridency, however, could not conceal the fact that Henry's parliamentary responses to mounting evidence of atrocities by Crown forces were unconvincing and 'perhaps the least satisfying aspect of [his] term of office.'[23] Badly briefed and evasive, he was forced to rely on RIC and military reports on incidents involving alleged reprisals and unwarranted shootings by Crown forces. As the conflict escalated in the early months of 1921 the political and personal pressures on Henry were intense. When he refused to discuss the alleged murder of men under army escort, his silence provoked vigorous protests by Liberal and nationalist MPs. Henry was also criticised by an official in Dublin Castle, Mark Sturgis, who alleged that he 'sat in London, afraid to set a foot in Ireland' at the height of the IRA campaign.[24] However, Henry's characteristic willingness to stand against the tide of Irish opinion and his later state-building role in Northern Ireland suggest that he did not lack personal courage. There is no doubt that his performance as Attorney-General was more impressive when explaining complex legislative matters such as the conditions of service of the RIC in Ireland, education and land purchase.

With Craig and his Ulster Unionist colleagues, Henry pointedly abstained on the second reading of the Government of Ireland Act (1920) which provided for partition and separate Home Rule parliaments, north and south. In the spring of 1921, as the government and Sinn Fein 'skirmished on the extreme edge of negotiation', he was amongst those in the cabinet in May 1921 who opposed a truce until the IRA had been defeated militarily. In the event of Sinn Féin refusing to operate the proposed Southern Irish parliament – a racing certainty – he was prepared to contemplate drastic action in the form of Crown Colony government.[25]

O'Connor, who knew Henry well at Westminster during this period, remembered him as:

> a tall, stout, red-faced man with a mane of hair rising high above his head and, in later years, very white. He had a strong face with a large nose and a very powerful jowl. If you did not know he was a distinguished lawyer you might take him for a squire of County Galway who had stood as a model to [the novelist] Charles Lever. The face indicated the nature, for though he was good-natured, he was also keenly alive to the good things of life, especially high position in his profession. These things he attained, but he had to go almost through blood and tears to reach them for he lived through a very stormy time in the history of his country.[26]

O'Connor added that, although Henry was often the subject of invective from nationalist MPs, he and they remained on friendly terms: 'they hated his politics but they did not – nobody could – hate the man.'

Lord Chief Justice

Any expectations of a respite from the pressures of public life were dispelled when, in August 1921, Henry was Craig's first choice for the position of Lord Chief Justice of Northern Ireland. He was sworn in before the Lord Chancellor for Ireland, Sir John Ross at a ceremony in Portrush Town Hall on 15 August 1921. Among the audience were Craig – now Prime Minister of Northern Ireland – and Henry's brother, Alexander Patterson Henry (known as 'Attorney' Henry), a local solicitor in Maghera. He was created a baronet in the same year.[27]

Henry's appointment came against the background of the July 1921 truce between the IRA and the British government, the Treaty negotiations, and the transfer of law and order to the Belfast authorities in November 1921. Northern nationalists continued to hope that the London negotiations would produce a united Irish state and showed little interest the appointment of a Catholic as head of the new judiciary. Dismissing Henry's appointment to 'the absurd northern judiciary', the *Irish News* commented caustically in August 1921: 'Sir James Craig's government cannot undertake any work with the degree of permanency attaching to it because they know that there can be no permanency in this partition.'[28]

To the deepening political uncertainty and politico-sectarian violence, which saw 450 people killed in Belfast during 1920–22, was added the urgent task of establishing new legal structures. The gargantuan task of creating the machinery of a new court system fell to Henry, now aged 57. He was active in the recruitment of officials to staff the new Northern judiciary, liaising with Dublin Castle and James Craig for whom he had 'a profound admiration' according to Lady Henry. One of Henry's first challenges was to ensure that the Northern Ireland Supreme Court, established under the 1920 Act, opened on 1 October 1921, the 'appointed day' laid down by Order in Council on which the separate Northern court system would come into existence.

Henry's colleagues on the new northern Court of Appeal were William Moore and James Andrews. Moore, a former Ulster Unionist MP and Carson's ally in the campaign against the third Home Rule Bill, had been a judge of the King's Bench Division in Dublin. Andrews was a brother of Craig's Minister of Labour, J.M. Andrews, and had served as standing counsel to numerous railway companies and corporations in Ulster. Sir Denis was well acquainted with his two High Court judges in the northern judiciary as both had served with him as Ulster Unionist politicians and law officers: D.M. Wilson had served as Solicitor General for Ireland while T.W. Brown had succeeded Sir Denis as Attorney-General.

While Henry was personally engaged in interviewing and appointing judges and court officials, he also took steps to secure appropriate premises for the Supreme Court of Northern Ireland. As the erection of a suitable court building would take time, he secured the use of the county courthouse on Belfast's Crumlin Road from its owners, Antrim County Council. Henry would not live to see the opening of purpose-built Law Courts in Chichester Street in 1933.

The frenetic amount of work involved in creating a new system of courts from scratch took its toll on the middle-aged jurist, already exhausted by the pressures of the Anglo-Irish conflict. As his colleague, William Moore has recorded:

> Henry did not spare himself in constant anxious work in setting up the courts and their administration, involving him in endless discussion and negotiation with the governments in Belfast and London, with the bar and the Law Society, council officials and many others. Added to his judicial work this made up a formidable workload.

His family believed that this formidable burden contributed to his death three years later at the early age of 61.[29]

As Lord Chief Justice, Henry was involved in several highly controversial cases which reflected the turbulent birth-pangs of the new state. In July 1922, he ruled against the plaintiff in a landmark case (O'Hanlon v. Governor of Belfast Prison) challenging the legality of the unionist government's Civil Authorities (Special Powers Act), 1922. The case concerned John O'Hanlon, a Portadown hotelier and former director of the Portadown Gas Company, who challenged his internment under the Act before the Northern Ireland High Court on two grounds: he contested the factual basis of any allegation against him by submitting an affidavit in which he denied involvement in any unlawful association or conspiracy, and he submitting that the introduction of internment under the Special Powers Act amounted to a suspension of *habeas corpus*, contrary to the terms of the 1920 Government of Ireland Act.

O'Hanlon's counsel, Thomas J. Campbell KC (later a nationalist MP at Stormont) argued that the draconian legislation under which his client was detained left captivity to the uncontrolled will of the Attorney-General which was 'a sweeping inroad on the old established guarantees for the liberty of the subject'. Henry's judgment was a predicable defence of the emergency law. Dismissing the factual basis of the plaintiff's claim, he ruled that: 'The only question the court has to decide … is whether … O'Hanlon is legally held. We have nothing to do with the consideration of whether there is any evidence against him.' Accordingly, Lord Chief Justice Henry ruled that O'Hanlon might be held so long as the executive desired.

Rejecting defence counsel's argument that the Special Powers Act breached the liberty of the individual, Henry held that the internment order was a 'modification of orders made in England almost every day by the Home Secretary there during the duration of the [First World] war dealing with persons of hostile origin or hostile association ...'. Consequently, the regulations were not *ultra vires*. The judgment prompted a blistering attack on Henry's judgment by the *Irish News* which described O'Hanlon as a respectable citizen who had been 'kidnapped in the name of the law'. It declared sarcastically that the Lord Chief Justice had been too 'careful of the feelings ... of Sir James Craig's "fair administration" ...'.[30]

In November 1923, Henry rejected claims for compensation for the victims arising over a notorious incident in Cushendall, County Antrim, on 23 June 1922 when three Catholic youths were shot dead by members of the 'A' Special Constabulary within hours of the IRA assassination of Sir Henry Wilson in London. While the police claimed that the men had been engaged in a paramilitary ambush, witnesses alleged they had been innocent while a private investigation by an English barrister, Robert Barrington-Ward KC rejected the Specials' version: 'My conclusion is that no one except the police and military even fired at all ... I am unable to accept the evidence of the Special Constabulary'. The unionist government, however, suppressed the report and ordered a fresh inquiry which vindicated the USC. In his judgment, Henry referred to the 'extraordinary conflict of testimony' between the police and the nationalist witnesses, but he rejected the claim for compensation on the grounds that the deaths arose out of an unlawful assembly.[31] Such adjudications reflected Henry's earlier defence of emergency legislation during the War of Independence and his instinctive support for the forces of law and order in their defence of the new sub-state.

The stresses and strains of the Irish Revolution years had taken their toll on Henry. He died, following a seizure, on 1 October 1925, at his home, 'Lisvarna', Windsor Avenue, Belfast. He was 61. In his final illness, he received the last rites of the Catholic Church from the local parish priest and the rector of Ardoyne Passionist monastery in Belfast. Tim Healy claimed that the dying judge 'had a priest after sixty years', suggesting that he had long abandoned religious practice. After a private Mass in the family home celebrated by his Jesuit brother William, Denis Henry was buried in his native place at Straw in the rolling Sperrins. In a tribute, Craig described him as 'one of Ulster's most distinguished sons.' His political opponents paid tribute to his personal qualities, his legal acumen and his compassion as a judge but, as O'Connor observed in an obituary, 'there remained some resentment among his co-religionists – and among nationalists generally – that this man of Celtic blood and of the Catholic creed should range himself in the ranks of the Orangemen.'³²

The career of Sir Denis Henry remains unique in an island where religious and political allegiances are often synonymous. Previous Catholic unionists like William Kenny and Father John Healy of Little Bray had come from the south of Ireland. Catholic unionists were always in short supply in the north. Henry's name was largely forgotten until the late 1960s when, in response to civil rights claims of anti-Catholic discrimination, unionist politicians trumpeted that the first Lord Chief Justice of Northern Ireland had been a Catholic. Yet attempts to broaden unionmist beyond its traditional Protestant base had little success in the divided state after his death and it was not until 1998 that another Catholic unionist was elected to the Northern Ireland Assembly.³³

Notes

1. A.D. McDonnell, *The Life of Sir Denis Henry, Catholic Unionist* (Belfast, 2000), pp 1–3; *Belfast Telegraph*, 2 Oct. 1925.
2. McDonnell, *Life of Sir Denis Henry*, pp 3–4; memo by Rev. William Henry SJ (Jesuit Archives, Dublin).
3. Ibid.; *Londonderry Sentinel*, 3 Oct. 1925; report on sale of the former Henry residence in *Irish News*, 26 Feb. 2010.
4. *Belfast Telegraph*, 2 Oct. 1925.
5. *Londonderry Sentinel*, 6 Jan. 1906.
6. *Derry Journal*, 29 July 1895.
7. Ibid.
8. John Biggs-Davison and George Chowdhary-Best, *The Cross of St Patrick: The Catholic Unionist Tradition in Ireland* (Kendal, 1984), p. 290.
9. McDonnell, *Life of Sir Denis Henry*, pp 11–16.
10. *Londonderry Sentinel*, 2 Jan. 1906.
11. McDonnell, *Life of Sir Denis Henry*, p. 14; Alvin Jackson, 'Irish Unionism' in Peter Collins (ed.), *Nationalism and Unionism: Conflict in Ireland 1885–1921* (Belfast, 1994), pp 40–41.
12. McDonnell, *Life of Sir Denis Henry*, pp 15–16; *Irish News*, 2 Jan. 1906.
13. Ibid., pp 20–26; Rev. W. Devine (Naval Chaplain) to Judge E.S. Murphy, 13 Mar. 1944 (in possession of author). In 1944, an Irish Catholic chaplain attached to British forces in Italy ministered to Captain (later Sir) James Henry, a wounded officer in the Royal Navy and the eldest son of Denis Henry. At James Henry's request, the priest wrote to the officer's 'black Protestant uncle', E.S. Murphy, a Belfast judge and former Ulster

Unionist MP, informing the family that James Henry was wounded but alive. The priest added humorously: 'He was very grateful that I should go so far to see him but I explained that I had once gone much further (from Maynooth as a student) to vote against his father in North Tyrone ... Young Henry ... is such a decent fellow that I was almost sorry I voted against his father.' Murphy, a prominent Orangeman, had married a sister of Denis Henry's widow and had been a close friend of the Catholic unionist.

14 *The Times*, 2 Oct. 1925.
15 *Northern Whig*, 20 Dec. 1909; Biggs-Davison and Chowdhary-Best, *Cross of St Patrick*, p. 292.
16 Certificate of Henry's marriage, 1 Oct. 1910 (General Register Office, London); obituary of Rev. W. Henry, *Irish Province News*, June 1928, pp 73–5.
17 McDonnell, *Life of Sir Denis Henry*, pp 30–31; T.J. Campbell, *Fifty Years of Ulster, 1890–1940* (Belfast, 1941), p. 136.
18 McDonnell, *Life of Sir Denis Henry*, pp 36–42.
19 *Irish News*, 22 Nov. 1917.
20 McDonnell, *Life of Sir Denis Henry*, pp 45–50; Eoin Walsh letter in *Irish News*, 13 July 1984.
21 McDonnell, *Life of Sir Denis Henry*, pp 53–60.
22 House of Commons Debates, 12 Apr. 1920, vol. 127, col. 1487; 19 Feb. 1920, vol. 125, col. 1171; 25 Apr. 1920, vol. 127, col. 2046–7.
23 McDonnell, *Life of Sir Denis Henry*, p. 71; Michael Hopkinson (ed.), *The Last Days of Dublin Castle: The Diaries of Mark Sturgis* (Dublin, 1999), p. 48.
24 McDonnell, *Life of Sir Denis Henry*, p. 72.
25 Thomas Jones, *Whitehall Diary, Volume III, Ireland, 1918–25*, edited by Keith Middlemas (London, 1971), pp 59, 71; McDonnell, *Life of Sir Denis Henry*, pp 66–7.
26 *Belfast Telegraph*, 2 Oct. 1925.
27 McDonnell, *Life of Sir Denis Henry*, pp 90–91.
28 Biggs-Davison and Chowdhary-Best, *Cross of St Patrick*, p. 355; *Irish News*, 6 Aug. 1921.
29 Cormac Moore, *Birth of the Border: The Impact of Partition in Ireland* (Newbridge, 2019), p. 107.
30 McDonnell, *Life of Sir Denis Henry*, pp 107–10.
31 Ibid., pp 110–14 Barrington-Ward's report indicting of the USC at Cushendall was not released until the late 1970s.
32 *Belfast Telegraph*, 2 Oct. 1925.
33 Sir John Gorman, a former senior RUC officer, was elected in North Down as an Ulster Unionist supportive of the Good Friday Agreement in 1998.

10

The Swanzy riots: Lisburn, 1920

CHRISTOPHER MAGILL

Introduction

In the summer of 1920 a series of riots erupted in parts of east Ulster, mainly in Belfast, Lisburn, Banbridge and Dromore. These events came as the IRA challenged British authority in Ireland and they signalled the loyalist backlash to the republican push for independence. Ulster in general had been relatively peaceful until the spring. In April, a major outbreak of violence occurred in Derry, continued intermittently until June, and involved gun battles between the IRA and UVF.[1] In July, serious communal strife manifested in Belfast and surrounding towns with violence continuing sporadically for the best part of two years in the city, killing at least 400 people.[2]

Much has been written about the violence in Belfast. This chapter focuses on an outbreak in a smaller urban setting, that of Lisburn in August 1920. These riots, initiated by loyalists against the local Catholic population, lasted between 22 and 25 August, and while they were in direct response to the IRA assassination of RIC District Inspector Oswald Swanzy in the centre of the town, they were shaped by wider Irish political and military events. The Lisburn – or Swanzy – riots were an important indicator of the interconnectedness of events in Ireland and this chapter will illustrate how community relations in the north-east were directly affected by events in the south. It will also highlight the plight of victims and bring a human dimension to what can only too easily be overlooked as just another violent historical event. And finally, this chapter will demonstrate the significance of these riots, in conjunction with violence in Belfast and elsewhere, in shaping political attitudes in the months leading up to the establishment of the first government of Northern Ireland.

The shooting of DI Swanzy

The rioting that broke out in Lisburn on 22 August 1920 had its roots in the opposite end of the island. It was in Cork that RIC District Inspector Oswald Swanzy became infamous in republican circles for his alleged role in the fatal shooting of the Sinn Féin lord mayor of Cork city, Tomás MacCurtain. On the night of 19 March 1920, a group of men, believed to be police officers, forced entry into MacCurtain's home and shot him dead. At the subsequent inquest it was discovered that the same men were seen entering Swanzy's home not long before the shooting, leading many to believe that Swanzy either directed the killing or failed to prevent it. Either way, he was named in the inquest as a responsible party, along with the British Prime Minister, David Lloyd George, the Lord Lieutenant of Ireland, Lord French, and other prominent members of the RIC.[3] Swanzy, therefore, became a key target for revenge, and a much more realistic one than the other alleged guilty parties. The Cork IRA had its chance to exact revenge on Swanzy soon after the death of MacCurtain. Florence O'Donoghue recalled that he encountered Swanzy one morning not long after MacCurtain was killed but decided against shooting him to avoid undermining the effect of the coming inquest verdict.[4] After his name was publicly read out in the coroner's report, the RIC transferred Swanzy to Lisburn, but it did not take long for the IRA to discover his new posting and confirm it via scouts.[5]

Plans were put in place for Swanzy's assassination. Originally, it was supposed to be carried out on 15 August, but was cancelled at the last minute when the car taking the gunmen from Belfast to Lisburn broke down. On the second attempt Roger McCorley, an IRA scout from Belfast, stayed in Lisburn in the days leading up to the operation to familiarise himself with Swanzy's movements and to ensure he could be properly identified. On the morning of 22 August, Sean Leonard, a republican from Sligo working as a taxi driver in Belfast, drove three IRA volunteers from Belfast to Lisburn. They were Sean Culhane and Dick Murphy from Cork, and Thomas Fox from Belfast. They met McCorley on the north side of Market Square, across from Railway Street where Swanzy lived. Leonard stayed in the taxi on Castle Street, which ran perpendicular to Railway Street. McCorley confirmed Swanzy had gone to church, so the men waited and made themselves as inconspicuous as possible, going as far as not speaking 'for fear our southern accents would betray us'.[6] It was at 12.30pm that Swanzy left Christ Church on Church Lane, less than half a mile from where the IRA gunmen waited. Swanzy set off home, joined by Major Gerald Valentine Ewart and Frederick Ewart, the major's father. They crossed Smithfield and Market Street, then onto Market Square.[7]

By now other churches had finished service and Sunday worshippers were filling the centre of Lisburn. It was something the gunmen had not expected and the crowded streets risked throwing their plans into disarray. McCorley recalled that he 'had never seen very many people at one time in the streets, but on this Sunday there were large numbers around.'[8] Fox confirmed 'many hundreds of people' were in the streets.[9] Despite this, they spotted their target and made their move at the corner of Railway Street. The republicans' attempts at remaining inconspicuous were successful as they came up behind Swanzy undetected. The Ewarts were unaware of the approaching assassins and both were pushed to the ground as Culhane fired the first shot into the back of Swanzy's head, using none other than MacCurtain's revolver.[10] Fox, McCorley and Murphy followed up with a volley of shots into Swanzy's lifeless body.

Across the road Lisburn cathedral had just finished service and its congregation was filing out onto Castle Street, creating a barrier between the gunmen and their getaway car. McCorley recalled 'the mob' turning angry and having to fire into it to get through.[11] One member of the congregation was ex-RAF captain Alex Woods who was standing on the north side of Castle Street waiting on his friend, Dr George St George, the chairman of Lisburn Urban Council and physician, who was exiting the gate of the cathedral. Woods recalled hearing something that he took to be a car backfiring, but soon realised the true source of the noise as he saw five men running in his direction holding revolvers. Woods may have been mistaken about the number of gunmen (IRA witness statements claim Leonard remained in the taxi), but he remembered clearly his own actions.

On seeing one of the assassins straggling behind, Woods, in his own words, 'rushed into the middle of the street and struck at him with my [blackthorn] stick.'[12] This was McCorley, who recalled being 'attacked by an ex-British Officer called Woods who seemed to have plenty of courage.' He pushed past Woods and, from only a few feet away, fired at him, 'by a fluke' shooting the stick out of his hand.[13] By now Dr St George reacted and made a late attempt for McCorley, but he was side-stepped, and the latter made a dash for the car. Leonard, however, had already started driving off and McCorley risked being left to the mercy of the Lisburn crowd. Luckily for him his comrades realised they were a member short and stopped so he could catch up.[14] A police chase failed and Swanzy's killers made good their escape. But they would not all evade justice. Dr St George managed to take note of the taxi number and report it to police. Without difficulty this was traced back to Sean Leonard who was later arrested and found guilty of his part in Swanzy's assassination. His sentence of death was later commuted to penal servitude.

Riots in Lisburn and other Ulster towns

It was in the immediate aftermath of this brutal shooting in front of so many shocked and horrified bystanders that rioting broke out. Yet, the Swanzy shooting occurred in a wider context that helps inform the loyalist backlash against Lisburn's Catholic population. By the summer of 1920 the Irish revolution had started to make a greater impact on north-east Ulster. IRA activity remained largely concentrated in the south, but the unionist press reported widely on it and the violence especially resonated amongst northern unionists when Protestant or Ulster police and military personnel were killed.[15] Politically, too, their antennae were twitching. In the January 1920 local urban elections, 44.7 per cent of the vote in Ulster went to non-unionist candidates in the form of republicans, constitutional nationalists, and labourites.[16]

This gave unionist leaders plenty to worry about as they viewed all three groups as one common enemy. James Craig felt Sinn Féin was 'working in conjunction with Bolshevik Forces', while the distinction between republicans and constitutional nationalists was unrecognised by his party and followers.[17] In the six counties that would become Northern Ireland, nationalists and republicans assumed control of ten urban councils, including Derry.[18] There were particular headline-grabbing results, such as in the overwhelmingly Protestant Lisburn where the first-preference vote poll was topped by a republican, William Shaw.[19] On the other hand, things were not quite as bad as unionists feared. The IRA were numerically and militarily weak in the north-east and the constitutional nationalists under Joseph Devlin held much greater sway than Sinn Féin among Catholics.[20]

Regardless, tensions within unionism heightened. On 12 July, Edward Carson delivered an inflammatory speech, often seen as a call to arms, in south Belfast. He said that unionists would 'take the matter into our own hands' if the government did not provide protection against the threat of the IRA.[21] Five days later the IRA assassinated the RIC divisional commissioner for Munster, Gerald B. Smyth, in Cork city in retaliation for his alleged support for shooting any civilian suspected of being in the IRA. Smyth was an Ulsterman from Banbridge and noted veteran of the First World War. His killing reverberated throughout the unionist community in the north.[22] On 21 July, Smyth's funeral took place in Banbridge while in Belfast industrial workers returned to their jobs after the Twelfth of July holidays.

In the Belfast shipyards, Protestant workers violently attacked and expelled their Catholic colleagues and some 'rotten Prods' whose loyalty was considered suspect. The incident sparked days of communal violence in the city in which 13 people died. In Banbridge, after Smyth had been laid to rest, loyalists attacked and burned down a newsagents owned by a Catholic, the alleged catalyst being the refusal of Catholic business owners to shut up shop for the duration of the funeral.[23] The following day Protestant employees of the Banbridge Weaving Company demanded the removal of Catholic workers. After succeeding, they made their way through the town coercing other businesses to follow suit.[24] Violence continued and culminated in a Protestant boy being shot, allegedly by a member of a well-known republican family whose house was being set upon by loyalists at the time.[25]

Rioting also broke out in other towns in the days following Smyth's funeral. Loyalists attacked Catholic-owned property in Dromore, including the Catholic Club and parochial house. The local priest, Father John O'Hare, was threatened at gunpoint to leave his home and during a second night of unrest a man was unintentionally shot by the police as they tried to disperse the crowd.[26] In Lisburn, a similar assault on Catholic homes and businesses began on 24 July, allegedly started by an influx of agitators from Belfast.[27] Again, symbolic Catholic buildings were targeted, including the Ancient Order of Hibernians hall and the convent, as well as property belonging to individual Catholic civilians.[28] After two days the police managed to put a stop to the upheaval.[29]

Therefore, Swanzy's assassination on 22 August occurred in a context of heightened tensions and uneasiness between unionists and nationalists. It was unsurprising that there was a severe loyalist reprisal. Some republicans even acknowledged that IRA operations in the north were too risky because of the potential of sectarian rioting that for so long had blighted Ulster. Ernest Blythe, a Protestant republican from Lisburn, stated decades later that although killing Swanzy was justifiable, to do it 'in a Lisburn street was a deed of lunatic recklessness' that led to 'disastrous consequences'.[30] Blythe, perhaps because he was a northern Protestant, understood the long established practice of sectarian rioting in the north-east and the ease with which it could be triggered.[31]

Immediately after Swanzy's death a hostile crowd numbering up to two thousand rapidly formed in the centre of Lisburn and started attacking property owned or occupied by Catholics.[32] First on the list were those who were either known to be active republicans or suspected as sympathisers. The confectionary shop of Isabella Gilmore on Cross Row, a stone's throw from where Swanzy's body lay, was first. Isabella's family were well known for their republican sympathies. Her deceased husband, Edward, had been a member of the Belfast IRB and raised their children in the republican tradition. One of her sons, William, had been GAA Ulster secretary between 1910 and 1911 when the family lived in Belfast. He and his brother Edward joined the Irish Volunteers and together attempted to take part in the botched Easter Rising in Ulster.[33]

Despite having to forego their GAA pastimes after moving to Lisburn (Gaelic sports were not played there after unionist outrage against them in

1904), their republican sympathies were well known in the town. In October 1919, Edward was arrested and court-martialled after a revolver and 50 rounds of ammunition were found in the Gilmore home on Cross Row.[34] Then in May 1920 Lisburn's unionist community received a reminder of the Gilmores' political persuasions when the *Lisburn Standard* reported that four Sinn Féiners, including William, had been nominated for the Lisburn Poor Law Board of Guardians.[35] It was unsurprising that the Gilmore shop and home were targeted first. The loyalist crowd raided the building and, failing to find the Gilmore men, emptied the furniture onto the street and burned it.

Next in line was Peter McKeever. Nothing is known of his political persuasion, but he was a Catholic and it is likely he was suspected of holding republican sympathies as he was targeted so soon in the riot. He was in his public house at the top of Bridge Street, just yards away from the Gilmore property, when it was attacked. The assault ended with him being shot and badly wounded. The crowd refused to allow an ambulance to attend to him, so McKeever was forced to escape through the cathedral graveyard that ran along the rear of his building. That afternoon the rioters visited another obvious target. William Shaw was Lisburn's only Sinn Féin councillor and well known for his politics, just like William Gilmore. Shaw was dragged onto the street outside his home on Haslem's Lane and badly beaten. His assailants then let him go and he made his way, presumably with some assistance, to the infirmary for much needed medical attention. His furniture, too, was taken outside and burned in the street. James Stronge, another republican nominated to the board of guardians, was also attacked on the first day of rioting.

Once the main republican figures in Lisburn were seen to, the loyalist crowd broadened its focus. Over the following two days the destruction continued, transforming from an assault on republicans to a crusade against Catholics and Catholic symbolism in general. The AOH hall on Linenhall Street was burned on Sunday evening and the convent and chapel were only saved by a guard of troops who arrived from Belfast not long after Swanzy was gunned down. Like events in Banbridge the previous month, there were industrial expulsions. Catholics were expected to take an oath of allegiance in many places of employment if they hoped to keep their jobs.[36]

Mitigation efforts were insufficient. The police were vastly outnumbered, and the military restricted its efforts to protecting key buildings, rather than risking an escalation with direct confrontation. The riots, therefore, continued unabated, as did the fires. The fire brigade struggled to hold back the flames, especially on Bow Street and Chapel Lane, thoroughfares where long stretches of terraced buildings were damaged. The Belfast fire brigade sent assistance on 23 August but stayed only a matter of hours, giving up after their hose was cut and repeated attempts were made to obstruct them.37 There were also peace efforts led by leading civilians and clergy. Canon W.P. Carmody convened a meeting of local notables in the cathedral in an attempt to devise a way to calm the situation in the town. Swanzy's cousin, Rev. Henry B. Swanzy, made his way to Lisburn on hearing of the trouble and attended the meeting. Those present offered their full support to Lisburn Urban Council and when the latter met arrangements were made to organise a peace patrol. Their aim was to calm the disturbances and, despite the presence of Rev. Swanzy on the patrol, rioters responded to the clergy by shouting 'an eye for an eye and a tooth for a tooth'.38

By Wednesday 25 August the riots had died out. The centre of Lisburn lay in ruins – described as a scene of 'absolute devastation' – and most of the town's Catholic population had been forced to flee.39 The scale of the destruction was enormous, with compensation claims amounting to £806,538. Although the figure the courts granted was significantly less, at £213,488, it was still too much for Lisburn Urban Council to cover.40 A debate about which local authorities were responsible for the cost of the riots (should Lisburn Urban Council pay it all or should neighbouring authorities shoulder some obligation?) was settled many months later when the Northern Ireland government footed the bill.41

Aftermath of the Lisburn riots

Undoubtedly, the Swanzy riots, and those a month earlier, had a major impact on the people of Lisburn. Experiences varied, as some emerged unscathed, some lost property as collateral damage, and Catholics were deliberately targeted. The historical record suggests that the rioters were not interested in murder. Only one unidentified charred body (believed to be a rioter) was discovered in the remains of Donaghy's Boot Factory. However, to those living through it there was a palpable fear for their lives. As previously mentioned, the publican Peter McKeever was shot early in the rioting. William Shaw, the Sinn Féin councillor, had no reason to doubt he might be killed as he was set upon. Although he was able to seek medical attention, he felt so unsafe in Lisburn that he discharged himself from the local infirmary against the wishes of Dr St George and was taken to Belfast by car. The nuns at the convent were also evacuated under military guard.42

Most Catholic victims were forced to flee the town as their homes and businesses were attacked. Their primary destination was Belfast, but to get there many took to the fields, perhaps to avoid any further harassment. Reports claim droves of Catholic refugees slept in the open fields outside Belfast.43 The conditions were terrible, especially for the elderly and those with disabilities.44 By the time they got to Belfast to seek assistance from the St Vincent de Paul Society at St Mary's Hall, their conditions were described as 'most pitiable'.45 One American observer commented they were 'the most hopeless-looking lot of people I have ever seen'.[46] But there was more than their physical expulsion from Lisburn to contend with. It was emotionally devastating, as most of the refugees lost everything they owned.

> I spoke to one old woman of seventy, very infirm, who never had any bad words with her neighbors [sic], and who was driven out of her house and could not get permission to take a thing with her. All her possessions, the accumulation of a lifetime, were lost in her house.[47]

A significant number of the refugees did not return home as the threat of renewed violence and harassment was too great. Some of those who remained in Lisburn or returned soon after the riots attended Mass under military protection.[48] In Banbridge (and likely Lisburn, too) Catholic businesses were boycotted, and the exclusion of Catholic workers was sustained throughout the summer.[49] For those who did return, the horror of the riots remained fresh. Donaghy's Boot Factory, situated in Graham Gardens off Bow Street in the centre of Lisburn, was the largest boot manufacturer in Ireland and was destroyed in the Swanzy riots. The family returned to rebuild the business but were again targeted in another, much smaller, outbreak of rioting 11 years later. In 1932 the family moved the factory to Drogheda in a major blow to Lisburn's economy.[50] On the night before their departure, the police called the family to inform them that the grave of Edward Donaghy, the founder of the family business, had been desecrated.[51]

There was a wide range of victims' experiences of the riots and, while it is impossible to capture all of these, there were some discernible examples that can be highlighted. Many families with strong republican links did not return to Lisburn. At the court hearing for Isabella Gilmore's compensation claim it was inferred that the Gilmores only had themselves to blame due to William's republicanism and Isabella said she would not return to the town for any amount of money.[52] The Gilmore family moved to Belfast and later Dublin, where they were joined by Isabella's brother, William Connolly, and his family. He had run a very successful pub in Lisburn, established by his father in 1854, and might have been suspected of being a republican as his nephew, William Gilmore, was a regular hand in his establishment.[53] Such people felt it unwise to return to Lisburn, for they would be the obvious targets in any renewed riots.

However, others must have wondered at their own victimisation. One such case was the Fusco family, headed by Peter and Alessandra. Both belonged to migrant Italian families from the Frosinone province south of Rome, who settled in Belfast's 'Little Italy' area near the city's docklands at the start of the century. In September 1905, Peter and Alessandra (née Forte) married in Belfast before moving to Lisburn where they established an ice-cream and confectionery shop and had seven children. Whatever their ignorance of Irish politics, their Catholicism set them apart from the Protestant majority. They were targeted in both the July and Swanzy riots, which must have come as a great shock to them. They had premises at Cross Row and Market Square and both were attacked in August, the latter being gutted. Alessandra claimed compensation of £10,000 but in court her claim was reduced to £3,529 as the Market Square property was owned by a landlord who lodged their own claim. The judge awarded the Fuscos £1,640.[54]

In the aftermath of the riots Peter and Alessandra were the subject of damaging speculation that they were Sinn Féin sympathisers. An explosion at the burnt-out Market Square shop in the autumn of 1920 was rumoured to have been caused by ammunition stored there. Alessandra was forced to place a notice in the *Lisburn Standard* clarifying that the blast's true cause was the bursting of a gas engine installed for commercial purposes.[55] But the intimidation continued as the following year they were subjected to continued harassment about their politics and Alessandra again took to the local outlet to make this clarifying point: 'A Denial: I am not a Sinn Féiner. I am a stranger in this country, and I can't be a Sinn Féiner or anything else. Hoping this will be the last, as I am tired of being called a Sinn Féiner. Mrs Fusco, Cross Row, Lisburn.'[56]

Alessandra's heartfelt insistence that they were not republicans was equalled by her family's determination to make a success of their business in Lisburn. She and her husband remained in the town for the remainder of their lives, becoming prominent local figures. Their ice-cream business was so successful that they broadened their commercial reach into spirits, buying up the Tavern Inn on Bridge Street in 1926. In addition, Peter became the president of Lisburn Star Football Club and oversaw a period of success there. These points were highlighted in Peter's obituary in 1947 while the riots and harassment his family experienced received no mention at all, despite the arguable point that his family's greatest achievement was facing down the suspicions of local loyalists and rebuilding their lives in Lisburn after the Swanzy riots.[57]

Intercommunal violence in modern Ulster is often posited as a binary struggle between Protestant unionists and Catholic nationalists, but this dichotomy is too simplistic. It is fair to argue that sectarian violence is perceived by many who experience it as representational – that acts of violence by republicans or loyalists are seen to be carried out on behalf of, or with the tacit approval of, the community from which the perpetrators come.[58] Yet, many instances of violence, such as that in Lisburn in August 1920, inevitably had such an impact that traditional loyalties must have been questioned. For instance, how did some republican-leaning Catholics in Lisburn feel about the assassination of Swanzy when the perpetrators must have reasonably expected a loyalist reprisal against defenceless

Catholics? Also, how did unionists feel about the rioters when their property was destroyed as collateral damage in the ensuing disturbances?

One such unionist with mixed feelings about the riots may have been Agnes Cherry, the owner of a haberdashery on Bow Street. In contrast to the Fusco family, the Cherrys had roots in Lisburn. Agnes (née Topping) married her husband, James, in Lisburn cathedral in 1877 and together they had six children. The family's politics, also in contrast to the Fuscos, were very public and staunchly unionist. Their son, James Alexander, was a member of the pre-war UVF and joined the British army in October 1914, gaining local publicity in the *Lisburn Standard* where his picture was printed alongside a narrative of his patriotic journey.[59] However, tragedy struck on 16 August 1917 when he was killed on the Western Front, prompting a stream of letters of condolences to the *Standard* which reflected the high regard with which he and his family were held in the town.[60] His father never got over his death, became withdrawn and passed away in May 1919. Nine months later Agnes's eldest daughter, Jennie, also died suddenly at the family home.[61]

Agnes may have felt herself safe from the riots that were clearly aimed at her Catholic neighbours, but on the first night of the outbreak after the shooting of Swanzy she lost her shop to fire. It happened after arsonists attacked Thomas Caldwell's pub on Bow Street, two doors down from Agnes's haberdashery. Five buildings adjacent to Caldwell's were either damaged or destroyed. Unlike many other victims, Agnes's plight attracted the sympathy of the press as it was acknowledged that 'few families have suffered more within a short space of time.'[62] With this suffering must have come great sorrow at the loss of everything they owned in the shop, leaving only the memories of the place she shared with her deceased loved ones. While Agnes and her family remained in Lisburn, it is hard to imagine they did so with any sympathy, never mind support, for the militant loyalists who destroyed her shop.

Another loyal family that had little support for the riots was the Swanzy family. District Inspector Swanzy was unmarried, but he left behind a devoted sister, Irene, and his elderly mother. Through Rev. Henry B. Swanzy, Irene made futile appeals for calm during the riots. There certainly was no justice to be gained from the reprisals as the family mourned their loss. Oswald and Irene's mother died two years later, Irene recalling that 'her heart was broken, but I never saw her without a smile.'[63] Irene herself could not bear to stay in the town, or the country for that matter. She travelled the world for over seven years, spending time in east Asia, the US, north Africa and Europe.[64] Finally, she settled in Fiji, from where she sent annual notices to the *Irish Times* in memory of her brother.[65]

As in many parts of Ulster, the spectre of renewed violence in Lisburn after August 1920 hung heavy over everyone's head. The Swanzy riots did not erupt out of nowhere. They followed a long tradition of intercommunal conflict in the province and they had clear, albeit unspoken, objectives. Sectarian violence was often inextricably linked to territory. Throughout Ulster geographical spaces were unofficially demarcated Catholic or Protestant, although there were varying degrees of permeation. Cultural and political activities were tolerated within an area only if subscribed to by the dominant religious group. Loyalists, for instance, took less issue with the activities of the GAA if they occurred in predominantly Catholic areas, because loyalists had no way of stopping the activities outside their own territory and their own cultural and political sphere remained unthreatened. However, it was contentious once activities impinged on the boundary between Catholic and Protestant communities. For instance, in 1904 unionist residents protested at the staging of hurling matches in Blaris, two miles from Lisburn, with one complaining that 'this mixture of shinny-playing and Fenianism is a mushroom growth in Lisburn' and that visiting spectators were 'making use of provocative rebel expressions when passing through the heart of an Orange district.'[66] In short, Blaris was Protestant and the GAA had no place there.

The shooting of Swanzy was interpreted as a republican incursion into loyalist territory and the subsequent riots were an attempt to re-assert Protestant and unionist dominance in what was seen as a Protestant and unionist town. In Belfast and Derry violence was often conducted to maintain the boundaries between largely segregated communities, but in Lisburn there was no neat separation. The town was three-quarters Protestant with Catholics residing throughout, although there was an area that could be deemed the centre of the Catholic community on Chapel Hill. The chapel was situated there, as was the largest proportion of the town's Catholic community. When rioting broke out in both July and August 1920 loyalists sought to affirm their supremacy over their Catholic neighbours, although this fell well short of an attempt to ethnically cleanse the town. It was more akin to a territorial claim, something that occurred often in east Ulster during the revolutionary period.

In Lisburn, loyalists painted the words 'New Orange Hall' on the Parochial House, as if annexing the building for Protestantism. In other districts councils debated raising the Union flag above public buildings to declare their towns British and bastions of unionism. It is also significant that as early as 1922 a statue of the imperial hero John Nicholson was erected and unveiled at substantial cost in Lisburn before the town was fully rebuilt. These forms of expression and the violent expulsions of Catholics from Banbridge, Dromore and Lisburn were impositions of Protestant dominance that did not require the killing of scores of Catholics. This contrasts with Belfast, where Catholics lived in greater numbers and were more concentrated, offering greater resistance to loyalism.[67] Therefore, the violence in Belfast escalated to a level unseen in Lisburn.

The Lisburn rioters did not so much impose as reinforce their dominance over Catholics as it had never been under serious threat. It must be remembered that Swanzy was killed not by local republicans, but by outsiders. Nevertheless, there persisted a desire to demonstrate the Protestant community's supremacy with renewed low-scale and brief, albeit doubtlessly terrifying, anti-Catholic violence in 1921 and 1931. They did succeed, however, in making Lisburn more Protestant as the Catholic population dropped by 26 per cent between the two census years of 1911 and 1926. A similar decline occurred in Dromore (29 per cent) while in other towns where Catholics already comprised greater proportions of the population their share grew – Ballycastle (20 per cent increase) and Warrenpoint (29 per cent) being two examples. In fact, inter-communal violence led to a sharpening of residential segregation across the north-eastern six counties that became Northern Ireland.[68]

The violence also had enduring political consequences. As has already been noted, many Catholics returned to Lisburn after the Swanzy riots. Not only did they have to face the local threat of renewed loyalist violence, they also faced wider discrimination by the incoming unionist government. It should be noted that not only did the government lack any sympathy for Catholic victims of loyalist militancy, but their policies were very much influenced by the violence of 1920. At the very least, the IRA campaign across Ireland and the loyalist backlash in the north-east created the toxic atmosphere into which the Northern Irish state was born.

Catholic victims of loyalist violence did not hold much optimism for their place under a unionist government. A key figure, who would play a major role in determining how security policy in Northern Ireland affected Catholics, was Richard Dawson Bates. He would become the Minister of Home Affairs in the first Northern government and his opinion of the Catholic victims was made clear when he wrote of the Belfast shipyard expulsions in July 1920:

> The immediate cause of the disturbance was the objection (and we consider a proper objection) of the shipyard men to work alongside Sinn Féiners who had taken the place of Protestants who had gone to war. There can be no doubt that the method adopted for making the Sinn Féiners leave their work was done in a more or less orderly way.[69]

Bates makes no distinction among the victims. They were all 'Sinn Féiners'. All republicans. All a threat. This was echoed by Fred Crawford, former UVF gunrunner, who described those driven out of Lisburn as 'rebels or their sympathisers'[70] As troubling for Catholics, however, was the defence of loyalist militancy. The shipyard expulsions were 'orderly', not violent. Bates reiterated this to James Craig, adding that the expulsions were carried out by 'a most respectable class of individual, who feel they are quite justified in taking the law into their own hands.'[71] In fact, it was believed loyalists were forced into taking action because of the security shortcomings of the government and, in this context, workplace expulsions met 'with practically the approval of everybody here.'[72] Bates was correct that there was support among his political colleagues for the loyalist militancy in the summer of 1920. In October, unionist leaders offered their approval to the shipyard workers in a series of visits to the yards. James Craig, a more temperate figure than Bates, gave a speech at the shipyards in which he defended the right of loyalists to protect themselves against the republican threat. He then roused his audience, interrogating first their loyalty, and then his own: 'Do I approve of the action you boys have taken in the past?' he asked. His answer, 'Yes,' was met with cheers and followed by the unfurling of a large Union flag.[73]

While displaying antipathy to Catholics, unionists used loyalist violence as evidence that the government had not done enough to protect Protestants. Wilfrid Spender, a former army officer placed in charge of the revived UVF in 1920, wrote in August: 'All over the country the men have become desperate & intend to take matters into their own hands.'[74] It was feared by Craig and his party that what occurred in Belfast, Lisburn and other east Ulster towns could be repeated across the province. An inability to control their own followers could have an adverse effect on British opinion. The risk was real. Loyalist violence was not driven by their political leaders, as shown in Lisburn after Swanzy was shot. Craig's words and those of his colleagues could not prevent violence, nor were they a prerequisite for initiating it.[75]

On 2 September, Craig met with members of the British cabinet and secured agreement on key aspects of the framework for the new northern state. It included the establishment of the Ulster Special Constabulary (USC), a force into which loyalists could be recruited and subjected to some degree of hierarchical control.[76] Even unionist hardliners, like Bates, were anxious to assert effective control over their followers and felt a centralised force was necessary. Prior to the USC's establishment, some special constable schemes were initiated by local authorities, but these proved to be inadequate. In Belfast, special constables were arrested for looting, while in Lisburn as many as 300, who were raised in response to the Swanzy riots, mutinied when some of their number were found guilty by a court of partaking in said riots.[77] In the latter incident, the special constables' threats to resign were removed only after the leader of the force promised to use his influence to affect the sentences of the men charged with riot.[78] This clearly demonstrated the limits of the tentative peace that the USC offered.

Loyalist satisfaction with the force was continually dependent on the uneven dispensation of justice and tacit safeguards against prosecution. In

August 1921, the USC was still under British government control and was suspended pending peace negotiations between Sinn Féin and the British government, much to the dissatisfaction of its members.[79] Without control transferred to Belfast and the resumption of duty by special constables, loyalists 'found vent, amongst other things, in the formation of Provisional Committees, and the organisation of armed Loyalists to supply the protection which they consider is withheld by the Authorities.'[80]

By acting as a kind of safety valve on loyalist militancy, the USC could be seen as a successful mechanism through which the Unionist Party reduced violence.[81] It did, however, lend a degree of legitimacy to subsequent loyalist transgressions, shrouding sectarian motivations in a cloak of state security. The USC armed over 19,000 'A' and 'B' Specials across Northern Ireland within its first year, meaning Catholics everywhere were subject to the whims of their armed Protestant neighbours. This was particularly alarming in the context of security policy from spring 1922 onwards. In April of that year, the Northern Ireland government passed the Special Powers Act which bestowed upon the Minister of Home Affairs, none other than Richard Dawson Bates, the power 'to take all such steps and issue all such orders as may be necessary' to maintain peace.[82] Under this act Bates introduced internment, which was used almost exclusively against suspected republicans and only rarely against loyalists.[83]

The communal violence across north-east Ulster in the formative years of Northern Ireland cannot be viewed as isolated incidents. Nor can they be viewed as renewals of traditional sectarian bitterness in the province. Both explanations are too simplistic. While it is true that each outbreak had its own immediate cause, each were heavily characterised by its context within the Irish revolution. The IRA's credible threat to British authority in Ireland heightened tensions in the north-east. It also struck fear into the unionist community which reacted with greater ferocity than usual. In Belfast the violence was much more intense than that described in this essay, but even the violence in Lisburn was more brutal and consequential than previous outbreaks of communal unrest. The riots did not pass without bringing change, such as the removal of thousands of Catholic residents, the destruction of many buildings in the centre of Lisburn and the general collapse in law and order which resulted in the creation of a sectarian, auxiliary police force almost entirely antipathetic to the intended victims of the riots. The Swanzy riots, in conjunction with communal violence elsewhere, also hardened anti-republican attitudes within the Unionist Party at a crucial period of political change in Ireland, influencing the first security policies of the new northern government and ushering in decades of suspicion and resentment in the relationship between that government and its nationalist minority population.

Notes

1. For the Derry violence, see Jonathan Bardon, *A History of Ulster* (Belfast, 2001), pp 467–9.
2. Peter Hart, *The IRA at War, 1916–1923* (Oxford, 2003), p. 248.
3. Christopher Magill, *Political Conflict in East Ulster, 1920–22: Revolution and Reprisal* (Woodbridge, 2020), pp 1–4.
4. John Borgonovo (ed.), *Florence and Josephine O'Donoghue's War of Independence: A Destiny that Shapes Our Ends* (Dublin, 2006), pp 95–6.
5. Statements of Sean Culhane and Sean Cusack (BMH WS 746 and 402).
6. Statement of Sean Culhane (BMH WS 746).
7. Testimony of Major Ewart at court martial of Sean Leonard, 31 Jan. 1921 (TNA, WO 71/362).
8. Statement of Roger McCorley (BMH, WS 389).
9. Statement of Thomas Fox (BMH, WS 365).
10. Statement of Roger McCorley (BMH WS 389).
11. Ibid.
12. Testimony of Captain Alex Woods at court martial of Sean Leonard, 31 Jan. 1921 (TNA, WO 71/362).
13. Statement of Roger McCorley (BMH WS 389); testimony of Captain Alex Woods at court martial of Sean Leonard, 31 Jan. 1921 (TNA, WO 71/362).
14. Statement of Roger McCorley (BMH WS 389); testimony of Dr George St George at court martial of Sean Leonard, 31 Jan. 1921 (TNA, WO 71/362).
15. Charles Townshend, *The Partition: Ireland Divided, 1885–1925* (London, 2021), p. 155.
16. Éamon Phoenix, *Northern Nationalism: Nationalist Politics, Partition and the Catholic Minority in Northern Ireland 1890–1940* (Belfast, 1994), p. 74.
17. James Craig memo, 1 Sep. 1920, (PRONI, Ministry of Finance, FIN/18/1/11); Magill, *Political Conflict in East Ulster*, pp 140–41.
18. Bardon, *A History of Ulster*, p. 468.
19. *Lisburn Standard*, 23 Jan. 1920.
20. RIC county inspector report, Down, Feb. 1920 (TNA, CO 904/111); Robert Lynch, *The Northern IRA and the Early Years of Partition 1920–1922* (Dublin, 2006), pp 22–3. For relative strengths of the Irish Parliamentary Party and Sinn Féin, see membership levels of Ancient Order of Hibernians and Sinn Féin clubs in RIC county inspector report, Antrim, Jan. 1920 (TNA, CO 904/111).
21. Bardon, *A History of Ulster*, pp 470–71.
22. For more on Smyth's assassination, see Magill, *Political Conflict in East Ulster*, pp 41–2.
23. *Dromore Leader*, 24 July 1920.
24. *Lisburn Standard*, 23 July 1920.
25. *Belfast Newsletter*, 23 July 1920.

26 *Irish News*, 26 July 1920; *Dromore Leader*, 31 July 1920.
27 *Lisburn Standard*, 30 July 1920.
28 Pearse Lawlor, *The Burnings 1920* (Cork, 2009), pp 85–9.
29 *Irish News*, 26 July 1920.
30 *Irish Times*, 4 Jan. 1975.
31 For a brief overview of this practice, see Townshend, *The Partition*, pp 20–23.
32 *Belfast Telegraph*, 23 Aug. 1920.
33 Pearse Lawlor, *Lisburn's Forgotten Families from the Burnings 1920* (unpublished transcript, Irish Linen Centre & Lisburn Museum, 2017), n.p.
34 *Lisburn Standard*, 17 and 24 Oct. 1919.
35 Ibid., 7 May 1920.
36 *Ballymoney Free Press*, 26 Aug. 1920.
37 This narrative of events of the Lisburn riots is constructed from *Lisburn Standard*, 27 Aug. 1920 and *Belfast Telegraph*, 23–26 Aug. 1920.
38 *Lisburn Standard*, 27 Aug. 1920.
39 Testimony of Mrs Annot Erskine Robinson in Albert Coyle (ed.), *Evidence of Conditions in Ireland Comprising the Complete Testimony, Affidavits and Exhibits Before the American Commission on Conditions in Ireland* (Washington DC, 1921), p. 570.
40 *Irish News*, 28 Feb. 1921.
41 Lawlor, *The Burnings*, p. 212.
42 *Belfast Telegraph*, 25 Aug. 1920.
43 *Irish Weekly and Ulster Examiner*, 28 Aug. 1920.
44 Ibid., 5 Mar. 1921.
45 Ibid., 28 Aug. 1920.
46 Testimony of Mrs Annot Erskine Robinson in Coyle (ed.), *Evidence of Conditions in Ireland*, p. 571.
47 Ibid., p. 571.
48 *Irish Weekly and Ulster Examiner*, 18 Sep. 1920.
49 Ibid., 28 Aug. 1920.
50 *Lisburn Standard*, 20 May 1932.
51 Unpublished memoirs of Joan Cassidy, n.d. (Irish Linen Centre & Lisburn Museum).
52 Glenn Patterson, *Once Upon a Hill* (London, 2008), p. 161.
53 Lawlor, *Lisburn's Forgotten Families*, n.p.
54 *Lisburn Standard*, 3 Dec. 1920.
55 Ibid., 15 Oct. 1920.
56 Ibid., 27 May 1921.
57 Ibid., 1 Aug. 1947.
58 T.K. Wilson, *Frontiers of Violence: Conflict and Identity in Ulster and Upper Silesia, 1918–1922* (Oxford, 2010), pp 99–100, pp 197–8.
59 *Lisburn Standard*, 2 Oct. 1914.
60 Ibid., 24 and 31 Aug. 1917.

61 Ibid., 20 Feb. 1920.
62 Ibid., 27 Aug. 1920.
63 Irene Swanzy to Sergeant McCarthy, 21 Oct. 1958 (Irish Linen Centre & Lisburn Museum, Swanzy Collection, LMILC.2021.226).
64 Ibid.
65 Magill, *Political Conflict in East Ulster*, p. 6.
66 *Northern Whig*, 19 Apr. 1904.
67 Magill, *Political Conflict in East Ulster*, pp 64–8.
68 Ibid., pp 167–9.
69 Richard Dawson Bates to James Craig, 24 July 1920 (PRONI, Department of the Prime Minister, PM/1/70/3).
70 Fred Crawford diary, 26 Aug. 1920 (PRONI, Fred Crawford Papers, D640/11/1).
71 Bates to Craig, 26 July 1920 (PRONI, Department of the Prime Minister, PM/1/70/3).
72 Bates to Craig, 28 July 1920 (ibid.).
73 *Belfast Newsletter*, 15 Oct. 1920; Bates also visited the shipyards in October – see Bates to Craig, 6 Oct. 1920 (PRONI, Department of the Prime Minister, PM/1/70/3).
74 Wilfrid Spender to Craig, c. late Aug. 1920 (PRONI, Department of the Prime Minister, PM/1/70/2).
75 Magill, *Political Conflict in East Ulster*, p. 57.
76 David W. Miller, *Queen's Rebels: Ulster Loyalism in Historical Perspective* (Dublin, 1978), p. 126.
77 Bates to Craig, 28 Aug. 1920 (PRONI, Department of the Prime Minister, PM/1/70/3); Magill, *Political Conflict in East Ulster*, p. 54.
78 Magill, *Political Conflict in East Ulster*, p. 54.
79 'Report by Secretary of the Cabinet on visit to London', 10 Aug. 1921 (PRONI, Cabinet Conclusion File, CAB 4/14/13).
80 Cabinet memorandum, 12 Sept. 1921 (PRONI, Cabinet Conclusion File, CAB 4/19/14).
81 Wilson, *Frontiers of Violence*, p. 94.
82 Alvin Jackson, *Ireland, 1798–1998: War, Peace and Beyond* (Malden, 2010), p. 334.
83 Michael Farrell, *Arming the Protestants: The Formation of the Ulster Special Constabulary and the Royal Ulster Constabulary, 1920–7* (London, 1983), pp 177–8.

11

Perceptions of the king's visit to Belfast, 22 June 1921

HEATHER JONES

One of the many questions about the partition of Ireland and the creation of Northern Ireland is why did northern unionism never establish any annual commemorative date to mark Northern Ireland's foundation.[1] This appears all the more strange when we consider that unionism traditionally made extensive efforts to annually mark key dates in its history, such as the two world wars or the Battle of the Boyne. As historian Robert Lynch has put it: 'the lingering impression that partition was an interim solution meant that Ireland was permanently partitioned almost by stealth. There would be no defining partition moment.'[2] There is a rich historiography on the significance of national days in moulding popular support and legitimacy for continental European states and governments.[3] In contrast, Northern Ireland never had one.

King George V's visit to Belfast to open the new Northern Irish parliament on 22 June 1921, a date which effectively marked the official ceremonial 'birth' of Northern Ireland and provided a royal imprimatur for the new regime, offers a valuable case study as to why. This chapter will set out how the events of the king's visit and opening of parliament, outwardly a moment of unionist celebration, actually posed deeply problematic questions for unionism. It looks at different elements of the day itself and the varying ways that contemporaries perceived it, in order to argue that 22 June 1921 raised multiple ambiguities and insecurities which reflected those inherent in the structures of the new Northern Ireland. Ultimately, 22 June 1921 drew attention to issues that undermined the unionist myths and hopes upon which the new Northern Ireland was being built and justified and could never provide a coherent foundation narrative to commemorate.

Unionist disunity

Among the major issues was that the opening of the new Northern Irish parliament very visibly highlighted divisions in Irish unionism. It finalised the rupture between northern and southern unionists which had been looming since the rise to dominance, in the period from 1910 on, of the Ulster Unionist Council within Irish unionism and the 1919 split between north and south in the Irish Unionist Alliance. Ironically, unionism was one of the first bodies in Ireland to be 'partitioned', prefiguring the division of the island itself by a border. 22 June 1921 also symbolically marked a new split within Ulster unionism as the unionists of three Ulster counties – Donegal, Cavan and Monaghan – were now outside the new Northern Ireland, deliberately excluded to safeguard its Protestant population majority. Symbolic of this split, Sir Edward Carson, born in Dublin, did not attend the opening of the new parliament, sending his wife in his stead, claiming work commitments kept him in London.[4] He had retired in spring 1921, telling a meeting of the Ulster Unionist Council on 4 February 1921 that 'you have got your own parliament'.[5] This wording, 'you' and 'your parliament' rather than 'we' and 'our parliament' was revealing. This was a parliament for northern unionism only, not Southern Unionists like Carson who had once hoped to preserve all of Ireland in the union.

It was claimed Carson stayed away in order not to overshadow his successor Sir James Craig, the new Ulster Unionist leader and premier of Northern Ireland. However, by not attending Carson only drew increased attention to himself and away from Craig. Sir Nevil Macready noted of 22 June that

> one looked in vain for the man whose name for so many years had been so closely identified with the province of his adoption. It seemed incongruous that he should have withdrawn himself at a time when the North was about to enter on a phase of existence beset with difficulties and dangers greater than those in which he had played the leading role in the past.[6]

The Irish Catholic even suggested Carson avoided the inauguration because 'he foresaw the failure of the freak parliament and made up his mind to wash his hands of the whole business.'[7] Carson was certainly aware of the potential dangers of unionist-majority rule: on 4 February 1921 he had presciently warned the Ulster Unionist Council that it now must transition from being 'an organization for a party. You will be a parliament for a whole community' and that it must be careful to show that 'the Catholic minority have nothing to fear from a Protestant majority.'[8]

The majority of Southern Unionists opposed partition; northern unionist celebrations on 22 June 1921 left them feeling abandoned by their erstwhile comrades. The fate of the Southern Unionists was uncertain at the moment of the king's visit to Belfast. They believed that the Government of Ireland Act was unworkable as it did not have majority support on the island. The earl of Donoughmore pointed out in the House of Lords on 16 June 1921 that:

> In the House of Commons not one single Irishman registered a vote for it. In the House of Lords our Ulster friends voted for the Bill, but not one Southern Irishman who was not a member of the Government voted for the Bill here. Is it quite fair comment to describe an Act with such a history as 'recognising the aspirations of the great bulk of the Irish people'?[9]

The king's privy counsellor, Sir Almeric Fitzroy, noted on 19 June that: 'The autonomy of the six counties … is hateful to the great majority of Irishmen, and to no section of them so distasteful as the loyalists of the South and West.'[10]

Sectarianism

Despite northern unionist attempts to project the parliament opening as a celebration, the royal visit also drew both British and global attention to the violent divisions that partition was creating in Belfast, and across Northern Ireland more widely, along polarising religious-political lines, which threatened a civil war between northern unionists, who supported the new regime, and the north's Roman Catholic minority who rejected it. By summer 1921 these divisions were driving intense internecine, often sectarian, violence. In Belfast, where the Catholic minority was significantly outnumbered, this period saw a string of killings, mob riots and arson attacks. Just days before the royal visit, on 10 June, the IRA killed Constable James Glover. This resulted in multiple reprisal killings of Catholics and attacks on their homes. A week before the royals arrived, MP Joe Devlin raised the case in the House of Commons of three Catholic men taken from their homes on 12 June by a suspected police gang and shot dead, one of whom, Malachy Halfpenny, was a First World War British army veteran.[11]

On the morning of the king's arrival, the *Irish News* referred to the recent eviction of around 150 Catholic families from their homes and described Belfast as both 'beflagged' and 'besmirched.'[12] The *Derry Journal* referred to 'King George's visit to Carsonia.'[13] In a letter to the king's private secretary, Lord Stamfordham, ahead of the visit 'the editor of the *Catholic Herald* urged that the King's ceremonial route in Belfast should not avoid "streets where the homes of large numbers of Catholics had been destroyed, simply because they were Catholics."'[14] However, the event's planners wanted to hide discord in how they routed the procession and to present to the world an image of a successful, secure, prosperous and above all, British, Northern Ireland. The reality was grimmer: there were such fears that the unionist crowds might get drunk and provoke disorder that the sale of alcohol was prohibited during the king's visit.

Deaths occurred on all sides as partition was implemented between 1920 and 1923 – there was an IRA campaign against border unionists, for example. Belfast's Catholic population, predominantly nationalist and already hostile to the Government of Ireland Act and partition policies, was deeply alienated from the new northern parliament and the king's visit by violent attacks on them by supporters of Northern Ireland trying to impose unionist-majority rule by force, who conflated reprisals against the IRA with indiscriminate attacks on Catholic areas. Unionists were deeply suspicious of the Catholic minority; many saw its objections to the royal visit as part of a wider IRA plot to destroy the new Northern Ireland. Ironically, several Belfast areas had been among the last outposts of the moderate, pro-Home Rule Irish Parliamentary Party in the 1918 general election, a party that was far less anti-monarchist than republican Sinn Féin; Irish Parliamentary Party MP Joe Devlin was a key voice in decrying sectarian violence in the House of Commons in June 1921.

It remains unclear the extent of active support for the IRA among Belfast Catholics by summer 1921, although it did exist. What is certain, however, is that the incidents of indiscriminate sectarian violence that Catholics experienced – and the deliberate police inaction to protect them – only served to increase it. Both loyalty to wider Irish nationalism and the fears and experiences of being a minority under attack by 1921 ensured that northern Catholics boycotted the royal visit and opening of the new parliament. According to Mary Kenny, only two attended.[15] The Catholic primate, Cardinal Michael Logue, was invited but diplomatically pleaded a prior engagement.[16] The Catholic hierarchy also issued a statement condemning the new parliament.

The new northern parliament contained no significant political opposition party or, until 1925, when a handful of nationalists led by Joe Devlin entered it, any Catholic minority representation. This was a visibly problematic start, a colossal democratic deficit for a parliament supposedly modelled on Westminster traditions of democratic parliamentary representation, opening against the backdrop of post-First World War extended suffrage and greater egalitarianism within Britain itself. With no significant opposition, Sir James Craig would remain Prime Minister of Northern Ireland for another 19 years until his death. The king himself warned of the risks of minority exclusion in his Belfast speech, directing those present to do their 'utmost' to ensure the new parliament became 'an instrument of happiness and good government for all parts of the community which you represent' and to manage Northern Ireland 'with fairness and due regard to every faith and interest.'[17] However, the implementation of the Government of Ireland Act's partition had visibly exacerbated rather than calmed community tensions. Renewed violence broke out rapidly once the royals left and within two weeks, on 10 July 1921, Belfast would experience the intercommunal violence of 'Bloody Sunday'.

Security

The ongoing war between the IRA and British forces meant that extreme precautions had to be taken for the king's safety, drawing attention to the fact that Ireland was now too dangerous even for the monarch – something that was both embarrassing for unionists and also a worrying indication of the deep vulnerability of the new Northern Ireland. The British government in 1921 was keen to emphasise Britain's internal stability, military prowess, law and order in the face of the rise of Bolshevism and revolution elsewhere on the continent. The press coverage of the royal visit, which openly emphasised the dangers the king faced, undermined all this. It was considered too risky for the king to spend a night in Northern Ireland: *Freeman's Journal* reported that his visit lasted only four and a half hours; organiser Nevile Wilkinson claimed seven.[18]

Queen Mary accepted Sir James Craig's last-minute invitation to accompany the king largely since she believed George V might be a target for the IRA and that her presence might, at best, make this less likely because they might be reluctant to attack a woman and, at worst, would mean she would be immediately on hand if anything happened to him. For security reasons, the Chief Secretary of Ireland was not allowed to join the royal procession, travelling to Belfast City Hall by another way. There were special detectives brought over from London, and the procession route was lined with British troops. All access to rooftops for the general public was meant to be prohibited and Sir Nevil Macready noted in his memoirs that 'soldiers were placed on the roofs of houses with orders to shoot if they saw people on the roofs along the route of the procession.'[19]

Many British establishment figures were aghast that the king would risk travelling to Ireland and called for the visit to be called off. Stamfordham himself wrote to Craig in late May that the visit was not definitely confirmed yet as 'there is a very strong difference of opinion about the King going to Belfast and many Irishmen, including those residing in that country, tell me that His Majesty is running considerable risk in going.'[20] Upon his return to London, huge crowds gathered to cheer the king and queen as the trip was perceived as an act of direct personal bravery. The queen's lady-in-waiting, Lady Airlie, referred constantly to security fears in her account – for example, her shock at seeing an armed guard posted outside the door of the queen's retiring room in Belfast City Hall and the relief when the royal party returned safely to their yacht, where the queen remarked to her that 'they could have got any of us.'[21]

The fears were well-grounded. Two days after the royal visit, a troop train to Dublin, carrying soldiers and horses that had taken part, including the four white horses that had drawn the royal carriage, was deliberately derailed in an IRA ambush in Armagh. Three soldiers and a railway guard were killed, along with 50–80 horses; a local farm labourer was later shot by soldiers in the aftermath for failing to stop when challenged and died in hospital.[22] Newspaper reports noted that among the horses left dying in pain was 'Titch', a regimental mascot who had survived the First World War in France, greatly upsetting soldier witnesses.[23] One IRA captain involved in the ambush, John Grant, believed the original plan was even more ambitious: to attack a number of trains leaving Belfast 'at different points.'[24] There were also other plots to disrupt the royal visit that the IRA was forced to abandon due to the heavy security, including one to burn the city's GPO after the king's arrival in Belfast.[25]

The extent of the coverage of the security measures for the visit and the risks that the king ran in coming effectively highlighted the precarity and instability of Northern Ireland. The message was not one of a new state secure in its future or of unionist success but of a parliament opened under threat and in a situation of widespread unionist fear for the future. This was evident in the audience reactions to the king's speech – 'some of the women wept' according to Countess Airlie.[26] This helps explain why it was a moment that unionism preferred not to commemorate – one of weakness and vulnerability rather than strength.

Royal interventionism

The role of George V also proved problematic. While unionists traditionally claimed steadfast loyalty to the British monarch, the king was personally not very popular with them. In 1914, he had resisted unionist petitions to refuse his assent to the third Home Rule Bill, leading to 'protests against the king' by some Ulster Unionists.[27] Nora Roberts, an Anglo-Irish grandee living in County Cork, recalled that 'Many agreed with the Ulsterman who complained "The King is no good. He's not loyal."'[28] Nevil Macready noted of 22 June 1921 that

> I could not help contrasting it with the Belfast of seven years ago, when that hall had been a focus of resistance to the King's Government, and many of the men whom I saw making obeisance to the King had been foremost in promoting what in reality was nothing less than a threat of armed rebellion.[29]

George V was also seen as a monarch who had reached out to Irish Catholics, visiting Maynooth seminary during his 1911 trip to Ireland, hosting the 1914 Buckingham Palace Conference and getting the anti-Catholic clause annulled from his coronation oath.[30] Behind the scenes he had asked for assurances that the Roman Catholic minority in the new Northern Ireland would not be mistreated and also strongly disapproved of his Prime Minister David Lloyd George's policy of reprisals in Ireland.[31] Dublin Castle civil servant Mark Sturgis reported that when the Chief Secretary of Ireland Sir Hamar Greenwood and his wife lunched with the king in May 1921, the latter was 'mighty displeased with the lot of us and all our works. Pitched into the Government all through lunch and said he hated the idea of the "Black and Tans".'[32]

Yet, monarchism as a cultural ideology still deeply mattered to unionists, regardless of personal feelings towards an individual monarch. Loyalty was due to the institution of the Crown and the First World War had increased its symbolic importance. Ulster Unionists believed that their menfolk had sacrificed, served and died 'For King and Country' in the war. Britishness itself was defined both legally and culturally as being a subject of the king-emperor. Lord Londonderry also told Stamfordham of resentment among Belfast unionists that the king had visited all the major UK shipyards during the war except the Belfast ones.[33]

For all of these reasons, in 1921, the king was needed to lend imperial and national grandeur, and to sacralise the opening of the new parliament with royal ceremonial. His presence was a tremendous boost to Ulster Unionist morale at a time of crisis and insecurity. Nevile Wilkinson, who was Ulster King at Arms, recalled 'the fairy-like scene which greeted Their Majesties' a scene captured by the Ulster artist William Conor who produced a famous painting of the opening of parliament.[34] More prosaically, Wilkinson also lost sleep over whether the lord mayor's two small children or Sir James Craig's daughter should present the queen with a bouquet.[35] Lady Craig described the Belfast streets as: 'bunting and flags and the pavement and lampposts painted red white and blue, really most touching, as a sign of their loyalty. Imagine Radicals in England thinking they would ever succeed in driving people like that out of the British Empire or wanting to!'[36] The comments are indicative of a unionist double-siege mentality – the fear of being absorbed 'out' of the empire into an encroaching independent Ireland, but also of being driven out of it by those in Britain who felt no loyalty to a British Ulster. The effusive displays of Britishness were heartfelt – monarchism was a core unionist cultural identity – but also politically expedient, a means of countering the many voices who did not support the new Northern Ireland in Britain itself.

The drafting of the king's speech also reveals that the involvement of the king in the historic occasion was not without problems for unionism. Sir

James Craig wanted the king's speech to set out the policies of the new Northern Irish government – similar to the speech that the monarch would make at the opening of parliament in Westminster. However, civil servants feared this might undermine the king's status and set problematic precedents. For the monarch to present Northern Irish policies risked that every other parliament across the empire might request the king open their legislature too. Although the king had opened the first Australian parliament after federation in 1901, this had occurred while he was still duke of York. Moreover, the Northern Irish parliament was not even a full dominion parliament nor was it a national one, being only a form of devolved home rule within the UK with certain powers, such as foreign affairs, remaining at Westminster. The king risked appearing inappropriately involved in trivial matters of local government if his speech saw him presenting policy plans that were very local to Ulster. On 15 June, civil servant Tom Jones and cabinet secretary Maurice Hankey met to discuss 'the constitutional position. Ought the king to be advised by the Imperial P.M. or by Craig?'[37]

The second concern of both monarch and courtiers was that the king might be seen as partisan, vocalising the demands and desires of Ulster unionism if he gave a speech prepared by Craig. This risked jeopardising the very rationale for the king opening the Northern Irish parliament in the first place, which was that the monarch was believed in Britain to be a revered symbol, 'above' politics and non-partisan, whose sacrosanct status would carry weight with a range of disparate groups, unionists and nationalists and those British Tory hardliners who still rejected any devolution, winning them round to Lloyd George's Government of Ireland Act. Sir Edward Grigg, Lloyd George's private secretary and one of his key advisors on Ireland, even assured the latter in a note, on 14 June 1921, that 'Ireland is very sentimental and like India monarchist to the core.'[38] He clearly underestimated how much republicanism – and Dáil Éireann – already dominated Irish nationalism by 1921.

The king's opening of the Northern Irish parliament was also meant to seal northern devolution as the final resolution of the Ulster question so that London could focus instead on pacifying the south. The British cabinet was deeply divided in early June between those who favoured increasing the use of repression in Ireland to force through the Government of Ireland Act in the south, against the will of the Dáil and IRA, and those who wanted to negotiate a truce in order to find an alternative solution. Lloyd George's view in late May-early June was that the Government of Ireland Act's provision for two devolved parliaments was as far as he was prepared to go; he favoured forcing this solution through by crushing the IRA militarily over agreeing a truce, but had not stopped various secret ongoing peace feelers with the republican leadership, most of which, including those by Lord Derby and Dublin Castle's Andy Cope, still revolved around various forms of advanced Home Rule solutions and ways to salvage the Government of Ireland Act solution.[39]

Drafting the king's speech to open the new northern Irish parliament proved tortuous, with multiple drafts discarded. One found in the Public Record Office of Northern Ireland differs substantially to the final speech. It focused more on economics, condemning violence as retarding prosperity and emphasising that the new Northern Ireland would 'ensure a brighter future for the great masses of workers.'[40] It suggested that the Council of Ireland – a part of the Government of Ireland Act that provided for a north-south body to discuss issues that concerned the whole island – would be enough to restore peace and referred to a 'race proud of the Empire and traditionally loyal to Throne and Constitution' and how 'wise and just' future Northern Irish governments would guard the safety of all persons' and contribute to the 'healing of differences that have long disturbed Ireland.'[41] It is unclear who drafted this early version, possibly prepared for Craig, but it is notably shorter and less personal than the final royal speech and significantly there is no mention of the southern parliament at all.

What is clear is that by 13 June 1921, the king had become aware of a draft speech prepared for him by Craig.[42] This had 'greatly distressed' the king who feared he was to be made 'a mouthpiece of Ulster' in the speech, rather than that of the empire and who had been insisting in May that he should open both the northern and the southern parliaments if he went to Ireland, in order to be seen as even-handed.[43] The king invited Jan Smuts, the Prime Minister of South Africa, who was in London to attend the Imperial Conference in June, to lunch at Windsor and asked Smuts to help draft the speech. It is not clear if the king sought the permission of his cabinet in London for Smuts' involvement. In any case, it meant that Craig's text was dropped. The day after meeting the king, 14 June, Smuts produced a text that called for peace and reconciliation and openly suggested a dominion status solution for the south of Ireland – and Lord Stamfordham telephoned Lloyd George on the king's behalf to advocate for Smuts' text.

For a speech of this importance, constitutionally, the government in London was responsible for the final approval of the text. The cabinet's Irish Situation Committee rapidly convened on 16 June to discuss Smuts' script, notably with Stamfordham present, and found it unacceptable, requesting former Prime Minister Arthur Balfour to draft an alternative. Balfour's text, ready by 16 June, proved much more unionist in tone, claiming that Ireland had already 'long enjoyed full political and religious freedom' under Britain.[44] However, in a highly unusual exercise of royal power, George V rejected Balfour's draft. Following royal advice on 17 June, Lloyd George finally accepted a new version was needed.[45] He instructed Edward Grigg to come up with a new wording that the king would accept.

Lloyd George's mistress, Frances Stevenson, noted in her diary on 18 June 1921 that Lloyd George had met Smuts that day and that the latter is 'inclined to be very tiresome over Ireland & suggests we should give them Dominion Home Rule. D.'s reply was: The British Isles are a federation: you do not contemplate giving Dom. Home Rule to Natal, or the Orange States. Why then do you suggest it for us?'[46] Grigg – who had conciliatory views on Ireland – duly melded elements of Smut's and Balfour's texts together, along with a section personally added by the king on his own desire for peace. This was the final version that the king ultimately delivered on 22 June 1921. The speech became to all intents and purposes, a very thinly veiled royal message that the British side was now interested in a truce with the IRA.

The wording of the king's speech also reflected the British aspiration that partition would not be permanent, with the hope that the two Irish northern and southern devolved parliaments would later reunite, albeit still under the aegis of UK, or even British imperial dominion, rule. The king's speech was ambiguous about whether the new Northern Ireland would be permanent and contained lines that surely alarmed rather than consoled unionism: 'May this historic gathering be the prelude of a day in which the Irish people, North and South, under one Parliament or two, as those Parliaments may themselves decide, shall work together in common love for Ireland.'[47] Its central references were to the king's 'Irish' people and 'Ireland' rather than to any unionist identity as such. It also shifted attention away from the north to the south. The speech also overtly referenced the north's sister Government of Ireland Act parliament in Dublin – a parliament that everyone in Ireland knew by this point was a fantasy solution that would never work, given the pre-existence of the Dáil and the fact that republicans had used the May 1921 elections to the southern Government of Ireland parliament as elections to the second Dáil.

By 24 June, British civil servant Mark Sturgis in Dublin feared the southern parliament would open with 'the ridiculous farce of a Ceremony of bare benches.'[48] If the two parliaments were essentially conceived of as twins, the Dublin parliament's imminent stillbirth could not but raise fears for the frail living northern sibling. Ultimately, only 15 senators and four of the MPs elected, the unionist members for Trinity College Dublin, showed up for the opening of the southern parliament in June 1921. Otherwise boycotted, in July it voted to adjourn itself and, in 1922, following the Anglo-Irish Treaty, was dissolved.[49] Moreover, the king opening the northern parliament invoked the embarrassing contrast that there would be no royal opening of its southern counterpart. As Mrs Pope-Hennessy wrote to the Palace after the royal visit to Belfast: 'to identify Monarchy with the North is tacitly to admit the claim of Independence with the South.'[50] The Palace were slow learners in this regard: in 1922, the king offered to ceremonially open Dáil Éireann following the establishment of the Irish Free State, an offer 'brusquely rejected' as in contradiction with that parliament's republican aspirations.[51]

Thus, the decision that the king should open the northern parliament had unexpected consequences – it led to a royal intervention behind the scenes advocating recognising the 26 counties of Ireland becoming an independent dominion, which was ultimately what would be the outcome of the Treaty talks several months later in December 1921. In fact, the king's speech even tacitly trailed the offer of dominion status, calling for 'every man of Irish birth, whatever be his creed and whatever be his home' to 'work in co-operation with the free communities on which the British Empire is based,' and referring to 'new nations' that had recently 'come to birth' within the Empire in 'the lifetime of the youngest in this hall' – clearly a reference to the dominions of Australia (1901), New Zealand (1907) and South Africa (1910), and referring to how the 'future lies in the hands of my Irish people themselves.'[52] Here were hints of Smuts' proposal of dominion status.

Smuts believed the South African peace accords at the end of the Second South African (Boer) War with the Boer republics might be a model for the Irish situation.[53] In fact, there is a possibility that Smuts was influenced by Irish republicans, having already established contact with Éamon de Valera through intermediaries and also receiving a memo on a solution to the war in Ireland from Irish republicans in South Africa.[54] While the London cabinet did not want the king's speech to be drafted by Craig, they never anticipated that royal pressure would push them to accept the final version it took which was more of an olive branch to nationalism than a celebration of their Government of Ireland Act and its two proposed devolved parliaments as originally planned. This helps explain why the Lord Chancellor made a bitter speech in the House of Lords calling for all-out force to repress the Irish, while the king was in Belfast, something that greatly angered the monarch.[55]

The unexpectedly reconciliatory tone of the king's speech was viewed positively by many nationalists. *Freeman's Journal* pointedly described it as 'in remarkable contrast with the utterances of his ministers.'[56] Northern-born Ernest Blythe wrote approvingly of how he had heard that the British cabinet 'had prepared a war to the hilt speech' but the king had refused to give it.[57] Dáil cabinet minister and Longford IRA commander Seán Mac Eoin, who was in prison awaiting execution in June 1921, remembered it as 'a goodwill speech.'[58] The speech crucially triggered a positive reaction from Éamon de Valera and the national leadership of the republican campaign for independence. The earl of Midleton recalled how, to his 'astonishment', he received a telegram two days later from de Valera inviting Midleton and three fellow Southern Unionist leaders to talks in Dublin on how to respond to the king's overture.[59]

Lloyd George was instantly pushed by the king's call for reconciliation into a public position of accepting a truce and negotiations. On his return to London the king immediately sent him a message warning him not to lose the opportunity the speech had created. There was now a real risk to the king's reputation and national and international status should his personal appeal for peace be ignored. This led the British cabinet to decide to invite de Valera to London for peace talks, only to discover, to their embarrassment that he had just been arrested in Ireland; he was promptly released. By 11 July there was a truce. The ultimate result would be the Anglo-Irish Treaty, with its creation of an independent Irish Free State dominion, which would in effect be run by the very republicans the northern unionists abhorred, and its promise of a boundary commission to renegotiate the border. Bringing the king to Belfast was not, therefore, behind the scenes an unmitigated unionist success story.

Empire discontents

The imperial context also proved problematic. Originally Craig had hoped that the dominion premiers, in London in June 1921 for the Imperial Conference, might attend as this would be 'desirable for every reason and especially on political grounds.'[60] The plan was to frame the opening of the Northern Irish parliament as an imperial success story, timing it to open during the Imperial Conference. The dominion premiers attending would have lent the opening imperial grandeur and status and imperial approval and support. But while there was some personal connection to unionism – New Zealand premier Bill Massey was Ulster-born – most dominion premiers saw the conflict in Ireland as deeply damaging to the empire's reputation and to the whole British imperial project and kept their distance. They feared the new parliament was a partisan solution to the Irish problem, might not survive, that attendance might worsen their relations with Irish nationalism, and felt that as dominion premiers it was inappropriate for them to attend the opening of a lesser-status parliament – a devolved home rule parliament within the UK. The disenchantment went both ways. Many northern unionists, who viewed the IRA as criminal murderers, were far from happy at Smuts' influence on events. They had wanted imperial solidarity; they got imperial interference. Even the parts of the king's speech directed towards imperial public opinion were less than sensitive, referring to Ireland as an embarrassment:

> everything which touches Ireland finds an echo in the remotest parts of the Empire. Few things are more earnestly desired throughout the English speaking world than a satisfactory solution of the age long

Irish problems, which for generations embarrassed our forefathers, as they now weigh heavily upon us.[61]

The unionist *Belfast News Letter* was left to claim that the king and queen's presence itself bestowed imperial status, setting: 'the seal of their presence upon our new parliament and thereby brought it in visible among the Parliaments of the Empire which acknowledge their rule and give them liege service.'[62] There was frustration among unionists regarding the lack of imperial solidarity. As Hugh MacDowell Pollock, the north's incoming Finance Minister, told the journalist Wilfred Ewart in May 1921: 'English people are stupid. Why can't they see that Ulster is the only bulwark between them and complete dissolution of the British Empire? Once concede independence to Ireland and you'll have Egypt, South Africa, India claiming it too.'[63]

The comment was prescient. This too, however, would add to the reasons why the opening of the new Northern Irish parliament was problematic to commemorate. As the British Empire disintegrated in the post-1945 period, it became expedient *not* to remember the imperial context for the 22 June 1921 opening, or the imperial identity that had been so important to both unionists and the king on the day. The 'frontier' of empire mentality praised in the unionist press in June 1921 now looked deeply problematic, with the British Empire increasingly seen as an historical structure that had oppressed indigenous peoples, while the collapse of the imperial framework, which had underpinned the whole Government of Ireland Act solution, risked raising questions about the north's future.[64]

Conclusions

Ultimately, the introduction of direct rule in 1972, which occurred in the face of civil unrest and a renewed IRA campaign, ended the original Northern Irish parliament that had been opened in 1921. Yet even before that parliament became obsolete, the realities of its opening were always more convenient to forget than commemorate. They raised complicated questions about the limitations of Northern Ireland's parliamentary democratic reach, the role and fate of its Catholic minority, the bitter splitting of Irish unionism, imperial interference, and the vulnerability and contingency of unionism's future in 1921. The king's suggestion of potential Irish reunification was also anathema to northern unionists who would go on to reject the Council of Ireland clause in the 1921 Anglo-Irish Treaty and the Boundary Commission. Perhaps unsurprisingly then Northern Ireland would never establish any civic commemoration of its foundation and the ruptures and traumas of the partition period.

Notes

1. For more discussion on issues of commemoration see: Edna Longley, 'Northern Ireland: commemoration, elegy, forgetting' and also Ian McBride, 'Introduction: memory and national identity in modern Ireland' in Ian McBride (ed.), *History and Memory in Modern Ireland* (Cambridge, 2001), pp 1–42 and pp 223–53.
2. Robert Lynch, *The Partition of Ireland, 1918–1925* (Cambridge, 2019), p. 113.
3. For some examples of what is a large historiography, see: Nadine Rossol, '"Ein Hoch auf die Republik!" Die Feiern des Verfassungstages in der Weimarer Republic' in D. Schumann, C. Gusy and W. Mühlhausen, *Demokratie Versuchen: Die Verfassung in der politischen Kultur der Weimarer Republik* (Berlin, 2021), pp 203–24; Eugen Weber, *Peasants into Frenchmen: The Modernization of Rural France* (Stanford, 1976); Christoph Mick, 'Nationale Festkultur in Lemberg vor dem Ersten Weltkrieg' in M.G. Müller and R. Schattkowsky (eds), *Identitätenwandel und nationale Mobilisierung in Regionen ethnischer Diversität. Ein regionaler Vergleich zwischen Westpreußen und Galizien am Ende des 19. und Anfang des 20. Jahrhunderts* (Marburg, 2004), pp 113–32.
4. John Horne, 'Carson's farewell to Ulster', 6 May 1921 (https://www.creativecentenaries.org/blog/carson-s-farewell-to-ulster, accessed 20 July 2022).
5. Ibid.
6. Nevil Macready, *Annals of an Active Life* (London, 1924), vol. 2, p. 567.
7. *The Irish Catholic*, 25 June 1921, cited in Mary Kenny, *Crown and Shamrock: Love and Hate between Ireland and the British Monarchy* (Dublin, 2009), p. 350.
8. Horne, 'Carson's Farewell to Ulster'.
9. House of Lords Debates, 16 June 1921, vol. 45, col. 609.
10. Almeric Fitzroy, *Memoirs*, vol. 2 (London, 1925), p. 753.
11. House of Commons Debates, 14 June 1921, vol. 143 col. 334–79.
12. Alan Parkinson, 'Loyalist Belfast had been keenly awaiting the royals in 1921 when the king opened Northern Ireland's new parliament', *Belfast Newsletter*, 27 Apr. 2021 (https://www.newsletter.co.uk/news/opinion/columnists/loyalist-belfast-had-been-keenly-awaiting-the-royals-in-1921-when-the-king-opened-northern-irelands-new-parliament-3215013, accessed 25 July 2022).
13. 'King George's Visit to Carsonia', *Derry Journal*, 20 June 1921, p. 3.
14. James Loughlin, *The British Monarchy and Ireland, 1800 to the Present* (Cambridge, 2007), p. 317.
15. Kenny, *Crown and Shamrock*, p. 350.
16. David Torrance, 'Parliament and Northern Ireland, 1921–2021' (21 Dec. 2020), pp 25–6 (House of Commons Library, Briefing Paper CBP-8884).

17 Harold Nicolson, *King George the Fifth: His Life and Reign* (London, 1952), p. 353.
18 'King George in Belfast', *Freeman's Journal*, 23 June 1921, p. 3. Nevile Wilkinson, *To All and Singular* (London, 1926), p. 265.
19 Macready, *Annals of an Active Life*, vol. 2, p. 567.
20 Kenny, *Crown and Shamrock*, p. 158.
21 Mabell Airlie, *Thatched with Gold: The Memoirs of Mabell, Countess of Airlie*, edited by Jennifer Ellis (London, 1962), p. 149.
22 Eunan O'Halpin and Dáithí Ó Corráin, *The Dead of the Irish Revolution* (New Haven and London, 2020), p. 491.
23 'Rebel Railway Outrage,' *Londonderry Sentinel*, 25 June 1921, p. 8.
24 Statement of John Grant (BMH WS 658).
25 Statement of Art McGann (BMH WS 431).
26 Airlie, *Thatched with Gold*, p. 149.
27 Heather Jones, *For King and Country: The British Monarchy and the First World War* (Cambridge, 2021), p. 252.
28 Nora Roberts, *Crowned Harp: Memories of the Last Years of the Crown in Ireland* (Dublin, 1960), p. 83.
29 Macready, *Annals of an Active Life*, vol. 2, p. 567.
30 Jones, *For King and Country*, p. 268.
31 Ibid.
32 Michael Hopkinson (ed.), *The Last Days of Dublin Castle: The Diaries of Mark Sturgis* (Dublin, 1999), p. 176 (11 May 1921).
33 Kenny, *Crown and Shamrock*, p. 157.
34 Wilkinson, *To All and Singular*, p. 267. Loughlin, *The British Monarchy and Ireland*, p. 315.
35 Wilkinson, *To All and Singular*, p. 266.
36 Lynch, *The Partition of Ireland*, p. 133.
37 Thomas Jones, *Whitehall Diary: Volume III: Ireland, 1918–1925*, edited by Keith Middlemas (Oxford, 1971), p. 75.
38 Note from Sir Edward Grigg to David Lloyd George, 14 June 1921, p. 3 (Parliamentary Archives, LG/F/86/1/5).
39 Jones, *Whitehall Diary*, p. 76.
40 PRONI, PM/8/1/12, n.d. I am grateful to Marie Coleman for alerting me to this source.
41 Ibid.
42 It remains unclear what was in this draft. It may possibly be the version found in PRONI, PM/8/1/12, but as this is not dated or signed this is uncertain.
43 Kenny, *Crown and Shamrock*, p. 158.
44 Jones, *Whitehall Diary*, pp 76, 247.
45 Ibid., p. 78.
46 Frances Stevenson, *Lloyd George: A Diary by Frances Stevenson*, edited by A.J.P. Taylor (London, 1971), p. 221.

47 Loughlin, *The British Monarchy and Ireland*, p. 318.
48 Hopkinson (ed.), *The Last Days of Dublin Castle*, p. 191.
49 David Torrance, 'Parliament and Northern Ireland, 1921–2021', p. 27.
50 Kenny, *Crown and Shamrock*, p. 162.
51 Ibid., p. 117.
52 Nicolson, *King George the Fifth*, p. 353.
53 He was not alone. See the references to South Africa in the debate in the House of Lords: 16 June 1921, vol. 45, col. 618; O. Geyser, 'Irish independence: Jan Smuts and Eamon de Valera', *The Round Table*, 348 (1998), pp 473–84.
54 Roy Maclaren, *Empire and Ireland: The Transatlantic Career of the Canadian Imperialist Hamar Greenwood, 1870–1948* (Montreal and Kingston, London, Ithaca, 2015) pp 228–9; statement of J.J. Moran (BMH WS 1492); Geyser, 'Irish Independence'.
55 Jones, *For King and Country*, p. 273.
56 'King George in Belfast', *Freeman's Journal*, 23 June 1921, p. 3.
57 Statement of Ernest Blythe (BMH WS 939).
58 Statement of Seán Mac Eoin (BMH WS 1716, pt 2).
59 William Broderick, Earl of Midleton, *Records and Reactions, 1856–1939* (London, 1939), p. 258.
60 Kenny, *Shamrock and Crown*, p. 157.
61 Nicolson, *King George the Fifth*, p. 353.
62 'Welcome,' *Belfast Newsletter*, 22 June 1921, p. 4.
63 Wilfred Ewart, *A Journey in Ireland, 1921* (London, 1922), p. 157.
64 Loughlin, *The British Monarchy in Ireland*, p. 316.

12

Lady Cecil Craigavon and the reclamation of history

DIANE URQUHART

> When the time comes for the writing of the history of the development of Unionism in Northern Ireland, the name of Lady Craigavon will be printed in huge letters throughout it.[1]

Ranked as one of 'the woman leaders of Ulster', Cecil Craig, Lady Craigavon (1883–1960) was, like many of her female contemporaries, sidelined from history.[2] Prime ministerial spouses have attracted some scholarly attention, but this is the first examination of the wife of a Northern Irish premier.[3] Coming to prominence during a period of women's emergence into formal politicking and the fights for suffrage and against Home Rule, Cecil married unionist MP Sir James Craig in 1905 and, came to view 'herself as an Ulsterwoman'.[4] The records of many 'ministerial consorts' were 'treated cavalierly since … [they] were "only" women', but Cecil's diaries, cross-referencing manifold volumes of press cuttings, survive, collectively chronicling the rise of popular unionism and the first decades of Northern Ireland's existence.[5] Cecil is also significant as she writes as both an outsider and insider: an Englishwoman of the upper-middle classes who married into the unionist elite.[6]

Although the original diaries were destroyed, over 480 pages of frank typescript extracts remain. Compiled for St John Ervine's 1949 biography of James Craig, the extracts cover the years from 1883–1900 and then, after a five-year hiatus, 1905–49.[7] In their current incarnation, Cecil's writings deviate from the diarist's usual preoccupation with privacy to recount 'personal experience on a given day … not necessarily addressed to someone other than the diarist.'[8] Referring to her spouse affectionately as 'J.', it is not known why the original diaries no longer survive or to what extent Cecil self-curated the extant extracts. However, reflections on events later deemed pivotal to the creation of Northern Ireland, like the establishment of the Ulster Volunteer Force (UVF), are included.[9] Cecil also considered using the diary extracts to write her reminiscences as Liberal prime ministerial wife, Margot Asquith, had in 1920.[10] Cecil's memoirs never transpired, but she clearly did not mistrust her own written word as was evident in diarists like Labour premier Ramsay MacDonald who prohibited the publication of his diaries in full, averring that their contents were 'meant as notes to guide and revive memory as regards happenings' rather than capture political policy.[11]

Home Rule to partition; 'feeling on Ireland was running very high'[12]

Lacking 'any political experience' at the time of her marriage, Cecil made her first public appearance in Ulster in 1906, and soon emerged as an able speaker.[13] This was relatively new female terrain and at odds with 'the aim of nearly every consort' of twentieth-century UK premiers 'to keep out of the limelight'.[14] By 1910 Cecil sardonically declared that she was 'capable of standing three-quarters of an hour and addressing an audience'.[15] James Craig concurred, claiming that his wife could 'take a meeting much better than I in an emergency'.[16] Evidence supports the latter as, when called to make an impromptu speech, Cecil rousingly addressed the crowd; 'We want … when the election result is declared to be able to say that Craig is your man, not by a three-figure majority, but by a four-figure one.'[17] The press also began to commend Cecil's abilities: 'Mrs Craig was no insignificant factor in the [electoral] contest. … The brief addresses she delivered proved as apt as they were stimulating.'[18]

Cecil's political interest augmented during the third Home Rule crisis of 1912–14. Attending the opening of parliament and going 'constantly to hear the debates in the House', she was often a lone female spectator: 'I was the only woman in the house all through this very interesting time, and wouldn[']t have missed it for anything.'[19] In this, Cecil was again dissimilar to the majority of UK prime ministerial wives, who, with the exceptions of Emily Palmerston and Lucy Baldwin, were 'not … politically minded'.[20] Cecil's diary, for example, revealed the discordant impact of Home Rule; 'there were constant scenes in the House [of Commons] and out of it, and many former friends in opposite political parties wouldn't speak to each other.'[21] This fostered a sense of community amongst the unionist elite. These communal ties tightened as unionism moved closer to solipsism and militarism in the aftermath of 1911 Parliament Act and passage but two-year suspension of the third Home Rule Bill in the following year. Cecil captured both widespread unionist consternation and mistrust of nationalists:

> Apart from their own detestation of the Bill in Ulster, it was a bad Bill for the rest of Ireland, the finance being absolutely unsound … There was, moreover, no desire for it in the South and West, except among political agitators, and ignorant peasants, who had been told that when they got Home Rule Ireland would flow with milk and honey, and be a kind of Utopia, such a thing as paying rent being unknown. The Nationalists had been repeatedly challenged to name any advantage which Ireland did not now enjoy that she would get under a Home Rule Parliament and … they were utterly at a loss to think of one.[22]

There was also a personal cost of resisting Home Rule. Cecil believed that 'the fight to save Ulster, to which J. devoted his whole life' sacrificed his Westminster career.[23] The formation of the UVF in 1913, more particularly its arming through gun-running, heightened fears of the unionist leaders' arrest. The Craigs were subsequently separated from their children:

> As rumours were prevalent that warrants were out for the arrest of Carson and J., Craigavon [the Craigs' home in east Belfast] had been turned into an armed camp, with masses of armed U.V.F … No one was allowed through the gates without a permit, and one of the most thrilling and interesting times I ever experienced took place; Colonel Sharman-Crawford very kindly took the three children and their nurses to stay with him at Crawfordsburn [County Down], as it was considered too dangerous to keep them at Craigavon.[24]

This provoked the sympathy of strangers; a Mrs Bagot writing from Levens in Cumbria acknowledged the strain of Cecil's position: 'I feel so sorry for you with such strenuous work to do, it is a responsible and yet a very unique position that you hold just now, I hope you will [have the] strength to carry it on as beautifully as you have begun it.'[25]

Despite such affirmations, early twentieth-century politics was subject to considerable sex segregation. Cecil could only attend the after-dinner speeches at London's Constitutional Club, 'the dinner itself being only a man's affair.'[26] Both she and Ruby Carson, wife of the unionist leader, were deemed the 'feminine element'[27] and defined in relation to their spouses; 'having husbands who are political leaders in Ulster, [they] take a deep interest in Ireland, and are as anxious as their menfolk for a settlement of a long vexed question'.[28] Yet, Cecil contributed to this trope, designating her position as ancillary to that of her spouse; 'the small role that falls to me is to accompany my husband, a duty which is a great pleasure, as it enables me to get to know better all the classes of the community.'[29]

However, in mid-1914, 'domestic politics receded ... The international situation became blacker and blacker ... The whole outlook changed immediately, and there is no doubt that the conflict between ourselves and Germany, saved Ulster ... from civil war.'[30] During the First World War, Cecil was involved in war work and ceremonial duties such as opening a ward of the UVF hospital in Belfast's Botanic Gardens.[31] The Craigs' home, Craigavon, was also used as neurasthenic hospital for shell-shocked soldiers from 1917. This caused further personal upheaval. As Cecil recorded; 'I dash over and empty the place in a week!, as they need it so urgently, with the result that a number of things get overlooked, and are put for sale by mistake'.[32] Despite the wartime political truce, Cecil's commentaries in the aftermath of the 1916 Easter Rising were emblematic of a hardening of unionist attitudes towards Westminster's ability and, more pertinently, willingness, to protect Ulster from Home Rule; 'Things in Ireland, outside Ulster[,] were very bad, as after the Easter rebellion Asquith had gone over to Dublin and shaken all the murderers in the gaols warmly by the hand!! ... people had more contempt than ever for the British Gov[ernmen]t.'[33]

Rallying unionist voters therefore gained a new urgency in the post-war election of December 1918, the first in which women could stand as candidates and, if duly enfranchised, cast a vote. Electioneering with her spouse, Cecil often attended multiple daily meetings and addressed female voters, but with an all-male unionist candidature, symptomatic of the party's entrenched conservatism, she could only urge women to vote for unionist men.[34] A further reminder that women's enfranchisement would not be wholly transformative came in the continued auxiliary depiction of Cecil's political work as rendering 'splendid aid' to her spouse.[35]

The political context was subject to a faster pace of change. Cecil's response to the 1919 Council of Ireland cabinet committee, even under the stewardship of former unionist leader Walter Long, to devise a solution to the vexed 'Irish question' was blunt; 'so they are at it again!!'[36] That committee's proposals became the 1920 Government of Ireland Act, partitioning both the island of Ireland and the nine-county province of Ulster. The six-county demarcation of Northern Ireland, excluding counties Cavan, Donegal and Monaghan with Protestant minorities totalling 70,000, was contentious but Cecil presented no political alternative:

> delegates from the three counties had magnanimously agreed to exclusion ... to save their fellows in the other six counties ... Parliament for the whole area would mean the parties being so evenly balanced, that it would very probably be soon submerged in

the Dublin one, or efforts to bring that about made, with civil war probably the result ... a six county area would be so strong that it would constitute an intensely loyal part of Ireland, pledged to Great Britain and the empire ... Furthermore[,] if Ulster rejected this [Government of Ireland] Bill[,] the 1914 Home Rule Act on the Statute Book would be enforced, and Ulster would be under a Dublin parliament.[37]

This was an uneasy remedy. As Cecil wrote: 'they would rather remain under the Union, but if that was not possible they had to do the best they could.'[38] Northern Ireland was, therefore, founded without unionist triumphalism in 1921. However, Cecil's later reflections on partition revealed a tempering of attitude:

partition of any country is a regrettable thing, and there is, consequently, a prima facie case for the removal of the Border. The Nationalist ... speaks of the border in the bitterest terms, as an insult to the Soul of Ireland, and you will find a similar fanatical note in some of the pronouncements of the I.R.A. We recognise the strength of these feelings and to a certain extent we share them. There are many Unionists in the South, and this brings home to us the unhappy division of Ireland. ... But we also face facts. There may be something inherently unsatisfactory about a divided country, but the union of peoples with different aims and ideals is even worse.[39]

Citing examples of 'highly successful' partitions in Benelux countries, Cecil could not envisage a similar fate for Ireland as the aims of the respective governments were 'so utterly at variance ... that union is unthinkable.' Unionists' conditional loyalty of the pre-partition era also remained: 'There is no more loyal part of the United Kingdom ... than Northern Ireland, but it would be mistaken to assume that our loyalty could bear the strain of betrayal' of a united Ireland.[40]

Premiership: 'this heavy task in Ulster'[41]

Despite Cecil's unionist allegiances, she had reservations regarding her spouse assuming the position of first premier of Northern Ireland in 1921. Her diaries relate a meeting with Ulster Unionist Council secretary, Richard Dawson Bates:

I point out that I know he [James] would really prefer to stay here [in England] ... and so would I, ... our two homes are now on this side, ... he is most highly thought of in the House [of Commons], and has undoubtedly a great and assured future before him here … Bates implores me to urge him to accept the invitation … the whole thing is very difficult and momentous![42]

Craig accepted the premiership only on the proviso that he was unanimously accepted.[43] Yet, despondency remained. Making his last Commons' appearance, Cecil wrote, 'we both feel very sad about it'.[44] The unionist elite rallied round; 'We leave for Belfast, the Carsons and the Herbert Dixons came over with us', and, guarded by 16 police, they stayed with Dawson Bates in Holywood, County Down.[45]

The Craigs were quickly politically enmeshed. On one day in 1921, for example, the Craigs attended:

> a big open air meeting in Comber, and shake hands after with hundreds of people. Dinner in the Reform Club at night, followed by a wonderful gathering of the U.U. [Ulster Unionist] Labour Association, with about 3000 people … We had met delegates from the Ulster Women's U.C. [Unionist Council], earlier in the day, so had covered a lot of ground![46]

This was indicative of Cecil's tireless interwar work. Many of her charitable interests were broad church and woman-focused and she unveiled countless war memorials, toured factories, opened bazaars, working men's clubs and Orange halls.[47] With 'people in and out of the house all the time',[48] there were also border tours and ceremonial events such as 'a big afternoon party to the members of the Senate and their wives, the members of the Commons and their wives, and the Permanent Officials and their wives, about 130 come.'[49] Moreover, when her spouse was incapacitated by illness, Cecil would often deputise. For example, opening a mine at Coalisland in County Tyrone she was one of 'only two women present in a vast gathering of all the principal businessmen of the Province, and some from Southern Ireland also.'[50]

Although occasionally 'fed up with politics',[51] many of Cecil's early 1920s diary entries were sanguine:

> A great new era was starting in Ulster, and they all looked forward to many reforms and benefits long overdue which their own local Parliament would be able to give its immediate attention to, and which were of necessity crowded out of business at Westminster owing to so much congestion of work and obstruction by the Nationalists.[52]

The royal visit to open the new Northern Ireland parliament in mid-1921 was Craig's political coming of age. With Carson deliberately absent to prevent eclipsing the new premier, Cecil organised an address to the Queen but only from the loyal women of Ulster, a move which was symbolic of divisions in the new state.

Given the levels of violence, with over 500 people killed in Northern Ireland from 1920–22, Cecil espoused the defensive mentality common to many unionists; 'permanent vigilance [was] … the motto of the new regime'.[53] Writing of the 'shocking outrages taking place in Belfast', she depicted it as 'still seething, and terrible things are happening there.'[54] The threat to the Craigs' personal safety amplified as they prepared to move into Stormont Castle in 1922: 'The Shinnies [Sinn Féin] thinking we had gone straight to the Castle on our return, attack it.'[55] Four days later, 'The Shinnies attacked the [Herbert] Dixon[']s house tonight, where we had been staying, thinking we were still there!'[56] Cecil commonly used an exclamation mark when recording such occurrences. This was not a means to trivialise the events but to indicate her strong feelings. Cecil also began to wait for her spouse outside events as 'it was less worrying than sitting at home, and perhaps letting one's imagination run away with one'.[57] She thus had much in common with Julia Peel who 'shared fully in all the anxieties attached to' her spouse's premiership.[58]

However, travelling to Dublin for Craig's meeting with de Valera in 1921, security concerns were such that Cecil was deterred from her usual practice.[59] This controversial meeting, depicted by Cecil as 'very distasteful' to Craig, aimed 'to stop the terrible reign of terror and atrocities': 'his [Craig's] extremists will be very annoyed with him. He never … bothered his head as to whether a particular line of action was a popular one or not, if he thought it was the right thing to do, he did it regardless[.]'[60] Cecil was frustrated by some subsequent reactions, determining that her spouse's past record proved his fidelity; 'I was so disgusted and angry that there should be any question about it, that I … let fly at a good many people, telling them exactly what I thought of them!! However, they were really only a comparative few.'[61]

Craig's 1922 meetings with Michael Collins caused similar censure due to fears that this signalled a dual process of southern involvement in and British retreat from Northern Irish governance. The meetings resulted in two pacts which Cecil felt legitimised Northern Ireland:

> Mr Collins by signing the document with J. admitted, whether he realised it or not, the status of Ulster as a separate Government in Ireland, which was most important. … I feel sure every decent person will approve of them, and if Ulster does not want moderation and fairness … [she] may well expect J. to resign, and make way for … the extremists. … The Orangemen who stand for civil and religious liberty can hardly object.[62]

Yet, this was countered in her next diary entry:

> What makes me so raging is the lack of guts of all of them, none of the people who heartily approve of his [Craig's] action have the courage to ... say so ... It makes one wonder whether they are worth slaving ... almost to death for. How I wish sometimes we had stayed in England, where he [J.] is so much appreciated, of course I know the people themselves all adore him, one can tell by going round everywhere with him as I have done.[63]

Neither pact impeded the violence: 'when one side is attacked the others retaliate with compound interest, and so it goes on'.[64] Two months later, Cecil was more partisan, echoing the Northern Irish government's absolution of 'loyalist mob violence';[65] 'Everyone is very afraid of retaliation by "our people" who are behaving really splendidly at the moment, considering what they have had to put up with.'[66]

Despite hegemony of both parliament and government, the looming Boundary Commission, enshrined in Article 12 of the 1921 Anglo-Irish Treaty, due to report in 1925, lent a sense of impermanency to northern unionists. To Cecil the commission's 'whole history ... was a disgrace to and blot on the honour of those statesman who signed it.'[67] Attending a 1922 party for the royals, Cecil broached the boundary issue with Churchill, underscoring the continued potency of socio-political entertaining:

> My chat with Winston was most interesting, and he assured me that we in Ulster would come out on top, and none of them would stand more than a rectification of the boundaries, they, the British Gov[ernmen]t. stooped to win Sinn Fein Ireland, and he said Sinn Fein Ireland would have to stoop to win Ulster. If not he said, we will use economic pressure, and as last year Southern Ireland exported 205 million pounds worth of stuff, and that 200 millions was to England, they would be ruined.[68]

With the Boundary Commission's report imminent, Cecil's rhetoric intensified: 'For the further mutilation of Ulster – which was already smaller than it should be ... anyone ... in his right mind' would not tolerate.[69] Her rallying calls to unionists 'to sink all their differences and to vote on the one important [boundary] issue. ... Did they want some of their brothers and sisters on the border to be sacrificed' provoked cries of 'No!' in Lurgan.[70] She also raised the possibility of armed defence; 'They were ... living in troublous [sic] times. They always wished for peace in Ulster, but if there should be any infringement of their rights and liberties, they would know how to act, as they had done in the past'. Deemed 'sinister' by the *Daily Herald*, this speech was misrepresented as 'the first threat of armed resistance to the law of the land from one in the fullest confidence of the Prime Minister' whilst denying Cecil's agency; 'it is not too much to presume that ... she was expressing the views of her husband. It is a nice commentary on the courage of the members of the Belfast Government that they allowed a lady to be the first to speak in that strain.'[71]

With the boundary secured, Cecil's diary revealed a new unionist sense of triumphalism:

> What a great triumph for James ... in the press that certain politicians have been saying that it is a great pity that the Ulster Prime Minister settled the Boundary by mutual agreement with Mr Cosgrave, if the Commission had issued its report Ulster would have come out much better. I can only suspect two things, of people who utter sentiments such as this ... that they are very devoid of intelligence, or ... they are deliberately trying to sow seeds of dissatisfaction in the minds of the Ulster people with the Government ... Neither side wanted a renewal of bloodshed, so the leaders did the statesmanlike and only thing they could do, which was to leave the Boundary exactly as it was. No other solution could ... James ... countenance, pledged as he was never to sacrifice one Loyalist.[72]

In return, Cecil demanded absolute allegiance to her spouse's administration and was chagrined by independent unionists, whom she deemed 'neither flesh, fish, fowl or good red herring. You cannot run with the hare if you hunt with the hounds'.[73] Opposed to a multi-party system: 'there was no room for more than two political parties in Ulster', Cecil upheld sectarian-sustaining divisions.[74] Such partisanship was evident in other prime ministerial wives like ladies Campbell-Bannerman and Palmerston; the latter considered intra-party differences as 'evidence of a wilful perversity.'[75] Moreover, when Cecil spoke of cross-class unity, it was only within the realm of unionism; 'In a small and intensely democratic country such as ours it is wonderful how easily all classes can combine to pull together for the common cause. Unity carries us forward and spells progress in capital letters; dissension spells retrogression and disaster. Let us stick fast to Unionist principles.'[76]

Responding to indictments of governmental bigotry, Cecil was defiant: 'There was no such thing ... but there was an intolerance of disloyalty which, she hoped, would always remain'.[77] This sense of an 'enemy within' never dissipated, leading Cecil to defend some of the most contentious legislation introduced in Northern Ireland including the Civil Authorities (Special Powers) Act of 1922; 'They had no feelings of ill-will towards any section of the community; they wanted all to share in ... prosperity',[78] but after 'two terrible years of insurrection [from 1920–22]; with claims for damages amounting to £3 million pounds from February to July [1922]' and 'the number of outrages averaged from ten to twenty a day ... we have had to face a barrage of anti-Ulster propaganda designed to secure the abolition of the border'.[79] Evoking 'democracy, and the rights of the majority',[80] Cecil portrayed the internment enshrined in the 1922 Act, allowing arrests and searches without warrant and imprisonment without trial (with 700 people detained without charges in its first two years of operation), as a defensive measure that met 'a great deal of unfair and misinformed criticism':

> cast in our teeth that these Powers are undemocratic and 'totalitarianism' ... and that the exercise of them strike at the liberty of the individuals and is contrary to the principles of British justice ... the object of these Special Powers Acts was to protect the freedom and indeed the personal safety of the law-abiding citizen against the outrages of the gun-bully. ... Where terrorism is concerned the ordinary processes of the law may be too slow ... Desperate cases call for desperate remedies and however much we may regret any departure from the principles of normal judicial procedure, any Government worthy of the name must take adequate steps to prevent the extension of violence and to protect the great mass of law-abiding citizens.[81]

Such unfailing defence of the Unionist Party was castigated by the nationalist press as a sign of weakness in Craig's administration. To the nationalist *Irish News*, Cecil was 'a party politician on the side of the Government'[82] and 'a valuable political asset ... A trained and polished speaker, with a graceful presence, a facile gift of language, and an effective delivery'. Yet, she provoked gendered scorn for 'putting up a case that indeed only a woman could put up on behalf of a Ministry whose only strength is the absence ... of an alternative Government to put in its place.'[83]

The Ulster Women's Unionist Council: 'Lady Craigavon's women'[84]

Elected president of the Ulster Women's Unionist Council (UWUC) in 1923, Cecil was 'perhaps prouder of [this] ... than anything else'.[85] Cecil had a long association with women's unionism, seconding the resolution to establish the UWUC in 1911 and serving as its vice-president from 1912, but the presidency afforded her an opportunity to air her political opinions more fully.[86] Although Cecil's presidential speech exhibited a characteristic modesty, hoping to 'be worthy of their confidence',[87] the press now acknowledged her not only 'as the wife of the Prime Minister, but also for her own qualities.'[88] Long ascribing to the belief that female politicking should be distinct from that of men, Cecil assigned a specific role for the unionist women: updating electoral registers; canvassing; holding public meetings and conducting 'missionary' work in England to convince voters of the efficacy of the unionist cause.

A separatist gendered stance was also apparent in the creation of the Ulster Women's Loyalist Volunteer Association, organised under the UWUC's auspices, in 1922. Seeking to train women to replace men in the civil service, police, Red Cross and St John's Ambulance and supply essential food, water, fuel and light, this body exposed unionist anticipation of widespread strikes and the renewed prospect of physical defence. Cecil was central to is organisation; 'I have a meeting in Belfast in connection with getting the City organised under the Ulster Women's Volunteer Association, and get things satisfactorily fixed up.'[89] The physical protection of the new state was also mooted as Cecil evoked Randolph Churchill's 'Ulster will fight' sentiment in the same year, claiming 15,000 men in London were 'waiting to take up arms in defence of Ulster':

> If the Sinn Fein party thought that their tactics were going to be the means of smashing Ulster then they were making a great mistake (Applause.) They might be able to brow beat their former friends in the ... British Government, but their methods would have no success in Ulster[.][90]

As socialism joined republicanism to threaten interwar unionism, Cecil's perceived need for vigilance justified the UWUC's continuance, deeming it 'a 'dangerous, futile ... insane thought' to think otherwise; 'if in the future Ulster's liberties should be attacked they could carry on and carry through to victory as they did in the past'.[91] Reorganising the UWUC from 1924, Cecil resolved to maintain the council as a separate body from its male counterpart, an initiative later praised by unionist MP Dehra Chichester as 'right ... she [Cecil] determined to see that their organisation should be maintained in its strength and increased in its strength.'[92] A key tenet of this scheme was to foster closer ties between urban and rural female unionist associations. Modelled on the idea of a political club, regional meetings of the UWUC's ruling body, the Executive Committee, were held. As Cecil resolved, 'instead of the country always coming to Belfast they should pay them the courtesy of going down to the country ... It made for a closer intimacy and a better understanding of one another, and also of the local conditions.'[93]

Conservative feminism was also strategically deployed as a mobilising tactic, initiating UWUC tuition in female citizenship with 'classes for training women unionists in the arts of discussion and of conducting meetings'.[94] Inviting Scottish unionist, Katharine, duchess of Atholl, the newly-appointed parliamentary secretary to the Board of Education in Baldwin's government and the first Conservative woman to hold cabinet office, to address the UWUC's annual meeting in 1925 was likewise designed to inspire unionist women. In a similar vein, continuing a trend to make unionism germane to women lives which was evident from the mid-1880s, Cecil encouraged the incorporation of domestic economy in women's unionist meetings; 'she was very keen on having lectures on subjects such as dressmaking, hygiene, and other matters that would be helpful to the women in their own homes.'[95]

Cecil believed that female unionists' work would be acknowledged by history; 'the part women had played in helping the men in the recent troubles times would, when they history of those times came to be written, compare favourably with the part played by the women of old'.[96] Sections of the contemporary press concurred, emphasising Cecil's role: 'She has been the motive power behind the Ulster Women's Unionist Council ... Her political duties have taken up a great deal of her time. She has given the time willingly and conscientiously she has gone to the smallest of meetings and addressed them with the same earnestness as she would a huge meeting ... She is an ideal hostess'.[97] Yet, despite her prominence and decades of work to politically educate and mobilise unionist women, this faith in history was ill-founded. Ervine's comment that Cecil was her spouse's 'helpmeet in an extraordinary degree' is the fullest acknowledgement that her work received mainstream unionist histories.[98]

'The heart of her husband doth safely trust in her'[99]

Cecil preserved an undated letter from an anonymous Catholic woman in her diary extracts: 'Any little thing I did or could do, would never approach the edge of deep debt of gratitude owing to the Prime Minister and your self [sic], by my husband and my self [sic], and in fact by the Catholic people generally, which they will some day [sic] realise.'[100] This serves as a reminder of Cecil's vexation at charges of unionist bias and she called for self-reflection:

> They should pause occasionally to consider what they as a Government had achieved. They had set up the whole working machinery of Government from nothing; they had restored law and order; they had passed various measures of benefit to the community at large, and had won the respect of England and ... many of their political opponents over here.[101]

However, she lacked the frustration shown by Margaret Trudeau, wife of the Canadian premier, that she was 'more than just a rose in ... [her] husband's lapel'.[102] Cecil downplayed her political acumen, asserting that 'she was not gifted with the ability to take her husband's place or with her husband's ability and make a political speech'.[103] Even after replying to a vote of confidence in her spouse which she deemed 'quite a success', she noted 'it all of course [was] really meant for J.'[104] She thus markedly contributed to her portrayal as 'the loyal wife of the Prime Minister. At practically every meeting which she addresses she asks not so much for support her herself, but that the women of Ulster should support Lord Craigavon.'[105] However, one *Sunday Dispatch* article, 'which pleases J. very much', recorded her 'tremendous help to Lord Craigavon' and ability:

> those who have watched her at mass meetings, note the quality of her speeches, the charm of her personality, her great power of persuasiveness, will know that the debt of the Prime Minister and the Unionist Party is no light one ... She has subjugated herself to her party, she has enormously strengthened that party.[106]

Others applauded Cecil's 'splendid calm', but this was façade as she had to combat nerves.[107]

Within the gamut of roles ascribed to political wives, from 'all-embracing nurturer to stalwart partner, passive doormat, lickety-spit support staffer ... [to] mischievous saboteur', Cecil resides in the former two categories.[108] She is, therefore, comparable to the most politically active of UK prime ministerial wives – Hannah Rosebery, Margot Asquith and particularly Emily Palmerston.[109] Like Cecil, Lady Palmerston 'spent herself in helping' her spouse, 'in furthering his interest and upholding his political views and acts ... thought her husband always in the right' and demanded party loyalty.[110] Indeed, although displaying many of the defensive characteristics of interwar unionism, Cecil's loyalty to her spouse overrode dedication to any political ideology. Widowed in 1940, there was speculation that she would stand for election in her late husband's North Down seat, but she returned to England, 'too shattered' by her spouse's loss 'to take part in any public affairs, at any rate for a long time to come':

> also I would not have had my heart in working for the man who had been chosen by the Government to succeed him, and I felt sore at the way a comparatively small number of peevers were allowed to harass and pinprick by dear PM without his own solid backbenchers in the House having the guts to stand up and attack them. These had undoubtedly hastened his end, so I had no wish to have anything further to do with politics.[111]

Sections of the nationalist press, at times, ranked Cecil more highly than her spouse and his ministers; 'Viscountess Craigavon's little speeches at times are more significant than the laboured addresses of her husband and members of his Cabinet'.[112] This did not dampen Craig's admiration of his wife, admitting that he 'owed more [to her] in his private and political life than he could ever tell.'[113] Yet, Cecil was more than a political wife – she was a Unionist Party asset who strove to politically educate the first post-enfranchisement generation of unionist women and thus more than warrants her place in history.

Notes

1. *Sunday Dispatch*, 18 Dec. 1932. Thanks to Prof. Ian McBride for prompting me to write further on Cecil Craig.
2. *Morning Post*, 26 Mar. 1923. Fifty-nine volumes of press cuttings survive. A baronetcy was conferred on James Craig in 1917. A viscountcy followed in 1927 and Cecil subsequently became Viscountess Craigavon.
3. In a UK context, see, for example, Elizabeth Lee, *Wives of the Prime Ministers, 1844–1906* (London, 1918) and Mark Hichens, *Prime Ministers' Wives – and One Husband* (London, 2004). For early examples of biographies of prime ministerial wives, see Desmond MacCarthy, *Lady John Russell* (London, 1910), Mary Drew, *Catherine Gladstone* (London, 1919) and Lucy Herbert, *Mrs Ramsay MacDonald* (London, 1926).
4. *Belfast Newsletter*, 9 Jan. 1935. Cecil was the daughter of Sir Daniel Tupper, assistant comptroller of the Lord Chamberlain's Office, who, as part of the king's household, resided in St James' Palace, and Mary Cholmondeley Dering of Kent. Parental divorce whilst Cecil was young, saw her live with her father and grandmother. Educated at a Bournemouth boarding school and in Windsor, in 1899 Cecil went to Switzerland, likely to finishing school, and came out in the season of 1900. Cecil met Craig at a Benburb shooting lunch. Engaged in early 1905, they married six weeks later. In 1906, she bore twin boys and a daughter was born in the following year.
5. Elspeth Cameron, 'Ladies of the Hill', *Maclean's*, 104:43 (28 Oct. 1991), p. 97. For example, sources are scarce for Lady Derby, wife of the UK Prime Minister in 1852, 1858–9 and 1866–8 and Lady Abbot, wife of the Canadian premier from 1891–2.
6. Lynn Lemisko, 'The inside out: diaries as entry points to historical perspective-taking', *Canadian Social Studies*, 44:1 (Fall, 2010), pp 38–54. Cecil's social class befits the profile of most UK prime ministerial wives although some, like Catherine Gladstone, Caroline Lamb and Dorothy Macmillan, were upper class.
7. St John Ervine, *Craigavon: Ulsterman* (London, 1949).

8 Irina Paperno, 'What can be done with diaries?', *The Russian Review*, 63:4 (Oct. 2004), p. 562.
9 For example, Cecil wrote that the UVF 'after they were armed ... undoubtedly saved Ulster for the empire', Cecil Craig diary extract (hereafter CCD), 17 July 1913 (PRONI, D1415/B/38). James Craig was the UVF's political staff officer.
10 Margot Asquith, *Autobiography* (London, 1920).
11 TNA, PRO 30/69/1753/1.
12 CCD, 17 Jan. 1913.
13 Ervine, *Craigavon*, p. 108.
14 Margot Asquith is an exception to this reticence (Hichens, *Prime Ministers' Wives*, p. 10).
15 *Belfast Newsletter*, 18 Dec. 1909.
16 *Daily Mail*, 21 Jan. 1938.
17 *Belfast Newsletter*, 12 Dec. 1910.
18 CCD, 10 Dec. 1910. James Craig's majority increased by 728 to 1698 votes in this 1910 election.
19 CCD, undated and 20 Mar. 1914.
20 Hichens, *Prime Ministers' Wives*, p. 9.
21 CCD, 17 Jan. 1913.
22 *Belfast Newsletter*, 17 Jan. 1914.
23 CCD, 23 Sep. 1911.
24 CCD, 20 Mar. 1914. Sharman-Crawford was elected as a unionist MP in 1914.
25 Cited in CCD, 30 Mar. 1912.
26 CCD, 25 June 1914. Established in 1883, members of this gentleman's club pledged support for the Conservative Party.
27 *The Tatler*, undated [1911] in Craigavon press cutting book (PRONI, D1415/A/3).
28 *Ladies Pictorial*, 2 Feb. 1918.
29 *Belfast Newsletter*, 30 May 1911.
30 CCD, 22 July 1914. James Craig was appointed Lieutenant Colonel of the 36th (Ulster) Division and served in the second wartime coalition from 1916–17 as Treasurer of the Household and a whip before resigning to join the 1917 Irish Convention.
31 CCD, 2 Feb. 1917.
32 This included a grand piano. CCD, Apr. 1917. Cecil opened the hospital in July 1917. Craigavon was sold in 1920.
33 CCD, undated.
34 *Belfast Newsletter*, 13 Dec. 1918.
35 *Morning Post*, 9 Dec. 1918.
36 CCD, 25 Sep. 1919.
37 CCD, 6 Mar. 1920.
38 *Northern Whig*, 7 Apr. 1919.

39 Cecil Craig speech, Ashridge Bonar Law Memorial College, 1 Aug. 1939 included in CCD. Ashridge offered political training. See Clarisse Berthezene, *Training Minds for the War of Ideas: Ashridge College, the Conservative Party and the Cultural Politics of Britain, 1929–54* (Manchester, 2015).
40 Cecil Craig speech, Ashridge Bonar Law Memorial College, 1 Aug. 1939 included in CCD.
41 CCD, 18 Jan. 1921.
42 CCD, 24 Jan. 1921. Bates was a unionist member of the NI parliament from 1921 and Minister of Home Affairs, 1921–43. Craig was Parliamentary Secretary of the Ministry of Pensions from 1919 and appointed Financial Secretary to the Admiralty in 1920.
43 CCD, 26 Jan. 1921.
44 CCD, 18 Mar. 1921.
45 CCD, 2 Feb. 1921. In 1921, the Craigs moved to Cabin Hill in east Belfast. Herbert Dixon was a unionist MP in Westminster and Stormont. A unionist chief whip in the latter assembly, he was parliamentary secretary to the Minister of Finance, 1921–42 and Minister of Agriculture, 1942–3.
46 CCD, 5 Feb. 1921. The Reform Club admitted women in 1929, following the passage of universal suffrage in 1928.
47 Cecil supported the non-denominational evangelical Belfast's Midnight Mission Rescue and Maternity Homes, the Salvation Army and the Samaritan Hospital for Women. Cecil was president of the Ulster Hospital in Belfast from 1930, the Midwives' Association for Ulster from 1935 and the Ulster Ladies' Work Depot from 1936. UK prime ministerial wives, Catherine Gladstone and Lucy Baldwin were also prominent philanthropists (Hichens, *Prime Ministers' Wives*, p. 100).
48 CCD, 7 Dec. 1924. For example, former Conservative premier, Stanley Baldwin and the Churchills stayed at Stormont in 1924 and 1926, respectively.
49 CCD, 13 Mar. 1922. For instance, a three-day tour of border areas, encompassing Down, Armagh, Tyrone and Fermanagh, covered 382 miles in 1922.
50 CCD, 25 July 1925. Cecil also deputised for Craig in 1933 and 1937 elections.
51 CCD, 17 Dec. 1921.
52 *Belfast Newsletter*, 23 Apr. 1921.
53 Brendan O'Leary, *A Treatise on Northern Ireland: Volume II: Control* (Oxford, 2019), p. 18.
54 CCD, 24 and 25 Nov. 1921.
55 CCD, 19 June 1922.
56 CCD, 26 June 1922.
57 CCD, 3 May 1921.

58 Julia Peel to Sir Robert Wilson, 1846 cited in Lee, *Wives of the Prime Ministers*, p. 53.
59 CCD, 3 and 5 May 1921. Catherine Gladstone also accompanied her spouse 'on all his political campaigns' (Lee, *Wives of the Prime Ministers*, p. 192).
60 CCD, 3 May 1921.
61 CCD, 5 May 1921.
62 CCD, 23 Jan. and 31 Mar. 1922.
63 CCD, 4 Apr. 1922.
64 CCD, 24 Mar. 1922.
65 O'Leary, *A Treatise on Northern Ireland*, p. 53.
66 CCD, 22 May 1922.
67 *Belfast Newsletter*, 14 Jan. 1925.
68 CCD, 9 Mar. 1922. This was hosted by the 7th marquess and marchioness of Londonderry.
69 *Irish Telegraph*, 28 Nov. 1925.
70 *Belfast Newsletter*, 2 Apr. 1925.
71 *Daily Herald*, 16 June 1924. Cecil previously spoke of physical defence, see *Northern Whig*, 24 Mar. 1922.
72 Notes in CCD, 3 Dec. 1925.
73 *Belfast Telegraph*, 9 May 1929.
74 *Belfast Newsletter*, 5 Mar. 1929.
75 Lee, *Wives of the Prime Ministers*, p. 239.
76 Cecil Craig, 'Women's Influence', *Northern Ireland. Home and Politics*, vol. 1, no. 2, March 1926, front page.
77 *Belfast Newsletter*, 9 Jan. 1935.
78 *Belfast Evening Telegraph*, 11 May 1928.
79 Cecil Craig speech, Ashridge College, 1 Aug. 1939 included in CCD.
80 O'Leary, *A Treatise on Northern Ireland*, preface and p. 58.
81 Cecil Craig speech, Ashridge College, 1 Aug. 1939 included in CCD. The vast majority of those interned were Catholic men (O'Leary, *A Treatise on Northern Ireland*, p. 29). The Special Powers Act was repealed in 1973.
82 *Irish News*, 20 Jan. 1926.
83 *Irish News*, 22 Apr. 1926.
84 *Spectator*, 22 Jan. 1938.
85 *Northern Whig*, 17 Oct. 1936. Cecil was also first president of East Down Women's Unionist Association (WUA) from 1911, and president of Mid-Down WUA from 1919. Cecil retained the UWUC presidency until 1942 and remained a UWUC vice-president until her death in 1960.
86 The resolution was proposed by Edith Mercier Clements.
87 CCD, 2 Mar. 1923.
88 *Belfast Telegraph*, 3 Mar. 1923.
89 CCD, 11 July 1922. The association was modelled on Edith, 7th marchioness of Londonderry's wartime Women's Legion and she led this new body which, by the end of 1922, had 230 recruits.

90 *Northern Whig*, 24 Mar. 1922.
91 CCD, 21 Jan. 1927.
92 Ibid., 20 Jan. 1925.
93 *Irish Independent*, 16 Oct. 1924.
94 *Morning Post*, 31 Oct. 1924.
95 *Belfast Newsletter*, 19 Dec. 1923.
96 CCD, 21 Jan. 1927.
97 *Sunday Dispatch*, 18 Dec. 1932.
98 Ervine, *Craigavon*, p. 538.
99 Inscription on a silver writing set presented to Cecil from members of the Commons and Lords by Austen Chamberlain in 1921 (CCD, 3 Aug. 1921).
100 CCD, 30 Dec. 1911.
101 *Belfast Newsletter*, 19 Dec. 1923.
102 Cameron, 'Ladies of the Hill', cited p. 97. Pierre Trudeau was Canadian premier from 1968–79 and 1980–84.
103 *Belfast Newsletter*, 8 Dec. 1921.
104 CCD, 16 Mar. 1922.
105 *Daily Express*, 29 Jan. 1932.
106 *Sunday Dispatch*, 18 Dec. 1932.
107 Lady Dolly Abercorn to Cecil, 1922 cited in CCD, 27 Nov. 1922.
108 Cameron, 'Ladies of the Hill', p. 97.
109 Hichens, *Prime Ministers' Wives*, p. 10.
110 Lee, *Wives of the Prime Ministers*, pp 109, 119. *Belfast Evening Telegraph* acknowledged in an article on Cecil that, 'Those who are in the hurly-burly of political life are not called upon to make all the sacrifices. The strain and the anxiety cast on those behind the scenes is no less than on the chief actors' (18 Dec. 1925).
111 CCD, undated [1940].
112 *Irish News*, 13 Oct. 1927.
113 CCD, 15 Apr. 1934.

13

The Boundary Commission and border minorities

CORMAC MOORE

The Boundary Commission hung over Northern Ireland and its border areas from the moment it became part of the Anglo-Irish Treaty of December 1921 up to the tripartite government agreement four years later in December 1925 when the British, Irish Free State and Northern Ireland governments agreed to shelve the Commission report and to retain the status quo. For nationalists, the Boundary Commission gave, what turned out to be false, hopes for the transfer of large tracts of territory and people from Northern Ireland to the Irish Free State. They felt they could continue to ignore and obstruct the institutions of Northern Ireland, particularly in areas of nationalist majorities. For unionists, the Boundary Commission was a source of instability and threat to the new entity of Northern Ireland so soon after its foundation. It contributed to the vulnerability and paranoia of unionists. When the Boundary Commission finally did convene from late 1924, the three commissioners conducted informal and formal hearings, interviewing more than 500 witnesses based on written statements submitted in advance. This essay looks at how both the unionist and nationalist communities reacted and dealt with the Boundary Commission, with a particular focus on the main submissions from minority communities in border areas, both unionists and nationalists, those trapped, as they saw it, on the wrong side of the border. The submissions provide an invaluable source on how the border was interpreted and experienced by people in the border areas so soon after its creation.

Article 12 of the Treaty

The Anglo-Irish Treaty was signed in the early hours of the morning of 6 December 1921 between negotiating teams from the British government and Sinn Féin. Its main provision relating to Ulster was Article 12. It stipulated that if Northern Ireland, which had been in existence since the summer of 1921, opted not to join the Irish Free State, as was its right under the Treaty, a Boundary Commission would determine the border 'in accordance with the wishes of the inhabitants, so far as may be compatible with economic and geographic conditions'.[1] Unsurprisingly, Northern Ireland took the first opportunity to remain outside of the Dublin jurisdiction in December 1922, thus triggering the establishment of the Boundary Commission. Interestingly, in an early draft treaty the British submitted to the Irish negotiators on 16 November, a Boundary Commission would be appointed 'to determine in accordance with the wishes of the inhabitants the boundaries between Northern Ireland and the rest of Ireland'. There was no mention of economic or geographic factors being considered which, four years later, in the words of Lord Longford, ultimately proved 'decisive in losing the Irish Free State every atom of anticipated benefit'.[2]

The idea of a Boundary Commission was not a new one nor necessarily a bad one from Sinn Féin's perspective, although the belief that the transferring of large areas from the north to the south would leave the remaining territory an unviable rump, was deeply flawed, as the industrial heartbeat of Northern Ireland was Belfast and its hinterlands, not the west and south of the six counties. Northern Ireland could have survived economically without counties Fermanagh and Tyrone. Also, and paradoxically, the more the Boundary Commission favoured the nationalist case, the smaller the nationalist population that would remain in Northern Ireland, and thus the case for national unity would be diminished, something those nationalists furthest away from the border, in places like Belfast, were acutely aware of.

While the Boundary Commission was viewed as a major concession to Sinn Féin, the details and wording of the clause agreed to in the Treaty proved to be disastrous for Sinn Féin and particularly for northern nationalists close to the border. Sinn Féin floundered greatly by acceding to such an ambiguous clause and by not insisting on similar terms for a Boundary Commission to the ones that had convened in post First World War Europe. What is particularly surprising is the lack of scrutiny nationalists of all hues on the island gave to the vague Boundary Commission clause and how it compared or not to other boundary commissions in Europe. It was just accepted by most that large parts of Northern Ireland would be transferred to the Irish Free State.

The Boundary Commission clause was riddled with ambiguities. No timetable was mentioned or method outlined to ascertain the wishes of inhabitants, 'how exactly economic and geographic conditions would relate to popular opinion, and which would prove most important'.[3] The areas and sizes of the units (small areas like district electoral divisions or entire counties) to be considered for transfer were not decided upon. Could Free

State territory be transferred as well as northern territory? No plebiscite was asked for. Essentially, the clause was open to many different interpretations. While the Sinn Féin plenipotentiaries were not partitionists and genuinely sought a united Ireland, they blundered enormously in acceding to such an indefinable Boundary Commission, which ultimately was the primary reason for the original border being retained as it was, as it still is. And while it was understandable for most northern nationalists to accept the formation of a Boundary Commission under the Treaty as a tolerable resolution to the border issue, it was foolhardy and naïve not to scrutinise and toothcomb its clauses.

Ulster Unionists were vehemently opposed to the Boundary Commission. Speaking to the British Secretary of State for the Colonies, Winston Churchill, in May 1922, the Northern Ireland Prime Minister, James Craig, claimed:

> The Boundary Commission has been at the root of all evil. If you picture Loyalists on the borderland being asked by us to hang on with their teeth for the safety of the Province, you can also picture their unspoken cry to us, 'if we sacrifice our lives and our property for the sake of the Province, are you going to assent to a Commission which may subsequently by a stroke of the pen, take away the very area you now ask us to defend?'[4]

Although they were not party to the Treaty, Ulster Unionists were now obliged to adhere to its clauses. The Boundary Commission reopened uncertainty and put Northern Ireland's future in doubt, at least significant parts of it, yet again. It revived the border question, believed closed by Ulster Unionists through the Government of Ireland Act 1920 and the establishment of Northern Ireland in the summer of 1921. Craig told the British Prime Minister, David Lloyd George, he would refuse to co-operate with the Commission as there was 'no precedent in the history of the British Empire for taking away territory from an established government without its sanction'.[5]

Even though, in 1919, Craig had suggested the establishment of a commission to examine the border area for Northern and Southern Ireland under the Government of Ireland Act 1920, to avoid the jurisdiction of the Northern parliament extending over the whole nine counties of Ulster, by 1921 he emphatically opposed the 'odious' Boundary Commission.[6] By that stage he had his northern 'citadel' which he intended to sit on 'like a rock'.[7] Craig also contended that the establishment of a Boundary Commission prolonged the period of unrest in the north and he insisted that the charges for maintaining the Ulster Special Constabulary must be borne by the imperial government until the border question was settled.[8]

Still citing fear of unrest because of the Boundary Commission, he opposed any disbandment of the Specials in 1925.[9] It is important to note that while unionists in the six counties were strongly opposed to the Boundary Commission, it offered 'a beam of hope for those Protestants living in border areas' in counties Monaghan, Cavan and Donegal who sought inclusion in the northern jurisdiction.[10] Instead of the Boundary Commission being the 'root of all evil' for unionists, it resulted in uniting unionists and leaving the boundary unchanged. The

> seeming threat it represented to the integrity of Northern Ireland greatly strengthened the Ulster Unionist Party, as it adopted the role of aggressive defender of the territorial status quo, uniting all shades of Protestant opinion behind it on the single agenda of maintaining intact the 1920 boundary.[11]

For northern nationalists, however, the Boundary Commission turned out to be the root of much evil. It gave false hopes for the transfer of large tracts of territory and people from Northern Ireland to the Irish Free State. The policy of ignoring and obstructing the institutions of Northern Ireland was promoted and supported by senior Sinn Féin figures such as Michael Collins and Eoin MacNeill. MacNeill, who subsequently came in for much ire from northern nationalists for his performance as Free State boundary commissioner in 1925, met a delegation of northern nationalists in Dublin a day after the Treaty was signed, on 7 December 1921, and asked them to adopt 'a practical programme of passive resistance' to the Northern government's authority, involving non-recognition of the courts, the non-payment of taxes and particularly 'non-recognition of the educational authority of the Belfast Parliament'.[12]

With the Boundary Commission, nationalist leaders in the six and 26 counties believed many areas in Northern Ireland would be transferred to the Irish Free State, including the entire counties of Tyrone and Fermanagh, as well as Derry City and Newry, and large parts of south Armagh and south and east Down.[13] Historian Denis Gwynn wrote that the 'suggestion of a Boundary Commission seemed naturally to imply that the Ulster Unionists would not be allowed to retain the full Six-County area if they did refuse to enter the Free State'.[14] His father Stephen Gwynn, former Irish Parliamentary Party MP and persistent critic of Sinn Féin, believed that if Dáil Éireann ratified the Treaty, 'then it is certain that before long Ulster will fall into its normal place … Almost certainly Ulster will end as a counterpart to Quebec within the Irish Free State'.[15] The nationalist optimism over the Boundary Commission, in many ways, explains the fraction of time devoted to partition during the acrimonious Dáil debates over the Treaty. Both the pro- and anti-Treaty sides supported the Boundary

Commission as a means to end or at least limit partition. Both sides 'were complacent about the vague terms of reference for the Boundary Commission and the lack of provision for plebiscites even in border areas'.[16]

For northern nationalists, the Treaty left many of them confused and dismayed. While those in the south were tearing themselves apart over the sovereignty issue, for those in the north it was of secondary importance compared to the issue of partition. The role of the proposed Boundary Commission was of primary interest. While nationalists living in the border regions, particularly in Fermanagh and Tyrone, were optimistic they would be quickly transferred to the Free State, those living in Belfast and east Ulster knew they would remain in Northern Ireland, regardless of the generosity of the Boundary Commission.[17]

The Treaty resulted in differing opinions and strategies being adopted by nationalists within Northern Ireland. Unlike within Ulster unionism, there was a lack of consensus amongst northern nationalists in general regarding the policy to be adopted towards partition and the Northern Ireland government. The split within Sinn Féin over the Treaty compounded the confusion of northern nationalists and effectively prevented the formulation of a policy which might have unanimous support. While local authorities such as Fermanagh County Council, and some in south Down and south Armagh remained defiant and refused to recognise the Belfast parliament, others such as Tyrone County Council acknowledged the *de facto* jurisdiction of that parliament in view of what was described as 'the temporary period during which the northern parliament is to function in this area'.[18] The main argument put forward by local authorities who believed in recognising the northern jurisdiction and leading Sinn Féin figures like Arthur Griffith and W.T. Cosgrave was that they would lose nationalist control and would rob whole nationalist tracts of effective representation in the face of the Boundary Commission. It was also 'clear that any adoption of a full-blooded recognition policy would be opposed by a section of border nationalists who held that it would weaken their case before the Boundary Commission, and by a considerable anti-Treaty section in Belfast Sinn Féin'.[19]

The Northern Ireland government decided to act against the 'recalcitrant' local authorities.[20] Over 20 nationalist-controlled authorities were suspended by April 1922.[21] Paid commissioners were put in place to run the affairs of these local authorities. On top of suspending such authorities, the government looked to take back control of them. It did this by abolishing proportional representation, compelling councillors to pledge an oath of allegiance to the crown and the Belfast parliament, and by the rearranging of local government boundaries.[22] Michael Collins, chairman of the Provisional Government of the Irish Free State from January 1922, complained to Winston Churchill that some of the decisions were made in anticipation of the Boundary Commission's work, 'to paint the Counties of Tyrone and Fermanagh with a deep Orange tint'.[23] All of these decisions that transformed the electoral landscape of Northern Ireland were evident when the Boundary Commission finally did meet in late 1924.

The Boundary Commission finally meets

The convening of the Boundary Commission was delayed by almost two years from the moment Northern Ireland opted out of the Irish Free State in December 1922. The Irish Civil War was a contributory factor in the delay, as were the non-cooperation of the Northern government and several changes of government in Britain.[24] (Between 1922 and 1924 there were three general elections and four governments in Britain.)[25] The Free State government was the first to appoint its commissioner, Eoin MacNeill, the Minister of Education, in July 1923. Almost a year later, in June 1924, the British government appointed the chairperson, Richard Feetham, a British-born judge based in South Africa. With the Northern government refusing to appoint its commissioner, the British intervened by selecting Joseph R. Fisher, a barrister and former editor of the Belfast unionist-leaning newspaper, the *Northern Whig*. While both Feetham and Fisher were from legal backgrounds and were devoted full-time to the Boundary Commission for its duration, MacNeill had no legal experience and retained his position as Free State Minister of Education, meaning he could only deal with the Boundary Commission on a part-time basis.

One of the most fatal anomalies from an Irish nationalist perspective was that the Irish Boundary Commission was the only one of the post First World War European boundary commissions that convened which did not have an independent chairperson, and with its vague wording, the ambiguity was to be determined by a British-appointed judge. By contrast, the other boundary commissions in Europe were presided over by chairpersons from countries with no vested interest in the disputed territories. The British argument that this was an intra-empire dispute wears thin given that the imperial government was the British government, one of the contesting parties.[26] With the Irish Free State and Northern Ireland commissioners cancelling each other out, the decision by the Sinn Féin representatives in 1921 not to contest the appointment of the judge by the British proved decisive. The acceptance of the Boundary Commission terms by pro- and anti-Treatyites and by most northern nationalists compounded this mistake. Practically all of Feetham's interpretations and decisions favoured the unionist over the nationalist case. In nationalist circles he became known as 'Feetham-Cheat'em'.[27]

The Commission met for the first time in November 1924. At the inaugural meeting it was agreed unanimously that 'The Commission resolved that no statement should be made for publication as to the work or proceedings of the Commission except with the authority of the Commission'.[28] It is clear, that while MacNeill stood rigidly to this, Fisher was in constant communication with the wife of Ulster Unionist MP David Reid, providing updates on the Commission proceedings which was then filtered through the Ulster Unionist ranks.[29] Much to the dismay of nationalists, Feetham decided not to conduct a plebiscite, 'choosing instead to assume a quasi-judicial approach' and ruling out wholesale transfers.[30] This was markedly different from the approach taken by other European boundary commissions where plebiscites were held to determine the wishes of the inhabitants. From December 1924 to July 1925, the three commissioners conducted informal and formal hearings, interviewing more than 500 witnesses based on written statements submitted in advance. The submissions focused on three areas mainly; the wishes of the inhabitants, economic conditions and geography.

Wishes of the inhabitants

The main argument used by nationalists looking to be transferred to the Irish Free State was that the wishes of the inhabitants should override any economic and geographic factors; since Catholics made up the majority in most of those areas, they should be transferred to the Irish Free State. [31] This was not how Justice Feetham interpreted Article 12 of the Treaty, stating that 'Under the terms of the Article the wishes of the inhabitants are made the primary but not the paramount consideration', and that the Commission should 'avoid drawing a boundary line which, by its defiance of economic or geographic conditions, would involve, as the result of its adaption, serious economic detriment, or geographic isolation, to communities on either side of it'.[32]

As no plebiscite was carried out, the Boundary Commission relied on the 1911 census figures (the last census taken in Ireland before the Commission convened), election results and evidence provided by witnesses to determine the wishes of the inhabitants. Paul Murray argues that it made 'little sense for nationalists to base their main arguments on the wishes of inhabitants as these figures, by and large, were already known'.[33] Feetham generally supported the assumption that all Catholics tended to be nationalists who sought inclusion in the Free State and all Protestants tended to be unionists who sought inclusion in Northern Ireland.[34] Based on submissions to the Boundary Commission, in most cases, this rule held through. Feetham ignored claims by some unionists that many Catholics wanted to stay in Northern Ireland and by some nationalists that many Protestants wanted to be transferred to the Free State, including a claim by James Craig when he met Feetham in July 1924 'that the vast majority of Roman Catholics had no wish for transfer, though owing to fear of intimidation they would doubtless vote for it in case of a referendum on the subject'.[35]

Submitting evidence on behalf of the Newry Urban District Council, spirit merchant Robert O'Rorke claimed, 'It is nearly entirely on the religious division. The entire Protestant population want to be included in the Northern Government, and I might say 999 Catholics out of every 1,000 are easily in favour of inclusion in the Free State'.[36] George Bennett was an exception, a Protestant who supported the inclusion of south Down and south Armagh in the Irish Free State, stating, 'I am myself a Protestant in religion but I am an Irishman and share the political opinions of the majority of my Countrymen. I desire inclusion in the Irish Free State and know that the majority of the people in South Down & South Armagh desire to be with their Southern neighbours'.[37] The primary reason cited for inclusion in the Free State by the overwhelming majority of nationalists who submitted evidence was that most of the people living in the areas they represented sought as much.

Many of the submissions from nationalists provided the Commission with the 1911 census returns to prove their areas had 'an unanswerable case' for inclusion in the Free State. The wishes of the inhabitants must override all other considerations according to nationalist representations from Tyrone, Magherafelt, Armagh Urban District Council, the electoral divisions of Middletown and Keady in Armagh, and the poor law unions of Newry including Crossmaglen and Kilkeel.[38] Nationalist ex-servicemen from Omagh claimed that 'the vast majority of the people of this District (Omagh) and of the whole county of Tyrone are Nationalist and Catholic and it is their desire that they should be incorporated with the Nation to which they belong and which has been set up as the Irish Free State'.[39]

A committee representing the nationalists of County Fermanagh, stated that, based on the census of 1911, and on local and national election results in 1918, 1920, 1922 and 1923, the 'claim of Fermanagh for inclusion in the Free State ... is grounded upon the democratic principle of the peoples' will'.[40] According to the 1911 census figures, 74.6 per cent of the population of Newry were Catholic, and were, therefore, overwhelmingly in favour of being included in the Free State.[41] Likewise, Father Felix Canon McNally, parish priest in Upper Killevy and Catholic chaplain to the Newry union workhouse, claimed the district electoral division of Killevy in south Armagh had a total population of 2,305 in 1911 made up of 2,283 Catholics and just 22 from all other denominations.[42]

Many nationalists believed they could only be retained in Northern Ireland through coercion and referred to their political rights being removed by the Northern government, highlighting the suspension of nationalist-controlled local authorities by April 1922 and the decision not to contest the local elections of 1923 when those taking their seats were obliged to take an oath of allegiance to the crown and the government. As a result, bodies such as Fermanagh County Council, Derry City Corporation, Newry Rural District Councils 1 and 2, and Kilkeel Rural District Council, which had been controlled by nationalists, were taken over by unionists 'without any Authority from the majority of the Inhabitants' according to Patrick Connolly, an ex-poor law guardian and former rural district councillor from Newry.[43]

Unionists countered that the non-compliant local authorities were rightly suspended for 'their refusal to perform the duties imposed on them in pursuance of the Local Government (Ireland) Acts' and in any event they would have won their seats in a contested election.[44] Many nationalists seeking to be transferred to the Free State highlighted moves made by the Northern government to undermine their civic rights through the abolition of proportional representation and the gerrymandering of electoral districts. The Derry Nationalist Registration Association claimed that after a re-adjustment of ward boundaries in the city, 'Catholics being 56.21 per cent of the population get 40 per cent of the representation, and all others (Protestants), 43.79 per cent of the population, get 60 per cent of the representation'.[45]

Most unionist submissions to the Boundary Commission did not focus on the wishes of the inhabitants but some points were raised on the levels of unity within the Catholic community. J. Moore Boyle, a solicitor representing the Newry Chamber of Commerce, claimed that Catholics were divided between those who sought a republic and those who favoured inclusion in the Free State.[46] Robert Forsythe, chairman of Kilkeel Rural District Council, also asserted that the Catholics of the Kilkeel Union were 'divided in their political outlook as a large section of them are republican and the leaders of the republican party are against the fixing of a boundary line in Ireland'.[47] When unionists did refer to wishes of the inhabitants, many believed differences should be accounted for between permanent residents and those who crossed the border temporarily for seasonal work (mainly Catholics); and those who paid the most rates (mainly Protestants). Such a case was made by some unionists in Warrenpoint and Newry who claimed that people should be differentiated based on the rates and taxes they contributed, and that those who paid the most were in favour of retention in Northern Ireland.[48]

Even though, according to the 1911 census, there were 264 Catholics and 184 Protestants living in Drummully, a locality in County Monaghan almost completely cut off from the rest of Monaghan by the Fermanagh districts of Clonkeelan and Derrysteaton, the Protestant inhabitants of Drummully claimed to the Commission that they owned 38 of the 63 farms in the area and paid seven-eighths of the taxes. They believed 'it was their right that their wishes should be consulted as to the government under which they were to live'.[49] The Donegal Protestant Registration Association argued that in many parts of the county 'the only really permanent element in the population were the landowners and the prosperous farmers. The servants employed by them – mostly Catholics – were hired on a Six Months Contract and generally left at the end of their time for some other district'. Nationalists in Donegal disagreed, claiming 'that these considerations were partly unfounded, as in many cases labourers often remained on the same farm for years, or at the most moved to another farm in the same district. One witness pointed out that as there were many marriages in this class, this would of itself necessitate a certain permanence of abode'.[50]

The Cliff district electoral division in Donegal, close to Belleek in Fermanagh across the border, comprised 169 Catholics and ten non-Catholics in 1911. However, the loyalists insisted that 'the Unionists are the largest property owners in the area, and consequently pay the greatest proportion of the rates', and therefore should be included in Northern Ireland.[51] Countering the unionist argument that those who occupy the 'greater part of the land and pay the major portion of the rates' should have a disproportionate say on where they lived, Fermanagh nationalists stated, 'the poor are members of the national community equally with the rich; they are the real component living members which constitute through the family the living body. It would be irrational to neglect one portion of the citizens and favour another'.[52] Much to the dismay of Fermanagh nationalists and all other nationalists who made submissions to the Boundary Commission, Feetham believed

> a distinction may, I think, fairly be drawn between different classes of the population, on the principle that the more permanent elements of the population of a particular area have a greater interest in the destiny of that area, and that their wishes are therefore entitled to greater weight.[53]

Economic conditions

Unionists mainly focused their cases for inclusion in Northern Ireland on economic factors, with almost all submissions claiming their regions were intrinsically linked economically with Northern Ireland. It is important to note, as Terence Dooley has, that 'some of the evidence submitted on economic grounds was used merely as a pretext. The real motivation for transfer to Northern Ireland (or to stay in Northern Ireland) may have been based on political factors'.[54] While both nationalists and unionists in Donegal agreed on the importance of Derry city to the county, nationalists insisted Derry should be in the Free State while unionists insisted that Donegal, at least the parts of the county with large unionist numbers, should be transferred to Northern Ireland. They insisted that the main distributing centre for Donegal was Derry, stating

> the economic importance of Derry to Donegal cannot be sufficiently emphasised ... Such towns as Letterkenny, and to a lesser extent, Stranorlar, may serve as local retail centres, but the fact remains that the whole district, and it is not going too far to say the whole county, appears to be economically dependent on Derry. Derry is the natural port of Co. Donegal.[55]

The case of Middletown district electoral division in County Armagh demonstrates how economic arguments were closely aligned with political wishes. While the nationalists claimed that, economically, Keady, Monaghan and Glaslough were Middletown's principal market towns, and that Armagh city was only a market for flax, unionist inhabitants refuted such claims, stating that Middletown was not economically connected with County Monaghan, that the principal cattle fair was Killylea, and that the great bulk of the district's farm produce was marketed in Armagh. It even obtained its bread from Armagh. They asserted that Armagh was an economic unit entirely bound up with Northern Ireland and that 'those Catholics who have a stake in the district are opposed to inclusion in the Irish Free State'.[56]

William Johnson, a solicitor based in Newry, claimed 'it could materially interfere for a considerable length of time with our tourist trade that we enjoy here from Northern Ireland' if Warrenpoint was transferred to the Free State.[57] Martin Hamilton, general manager of the linen firm Bessbrook Spinning Company, asserted they had no economic links with the Free State.[58] Coal importer and ship owner Frank Fisher believed Newry would lose its coal and linen trade if it was transferred to the Free State. He also mentioned the higher cost of living in the Free State compared to Northern Ireland, stating, 'A £1 note can at present buy more in Newry than in Dundalk and this fact has a bearing on local wages'.[59] A special committee established by the Newry Urban District Council countered that the linen industry was in steep decline, claiming:

> it is well known that the linen industry in Northern Ireland instead of making progress is retrogressing for at the time we prepare this statement out of the three Spinning Mills in the town of Newry one has been entirely closed down for two or three years and the other

two are working half-time while the Mills of Bessbrook Spinning Co. Ltd. in spite of the fact, that they are at present situated in Northern Ireland are not working full time and are not working to capacity.[60]

Feetham looked at economic conditions as they prevailed in 1924/25 and not how they were interpreted by the Treaty signatories in 1921. In fact, Feetham refused to hear any evidence on how the Treaty signatories interpreted Article 12, despite its obvious ambiguities.[61] This proved highly damaging for the Free State cause. Unionists either looking to be transferred to or to remain within Northern Ireland were quick to point out the higher taxation and generally higher cost of living in the Free State, partly caused by the crippling civil war that engulfed the Free State after the Treaty was signed.[62]

The northern government began construction on a reservoir to supply water to the residents of Belfast in Silent Valley in the Mourne mountains in 1923. This was used as an argument to retain all of County Down in Northern Ireland. The Belfast City and District Water Commissioners, who were responsible for the Belfast water scheme in Silent Valley, objected to any part of south Down being included in the Free State as it 'would expose the Commissioner's Works to easier attack and necessitate continuous protection' and placing 'the Commissioners Works under a jurisdiction different from that under which the Area served' would lead to 'interference with the undertaking', 'restrictions in the use of the water' and 'increased taxation'.[63]

Arguably more damaging was the decision by the Free State government to introduce a customs barrier between the Free State and Northern Ireland in April 1923.[64] Feetham, describing it as 'the terrors of the Customs Barrier', continuously referred to it in his questioning and to the damaging consequences it would cause if the boundary line underwent further changes.[65] Both unionists and nationalists went into some details on the affects the barrier had on their daily lives and livelihoods. Major R.L. Moore, who owned land in Cliff in Donegal, claimed that since the customs barrier was erected, his tenants looking to make the one-mile-long journey to Belleek in Fermanagh via motor car were no longer able to use the 'unapproved' road where he lived and instead had to make a 'round-about' journey through Ballyshannon, nine miles away, to get to Belleek.[66] Similarly, Thomas Johnston from Pettigo, partly in Donegal and partly in Fermanagh, claimed that in order to get to Kesh from the Donegal side of Pettigo, a distance of four miles, 'we must first go to Belleek, 12 miles, and then on to Enniskillen, 20 miles, and back on that journey 20 miles to Kesh'.[67]

Border towns like Pettigo and Clones in County Monaghan were 'singled out by the Boundary Commission as being most likely to suffer from the adverse social and economic effects of the border it now found on its very doorstep'.[68] Matthew H. McCann, a baker based in Newry, stated that output from his bakeries had 'been considerably reduced owing to the fact that the confectionery made by my firm cannot now be carried by my carts over the customs barrier'.[69] John Foster, a draper also based in Newry claimed that 'Since the Customs Boundary was put up a lot of people come to Newry to buy boots and wear them home and do not pay duty on them'. He also believed 'a barrier north of Newry would very seriously affect the shipping trade. Anything that affects the prosperity of the town affects the retailer. There is no doubt that farmers north of Newry, if the barrier were between them and Newry, would not cross it'.[70] While unionists believed the placing of a customs barrier north of where they lived would lead to large financial losses and considerable inconvenience, nationalists claimed they were already suffering from the effects of the barrier by losing customers from their hinterland in the Free State. Asserting their economic prosperity lay with the Free State, nationalists sought for the boundary line to be drawn northwards.[71]

Nationalists in border areas stated there were no economic conditions incompatible in those areas from being transferred to the Free State. Nationalists in Keady in County Armagh claimed the village was cut off from a considerable area in County Monaghan which had formed part of its economic sphere. One witness also claimed that if 'free communication were established with the port of Dundalk which is much nearer to Keady than Belfast, Keady would benefit considerably'. Industries such as linen, baking and tailoring in Keady, which had suffered considerably because of the customs barrier, would survive and flourish if Keady was included in the Free State.[72] Edward A. Lamb, secretary of Newry Port and Harbour Trust, claimed that 'the interests of the port of Belfast will always be paramount and receive preferential treatment from every authority in Belfast including the Government of Northern Ireland to the detriment of the port of Newry'.[73] Joseph Johnston, an economist based in Trinity College Dublin, believed 'overwhelming economic considerations would have to be proved before the Commission would be justified in going against the wishes of the inhabitants'. He further contended that 'the commercial hinterland which is the background of Newry's activities is even under present conditions, to a greater extent in the present Free State area than in Northern Ireland', claiming the bulk of Newry's grain and flour trade was with Monaghan and Cavan in the Free State.[74]

Geography

With Feetham deciding that smaller units such as district electoral divisions, instead of large units such as entire counties or poor law unions, should form the basis of areas to be considered for transfer, geographic factors took on added significance. With the Catholic population more or less concentrated in the centre of Tyrone, the decision not to consider whole counties was detrimental to the nationalist case for inclusion for many districts in the county.[75] When Patrick O'Neill MP claimed all of south Down should be transferred to the Free State, Feetham contended that the town of Newcastle, with a Protestant majority, was not a small area and this would have to be considered.[76] Unionist inhabitants of Mullyash district electoral division in County Monaghan based some of their claims for inclusion in Northern Ireland on geographic considerations, arguing that if Mullyash was 'added to the present county (Armagh) area, the boundary of the County towards the Free State would be considerably shortened and straightened'.[77]

Unionists also contended that Carlingford Lough was a natural geographic boundary, with William Johnson stating that to transfer Warrenpoint 'into the 26 county area would not only be incompatible with the existing Geographical conditions but would be substituting for the present natural so well defined boundary of Carlingford Lough an unnatural and ill defined line of demarcation'.[78] This was refuted by Newry Urban District Council which claimed that south Down

> will be bounded both on the west and on the south by territory at present under Irish Free State jurisdiction and on the east by the sea. Of necessity it must touch Northern Ireland territory at some point and this will be confined to the Northern Boundary of the area. There is therefore no geographic condition which can be adduced to prevent the area from being retained in the Irish Free State.[79]

The county most affected geographically by partition was Donegal, almost completely isolated by the rest of the Free State. Most nationalist submissions from Donegal and Derry stressed the social, economic as well as geographic bonds between both places, with one witness, Rev. John O'Doherty, arguing 'that Donegal people viewed Derry as part of Inishowen and, as such, a part of Donegal'.[80] Unionists saw it differently, with submissions seeking Inishowen to be attached to Derry city, and others looking for the transfer of the eastern part of Donegal, and in some cases the entire county, to Northern Ireland.[81]

Conclusion

The work completed by the Boundary Commission would not be revealed for decades due to the leaking of the (by-and-large accurate) recommendations by the pro-unionist newspaper the *Morning Post* in November 1925. Much to the surprise of many nationalists, no large-scale transfers were on offer. In fact, parts of the Free State were to be transferred to the north, including 'a rich portion of East Donegal'. The leaked report recommended the shortening of the border by 50 miles, transferring 286 square miles to the Free State and 77 square miles to Northern Ireland, which would have moved 31,219 people to the former and 7,594 to the latter.[82] Parts of south Armagh, including Crossmaglen, were recommended to be transferred to the Free State with some areas in north Monaghan being recommended for transfer in the opposite direction. No part of Down was deemed to have met the criteria for transfer. People in Donegal were particularly crestfallen: 'Donegal was blockaded: they could not leave the county without passing through the Six Counties'.[83]

The leak caused outrage in Dublin, leading to the Free State commissioner Eoin MacNeill resigning from the Commission, the Free State government and the Dáil, claiming as he departed that 'he wasn't the most suitable person to be a commissioner'.[84] According to Ted Hallett, MacNeill erred by not making a stand 'when he realised that an award corresponding to Free State expectations was not going to emerge' either in September or October 1925, during the Boundary Commission's deliberations, and by 'his lack of frankness with his Executive Council colleagues following the *Morning Post* leak'.[85] Realising the danger, the crisis posed to the Free State government, the President of the Executive Council, W.T. Cosgrave, dashed over to London to have the report put on hold. A tripartite agreement was signed by the British, Free State and Northern Ireland governments that shelved the Boundary Commission report and maintained the border as it was, and as it is to the present day. While the work of the Boundary Commission ultimately proved fruitless and resulted in the transfer of neither people nor territory, the volume of work it produced and the submissions it received offer great insights on what life was like for both unionists and nationalists at the time of the creation of the border.

Notes

1. Cormac Moore, *Birth of the Border: The Impact of Partition in Ireland* (Dublin, 2019), p. 63.
2. Lord Longford (Frank Pakenham), *Peace by Ordeal: The Negotiation of the Anglo-Irish Treaty, 1921* (London, 1935), p. 184.
3. Robert Lynch, 'The Boundary Commission' in John Crowley, Donal Ó Drisceoil and Mike Murphy (eds), *Atlas of the Irish Revolution* (Cork, 2017), p. 828.
4. Robert Lynch, *Revolutionary Ireland, 1912–25* (London, 2015), p. 107.
5. Michael Hopkinson, 'The Craig-Collins pacts of 1922: two attempted reforms of the Northern Ireland government', *Irish Historical Studies*, 27:106 (Nov. 1990), p. 146.
6. Moore, *Birth of the Border*, p. 22.
7. Ronan Fanning, *Fatal Path: British Government and Irish Revolution 1910–1922* (London, 2013), p. 264.
8. Cabinet Conclusion File, 10 Jan. 1922 (PRONI, CAB/4/29).
9. Cabinet Conclusion File, 23 Apr. 1925 (PRONI, CAB 4/140).
10. Terence A.M. Dooley, 'From the Belfast Boycott to the Boundary Commission: fears and hopes in County Monaghan, 1920–26', *Clogher Record*, 15:1 (1994), p. 95.
11. Paul Murray, *The Irish Boundary Commission and its Origins 1886–1925* (Dublin, 2011), p. xix.
12. Éamon Phoenix, *Northern Nationalism: Nationalist Politics, Partition and the Catholic Minority in Northern Ireland 1890–1940* (Belfast, 1994), p. 156.
13. Paul Murray, 'Partition and the Irish Boundary Commission: a northern nationalist perspective', *Clogher Record*, 18:2 (2004), p. 182.
14. Denis Gwynn, *The History of Partition (1912–1925)* (Dublin, 1950), p. 203.
15. A.C. Hepburn, *Catholic Belfast and Nationalist Ireland in the Era of Joe Devlin 1871–1934* (Oxford, 2008), pp 230–31.
16. Jonathan Bardon, *A History of Ulster* (Belfast, 2001), p. 486.
17. James A. Cousins, *Without a Dog's Chance: The Nationalists of Northern Ireland and the Irish Boundary Commission, 1920–25* (Kildare, 2020), p. 213.
18. Phoenix, *Northern Nationalism*, p. 155.
19. Ibid., p. 212.
20. Cabinet Conclusion File, 1 Dec. 1921 (PRONI, CAB 4/28).
21. Bardon, *A History of Ulster*, pp 499–500.
22. Brendan O'Leary, '"Cold house": the unionist counter-revolution and the invention of Northern Ireland' in Crowley, Ó Drisceoil and Murphy (eds), *Atlas of the Irish Revolution*, pp 821–2.
23. Bardon, *A History of Ulster*, p. 500.
24. Peter Leary, *Unapproved Routes: Histories of the Irish Border, 1922–1972* (Oxford, 2016), p. 34.
25. Ivan Gibbons, *Drawing the Line: The Irish Border in British Politics* (London, 2018), p. 49.

26 Murray, *The Irish Boundary Commission and its Origins*, p. 244.
27 Ibid., p. 244.
28 Boundary Commission minute book, 6 Nov. 1924 (TNA, CAB 61/1).
29 Murray, *The Irish Boundary Commission and its Origins*, p. 210.
30 Leary, *Unapproved Routes*, p. 35.
31 Murray, *The Irish Boundary Commission and its Origins*, p. 108.
32 Boundary Commission minute book, 16 Dec. 1925 (TNA, CAB 61/1).
33 Murray, *The Irish Boundary Commission and its Origins*, p. 177.
34 Boundary Commission minute book, 7 Dec. 1925 (TNA, CAB 61/1).
35 Cabinet Conclusion File, 4 July 1924 (PRONI, CAB 4/117).
36 Newry Urban District Council, vol. 2, 9 Mar. 1925 (TNA, CAB 61/120).
37 Warrenpoint Urban District Council, 12 Mar. 1925 (TNA, CAB 61/158).
38 See summaries of cases put forward in support of claims submitted to the Commission (TNA, CAB 61/159).
39 National Ex-Service Men of Omagh, 28 Feb. 1925 (TNA, CAB 61/122).
40 Fermanagh Nationalist Committee, vol. 1 (TNA, CAB 61/67).
41 Newry Urban District Council, vol. 1, 17 Feb. 1925 (TNA, CAB 61/119).
42 Newry Union (Armagh) (TNA, CAB 61/113).
43 Newry Union (Down) (TNA, CAB 61/113).
44 Newry Chamber of Commerce (TNA, CAB 61/115).
45 Londonderry Nationalist Registration Association (TNA, CAB 61/95).
46 Newry Chamber of Commerce, 24 Mar. 1925 (TNA, CAB 61/115).
47 Kilkeel Rural District Council, 21 Feb. 1925 (TNA, CAB 61/86).
48 Newry Chamber of Commerce (TNA, CAB 61/115); Principal Property Owners, Traders, Lodging House-Keepers and Residents, Urban District of Warrenpoint (TNA, CAB 61/157).
49 Dooley, 'From the Belfast Boycott to the Boundary Commission', p. 98.
50 Summaries of cases put forward in support of claims submitted to the Commission (TNA, CAB 61/159).
51 Ibid.
52 Fermanagh Nationalist Committee, vol. 1 (TNA, CAB 61/67).
53 Report of the Irish Boundary Commission, p. 61 (TNA, CAB 61/161).
54 Dooley, 'From the Belfast Boycott to the Boundary Commission', p. 101.
55 Summaries of cases put forward in support of claims submitted to the Commission (TNA, CAB 61/159).
56 Middletown, Committee of Inhabitants (TNA, CAB 61/106).
57 Principal Property Owners, Traders, Lodging House-Keepers and Residents, Urban District of Warrenpoint, 12 Mar. 1925 (TNA, CAB 61/157).
58 Bessbrook Spinning Company Ltd, 21 Mar. 1925 (TNA, CAB 61/32).
59 Newry Chamber of Commerce (TNA, CAB 61/115).
60 Newry Urban District Council, vol. 1, 17 Feb. 1925 (TNA, CAB 61/119).
61 Newry Chamber of Commerce, 11 Mar. 1925 (TNA, CAB 61/115).
62 See, for example, Pettigo Unionist Inhabitants (TNA, CAB 61/125).

63 Belfast City and District Water Commissioners, 24 Dec. 1924 (TNA, CAB 61/28).
64 See Moore, *Birth of the Border*, pp 126–33.
65 Principal Property Owners, Traders, Lodging House-Keepers and Residents, Urban District of Warrenpoint, 12 Mar. 1925 (TNA, CAB 61/157).
66 Major R.L. Moore, 30 Dec. 1924 (TNA, CAB 61/109).
67 Pettigo Unionist Inhabitants, 1 May 1925 (TNA, CAB 61/125).
68 Dooley, 'From the Belfast Boycott to the Boundary Commission', p. 98.
69 Newry Union (Armagh) (TNA, CAB 61/113).
70 Newry Chamber of Commerce, 11 Mar. 1925 (TNA, CAB 61/115).
71 See, for example, Newry Urban District Council, vol. 1, 17 Feb. 1925 (TNA, CAB 61/119).
72 Keady, Committee of Inhabitants of the Town End (TNA, CAB 61/81).
73 Newry Urban District Council, vol. 1, 17 Feb. 1925 (TNA, CAB 61/119).
74 Ibid.
75 See, for example, Nationalist Inhabitants of County Tyrone, vol. 2 (TNA, CAB 61/146).
76 Committee of Nationalist Inhabitants of East Down, 18 Mar. 1925 (CAB 61/55).
77 Summaries of cases put forward in support of claims submitted to the Commission (TNA, CAB 61/159).
78 Principal Property Owners, Traders, Lodging House-Keepers & Residents, Urban District of Warrenpoint, 12 Mar. 1925 (TNA, CAB 61/157).
79 Newry Urban District Council, vol. 1, 17 Feb. 1925 (TNA, CAB 61/119).
80 Okan Ozseker, *Forging the Border: Donegal and Derry in Times of Revolution* (Dublin, 2019), p. 198.
81 Ibid., p. 200.
82 Moore, *Birth of the Border*, p. 80.
83 Ozseker, *Forging the Border*, p. 2.
84 Moore, *Birth of the Border*, p. 81.
85 Ted Hallett, 'Eoin MacNeill and the Irish Boundary Commission' in Conor Mulvagh and Emer Purcell (eds), *Eoin MacNeill: The Pen and the Sword* (Cork, 2022), p. 230.

Index

Abercorn, duke of, 26, 90
Aberdeen, Lord, 5, 9, 17
Adams, Jennie, 5
Adams, W.G.S., 98–9
Agnew, Samuel, 116
Airlie, Lady, 2, 209
Ancient Order of Hibernians, 61, 67, 68, 153, 154, 191, 192, 201 n20
Anderson, R.N., 90
Andrews, James, 182
Andrews, John Miller, 90, 108 n63, 182
Anglo-Irish Treaty, 74, 77, 154–5, 164, 166, 213–16, 227, 238–44, 249
Anglo-Irish War, 149, 150, 153, 156, 162, 180, 183–4
Annaghmore (Co. Armagh), 132
Armagh (city), 43, 50, 62, 245, 248
Armour, J.B. (James Brown), 1–18
Armour, J.S.S., 2–3, 4, 18 n5
Armour, Kenneth, 4, 5
Armour, Max, 2, 4, 5, 17
Armour, William S., 4, 5
Armour, William, 4
Armstrong, H.B., 90
Ashbourne, Lord, 12
Asquith, Herbert, 1, 2, 9, 10, 28, 31, 36, 66, 180, 223
Asquith, Margot, 221, 232
Atholl, duchess of, 231
Auxiliaries, 180

Bagot, Mrs, 222
Bailie, Hugh, 115, 117, 120, 122
Baldwin, Lucy, 221, 235 n47
Balfour, Arthur, 212–3
Ballymacarrett (Belfast), 132, 136–45, 150
Ballymena, 54

Ballymoney, 1–2, 4–5, 7, 8–9, 10–12, 14, 15–16, 20 n51
Ballyshannon, 115, 123, 249
Banbridge, 137, 149, 187, 190–91, 192, 194, 197
Bangor, 51, 114, 149
Barbour, John Milne, 90
Barnes, Jerry, 74
Baronscourt, 26
Barrington-Ward, Robert, 184
Barrie, Hugh Thom, 84, 86, 89, 92–102, 108 n63
Barry, Redmond, 176
Bates, Richard Dawson, 89, 95, 100, 198–9, 200, 224–5, 235 n42
Baxter, John, 12
Baxter, Sir William, 10
Beadle, J.P., 47
Beaverbrook, Lord, 24
Belfast Cenotaph, 55
Belfast City and District Water Commissioners, 249
Belfast City Hall, 47, 91, 208–09
Belfast Corporation, 115, 118
Belfast Labour Party, 62
Belfast Old Town Hall, 44, 93, 97
Belfast Protestant Association, 161
Belleek, 156, 247, 249
Bennett, George, 245
Beragh, 73
Bernard, John, 96
Bigger, F.J., 10, 12
Birrell, Augustine, 9
Black and Tans, 180, 210
Blythe, Ernest, 65, 77, 191, 214
Board of Erin, 67
Booth, Frank, 65, 67, 68, 73, 74
Boundary Commission, 154, 162, 165–6, 215–16, 227, 238–52

256

Boyle, D.D., 9
Boyle, J. Moore, 246
British Legion, 48, 55
Brooke, Basil, 150, 158–9, 165
Brown, Jane, 4
Brown, T.W., 183
Brown, William, 4
Bureau of Military History, 62
Burke, C.E., 138
Burns, Jim, 68
Burns, Peter, 64, 65–6, 68, 72–4

Caldwell, Thomas, 196
Cameron, Sir Charles, 117
Campbell, Georgina, 142
Campbell, Lloyd, 90
Campbell, Thomas J., 183
Campbell-Bannerman, Lady, 228
Cardinal Tomás Ó Fiaich Memorial Library and Archive, 62
Carolon, Mick, 74
Carson, Sir Edward, 2, 11–14, 16, 22, 24, 25, 27–8, 31–7, 39 n2, 44, 55, 66, 69, 75, 84–6, 96, 98–9, 102, 141, 174, 179, 182, 190, 205, 222, 225–6
Carson, Robert, 13
Carson, Ruby, 222
Casement, Sir Roger, 2, 10–13, 15–16, 19–20 n32, 71, 178
Chamberlain, Joseph, 176
Chamberlain, Neville, 50
Chambers, T., 90
Cherry family, 196
Chestnutt-Chesney, Frederick, 138–9, 143
Chichester, Dehra, 230
Chichester, Robert, 178
Childers, Erskine, 15, 168 n41
Churchill, Randolph, 230
Churchill, Sir Winston, 11, 22, 24, 36, 154, 156, 165, 227, 240, 243
Clark, Lt-Col., 90
Clark, Ernest, 152, 158
Clark, Sir George, 89, 98, 101, 108 n63

Clarke, Helen, 116
Clarke, Thomas (Tom), 65, 69, 71
Clear, Tom, 65, 68, 74
Clones, 120, 124–7, 155, 161, 249
Coalisland, 65–6, 71–4, 76, 225
Coleraine, 10, 15, 21 n54
Collins, Michael, 78, 153–7, 162, 164, 226, 241–3
Comrades of the Great War, 48–9
Connaught Rangers, 45, 53
Connolly, Alex, 74
Connolly, Ina, 72
Connolly, James, 70–72
Connolly, Joseph (Joe), 63, 65, 67, 74
Connolly, Nora, 72
Connolly, Patrick, 246
Connolly, William, 194
Conor, William, 5, 210
Conservative Party, 25–6, 32, 35–7, 66, 153, 173
Conway, John, 179
Cookstown, 73, 118, 120–22, 126–7
Cope, Sir Alfred (Andy), 77, 212
Corr, Elizabeth, 72
Corr, Nell, 72
Cosgrave, W.T., 228, 242, 252
Cotton, Alf, 65, 71, 74
Craig, Cecil (Lady Craigavon), 210, 220–33
Craig, Sir James (Lord Craigavon), 7, 22, 55, 66, 85, 86, 144, 150, 153–8, 161–2, 164–5, 176, 179, 181, 182, 184, 190, 198, 199, 205, 207, 208, 210–11, 212, 214, 215, 220–33, 240, 245
Crawford, Fred, 30, 198
Crawford, Lindsay, 10
Crawford, Oliver, 116
Crolly, George, 140
Crossmaglen, 245, 252
Crozier, John, 84, 90
Crumlin Road gaol, 71, 114
Crummey, Frank, 68, 75
Culhane, Sean, 188, 189
Cumann na mBan, 72
Cunningham, Seán, 53, 75

Curragh Mutiny, 2, 28, 30, 35, 37, 69
Cusack, Sean, 65, 67, 68, 73
Cushendall, 159–60, 184

D'Arcy, Charles, 55
Dáil Éireann, 150, 153, 180, 211, 214, 241
De Valera, Eamon, 7–8, 157, 214–15, 226
Dempsey, Dan, 68
Dering, Mary Cholmondeley, 233 n4
Derry (city), 90, 114–16, 124–5, 127, 136, 152, 155, 187, 190, 197, 241, 246, 248, 251
Derry Nationalist Registration Association, 246
Derrykeighan, 135
Devlin, Bernard (Bertie), 52
Devlin, Joseph (Joe), 22, 61, 66–70, 75, 94, 102, 153, 180, 190, 206–07
Dickson, John, 49
Dinsmore, John, 13–14
Dixon, Herbert, 225, 226, 235 n45
Dobbyn, Henry, 63, 72, 74
Dobbyn, Seamus, 63, 65, 73, 74
Dodd, William, 175–6
Donaghy, Edward, 194
Donegal Protestant Registration Association, 247
Donnelly family, 155
Donoughmore, earl of, 206
Dougherty, Sir James, 12
Draperstown, 172
Dromore (Co. Down), 149, 187, 191, 197, 198
Drummully, 246–7
Duffin, Adam, 95–6
Dundalk, 173, 248, 250
Dunfanaghy, 115
Dungannon Clubs, 62, 64–5
Dungannon, 13, 72, 114, 115, 118, 122, 123
Dunning, William, 52

Easter Rising, 6, 16, 42, 60, 65, 70–76, 78, 81, 86, 103, 178, 191, 223
English, Thomas, 118
Enniskillen, 27, 53, 54, 114, 155, 249
Ewart, Frederick, 188–9
Ewart, Gerald Valentine, 188–9
Ewart, Wilfred, 216

Feetham, Richard, 243–5, 247, 249, 251
Fianna Éireann, 63–4, 65, 75, 76
First World War, 6, 30, 42–56, 70, 75, 76, 87, 120, 124–5, 132–6, 146, 184, 190, 206, 207, 209–10, 223, 239, 243
Fisher, Frank, 248
Fisher, Joseph R., 243–4
Fitzpatrick, Rory, 75
Fitzroy, Sir Almeric, 206
Forsythe, Robert, 246
Foster, John, 250
Fox, Thomas, 75, 76, 188–9
Fraser, Lovat, 25–6
Freedom Club, 62, 64–5, 66–7
Frongoch, 74
Fusco family, 194–6
Fyfe, H. Hamilton, 29, 31

Gaelic Athletic Association, 63–4, 67, 76, 191–2, 197
Gaelic League, 62–3, 64, 67
Gallipoli, 45, 46, 70
Garvin, J.L., 24, 32–4
Gaynor, Liam, 65, 73
Gaynor, Sean, 65
George V, 153, 204–16
Gilmore family, 191–2, 194
Gladstone, William, 6, 34, 174
Glaslough, 248
Glendinning, John, 90
Glendinning, R.G., 9–10
Glenties, 115
Glover, James, 206
Grant, John, 209

Graves, Charles, 118, 121, 122, 126
Grayson family, 47–8, 50
Green, Alice, 111–13
Greenwood, Sir Hamar, 180, 210
Gregg, J.A.F., 145–6
Grierson, Charles, 137, 142–3
Griffith, Arthur, 75, 122, 242
Grigg, Sir Edward, 211, 212–13
gun-running, 28, 30–31, 36, 38, 51–2, 65, 69, 222
Gwynn, Denis, 84–5, 241
Gwynn, Stephen, 83, 93, 104 n13, 241
Gwynne, H.A., 24, 35–6

Haddick, J.E.K., 139
Hales, Seán, 162
Hamilton, A.M.S., 5
Hamilton, Martin, 248
Hands, Charles E., 29
Hankey, Maurice, 211
Harmsworth, Alfred, 24–5, 29–31
Harmsworth, Cecil, 81–2, 92
Haskins, Rory, 64–5, 68, 74
Healy, John, 25
Healy, John (Rev.), 184
Healy, Tim, 178, 184
Helen's Tower, 55
Henry (née Holmes), Violet, 177
Henry, Alexander Patterson, 182
Henry, James, 172–3
Henry, Sir Denis, 172–85
Henry, Sir James, 185–6 n13
Henry, William, 172, 173, 177
Herdman, E.T., 174
Heron, Archie, 65
Heron, Sam, 65, 74
Higgins, Martin, 63
Hillsborough, 54
Hobson, Bulmer, 62–5, 69
Holmes, Hugh, 177
Holywood, 114, 115, 133, 225
Hopkins, Gerald Manley, 173

Independent Labour Party, 62
Independent Orange Order, 9–10
Inniskilling Dragoons, 43
Irish (10th) Division, 45
Irish (16th) Division, 45–6, 51, 55, 134
Irish Citizen Army, 15, 70, 72
Irish Civil War, 78, 156–7, 163, 243, 249
Irish Labour Party, 62
Irish National Volunteers, 70, 75–6
Irish Nationalist Veterans' Association, 49, 52
Irish Parliamentary Party, 44, 60, 61, 66, 67, 69, 75, 76, 134, 207, 241
Irish Republican Army, 53, 56, 62–3, 66, 74, 75, 77–8, 137, 149–51, 153–66, 180–82, 184, 187–91, 198, 200, 206–09, 213–16, 224
Irish Republican Brotherhood, 61–76, 191
Irish Sailors' and Soldiers' Land Trust, 49
Irish Transport and General Workers' Union, 70
Irish Unionist Alliance, 205
Irish Volunteers, 8, 43–5, 53, 63, 65–76, 191
Irwin, J.A.H., 7–8
Irwin, John, 90

James Mackie & Sons Ltd, 113
Johnson, William, 248, 251
Johnston, James, 90
Johnston, John, 90
Johnston, Joseph, 250
Johnston, Thomas, 249
Johnstone, James, 74
Johnstone, Robert, 63
Jones, Tom, 211

Keady, 123, 245, 248, 250
Keating, Con, 71
Kelly, John, 74

Kelly, Sean, 65
Kenny, William, 176, 185
Kerr-Smiley, Peter, 10, 16
Kesh, 249
Kilbride, 145
Kilkeel, 245, 246
Killylea, 248
Knight, Michael, 89

Labour Party, 48, 180
Lamb, Edward A., 250
Larne, 36, 69, 114, 115, 118, 120, 121
Law, Andrew Bonar, 22, 25, 26, 30, 32, 66, 98
Leatham, Edward, 90
Lehane, Denis, 71
Lemass, Noel, 163
Lemass, Seán, 163
Leonard, Sean, 188, 189
Lester, Sean, 65
Letterkenny, 115, 119, 248
Liberal Party, 6, 8–9, 165
Lisbellaw, 155
Lisburn, 63, 114, 116, 139, 149, 187–200
Lloyd George, David, 2, 81, 86–8, 91, 96, 98, 99–100, 103, 151, 156–7, 164, 179, 188, 210–13, 215, 240
Local Government Board for Ireland, 114, 117, 118, 120–22, 123
Logue, Michael, 207
Londonderry (city), see Derry
Londonderry & Lough Swilly Railway, 115
Londonderry, 7th marquess of, 14, 82, 89, 91–6, 98–101, 108 n63, 210
Long, Walter, 176, 223
Lonsdale, Sir John, 86–9
Lowe, W.J., 142
Lurgan, 47–50, 114–16, 124, 127, 227
Lynd, Robert, 65
Lynn, W.J., 16
Lysaght, Edward, 93

Macafee, William, 10, 13
Macpherson, Ian, 180
Macready, Sir Nevil, 205, 208, 209
Magee College, 5
Magherafelt, 179, 245
Magowan, Anna, 116
Manning, George, 116
Markievicz, Countess, 63–4
Marmion, Mathew, 122
Massey, W.F. (Bill), 215
Maxwell, Henry, 85
McCance, Stouppe, 90
McCann, James, 146
McCann, Matthew H., 250
McCartan, Pat, 72–3
McCarter, Jeannie, 136
McCartney, Sean, 75
McCorley, Felix, 63, 75
McCorley, Roger, 63, 75, 77, 188–9
McCormick, Pat, 73
McCullagh, Sir Crawford, 90
McCullough, Dan, 63
McCullough, Denis, 62–74, 122
McCullough, Emma, 116
MacCurtain, Tomás, 188, 189
McDermott, Sean, 62, 65, 70–71
MacDonald, Ramsay, 221
MacDonnell, Lord, 92
McDowell, Sir Alexander, 90, 93–4
McDowell, Cathal (Charles), 68, 73, 74
McElderry, John, 12
McElroy, Samuel Craig, 8–9
Mac Eoin, Seán, 214
McGeown, P., 178
McGuinness, David, 63–4, 75, 76
McKeever, Peter, 192, 193
McKelvey, Joe, 63, 74, 75
McKenna, Seamus, 75
McKeown, Daniel, 50
McKiernan, Owen, 75
McMahon family, 142, 155, 159, 161, 163
McMaster, John, 13
McMeekin, John, 90
McNaghten, Helen, 15

McNally, Felix, 245
McNally, Tom, 61, 75
MacNeill, Eoin, 67, 73, 76, 241, 243–4, 252
McNeill, Ronald, 16, 84, 85
McRory, Joseph, 142
Meeke, John, 134–5
Megaw, John, 16
Megaw, R.D., 16
Mellows, Liam, 71
Methodist College Belfast, 116, 133
Middletown, 245, 248
Midleton, earl of, 84–5, 94, 96–8, 214
Milliken, Nurse, 126
Milner, Lord, 28, 29
Monaghan, Charlie, 71
Montgomery, Hugh de Fellenberg, 90–91, 93, 99–101
Montgomery, Sean, 75
Monypenny, William Flavelle, 29
Moore, Maurice, 75–6
Moore, R.L., 249
Moore, William, 9, 143, 182–3
Morgan, J.H., 6
Morrow, George, 63, 65
Morrow, Jack, 63, 65
Mosley, Mercedes (Dollie), 11
Mulcahy, Richard, 162
Murnaghan, George, 179
Murphy, Dick, 188
Murphy, E.S., 185–6 n13
Murphy, Kathleen, 72
Murphy, William Martin, 94
Murray, Joe, 63, 75

Nash, Pat, 74
National Association of Discharged Sailors and Soldiers, 48
National Federation of Discharged and Demobilised Sailors and Soldiers, 48
National Literary Club, 63
Neeson, Sean, 74
Newry, 114, 115, 117, 125–6, 127, 144, 241, 245–6, 248–9, 250, 251
Newsholme, Sir Arthur, 121–2
Newtownards, 114, 117, 132, 149, 155
North Antrim Land Purchase Association, 9
North Irish Horse, 43
Nugent, Sir Oliver, 54

O'Boyle, Neal John, 63
O'Brien, William, 83–4
O'Callaghan, ?, 68
O'Connor, T.P., 173, 178, 180, 181–2, 184–5
O'Doherty, John, 251
O'Doherty, Philip, 176
O'Donnell, Patrick, 69, 92, 94–5, 96, 100, 101
O'Donoghue, Florence, 188
O'Duffy, Eoin, 53
O'Hagan, Dan, 63
O'Hanlon, John, 183–4
O'Hare, John, 191
O'Hare, Patrick, 53
O'Kelly, Sean, 68
O'Malley, Ernie, 74
O'Neill, Patrick, 251
O'Neill, Sean, 75
O'Rorke, Robert, 245
O'Shannon, Cathal, 65, 68, 71, 74
O'Sullivan, Patrick, 116
O'Sullivan, Sean, 64
Officers' Association, 48
Oliver, F.S., 29, 33
Orange Order, 12, 16, 31, 37, 47, 61, 64, 67, 69–70, 84, 86, 89, 141, 174–5, 176, 178, 179, 185, 197, 226, 243
Orr, John, 145
Osborne, Harry, 72, 74
Osborne, Paddy, 72

Pamerston, Emily, 221, 228, 232
Patterson, William, 142
Pearse, Patrick, 66–7, 72, 73, 75
Peel, Julia, 226

Pettigo, 156, 249–50
Pim, Herbert Moore, 65, 73
Pinkerton, John, 8
Plumbridge, 175
Plunkett, Sir Horace, 81, 82, 84–5, 91, 92, 93–101
Pollock, Hugh MacDowell, 82–5, 90–92, 94, 96, 100, 104 n13, 216
Pope-Hennessy, Mrs, 213
Portadown, 49, 54, 114–17, 124, 127, 183
Porter, John, 90
Powell family, 47–8, 50

Queen's College/University, Belfast, 3, 5, 173

Rathfriland, 159
Redmond, Eleanor, 134–5
Redmond, Elizabeth, 132–3
Redmond, John (MP), 1, 6, 22, 44, 49, 60, 66, 68–9, 70, 75, 83, 84, 86–7, 88, 93–4, 96, 98, 101, 134, 173
Redmond, John (Rev.), 132–46, 150, 154, 162
Redmond, Johnston, 132–3
Redmond, William, 134–5
Reid, David, 178, 244
Rentoul, J.L., 5
Ricardo, Ambrose St Quintin, 159, 164
Ridges, Frances, 116
Robb, Gardner, 124
Roberts, Nora, 209
Robinson, Geoffrey, 25
Robinson, Joe, 64
Roseberry, Hannah, 232
Ross, Sir John, 182
Rosslea, 159
Rowlett, James, 124
Royal Air Force, 47
Royal Army Medical Corps, 124–5
Royal Flying Corps, 47
Royal Inniskilling Fusiliers, 43, 134
Royal Irish Constabulary, 53, 68, 77, 150, 151, 153, 156, 160, 165, 180, 181, 187, 188, 190
Royal Irish Fusiliers, 43, 46, 48, 50,
Royal Irish Rifles, 43, 45, 46, 48, 51, 52
Royal Ulster Constabulary, 165
Russell, George, 93, 94, 103
Russell, T.W., 9

Scott, C.P., 24
Scullion, James, 63
Selby, Sergeant-Major, 52
Sharman-Crawford, Robert, 90, 222
Shaw, Thomas, 51, 56,
Shaw, William, 190, 192, 193
Sheehy-Skeffington, Francis, 178–9
Sinn Féin, 6, 7–8, 52, 62, 64, 68, 74, 75–6, 81, 95, 114, 122, 137–8, 139, 141, 149, 150, 152–3, 154–5, 164, 165, 179, 180, 181, 188, 190, 192, 193, 195, 198, 200, 207, 226, 227, 230, 238–43
Smith, F.E., 27, 29
Smith, James, 74
Smuts, Jan, 212–15
Smyth, G.B., 137, 149, 190–91
Smyth, W.H., 142
Somme Museum, 132, 136
Somme, Battle of the, 42–55, 133, 141
Southborough, Lord, 91
Southern Unionists, 81, 82, 84, 88, 93, 94, 96, 101, 102–03, 174, 205–06, 214
Spender, Wilfrid, 199
St George, George, 189, 193
St Vincent de Paul Society, 125–6, 193
Stamfordham, Lord, 206, 208, 210, 212
Stead, W.T., 24
Stevenson, Frances, 213
Strabane, 114, 125, 175
Strachey, John St Loe, 37
Stranorlar, 115, 248
Stronge, James, 192

Stronge, Sir James, 90
Sturgis, Mark, 181, 210, 213
Sullivan, A.M., 178
Swanzy, Henry B., 193, 196
Swanzy, Irene, 196
Swanzy, Oswald, 139, 150, 163, 187–200

Taggart, Thomas, 10, 11, 21 n54
Tallents, Stephen, 157, 159, 163
Thompson, Dealtry, 90
Tierney, Edward, 74
Toomath, Mr, 139
Trinity College, Dublin, 89, 91, 138, 213, 250
Trudeau, Margaret, 232
Tullaniskin, 145–6
Tupper, Sir Daniel, 233 n4
Turnbull, Arthur, 178
Twaddell, William, 157

Ulster Covenant, 13, 14, 27, 33–8, 43, 47, 50, 66, 177
Ulster (36th) Division, 42–8, 50–51, 54–6, 88, 133–5, 141, 150, 234 n30
Ulster Ex-Servicemen's Association, 49, 55
Ulster Farmers and Labourers Union, 9
Ulster Liberal Association, 9, 10
Ulster Literary Theatre, 63
Ulster Special Constabulary, 53, 140, 142, 149–66, 180, 184, 199, 200, 240
Ulster Temperance Council, 141
Ulster Tower, 55
Ulster Unionist Council, 55, 66, 82–4, 86–92, 95–6, 101, 103, 141, 1150, 174, 176, 205, 224
Ulster Unionist Labour Association, 82
Ulster Unionist Party, 24, 54, 66, 98, 141, 144, 150, 157, 164, 200, 229
Ulster Volunteer Force, 14, 24, 26, 28, 30, 31–2, 36, 38, 43–8, 51, 53, 56, 64, 66, 67, 149–53, 187, 196, 198–9, 221, 222, 223
Ulster Women's Loyalist Volunteer Association, 230
Ulster Women's Unionist Council, 86, 93, 225, 229, 231, 232, 233, 241
United Irish League, 22, 67

Wallace, Robert Hugh, 89, 92
Walsh, Louis J., 179
Walsh, Sadie, 116
Walshe, Joseph, 52
war memorials, 47, 53–5, 225
Ward, V.E., 32
Warke, Jasper McCleery, 136
Warrenpoint, 198, 246, 248, 251
Watson, William, 34
Weygand, General, 55
Weyman, S., 29
White, John (Jack), 2, 10–12, 13, 15, 19 n24, 20 n43
White, Sir George, 11
Whitla, Sir William, 90
Wilkinson, Nevile, 208, 210
Wilson, Alec, 13–14
Wilson, D.M., 183
Wilson, Frank, 65, 66, 67–8, 69, 70, 72, 74
Wilson, Sir Henry, 155, 159–60, 184
Wilson, Thomas, 64,
Woods, Alex, 189
Woods, Eilis, 72
Woods, Philip, 51–2
Woods, Seamus, 74, 75, 77, 153, 158
Wylie, W.E., 177–8

Other titles from Ulster Historical Foundation
www.ulsterhistoricalfoundation.com

Other titles from Ulster Historical Foundation
www.ulsterhistoricalfoundation.com

Other titles from Ulster Historical Foundation
www.ulsterhistoricalfoundation.com

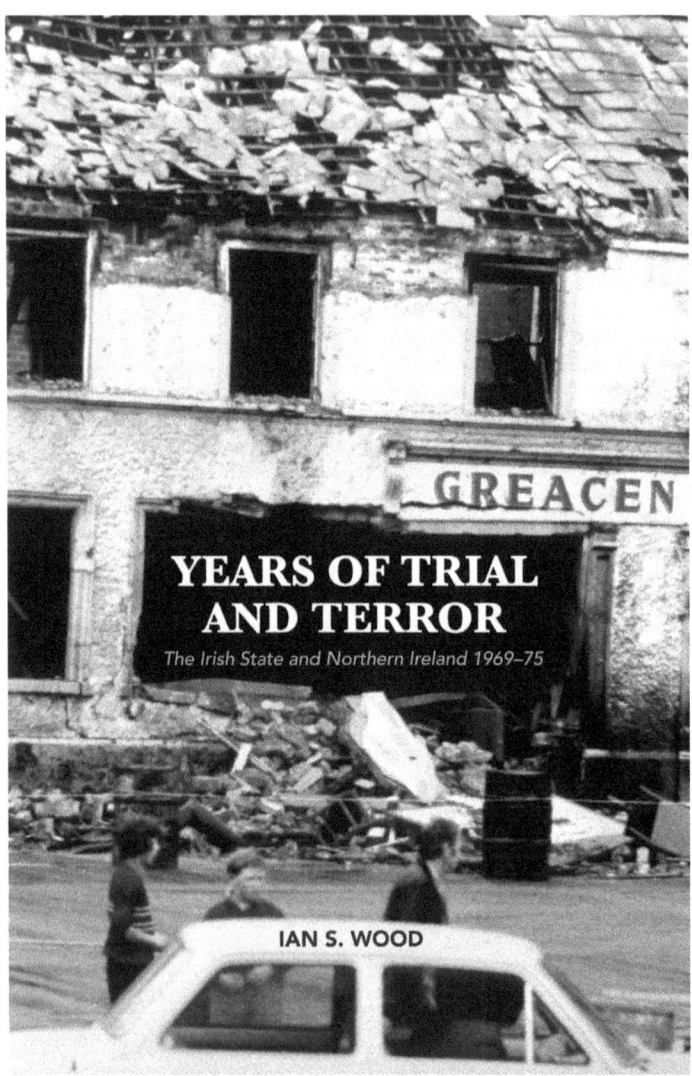

www.ingramcontent.com/pod-product-compliance
Lightning Source LLC
Chambersburg PA
CBHW041214130526
44590CB00061BA/4035